29.95

D0458115

UNSUNG SAILORS

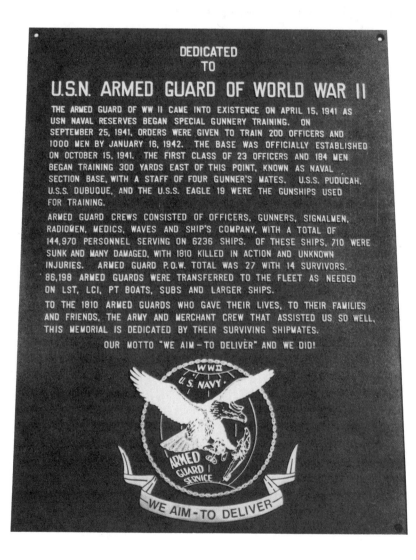

DEDICATED
TO

U.S.N. ARMED GUARD OF WORLD WAR II

THE ARMED GUARD OF WW II CAME INTO EXISTENCE ON APRIL 15, 1941 AS USN NAVAL RESERVES BEGAN SPECIAL GUNNERY TRAINING. ON SEPTEMBER 25, 1941, ORDERS WERE GIVEN TO TRAIN 200 OFFICERS AND 1000 MEN BY JANUARY 16, 1942. THE BASE WAS OFFICIALLY ESTABLISHED ON OCTOBER 15, 1941. THE FIRST CLASS OF 23 OFFICERS AND 184 MEN BEGAN TRAINING 300 YARDS EAST OF THIS POINT, KNOWN AS NAVAL SECTION BASE, WITH A STAFF OF FOUR GUNNER'S MATES. U.S.S. PUDUCAH, U.S.S. DUBUQUE, AND THE U.S.S. EAGLE 19 WERE THE GUNSHIPS USED FOR TRAINING.

ARMED GUARD CREWS CONSISTED OF OFFICERS, GUNNERS, SIGNALMEN, RADIOMEN, MEDICS, WAVES AND SHIP'S COMPANY, WITH A TOTAL OF 144,970 PERSONNEL SERVING ON 6236 SHIPS. OF THESE SHIPS, 710 WERE SUNK AND MANY DAMAGED, WITH 1810 KILLED IN ACTION AND UNKNOWN INJURIES. ARMED GUARD P.O.W. TOTAL WAS 27 WITH 14 SURVIVORS. 86,198 ARMED GUARDS WERE TRANSFERRED TO THE FLEET AS NEEDED ON LST, LCI, PT BOATS, SUBS AND LARGER SHIPS.

TO THE 1810 ARMED GUARDS WHO GAVE THEIR LIVES, TO THEIR FAMILIES AND FRIENDS, THE ARMY AND MERCHANT CREW THAT ASSISTED US SO WELL, THIS MEMORIAL IS DEDICATED BY THEIR SURVIVING SHIPMATES.

OUR MOTTO "WE AIM – TO DELIVER" AND WE DID!

WW II
· U.S. NAVY ·

ARMED
GUARD
SERVICE

–WE AIM – TO DELIVER–

UNSUNG SAILORS

The Naval Armed Guard

in World War II

Justin F. Gleichauf

NAVAL INSTITUTE PRESS

Annapolis, Maryland

Library of Congress Cataloging-in-Publication Data

Gleichauf, Justin F.
    Unsung sailors : the Naval Armed Guard in WWII / Justin F.
Gleichauf.
        p.   cm.
    Includes bibliographical references.
    ISBN 0-87021-770-4 :
    1. United States. Navy. Armed Guard—History. 2. World
War, 1939–1945—Naval operations, American. 3. World War,
1939–1945—Regimental histories—United States. 4. Sea-
men—United States—Biography. 5. United States. Navy—
Biography. I. Title.
D769.45.G57 1990
940.54′5973—dc20   89-13767

Printed in the United States of America on acid-free paper ∞
9 8 7 6 5 4 3

To the officers and men of the "Other Navy,"
The U.S. Naval Armed Guard, their Merchant
Marine shipmates, Army Armed Guards, and
volunteer gunners aboard ship, who played such
an important but little-recognized role in
delivering the troops, guns, and essential goods
of war to where they were needed throughout
the world.

CONTENTS

Preface   ix

Acknowledgments   xiii

1. The Great War (1914–1918)   1
2. The Road to War (1939–1941)   12
3. Naval Armed Guard Organization and Training   22
4. The "Other Navy" at Sea   49
5. The Ships They Sailed   69
6. Gallant Ships, Gallant Men   94
7. The Convoys   111
8. The Sea Raiders   123
9. Other Hazards   138
10. Relations with the Merchant Marine   156
11. Hell Below Zero: The Murmansk Run   170
12. The PQ-17 Disaster   190
13. Stranded in Russia: The Forgotten Convoy   210
14. Battle of the Atlantic   222
15. The "Yankee Turkey Shoot"   248
16. The Mediterranean   268
17. The Pacific   301

18. The War in Southern Waters   324
19. Japanese Submarine Warfare/Atrocities   349
20. Toward Victory in Europe   359
21. "The Navy Regrets . . ."   368
    Epilogue   377
    Notes   381
    Bibliography   409
    Index   419

PREFACE

The following is not a history book; it is the highly person-
alized story of a group of young men, some hardly more than
boys, who helped make history against the backdrop of two
world wars. They had no Ernie Pyle to record their achieve-
ments and sacrifices, but this account is a belated attempt to
tell the story of a long-unknown and unrecognized element
of the U.S. Navy. It is intended to pay tribute to the members of
the United States Naval Armed Guard (NAG), their shipmates of the U.S. Merchant Marine, Army Armed Guards,
and volunteer gunners, and the cadet/midshipmen of the U.S.
Merchant Marine Academy, Kings Point, and other fine nautical training schools with whom they lived and often died.

Victory in World War II required two seeming miracles:
the production of an incredible volume of planes, ships,
guns, tanks, and other goods of war, and the successful delivery of such vital necessities, worldwide, where needed. It
was in the latter capacity that the U.S. Naval Armed Guard
served in every theater of operations, and in some of the
most remote and hazardous regions of the world. An unpublished navy history, referred to frequently in this account,
states:

The Armed Guard met its supreme test in the voyages to North Russia, better known as the Murmansk Run. Without doubt, there were more hazards in these trips than in any other kind of naval duty . . . ships which left ports in the United States for Russia had about one chance in three of safe return . . .

In spite of its gallant record, the Naval Armed Guard has never been accorded the recognition and honor it deserves. Many former Armed Guards have had to suffer sneering remarks and questions such as: "What did you do during the war—guard buildings?" Even during the course of research in various areas of the Navy Department, the writer has been asked, "Were they really part of the Navy?", or "Weren't they actually in the Merchant Marine?"

It is in an attempt to correct this confusion and provide an authentic account of the important role of the Naval Armed Guard in two world wars that this book has been written. Admittedly, it is incomplete; a vast amount of historical record has been lost or destroyed over the passage of years. Fortunately, many long-forgotten and ignored dusty files concerning the service of the Naval Armed Guard in World War I were made available by a navy specialist at the National Archives, and they provide fascinating details of events of that era. The story of the NAG in World War II is also based on official records, many never published, including Armed Guard Officer Voyage Reports, which in their understated way often portray harrowing experiences of ordeals at sea, along with Summaries of Statements of Survivors. The bibliography furnishes a long list of historical references, but the principal sources are the personal accounts of former Armed Guards, often laboriously prepared in handwritten form, personal interviews at Armed Guard reunions across the country, nationwide correspondence and phone calls, supplemented on occasion by British, Canadian, and even German sources. Humor and tragedy are often balanced off, as they were in actual Armed Guard experience.

Chapter notes at the end of the book provide documentation on sources and text. Most sources are identified, with permission, but it is not the writer's intention to cause pain or embarrassment to individuals or their families, so a number are not identified, particularly those involving cases of harrowing death at sea.

Personal interviews were most gratifying. They involved reviewing many scrapbooks, whose yellowing pages are quite uniform: hometown newspaper clippings featuring their names, faded snapshops of boys in white hats or dress blues standing by their guns, or even peering somewhat glassy-eyed at the camera in pictures taken while on leave with their buddies. There are pictures of Mom and Dad, kid brothers and sisters, smiling best-girls, and precious documents certifying their training and advancements; invariably there will be that great document, their Honorable Discharge certificate. Their ranks are dwindling rapidly, but they become young again at Armed Guard reunions, where the names of remote and obscure ports of call, as well as major cities around the globe, are tossed about as casually as references to Brooklyn, New Orleans, or Treasure Island, from which they shipped out.

Eyes brighten, sometimes to be dimmed with tears when greeting an old shipmate, not seen for forty or more years, with whom they shared a lifeboat or raft in unforgettable and often tragic ordeals at sea after the sinking of their ships. Over a period of several years in which this account has been developed, the writer has formed the highest regard and respect for the men of the U.S. Naval Armed Guard. Their enthusiastic support and contributions of experience, so that their story may be told at long last and not lost in history, has been invaluable, as has that of many of their Merchant Marine shipmates, Army Armed Guards and volunteers, and families who lost members at sea during the war but made their often-tragic stories available.

While to many, World War II may seem the equivalent today of Caesar's Gallic Wars as regards relevance to our current world, it is hoped that the story of the United States Naval Armed Guard may prove not only an interesting piece of history, but a reference that might obviate repeating errors of the past, in which hard lessons of World War I were forgotten between the wars and had to be relearned at heavy cost in World War II. It is with such hope and respect that this account is presented.

ACKNOWLEDGMENTS

While there are many who have provided great assistance in the development of the story of the United States Naval Armed Guard service, it is possible to acknowledge only a few. Particular appreciation is due Vice Admiral G. W. Davis, Jr., USN, Commander Naval Surface Force, U.S. Pacific Fleet, for his authorization for the writer to spend several days at sea aboard the USS *Hewitt* (DD 966). The opportunity to observe and discuss operations enabled the writer to gain a much better understanding of ASW warfare and an appreciation of the many problems of Naval Armed Guards aboard merchant ships in World War II.

Thanks are also extended to Captain Stephen Loeffler, USN, commanding officer of the USS *Hewitt,* and to Lieutenant Commander James D. Hammontree, executive officer, for their generous hospitality and assistance and patient answering of innumerable questions. The junior officers, chiefs, and enlisted men could not have been more helpful in explaining their functions. Special thanks are also due Command Master Chief Jerry Rose, Naval Training Center, San Diego, for arranging the details of my visit and many courtesies.

The Naval Historical Center, Washington, D.C., has been of great assistance, particularly Bernard Cavalcante, Operational Archives Branch, who made available pertinent official records, including unpublished navy historical reports. John Vajda, assistant director, Navy Department Library, provided access to many important sources of information. Patty M. Maddocks, director, Library and Photographic Services, and Linda Cullen, photo editor/archivist, both of the U.S. Naval Institute, and Charles Haberlein, head of the Photographic Section, Naval Historical Center, were all of great help in gaining access to voluminous files of official navy photos. Alice C. Creighton, head of Special Collections, Nimitz Library, United States Naval Academy, was also most helpful, as were the navy specialists on the staff of the National Archives who provided official navy records, including Armed Guard Officer Voyage Reports, Summaries of Statements of Survivors of sinkings, and other documents.

Particular appreciation is due Captain Arthur R. Moore, author of the monumental study of American merchant ships lost in World War II, *A Careless Word . . . A Needless Sinking,* for his generous permission to quote from his work. Without his exhaustive research, vital data on many merchant ships referred to in this account would not have been available, or could not have been authenticated.

Thanks also to Dr. John Garver, Jr., senior assistant editor and chief cartographer, National Geographic Society, for the unusual privilege of being granted permission to reproduce a photograph of the Atlantic Ocean that appeared in the July 1941 issue of *National Geographic,* upon which President Franklin D. Roosevelt drew a line of demarcation indicating the area of the Atlantic that would be policed by the United States Navy, freeing Great Britain of convoy escort duty over a vast area.

Ms. Ann Frechette, communications advisor, Corporate Affairs Department, Exxon Company, International, furnished details of the operations of *Ships of the Esso Fleet in World War II,* referred to repeatedly in the text, and from which excerpts have been quoted.

Steve G. Stanford, director of public relations, Todd Shipyards Corporation, provided much useful information on the operations of Todd Shipyards in both world wars, and in the difficult period between wars.

C. Ted Baldwin, Public Affairs Department, Bethlehem Steel Corporation, furnished details of shipbuilding operations and numerous photos of Liberty-ship construction in Bethlehem yards, including the launching of the SS *Patrick Henry*, the first of over 2,700 Liberty ships built in World War II.

Robert B. Norling and the *Boston Globe*, kindly gave permission to quote from his article on the attack by Japanese kamikazes on the SS *Benjamin Ide Wheeler*, in which he served as signalman during the invasion of the Philippines. Mr. Norling also made numerous valuable research contributions concerning various ships and their Armed Guard personnel.

C. Brian Kelly, editor, *Military History*, granted permission to quote from an interview with General Lyman Lemnitzer concerning delays in launching Operation Torch, the invasion of North Africa, caused by losses of ships carrying supplies in the Battle of the Atlantic.

Frank O. Braynard, curator, American Merchant Marine Museum Foundation, U.S. Merchant Marine Academy, Kings Point, answered many questions and courteously furnished a photograph of the dramatic painting, *The Last Shot*, depicting the heroism of Cadet/Midshipman Edwin O'Hara during the epic battle of the SS *Stephen Hopkins* and the German raider *Stier*, a duel to the death in which both ships were lost.

James O. Hoffman, West Coast representative of the U.S. Merchant Marine Academy, provided valuable data on the academy and its great contribution to the war effort, as well as his ongoing support and referrals to worthwhile sources.

Particular appreciation is owed Charles A. Lloyd, chairman, U.S. Naval Armed Guard Veterans of World War II, for his warm hospitality and long hours of work on his computer, over a period of days, to provide the names of potential sources and the ships in which they served. His files include a roster of almost 6,800 former Armed Guards who served in some 6,000 merchant ships. Mr. Lloyd has been unstinting in his continued support and assistance. One of three brothers who served in the Naval Armed Guard, his elder brother Whitson was the last Armed Guard to die, in the last American merchant ship sunk by a U-boat, within sight of the East Coast, and just three days before the surrender of Germany.

Special thanks are also due ex-Able Bodied Seaman William Leonard Phillips, Royal Navy, Cheshire, England, who served in HMS *Opportune* and participated in seventeen convoys to North Russia, in addition to service in the Atlantic and Mediterranean. His experiences, described in voluminous correspondence with the writer, are referred to frequently in this account. They are not only appropriate, but one, involving the rescue of a baby, a number of Norwegian civilian refugees, and several Naval Armed Guards from the sinking SS *Henry Bacon* on the Murmansk Run, is particularly dramatic in its conclusion.

I am deeply grateful to the more than one hundred former Naval Armed Guards, Merchant Marine shipmates, Army Armed Guards, and volunteer gunners who contributed so much time and effort in relating their stories for this account. And special thanks are due members of the families of deceased veterans who have so generously given their assistance.

Special appreciation is extended to Paul W. Wilderson, acquisitions editor, Naval Institute Press, for his continuing support and advice, and to Carol Swartz, senior manuscript editor, for her patience and expertise in preparing the manuscript in its final form.

Last, but certainly not least, thanks to Yeoman First Class Michael A. Moncavage, USNR, who not only typed a major part of this record, but provided necessary and most valuable technical advice on the U.S. Navy to a "land-lubber."

UNSUNG SAILORS

CHAPTER ONE
THE GREAT WAR
(1914–1918)

*Navy gunners, manning Navy guns on
American merchant ships were sailing
the war zone before the U.S. declared
war. First to get into action, these
armed guards had more than 200 en-
counters with submarines, many of
them long-fought gun battles. First in
service, they were first in sacrifice . . .*[1]
—Josephus Daniels, Secretary of
the Navy

The dramatic story of the U.S. Naval Armed Guard Service (NAG) encompasses two world wars, in which it performed valiant and important service, but with such a lack of recognition that even today it is almost unknown. The arming of merchant ships by both Great Britain and the United States in World War I was brought about largely because of the unexpected and stunning success of a comparatively new weapon of war, the submarine. Although submersibles had been experimented with for many years and proven seaworthy by Simon Lake as early as 1897, neither the British Admiralty nor the German Naval High Command realized the full potential of the submarine in sea warfare. And across the Atlantic, U.S. Navy "battleship admirals" had shown no more foresight. Their considered opinion of the submarine was that it was no more than "a passing fad of a small group of wayward naval architects."[2]

Just before the outbreak of war in August 1914, a British admiral, called to a conference on potential U-boat problems, declared positively, "Gentlemen, it is child's talk to say that U-boats will ever amount to anything! Disregard them entirely!"[3] That confident assertion must have come home to haunt him; losses of Allied shipping were to mount at an astounding rate and skyrocket to over 6,000,000 tons in 1917, coming perilously close to knocking Britain out of the war before an effective system of convoying merchant shipping was belatedly adopted. Germany was also slow to realize the significance of U-boat warfare; U-boat commanders early on were given no orders to attack merchant shipping, but were merely told to select targets of opportunity. At the beginning of the war Germany had only about twenty boats, suitable mostly for short patrols and mine-laying. Nevertheless, this small force sank thirty-nine ships in less than three months. Germany began to build more submarines, but even in spite of their obvious successes, the effort was only half-hearted. On 1 January 1917 Germany had 133 U-boats, a year later only 144, a third of which were on station at a given time. Even so, the rate of sinkings increased steadily. In 1914 U-boats sank ships totaling 310,000 tons, in 1915 the toll rose to 1,301,000 tons, in 1916 to 2,322,000 tons, and in catastrophic 1917 losses rose to 6,270,000 tons.[4]

Most of the merchant ship losses were of vessels traveling alone, easy prey for U-boats. Germany's seagoing ace, Commander Lothar von Arnauld de la Perrierre, sank fifty-four ships in less than one month in 1916. In what has been described by British historian Captain B. H. Liddell Hart as "Britain's blindest blunder of the war," the Admiralty firmly held to the belief that it was not necessary to provide protection for ordinary merchantmen, and actually thought that convoying would prove more dangerous to them. A convoy was likened to a flock of sheep, easier for a wolf to attack. There were other objections: it was feared that reducing the speed of a convoy to that of the slowest vessel would lose valuable time, and the arrival of a convoy at one port at one time would jam unloading facilities and cause additional delay in getting the goods where needed. It was strongly felt that merchant ships could not possibly steam in close formation and at the speed required and would thus cause collisions. The clinching argument was that the Royal Navy could not spare escort vessels, especially destroyers, which were felt to be more needed to protect and screen the Grand Fleet at home.[5]

Junior officers at the Admiralty fought doggedly to change this policy, to no avail; one out of every four ships that left Britain did not return, and Britain's merchant fleet was being decimated. When Rear Admiral William S. Sims, USN, arrived in England to survey the situation in early 1917, Britain was down to food supplies for only six weeks, and Sir John Jellicoe, First Sea Lord, told Sims frankly, "It is quite impossible for us to go on with the war if losses like this continue . . ." Winston Churchill later wrote, "In April 1917, the great approach route to the southwest of Ireland was becoming a veritable cemetery of British shipping."[6]

Mounting pressure on senior officers of the Admiralty became so great that on 1 May 1917 they reluctantly agreed to go along with one experimental convoy, homeward-bound from Gibraltar. The success of that and a second experimental convoy brought about a complete change of policy, and the convoy system was soon expanded. A flotilla of American destroyers arriving in Ireland in early 1917, and operating under the command of a British admiral, assisted materially in reducing the losses of merchant vessels. By the end of 1917, the U-boat menace was largely overcome, and E. B. Potter, professor of naval history, U.S. Naval Academy, later wrote, "It is no exaggeration to state that adoption of convoy saved Britain from defeat in World War I."[7]

The Admiralty was not the only naval command that blundered; it was not until 1918 that the German Naval High Command ordered priority construction of several hundred U-boats, to be delivered in 1919, but it was much too late. A Commodore Herman Bauer had recommended earlier that a command submarine be stationed off the Western Approaches, to coordinate U-boat operations by radio (as practiced so successfully by the Dönitz wolfpacks in World War II before Allied defenses became effective). Bauer was not only turned down, but he was relieved of command, and Germany lost its best opportunity to bring Britain to its knees before American participation changed the balance of scales.[8]

The outbreak of war in 1914 was regarded by many Americans as "just another European war," and one that we should well stay clear of. President Woodrow Wilson enunciated U.S. national policy as absolute neutrality, "We must be impartial in thought, as well as in action," and he won a second term in 1916 on the slogan, "He kept us out of war." Both sides took actions that were offensive to the United States as a neutral; British search and seizure of American shipping was reminiscent of events leading up to the War of 1812. Wilson's personal physician, Rear Admiral Cary Grayson, USN, later wrote that Wilson was incensed at British actions. "At one time, if it had not been for the realization that Germany was the scourge of the world, he would have been ready to have it out with England. . ." Resentment of British actions extended to the U.S. Navy Department. Chief of Naval Operations Rear Admiral William S. Benson told Rear Admiral Sims prior to his departure on his mission to England, "Don't let the British pull the wool over your eyes. It is none of our business pulling their chestnuts out of the fire. We would as soon fight the British as the Germans."[9]

American public opinion shifted slowly in favor of the Allies, primarily because of the German policy of unrestricted submarine warfare, despite German claims that it had become necessary because of the arming of British merchant vessels and the use of "Q" ships, disguised armed freighters, that made it impossible for a submarine commander to determine if a ship were an ordinary unarmed merchantman or a man-of-war, capable of blowing his boat out of the water when its guns were run out. American resentment toward Germany flamed with the sinking of the British liner *Lusitania* off the coast of Ireland in May 1915, with the loss of 1,198 lives including 139 Americans. The "Lusitania Massacre," in effect, ended public debate in the United States on the relative merits of claims of Great Britain and Germany. Although Germany yielded to a virtual ultimatum by President Wilson and gave assurances that no liners would be sunk without warning and that some provisions would be made for the safety of noncombatants, the damage had been done. It was compounded by a fatal decision by the German High Command: in January 1917, at an official high-level conference at Pless, it was concluded that the resumption of unrestricted submarine warfare was the quickest and best way to bring Britain to its knees. It was a deliberate decision, with full understanding that it would bring America into the war, but with the calculation that the war could be ended before America's full power could be brought to bear. It was estimated that by sinking Allied shipping at the quite-possible rate of 600,000 tons per month, Britain would have to yield within no more than six months, and possibly as little as three. Therefore, on 31 January 1917, Ambassador Johann von Bernstorff informed Secretary of State Robert Lansing that, as of the next day, German submarines would sink on sight and without warning all merchant ships, including neutral vessels, entering its declared war zones.[10]

The United States government severed diplomatic relations with Germany on 3 February, but did not go so far as to issue a formal declaration of war. On 26 February Wilson asked Congress for authority to arm merchant ships on grounds that since diplomatic means had failed there was "no recourse but armed neutrality"; the Armed Ship Bill was quickly passed by the House of Representatives, 403-13, but ran into serious opposition in the Senate, which blocked it by a filibuster after bitter debate. A furious Wilson then exercised his constitutional powers and directed the navy to furnish guns, ammunition, and gunners to American ships clearing for ports in Europe and passing through declared German war zones. The navy objected, declaring that the idea was "fundamentally fallacious" and arguing that such policy would deprive the navy of scarce manpower, guns, and ammunition, all of which would have to come from the fleet, but to no avail.[11]

Following the navy's announcement that it was proceeding with arming merchant shipping, an official report was submitted to the department by Captain W. Pitt Scott, USN, who had been making a preliminary study of the problem. Dated 1 March 1917, his report covers a wide range of pertinent points: what vessels were to be armed, how to arm them, how to man the guns, rules for the conduct of merchant ships, rules for officers and men of the naval armed guard service assigned to duty on merchant vessels, and rules for masters of merchant vessels to which naval gun crews would be assigned. Captain Scott, who later became the organizer and chief operating officer of the Naval Armed Guard Section, recommended that armed guard crews at first be trained enlisted men of the navy, to be replaced later by specially trained men with short-term enlistments. He also recommended that no officers be assigned to the armed guard section—". . . 668 men immediately needed, including 149 petty officers . . . two guns should be supplied to each vessel, except larger vessels where four should be mounted, if supply permits." For all practical purposes, Captain Scott could be considered father of the U.S. Naval Armed Guard Service. His thorough and comprehensive report was in decided contrast to much of the conflict going on in official circles at the time.[12]

On 2 April 1917, President Wilson addressed a joint session of Congress and delivered an eloquent speech in which he stated, "Armed neutrality it now appears is impracticable. The German Government denies the right of neutrals to use arms at all within areas of the sea it has proscribed . . ."; he then called for a declaration of war on Germany, passed by Congress on 6 April 1917.

Prior to the declaration of war and for a short time after U.S. entry, the details of furnishing armed guards were handled by commandants of various navy yards, but it soon became evident that a central organization to provide administration and to supply the armed guards was necessary. A navy report dated 25 October stated, "The situation of having naval men associated on board a merchant vessel, under control of a merchant Master, is one without previous naval precedent . . . a new feature of naval administration and has brought forth many new and interesting problems."

It adds, "As it almost immediately developed that but little dependence could be placed on the merchant seamen to assist the AG in its special duty, the complement of AG has been made sufficient for a full gun's crew for each of the guns placed aboard, with sufficient additional men to provide an adequate and continuous lookout. Navy radiomen are also furnished on all vessels with Armed Guards." An earlier directive from the chief of naval operations stated, "It is desired, if practicable, without crippling the fleet personnel that at least one member of each guard be an expert signalman."[15]

The very first action of the armed guard occurred just three days before the declaration of war against Germany. The SS *Aztec,* carrying the first AG crew consisting of one officer and twelve men, was torpedoed by a U-boat off the island of Ushant, and quickly went down by the bow. John J. Eopolucci of Washington was the first man of the American armed services to lose his life in service against Germany. A few days later, Lieutenant Charles C. Thomas, commanding officer of the armed guard unit aboard the SS *Vacuum,* was the first officer of the AG to lose his life, along with four of his men. More action soon followed. On 19 April a shot from the SS *Mongolia* scored a direct hit on the periscope of a German U-boat. On 12 June 1917, the SS *Moreni* was attacked and sunk by a U-boat, but put up such a good fight that it elicited praise from the submarine's commander. Chief Boatswain's Mate Andrew Copassaki was cited for his almost unbelievable performance in the defense of the ship. Also in June, the SS *Norlina,* out of Baltimore, was struck by a torpedo that failed to explode. The gun crew took full advantage of its new lease on life and scored a direct hit on the submarine's periscope, and a second hit either sank or disabled the submarine. Other ships that engaged the enemy were the SS *Albert Watts* and the SS *John L. Luckenbach.* The AG-manned ship that had the longest fight with the enemy was the SS *Compana;* although finally captured and sunk by bombs placed aboard, the engagement with the *U-61* in the Bay of Biscay on 16 August 1917 lasted four hours and ten minutes. A report on the fight and subsequent treatment aboard the submarine was written by Chief Gunner's Mate James Delaney. It was so detailed and colorful that it was sent to the secretary of the navy for his personal review.[14]

Naval armed guards were placed upon passenger vessels, the first of which, the SS *Manchuria,* sailed from New York on 26 March 1917. Others served aboard a number of German passenger vessels that had been interned after the outbreak of war and were subsequently seized as prizes of war by the American government after the U.S. declaration of war. One of these was the brand-new *Vaterland,* then the largest ship afloat. Renamed the SS *Leviathan,* she became the largest liner ever to fly the American flag. Converted to a troop transport, she carried over 110,000 American troops to Europe. However, before she could enter troop service, she and the other confiscated German liners had to be thoroughly rehabilitated, as all had been extensively sabotaged by their crews prior to seizure. Following repair, the *Leviathan* made a shakedown cruise to Guantánamo. An unpleasant surprise was found upon her entry into tropical waters; the ventilating system had been sabotaged to work backwards and almost suffocated the crew in their bunks. One of the crewmen was a young signalman named Humphrey Bogart, later to achieve lasting film fame.[15] Bos'n Mate William C. Callahan, North Adams, MA, was gun captain of a nine-man gun crew aboard the SS *Mt. Vernon,* the former *Kronprinzessin Cecile,* and made twelve trips to Europe in her. In his nineties when interviewed by the writer, he furnished fascinating details of service in World War I. He passed away in July 1987.[16]

Joseph Lafferty was a seaman on the USS *Pennsylvania* when a request was made for volunteers to man the guns on newly armed merchant ships. He was getting bored with the routine life on the *Pennsylvania,* and he and twelve others volunteered for the new armed guard. His first ship was an old rusty tramp steamer that had formerly been under the Austrian flag but had been interned and was being put into U.S. government service. Two guns were placed aboard, a four-inch forward and a three-inch aft. A machine gun was installed on the bridge, and each man in the gun crew was issued a long-barrel forty-five Colt pistol. The gun crew consisted of a chief petty officer, two rated men, bos'n mate 1/c and a gunner's mate and ten seamen, five for each gun.

Heading out to La Rochelle with a cargo of rock phosphate, they tested the guns that had been taken off one of Admiral Dewey's old gun boats. The recoil spring broke on the forward gun and the firing pin gave way on the aft gun, leaving one machine gun and side arms to defend the ship. The gun crew continued to maintain watch on the useless guns, hoping that they might have a chance to turn the ship in time if a torpedo was sighted. They arrived safely in France, to be told that the day before a lifeboat had been picked up with only two survivors. Lafferty says that he wonders if the Germans had thought it was worth wasting a torpedo on the rusty old tramp.

Upon returning to the U.S. he found that the armed guard had grown and become a very important part of the navy. The service was in command of regular navy officers, with the same rules and regulations as on shipboard.

Lafferty's next trip was on the SS *Paulsboro,* a Sun Oil Company tanker. She was a nice ship with two late-model guns and good quarters, but she was so infested with roaches that they often fell into the food from above. Lafferty said he then realized why they were forced to keep things so clean on the *Pennsylvania.* After fighting heavy gales and narrowly evading several torpedoes, they arrived in England safely, but the return voyage was even worse. The entire civilian crew had quit, and the "new cooks couldn't cook and the bakers couldn't bake." Complaint to the captain did no good as he was forced to put up with the same thing. Finally some of the armed guard crew tried cooking some things for themselves when the galley was clear.

On Lafferty's next trip the weather was fine; no losses to submarines had been reported, and the *Paulsboro* left the convoy as she could make better time. He adds, "Then, lo and behold, a shell came streaking across our bow from a

German sub that had gotten between us and the sun and could not be seen. In quick order both our guns were in action. A couple of holes were put in the ship above waterline and one crewman was fatally injured. I went down with a dent in my skull and leg. How much later I came to I don't know, but the guns were silent and the sub was not in sight. I was told that it had been seen to turn up and go down stern first. We were instructed not to say anything about it when we went ashore, but the first thing that met our eyes was a newspaper with big headlines, "American Gun Crew Sinks German Sub."

Lafferty was put ashore to recover from his injuries, and then was felled by the Spanish flu during the epidemic that took a heavy toll of lives worldwide. Shortly after he left the hospital, the Armistice was signed. He was cited by Secretary of the Navy Josephus Daniels for his part in the submarine action, but only says, "We did what we were supposed to do and went where told." Now in his nineties, he was recently honored for his forty years of volunteer service to Letterman Army Medical Center, San Francisco, still going on.

During 1917–18, the navy furnished a total of 30,000 men to the AG. They compiled a record of 1,832 transatlantic crossings in AG status, 347 sightings of submarines, and 227 attacks by submarines, of which 197 were repulsed. Of 2,738,000 tons of American marine shipping on which they served, only 168,458 were lost. Attacks repulsed by the AG saved 1,140,000 tons. Not a single troop ship was lost, although over 300,000 men were transported to Europe per month. The AG gun crews, of fifteen to thirty-two men usually under command of a chief petty officer, served on practically every American vessel that plied the war zones, and according to Secretary of the Navy Josephus Daniels, "achieving a record for bravery and efficiency difficult to excel." [17]

Of the total of 384 ships carrying naval armed guards, 42 were lost—36 sunk by enemy action, and 6 others lost through other causes such as internal explosion, fire, mines, and grounding. A total of fifty-eight AGs were lost.

During World War I, the total tonnage destroyed by U-boats was ten times that destroyed by mines and twenty times more than by surface raiders. Planes sank only 8,000 tons, but "as a cloud no bigger than a man's hand," they offered a glimpse of what was to come in World War II. After the war the naval armed guard was deactivated; many men returned to fleet duty, others headed for home to resume civilian life. Unnoticed by anyone among the victorious Allies, an obscure young U-boat officer, Lieutenant Karl Dönitz, decided to remain in the tiny, weak postwar German Navy. He was fated to become all too well-known to the world a few years later.[18]

Many of the hard lessons learned during the war, most notably the vital importance of convoy, were forgotten by the Allies between wars and had to be relearned at great cost in World War II.

CHAPTER TWO
THE ROAD TO WAR
(1939–1941)

We must be the great arsenal of
democracy. . . .[1]
—Franklin D. Roosevelt (1940)

The Great War ended at the eleventh hour, of the eleventh day of the eleventh month of 1918, with the signing of the armistice in Compiègne, France. Shortly thereafter, an idealistic President Wilson went to Europe for peace-treaty negotiations, with high hopes that his "Fourteen Points" plan for unity of nations and permanent peace would be realized. He returned disillusioned and bitter, brought about by leaders of the Allies who were more interested in vengeance than in a just and lasting peace. At home, he campaigned strongly for the League of Nations, but became a broken man, defeated in his dream of America's joining the League and incapacitated by a stroke. For the rest of his term, he was virtually a president in absentia. He died only two years later.

The American public was confident that a prostrate Germany would never again pose a threat. Under the terms of the 1920 Peace Treaty of Versailles, Germany was almost totally disarmed. It was permitted an army of only 100,000 men, and to have no tanks or planes. The powerful but ineffective German High Seas Fleet—eleven battleships, five battlecruisers, eight light cruisers, and fifty destroyers—had been interned at Scapa Flow. The postwar German Navy was limited to ships of 10,000 tons' displacement and was prohibited from having any submarines. However, indicative of bitter resentment and events to come, on 21 June 1919, diehard German officers scuttled the fleet on station in Scapa Flow, to the vast embarrassment of Great Britain.

With the "war to end wars" concluded victoriously, the American public and Congress relaxed. The army and navy were sharply reduced, the naval armed guard, which had served valiantly, was no longer needed and was deactivated, E. B. Potter, professor of naval history, U.S. Naval Academy, wrote that both Congress and the public developed a spirit of "a plague on both your houses," as far as Europe's dissensions and rivalries were concerned. The Great Depression took a further heavy toll on U.S. armed forces. In 1934 the navy did not have enough billets to provide active duty for all of the graduates of the United States Naval Academy class of 1934. Many were released to civilian life.

During the thirties, a depression-wracked America took steps to insulate itself from the European powers' continuous bickering and friction. America wanted no part of the long succession of European wars and took steps to preclude being drawn into another. Although Adolph Hitler came to power in Germany in 1933 and gave early evidence of being a dangerous threat to peace in Europe, in 1935 an act of Congress forbade the sale or delivery of munitions to any belligerent nation. The following year it forbade loans to belligerents, and in 1937, Congress passed a new act that became known as the "Cash and Carry Act." It required that all sales to belligerents be made on a C.O.D. basis, payment to be made in cash, with the proviso that the goods had to be transported from the United States in non-American ships.

This action was taken in spite of the fact that on 7 March 1936, Hitler had announced that he had torn up the Treaty of Versailles. He then quickly moved troops into the forbidden Rhineland, without opposition. Hitler had previously announced that he was reintroducing compulsory military training and forming a new air force. Until then, Germany had begun rearming only by ruse and subterfuge.

World apathy was such that in 1936, Great Britain signed a pact with Germany agreeing to set German naval strength at one-third that of the Royal Navy, and also recognizing Germany's right to have submarines, expressly denied by the Versailles Treaty. Germany, given the green light to rebuild its navy, proceeded to do so in a hurry, notably by developing "pocket battleships," marvels of naval construction. By the outbreak of war in September 1939, Germany had three battleships, two battlecruisers, four cruisers, twenty-one destroyers and fifty-seven submarines.

As in 1913, the British were overconfident. They had a tremendous edge in naval tonnage, almost 2 million vs Germany's 235,000 tons. They also felt that with the development of new scientific techniques, including ASDIC (the precursor of sonar) and others, they could easily control the limited number of U-boats that Germany could be expected to produce. Radar, in which Britain was far advanced, was a revolutionary development that reportedly could "see through darkness, clouds, water and fog"; it eventually broke the back of the U-boat threat, but not until after a real scare and until it was greatly improved.[2]

Britain also was confident of the fact that she and her allies had an overwhelming advantage in the gross tonnage of merchant fleets of the leading nations at that time. The tonnage available to Great Britain and her allies, including the United States, was in excess of 46.3 million tons vs a total of 13.5 million tons available to Germany, Italy, and Japan. However, Britain's confidence was based on the same sands upon which France's faith in the "impregnable" Maginot Line was founded.

In the First World War, President Wilson had stated that American national policy was "impartial in thought as well as in action." In spite of the strong public isolationist sentiment in the U.S. and in Congress, as indicated by its continuing legislation, President Franklin D. Roosevelt had no such ideas, although he made numerous declarations of "neutrality." In an election campaign radio broadcast in Boston on 30 October 1940, he said, "And while I am talking to you mothers and fathers, I give you one more assurance. I have said this before, but I shall say it again, and again, and again, your boys are not going to be sent into any foreign wars!"[3]

At the time, he was actively engaged in maneuvering to get around the Neutrality Act. The act had been passed by

Congress and proclaimed by the president on 5 September 1939, almost immediately following the outbreak of war in Europe.

In his book on the history of the United States Navy, Professor E. B. Potter summarized Roosevelt's "devious means" of leading the country into rearmament and increasing aid to Germany's antagonists, step-by-step.[4]

- He established a Neutrality Patrol, to track and report on belligerent aircraft, ships, or submarines approaching the United States or West Indies.
- The U.S. Naval Reserves were called to colors and given training that prepared them for convoy escort duty.
- On 2 September 1940, Roosevelt arranged a ninety-nine-year lease with Great Britain for eight bases in the West Indies and Newfoundland in exchange for fifty World War I destroyers and ten Coast Guard cutters equipped for antisubmarine warfare.
- He eliminated the "cash" part of "Cash and Carry Act."
- He persuaded Congress to pass the Lend-Lease Act, to provide arms, war supplies, and other products to the Allies on a "loan" basis.
- He froze German and Italian assets in the United States.
- He authorized American vessels to carry lend-lease supplies to British ports.
- He began sending U.S. Navy ships to escort merchant shipping convoys to Iceland, later taking over convoy escort to the mid-Atlantic.
- He brought about the U.S.-British declaration of "Atlantic Charter," which set forth the war aims of both countries.
- He armed U.S. merchant shipping, and assigned U.S. Naval Armed Guards.

One of Roosevelt's early moves relieved the hard-pressed British and Canadian navies of the necessity of escorting merchant shipping all the way from Canada to the United Kingdom. In April 1940, the U.S. declared Greenland under its protection and arranged with the Danish government to permit U.S. naval and air bases there. In July, U.S. troops landed in Iceland to relieve Britain of the necessity of defending the area and to develop U.S. naval and air bases there.

During 1940, Churchill kept pleading for destroyers, "Each destroyer you can spare can be measured in rubies," he wrote Roosevelt in his usual colorful fashion. "Rubies" they might have been to him, but the four-stack, flush-deck antiques turned over to Britain were no jewels to the British sailors who had to man them. Rough-riding, incredibly cramped, and barely seaworthy, they were so hard to maneuver that twelve of them collided with friendly ships. Admiral Lord Ramsey, RN, wrote, "I really thought they were the worst destroyers I had ever seen, poor sea boats with appalling armament and accommodations. The price paid for them was scandalous." Lord Ramsey certainly did not think much of the arrangement, and in this he had some vociferous American agreement, but for different reasons.[5]

Although Roosevelt's actions in behalf of Britain today cannot be faulted, at the time of the destroyers-for-bases deal, there was a loud public as well as congressional outcry for his having bypassed Congress. The *St. Louis Post Dispatch* took out an advertisement in a number of major American newspapers stating, "Today, Mr. Roosevelt committed an act of war. . . ." Wendell Willkie, Roosevelt's election opponent, also denounced the bypassing of Congress as, "dictatorial and arbitrary," although reportedly favoring it in secret. Some years later, the outspoken Clare Booth Luce, noted playwright, member of Congress, and former ambassador to Italy, wrote that F.D.R. "had lied us into a war into which he should have led us."[6]

Shortly after gaining independence, the United States had engaged in an undeclared "Quasi-War" with France (1798–1801). In 1940–41, the United States was again engaged in an undeclared war, only this time with Germany, a war not without casualties. The first actual shots were not fired until 4 September 1941. The destroyer USS *Greer* had tracked a German submarine, the *U-652*, for several hours, acting as a spotter for a British patrol plane, which dropped some bombs. The *U-652* then fired a torpedo at the *Greer*, which responded with depth charges, neither action taking effect. However, action was soon to pick up. Five American destroyers came to the aid of a convoy attacked by a wolf-pack and in which several merchant ships were sunk. The USS *Kearny* was struck by a torpedo and sustained a loss of eleven men. Shortly thereafter, in October, the USS *Reuben James* was torpedoed; the whole bow was blown off and the *James* sank with a loss of over one hundred lives, the first United States warship to be lost in the Second World War. At this time, Admiral Harold R. Stark (CNO) declared, "The Navy already is in the war of the Atlantic, but the country doesn't seem to realize it . . . whether the country knows it or not, we are at war."[7]

The torpedoing of the *Kearny* gave Roosevelt the opening he had been looking for. He had previously drawn a line on a map of the *National Geographic* magazine indicating the expanded U.S. Navy's policing of the Atlantic and the convoying of merchant shipping to the mid-Atlantic, at which point the convoys would be turned over to the British and Canadian navies, relieving them of covering a vast expanse of ocean. Next he pressed the Senate for changes in the Neutrality Act, approving the arming of American merchantmen and permitting them to carry war supplies directly to English ports, previously denied. The *Kearny* torpedoing influenced Senate debate, and after a stiff fight by Senate isolationists, the Senate approved the bill 50-37, and it became law on 11 September 1941.[8]

American public opinion was also molded by an effective bit of public relations. Winston Churchill, ever the master craftsman of the English language, proved his skill again when he suggested that the term "U-boat" be applied to German underwater craft, and "submarine" to similar Allied vessels, on the grounds that "U-boats are dastardly villains who sink our ships, while submarines are those gallant and noble craft which sink theirs."[9]

Although Congress had previously denied its approval of arming merchant ships, the navy, prompted by the chief of naval operations, had directed that the training of naval reservists should be undertaken on a miniature scale by various naval districts, and such had been under way for a period of several months in early 1941.

In December 1940, in one of his popular "Fireside Chats," using his mellifluous voice and charm to the utmost, Roosevelt proposed to the country that we should act as a nation in the same way that an individual American would if a fire had broken out in a neighbor's house. "We would help them save their home," he said, referring to his proposal to inaugurate a program of "Lend-Lease" for the benefit of our allies. It was one of the most innovative programs ever developed by government to assist allies in time of war, but it took some doing and a lot of political sleight-of-hand.[10]

The Johnson Debt-Default Act of 1934 had forbidden any loans to governments that had defaulted on World War I debts—this meant all the Allies, with the exception of tiny Finland, which had met its obligations for years meticulously on each due date. During 1940, Churchill continuously asked for U.S. financial aid, saying that Britain had reached the bottom of the barrel in financial assets. Roosevelt had to come up with some device to overcome the Debt-Default Act and provide such aid. He directed the Treasury Department to draw up a solution, and the result was an imaginative approach that would give him sweeping authority to help any nation he designated. The resulting Lend-Lease Act permitted the president to authorize the manufacture of defense articles and "sell, transfer title to, exchange, lease, lend or otherwise dispose of" any article to any country whose defense he considered vital to the United States. The act was signed on 11 March 1941.

Goods and supplies furnished were considered "loans" rather than sales and thereby avoided problems of postwar debts, à la World War I, which had led to considerable ill feeling on the part of the American public toward their allies. Eventually, over 49 billion dollars in lend-lease shipments was distributed to the Allies, mostly to Great Britain and the U.S.S.R. "Reverse lend-lease," in the form of goods and services, considered payment in kind, primarily from Great Britain and the Empire, amounted to 7.7 billion dollars.[11]

The principal mission of the naval armed guard was to defend merchant ships carrying the flood of lend-lease supplies to the Allies. While preliminary training had begun in a number of navy armories early in 1941, the service did not actually become reactivated unofficially until 15 April 1941, when its first real training center was opened. Naval reservists began special gunnery training in a small, ill-equipped camp at Little Creek, Virginia. Other reserve officers received special training at the United States Naval Academy. On 17 September 1941, orders were received at Little Creek to train 200 officers and 1,000 enlisted men by 6 January 1942. The base was officially activated on 15 October 1941, the first class consisting of 23 officers and 184 enlisted men, with a staff of four gunner's mates at the start. However, the naval armed guard service, per se, was not officially activated until 17 November 1941, after Congress finally authorized the navy to man the supply ships with guns and men to protect the lives and cargoes on those vessels.[12]

The lend-lease program, the greatest foreign aid program the world had ever seen, was a prodigious effort that had a significant effect in achieving victory. Credit must be given to America's miracles of production and to the men who delivered the goods, the naval armed guard and the men of the American merchant marine, with whom they served and frequently died. However, not all of our wartime allies appreciated the assistance they received. The Great Soviet Encyclopedia refers to the program in part as follows:

"The deliveries made under lend-lease spurred U.S. production during the war and promoted the enrichment of the monopolies at the expense of the government. After the war, the USA used lend-lease and the settlement of lend-lease accounts for the economic and political penetration of many countries of Europe and Asia." It then complains that an agreement of October 1945 between the U.S. and the U.S.S.R.

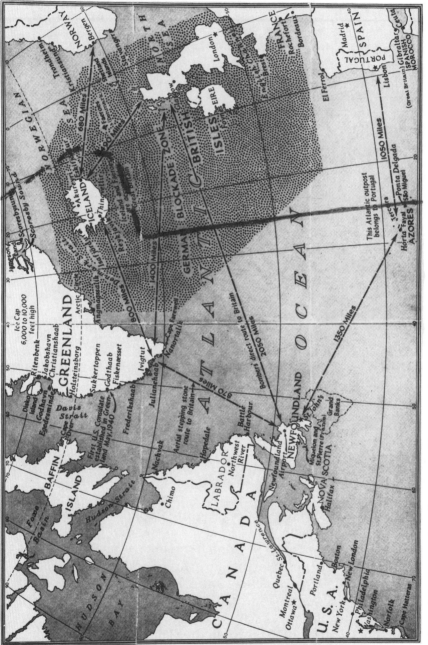

Line of demarcation drawn on National Geographic map in 1941 indicating Atlantic area that would be policed by U.S. naval and air patrols, relieving over-extended British escort vessels. The map was carried to Winston Churchill by Harry Hopkins, Roosevelt's special emissary. (Courtesy Franklin D. Roosevelt Library and National Geographic Society)

for delivery of equipment already on hand or on order under lend-lease, but not yet delivered ("the total amount being 244 million dollars") was not kept. "In December 1946, the USA which had already begun to display open hostility toward the U.S.S.R., unilaterally discontinued operations under the agreement, and later asked for 1.3 billion dollars in payments, overestimating expenditures in comparison to accounts with other countries." The reasons for the "display of hostility" were not mentioned, such as Soviet abrogation of wartime agreements.[13]

The Encyclopedia was little kinder to President Franklin D. Roosevelt, who had reopened diplomatic relations with the U.S.S.R. after years of nonrecognition and who had almost single-handedly pushed lend-lease through a reluctant Congress, referring to him as the "son of a wealthy landowner and enterpriser. . . . After taking office, under pressure from the toiling masses, the Roosevelt administration made some concessions in social legislation." It also reported that ". . . after U.S. entrance into the war, Roosevelt made an important contribution to the strengthening of the anti-Hitler coalition. . . ."[14]

The Soviet government's lack of appreciation for both American and British assistance as regards cost in lives, ships, cargoes, and human suffering in delivering aid to the U.S.S.R. will be covered in accounts of the "Murmansk Run."

CHAPTER THREE
NAVAL ARMED GUARD
ORGANIZATION AND
TRAINING

Ready—Aim—Abandon Ship!
—Sign in officer's club bar, Little
Creek, VA

To many members of the naval armed guard, World War II could have been divided into Parts A and B, with subdivisions for the various worldwide theaters of operations. Part A could generally be applied to the period from 1941 through mid-1943, and Part B from mid-1943 to the end of the war. As early AG Leonard Layton put it, "When I went into the AG, nobody wanted it, but when things cooled off, everyone wanted in. . . ." As before WW I, the United States was woefully unprepared for war, in guns, ammunition, and manpower. Training methods and equipment of the newly reactivated NAG were primitive, and immediately after Pearl Harbor confusion seemed to reign, with some unique results that appear in retrospect to be ludicrous but were then in dead earnest.[1]

Ed Quin, Orlando, Florida, enlisted in the navy as soon as he turned seventeen and could get his parent's permission. His best friend had become a navy signalman, and Quin wished to follow him, but the navy had other ideas and he found himself in Radio School in San Diego on 7 December 1941. The next day he was appointed "squad leader" and with a few fellow students was taken by truck to Point Loma, outside San Diego, and told to "guard" the area until relieved. Five days later, nothing had been heard from the navy, and no food had been received for the hapless guards, who had to rely on nearby residents for something to eat.

Having seen nothing, heard nothing, and eaten little, and not having had a bath or change of clothes, Quin gathered his brave little band and marched back to the navy base, rifles on shoulder, in cadence. Nobody had ever heard of their "mission," so they returned to radio school for sixteen weeks before some were assigned to the Armed Guard Center at New Orleans (NOLA). Quin was one of the first twelve sailors received at the center, after which he was assigned as a member of the commodore's communications staff on a brand new Liberty ship, the SS *Frederick L. Dau.* Quin's sea duty got off to an inauspicious start. The ship was ordered to New Orleans, "but it was so short of crew that the captain had to bail enough crewmen out of jail to get underway." [2]

George Prestmo, Mt. Vernon, Washington, was another early bird. He had enlisted in the navy in September 1941, and on 1 November, with 100 others, was assigned to the fledgling armed guard at Treasure Island. Immediately after Pearl Harbor, he reported along with other new AGs to fishing boats, yachts, and other craft along the West Coast to monitor possible radio contacts between Japanese sympathizers and enemy warships or planes, believed just offshore. Prestmo says that it was very good duty because there was plenty to eat, and owners took very good care of them, even to giving them Christmas presents. However, one young AG friend, finding himself alone on board a boat well stocked with food and spirits, got into the real spirit of Christmas. He began broadcasting over the boat's radio, singing and extending Christmas wishes to one and all and adding a few comments not appreciated by a navy monitor. He was picked up and brought before Captain's Mast on charges and sentenced to the brig. The story ends happily, however because before his brig time was up, he was transferred to the Brooklyn AG Center where he soon found another brig for sounding a false fire alarm, but he eventually became a hero for action against a German U-boat. [3]

The original NAG training center at Little Creek was soon found inadequate, and training was transferred to a larger base at Camp Shelton, Virginia. Floyd Jones of Natural

The U.S. Naval Armed Guard Center, Treasure Island, California, circa 1943. It was later destroyed by fire. (Courtesy C. A. Lloyd)

Bridge, Virginia, was one of the early arrivals at Little Creek. In November 1941, he was one of a group of twenty-one enlisted men sent to the new base. The only thing at Little Creek then was a mess hall, administration building, and one barracks. "All we did was train on a .30 caliber machine gun, that was all we had at the time. We didn't know what we were training for, but a few days later, they called us out to the flagpole and told us we were training for armed guard duty on merchant ships in case of war." Then they picked out three gun crews (6E, 7E, and 8E), part of the earliest wave of AG gun crews, soon to number in the hundreds. The three crews were then sent to the Brooklyn AG Center where they trained on .30- and .50-caliber machine guns until Pearl Harbor. On 10 December 1941, gun crew 7E, including Jones, went aboard the SS *President Monroe,* which was to bring officers and families back from Pearl Harbor. Jones made three trips on the *President Monroe* before moving on to merchant shipping and a lot of action in the South Pacific.[4]

The NAG, deactivated since World War I, had to be developed anew from scratch, and though mistakes were made, as was to be expected, the results were astounding. The arming of merchant ships in the early stages was a fearsome logistical task. The navy had to provide not only guns, ammunition, and manpower, but also storage space for the ammunition aboard ship and protection of the ship's bridge and radio shack. It had to make arrangements for darkening ship, install the guns and lookout stations, and squeeze an unexpected, and often unwelcome, AG gun crew into quarters already limited and provide messing for them.

The first gun, an obsolete 4-incher, was loaded aboard a merchant vessel in Hoboken, New Jersey, on 26 November 1941. It was the first such weapon on a merchant ship since WW I, but it was to be followed by many such antiques until production caught up with demand. Some "armed" vessels left port with creosote poles simulating guns; few had anything more deadly than a couple of WW I-vintage .30-caliber Lewis machine guns. The Lewis gun was beloved by the fighting men of the trenches in WW I, but could not be expected to be very effective against U-boat deck guns and torpedoes or armored enemy bombers.

Training the new armed guards, many of whom had never seen a ship before was no easier. Once again, there was a shortage of everything—most of all, guns. What heavy weapons were available at training centers were mostly for show. There was very little formal navy education in the early stages, and one brand-new gunnery officer remembers being told on his introduction to guns, "This is a 4-inch gun, and this is a 3-inch, and if you don't believe it, you can get a ruler and measure it." He adds that there were two Oerlikons for "training" approximately 500 men and officers.

The situation was repeated in many areas. At Little Creek, there were three tired old gunships used for training—the USS *Paducah*, USS *Dubuque*, and the USS *Eagle*. Live gunnery practice, however, consisted of only one day "at sea," observing gunnery drills and luckily perhaps getting to fire one round. Various divisions of the navy were involved, and there was no central control system of the NAG service

A training class at Treasure Island AG Center, 13 July 1942. (Courtesy Lt. Harold Bondhus, USNR)

until 31 January 1942, when the Arming Merchant Ships Section (later known as OP-236) was established in the Fleet Maintenance Division of the Office of Chief of Naval Operations. Individual divisions of the navy had previously handled pieces of the problem and proceeded on their own with little or no coordination. The Bureau of Naval Personnel handled the assignment of personnel and was charged with preparing curricula for training; the Bureau of Ordnance and Bureau of Ships supplied guns and equipment to merchant ships; training of AG personnel was under CominCH; the Maritime Commission–War Shipping Agency had responsibility for the installation of defense equipment aboard ship, in collaboration with local naval agencies at the shipyards; port chiefs were to make sure that each ship that left port was properly armed and equipped and manned with armed guards; Armed guard centers at Brooklyn, New Orleans, and

Treasure Island were responsible for records, mail, and pay accounts, as well as for discipline, issuing of proper clothing, and many other details. The AG Centers were the AGs' wartime duty stations when not attached to a ship.

The Arming Merchant Ships Section, under Captain Edward Cleveland, USNR, eventually assumed all functions formerly performed by the Fleet Training Division and the Naval Transportation Service, and was given primary interest in training from CominCH as of September 1942. It gradually pulled all the multitudinous details of the massive new AG program together. It should not be surprising that problems were many and serious, but what is surprising is that they were ultimately recognized, corrected, and improved, and solutions were found to rapidly occurring developments or conditions around the globe. It was a Herculean task, and one that converted the most hazardous service afloat to the best duty in the navy in the late stages of the war.[5]

To touch upon just a few of the many problems of the AG service, the New Orleans Center (NOLA) *Training Review* of October 1945 reported, "In the early stages, it was not uncommon for a man to board his first ship in the morning, and be a survivor in the evening . . . quite often the officer and a new crew were assigned to a ship without benefit of any military training." Early shortages of trained AG crews were soon overcome, but a major problem that lasted until much later in the war was the availability of proper guns for currently operating merchant vessels, and there were difficulties in developing new guns and producing arms and ammunition, as well as training AG crews in the new equipment. The flood of new ships pouring out of U.S. shipyards only made the problem worse.

As the navy ranks swelled with the flood of new enlistees following Pearl Harbor, many were eager to get into action and volunteered for the armed guard without knowing what it was or ever even having heard of it. When young Mike Molinari of Brooklyn, New York, a "graduate" of Depression CCC training, heard "Who wants to go to sea immediately?", he and others raised their hand. That is what they had enlisted for, and they wanted to get into the war. Within days they were off to sea, not in the "real" navy, but aboard an often old, filthy rust-bucket, to work with a frequently hostile merchant seaman crew.[6]

Al Gonzales of tiny Santa Rita, New Mexico, heard the same words across the country in San Diego, California. Although admittedly not speaking English too well at the time, that was what he had enlisted for and he raised his hand also. Then followed one week's training in "seamanship," mostly learning to tie knots, and another week in gunnery training, with no shots being fired until he put in his one day "at sea" observing firing practice. With that, he was off to war in the Pacific, first stop Guadalcanal, on a troop ship.[7]

All through boot camp, Irv Brownell, now of Florida, had heard of the "threat" of being assigned to the armed guard if involved in rule infractions. He and others took care to "keep your noses clean," but after completion of training, standing in formation alphabetically by name, he heard the dreaded words, "A through D to armed guard, E through . . . to destroyers or destroyer escorts. . . ." Then followed a week's introduction into the world of guns, ammunition, aircraft and ship recognition, and finally some actual practice with AA weapons. Then it was off to board his ship—"Good God! A tanker!"—running all alone, out of sight of land or any other ships, destination South America.[8]

One of the early "volunteers" was Herb Norch, formerly of the Bronx, New York, but now living in land-locked El Paso, Texas. He tells another story, not entirely to be believed. "We were standing in formation one morning, and some guy said, 'Those who want to volunteer for the Armed Guard take one step forward.' Well, I had never heard the words before and I was sort of sleepy, and never noticed the whole rank had taken one step backward. So, there I was out in front. . . ." Two days later, he was at Little Creek, Virginia. He was to go through more than his share of unfriendly treatment in various parts of the world without harm until he was transferred to fleet duty on a destroyer escort following VE-Day, and was seriously injured in a kamikaze attack.[9]

Like Firel W. Millhoupt of Grand Rapids, Michigan, some weren't "volunteers." His training was conducted at Great Lakes, and he reports that "my whole company (Company 37-32) of 120 men were shipped off to the Armed Guard."[10]

Of vital importance was the training of communications personnel, signalmen and radio operators. At the beginning of U.S. involvement in the war, there was such a serious shortage of communications personnel that the AG gunnery officers were also given a brief training in communications to assist the master in handling the wartime communications of the ship. This proved most unsatisfactory from a number of aspects: such officers were basically unskilled in the field, and in time of action the officer had more than enough to do in defending the ship from enemy attack. And with the rapidly expanding merchant marine, there were not enough commercial radio operators available to man necessary radio watches under wartime conditions. Merchant crews were not trained to assume the vast responsibility of handling communications in convoy. A naval directive of 20 October 1943 ordered that U.S. convoy commodores should have one liaison officer and four signalmen, with additional radiomen to be assigned as required.[11]

As the navy expanded, the shortage of trained radiomen became extremely serious, and a massive training program was established in a number of colleges and universities; under navy contract, a Naval Training School (Radio) similar to V-5 for flight training, V-12 for naval cadets and others, was also instituted.

The quiet southern Ohio town of Oxford was turned topsy-turvy when Miami University contracted for a radio-operator-training installation, following boot training. The period of training lasted four months and consisted of concentrated courses from typing to coding; bare plank tables were outfitted with transmitters, and the staccato sounds of dot-dash could be heard from early morning to late at night. The radio school at Miami turned out over 6,000 radio technicians, many of whom were destined for the AG, although the majority were sent to the fleet.[12]

From the outbreak of the war to 11 September 1945, the navy supplied 803 communication liaison officers to merchant ships and transports. It furnished 15,769 radiomen and signalmen in the same period. Radiomen were the "hermits" of the AG; they were largely isolated in the radio shack aboard merchant vessels and worked 50 minutes per hour. They also often served as signalmen and were familiar with flags and the international code.[15]

Jim Bennett of Oxnard, California, was one of those sent to Miami University. He relates his experience in training, "At boot camp I was selected for radio operators school by my performance on an aptitude test of matching audio sound groups. In August 1942, I reported to Class "A" Radio School at Miami University. As I remember, our instructors were members of the University's faculty. The subjects were Morse Code, typing, navy message procedure, and electronic theory. . . . The requirements for graduation in Morse Code were 25 words per minute in plain language and 18 words per minute in five-letter coded groups. Typing was 40 words per minute, with most of our spare time working on our Morse Code and typing. I graduated in February 1943, in the top ten percent of my class, with a third-class radioman rating. My fate was the Armed Guard, which at the time was a mystery to me and the other sailors assigned to that duty. Then I was shipped out to the Communications Pool School at Noroton Heights, Conn., for a short course in signalman training, because in the Armed Guard the Navy radioman also performed signalman duties under certain conditions. My instructor was a Chief signalman who had seen plenty of action in the early days of the war with the Armed Guard. We were taught flaghoist, semaphore and the use of various types of signal lights, using Morse Code which was a snap for the radiomen . . . Unlike most other branches of the military, we were prime targets in combat situations from the time we passed through the torpedo nets going out, until we passed through the nets coming home. The coasts off the Carolinas and Virginia weren't called "torpedo alley" for nothing. When I look back in retrospect, I believe that each man fought his own private war, with enough rationalization and make believe to keep from going bananas. Unfortunately, some did wind up in the rubber room."[14]

Gene Book from Chapman, Kansas, went into the navy in March 1943. After boot training, he was sent to U.S. Navy Class "A" Radio School at Northwestern University. On graduation, the high-performers were sent to the armed guard radio school in Los Angeles. Book says that at the time, none of his classmates had ever heard of the armed guard, and adds, "The best men were sent to AG training because we had a lot more to learn. Message format and radio procedures were entirely different in the merchant fleet. Also, we had no backup support; on a ship of the Fleet, there were many radio operators, including many with extensive experience, and Communications Officers to make most of the decisions. There were electronic specialists to take care of and repair the equipment. There were decoding machines and other equipment to assist in the operation of communications. On a merchant ship there were only two or three radio operators, and nothing else. These men were responsible for receiving and sending all radio messages, encoding and decoding messages (all manually) as well as maintenance and repair of the radio equipment."

Book goes on to say that radiomen were considered a "little odd" by many of the gunners on the AG crew. "For one thing, most of us were petty officers, considered somewhat apart, and even our schedule separated us." The principal reason for this was that all radio shifts were run on Greenwich Mean Time (GMT) rather than ship time (sun time). Radiomen had to work in a small dark room, full of equipment, protected by shielding that was intended to enable the radio operators to send out a distress signal. The international distress frequency was monitored continuously, but if a ship had only one or two operators, an alarm would sound if a distress call was picked up when an operator was not on duty. In case the ship itself was in distress, other than direct enemy action, an outgoing distress call was "SOS"; if under attack by aircraft, the opening signal would be "AAAA" repeated several times, and if by submarine, the distress signal would be "SSSS" repeated several times, followed by the call letters of the ship under attack. These calls could give warning to other ships and aid in locating the ship in distress.

In case of attack, a radio operator off duty could serve as a loader or even a gunner. In case of "abandon ship," he was responsible for getting an emergency radio kit into the appropriate lifeboat and for disposing of the codebook in heavily weighted sacks that would sink quickly.[15]

While Book's training was very thorough, he has spoken with radiomen whose training immediately following boot camp consisted of a six-week crash course in radio procedure, Morse Code, and signalman duties. Then they were assigned to a ship as the only communications man aboard. They had to serve as both radiomen and signalmen. This was early in the war, however, when there was a desperate need for communications people; later on, there was a vast expansion and improvement in the training of radio operators.

In the early stages of reactivation, the AG consisted largely of enlisted personnel transferred from other navy duties. The navy at that time was so short of commissioned officers that it followed the World War I practice of sending early AG crews to sea under the command of a junior non-commissioned petty officer, or even a seaman 1st class, a policy found wanting in many respects and later changed. The first NAG officer of World War II was Ensign R. Brinn, who volunteered for the first run to Murmansk. He mustered his gun crew (1E) and boarded the SS *Dunboyne*.[16] However, the *Dunboyne* encountered a number of problems that resulted in her being replaced by the SS *Expositor*, which sailed for Murmansk in early 1942 with an AG crew of four seamen and a signalman under command of Lieutenant Robert B. Hicks. She made that run with no problems, but the *Expositor* was later lost in the North Atlantic on a return run from North Russia, with a loss of six merchant seamen and three members of the AG crew.[17]

The NAG did not consist only of gun crews. Included in its roster were signalmen, radio operators, and pharmacist's mates (only on certain ships), plus members of ship's company, who provided the backstopping, training, and handling of the paperwork of an organization that eventually grew to over 140,000 men and a number of Waves. The latter proved of great value in later training, handling the simulators that would expose trainees to all phases of defense except actual explosion. Many later instructors were battle-hardened veterans of AG service who passed on their invaluable practical experience to the neophytes.

The men of the NAG were the most widely traveled of any branch of the armed services. The more than 6,000 ships upon which they served carried them into the most far-flung and isolated ports of the world and into inhospitable climates, ranging from the blazing heat of the Persian Gulf to the frigid Arctic blasts of the Barents Sea. A young AG's first time at sea might well develop into a months'-long trip around the world. Signalmen were the most mobile of all, as regards the number and variety of ships to which they were assigned, particularly if they served commodores of convoys. Each trip found them on a different ship and often under a variety of foreign flags.

Signalmen were required on all ships of a convoy, regardless of flag, to ensure uniform understanding and operations. During one tour of duty in New York–Caribbean convoys, C. A. "Pete" Burke of Philadelphia, Pennsylvania, sailed on seventeen tankers and four passenger vessels as a commodore's signalman. Lieutenant Commander Paul Kincade, USN (Ret.), from San Diego, California, sailed as an enlisted man on ten ships, five Panamanian-flagged, one each British, Norwegian, and Dutch, and only two American-flagged ships.

Burke enlisted in the navy in September 1941, and was sent to Navy Communications School in San Diego on 1 December 1941. "When Pearl Harbor blew up, all hell broke loose, everything was disrupted." He finally graduated from Radio School, and he and eighty-five other radiomen were sent to the AG Center in New Orleans, whence they were directed to Key West. There the chief said, "I don't need radiomen—every merchant ship has its own radiomen. What I need is signalmen." The entire draft was sent back to New Orleans to be converted into signalmen. Since they were already familiar with Morse Code, sound, and in some navy communication procedures, they were given a crash course in visual communications—flag hoists, semaphore, blinker light using Morse Code, etc. "Two weeks later we were sent back to Key West as signalmen and I was assigned to the communication staff of Commodore, Captain La Bounty, USN, and we went out on convoy in the Standard Oil tanker SS *John D. Archbold.* "All in all, I sailed on twenty-five ships, and not one of them was a Navy vessel. . . ." It was not until after the war, when Burke enlisted in the naval reserve, that he finally got to serve in a U.S. Navy ship, the USS *PC 1232* (on a two-week cruise to Bermuda).[18]

Lieutenant Commander Kincade made the navy a career, enlisting when he was only seventeen. He knew semaphore because his best buddy had become a signalman. Kincade applied for signal school and was immediately accepted. His entire class was assigned to the NAG. His first ship was the SS *Courageous,* which had been in the "boneyard" for ten years but was resurrected and brought back into service. Service in the *Courageous* was a nightmare. She had constant breakdowns, including her steering. It took two men to wrestle the jury-rigging of the rudder. Her problems were so bad she had to drop out of convoy, at which time she developed saltwater intrusion in the freshwater supply, putting salt into everything, including the food. It could be said that the most courageous feature of SS *Courageous* was the crew, having to risk their lives to keep her afloat, completely disregarding the enemy's activities.[19]

One of the smallest, yet one of the most important, elements of the NAG, was the pharmacist's mate section. These men, also known as "Corpsmen," were frequently and irreverently called "chancre mechanics" wherever they served. One such pharmacist's mate was Ph M 2/c Manley Michler from Olympia, Washington, who states that "Pharmacist's Mates were selected on the basis of aptitude tests, with good math and spelling being obligatory." They were called hospital apprentice 2/c at the beginning of training, which first involved being sent to a naval hospital to observe operations, a screening process to weed out those who couldn't take it. They then spent six weeks in training, three of which were in a naval hospital doing a variety of tasks to give them exposure to the real thing, e.g., first aid and hospital care. Their "bible" was a reference book called "*Handbook of Hospital Care, USN* (1939)," that contained over 1,000 pages of medical problems, physiology, symptoms of various diseases found worldwide, treatment, etc. With the exception of new medical drugs and practices, the *Handbook* is still relevant today.[20]

In 1942 as the war was escalating, the navy was pushing men into such training, and they were trained well enough to go out in the field by themselves and take care of the wounded.

After serving in the tanker SS *Cities Service Toledo,* in which he had been sunk and had barely escaped being incinerated by flaming waters, James D. Handy, Spring City, Tennessee, was ordered to receive a very little known type of training. He reports that "in July 1942, the NAG decided to start using barrage balloons on ships going into areas in which they would be subjected to air attacks, presumably because the English had had some limited success with them." Handy was part of a detachment of five officers and twenty enlisted men sent to a make-shift school at Parris Island. The idea was to put one man with a NAG gun crew to operate the balloon, which was supposed to snag the wing of an attacker at about 1,000 feet and blow up the plane with an explosive device. Training lasted six weeks, and the AG group was sent back to the Brooklyn AG Center. Handy never heard any more of the idea, however, although he served subsequently in four ships. Handy further stated that "I heard later that the Germans had developed a real good defense against them. They installed cable cutters on the wings of a fast-moving plane which was sent in to clip all the cables, thus rendering the balloons useless, but I have no personal experience with it."[21]

Training of naval armed guard officers, in the early

stages of the war, often appeared as cursory as that for the "men" (teenagers at best) who composed the gun crews. For the brand new officer, just learning about such strange things as watch bells, keeping station, and a wholly new concept of time (GMT) was confusing. One befuddled student confessed, "Now I am so balled up, I'll never know what day it is." Gunnery drills, safety precautions, machine-gun stripping, and countless other details added up to a frightening amount to absorb in a matter of just a few weeks.

One who didn't have so much to worry about was Stansel E. DeFoe of Independence, Missouri, now captain, USNR (Ret.). He attended a V-7 midshipman course at the United States Naval Academy and was commissioned an ensign in May 1941. Along with 100 other members of his class, he was assigned for further training as an armed guard gunnery officer. He was miles ahead in navy practice and procedure of most of the hastily trained new officers. His first AG cruise, aboard the SS *Robin Tuxford*, carried him around the world, via New York to Australia and then to South Africa and back to New York. He then added the Murmansk run to his travels.[22]

A young chemical engineer, Lieutenant Commander Norman Alston, USNR (Ret.), now of El Paso, Texas, was working for Henry Kaiser at the Permanente magnesium plant in early 1942 when he received a letter from the Office of Naval Officer Procurement. The interviewing officer explained how the navy needed experienced engineers for its new technical developments and assured Alston that he was what the navy needed for the radar program. He would be trained as a radar officer at Harvard or Northwestern and, in all probability, be assigned to an aircraft carrier. With such promises and dreams, as well as a direct commission as a lieutenant (j.g.), Alston was sworn in. Then came the shock of the orders: "You will report to the Armed Guard School in Boston. . . ." As Alston reports, "Armed Guard? What's that? I had no idea. What it turned out to be was three weeks of intensive training on gunnery, convoy procedures, and 'how to get along with a merchant crew,' liberally sprinkled with lectures on the horrors of the Murmansk run. Boston was followed by four weeks in Chicago with half of each day devoted to training equally inexperienced enlisted men, truly a case of the blind leading the blind. When I wrote home that I was going into the Navy, my mother replied, 'Thank God you are not joining the Merchant Marine.' Little did she know about the Armed Guard. From Chicago it was to the Armed Guard Center in New Orleans and on to a Houston shipyard to go aboard a brand new Liberty ship, the SS *Thomas J. Rusk*. There was an absolutely minimal test run, the ship floated, the engines operated, and the guns were fired. After a short trip to Puerto Rico, the ship was modified for the frigid Murmansk run and the men were outfitted with clothing for the coldest of weather. The *Rusk* loaded in Philadelphia with Lend-Lease materials intended for Russia." Alston and his crew were on their way, but not to Murmansk. Instead, it was to the Persian Gulf by way of Panama and Australia.[23]

Lieutenant Commander Harold J. McCormick of Fort Wayne, Indiana, took his AG training in Algiers, Louisiana. "Mostly gunnery, some communications, no seamanship or navigation." During three years aboard merchant ships, he reports that there was never a boat drill. When his ship, the Liberty SS *William Gaston,* was sinking following torpedoing in the South Atlantic, "most members of the crew had no idea about how to lower a lifeboat or launch a raft." This obviously important shortcoming was ultimately recognized by the navy, and the technique of abandoning ship was included in later AG training.[24]

President Roosevelt's famed "Fireside Chats," which were intended to boost national morale and soothe concern, did not always hit the mark. A young AG lieutenant vividly recalls one famous and supposedly inspiring quotation of the president's. Lieutenant Carl G. Ossman, USNR, now head of a prominent architectural firm in Topeka, Kansas, remembers, "Our class of officers, approximately 200, were in chow line or some similar formation in Boston about June 1942. One of the men appeared with a copy of a Boston paper and the quote of the President, as I remember it quite distinctly, was, '. . . and we will win for we will build ships faster than they [the Germans] can sink them!' You can imagine the feelings of us who were getting ready to report to these sinkable merchant ships."[25]

Gib Robinson, Salinas, Kansas, states, "I enlisted as a boot, but the Navy recruiter who checked over my papers told me I should apply for a commission. I did so and got a commission as LT (j.g.). I was sent to Princeton for training in small craft, but about that time, the Navy had decided it had made a judgment error in assigning many very young men as AG officers, and it was not working out too well. At that time, they were assigning more experienced, older men to the AG. At the close of our training period they reassigned about a third of our entire group to AG duty and sent us to Boston for some AG training. We spent about six weeks in Boston, then to AG Training Center in Gulfport, Mississippi, for a month or so of gunnery and related training. From there it was to New Orleans for ship assignment. I was assigned to two shakedown trips to South America, and then spent a lot of months, including two winters, battling the North Atlantic where I had more than my share of bad weather and submarine attacks while making many trips to Ireland, England and France."[26]

Former AG gunnery officer Lieutenant N. Paul Cronin, now an attorney in Aberdeen, Maryland, had a rather typical experience. "I was assigned to the NAG after indoctrination at Princeton, then followed training at the Fargo Building in Boston, and gunnery practice at Little Creek, Virginia. Upon reporting to the AG Center, Brooklyn, orders sent me to an officer pool at Londonderry, North Ireland, from where I was assigned to the SS *Samuel Parker*," later to become known as "Fighting Sam" because of its outstanding combat record in the Mediterranean.[27]

Lieutenant Irving Kaplan, USNR, from El Cerrito, California, came into the AG via a very circuitous route. When the war broke out, he held a commission in the army from his ROTC course in college. However, he preferred the navy and enlisted immediately. Based on his knowledge and experience in photography he was given a rate of photographer's mate 3/c, and after boot camp was assigned to the photographic squadron (FAPSA) in Norfolk, Virginia, in which he flew in PBYs along the eastern seaboard. After transfer to the "baby aircraft carrier," USS *Charger* (CVE), he applied for a commission, which was approved, and one day at sea, he was sworn in as a lieutenant (j.g.) by Captain Wall, in his quarters. Then it was off to Dartmouth College for officer's indoctrination where he received orders to the AG. After gunnery training he was assigned to the SS *Woodbridge N. Ferris.* He adds, "I recall at this late date that the training was basic and rapid. True training was acquired at sea." The SS *Woodbridge N. Ferris*'s AG crew was highly commended by the ship's master for its skill in fighting a fire that might have cost the ship.[28]

Lieutenant Harold Bondhus, USNR, of Oxford, Ohio, gives a graphic description of his training, or ". . . lack of training and decent equipment are my most vivid memories of my days in the Armed Guard. We reported to Treasure Island in San Francisco Bay on 13 July 1942. The people who were in charge of the operation were not prepared for us. It was like some of the classes in college when you were sure that the prof had first started to prepare for today's class the night before. There was no real continuity to anything. We had a Lt. Comdr. as the gunnery instructor. He had been a Warrant Gunner on the old battleships which had 14-inch guns. So, the bulk of our instructions were on 14-inch guns. It was the only gun for which there was any instructional material. We did march a lot, since they didn't seem to have anything else planned for us. We had liberty from Friday afternoon until Monday morning. So, you can see that there was no urgency about anything. I never stood a single watch during the four weeks that we were there. One day, we went down the coast to a firing range. We each fired a short burst from a .30 caliber machine gun. That was the total experience during the four weeks. We knew two things for sure when we got finished there: do not stand in front of the gun when it is fired and don't salute doormen. We then went off for four weeks at the Destroyer Base in San Diego. The training was of about the same quality. However, we did go to sea for three days—out in the morning and back in the afternoon. We got to walk around the decks and look in wherever we found something of interest. A crew of five fired three rounds from a 4″ gun. Another day, we fired three rounds from a 3″23. Since there were three of us in the crew, we got to shift to each position for one round. I forget when, but sometime during that trip they fired off a couple of depth charges. So, we were not a heck of a lot smarter when we returned to San Francisco.[29]

Lieutenant William C. Schofield, USNR, in his excellent book, *"Eastward the Convoys,"* reports being told while in training at Little Creek, "Many of you will be lost—all of you will be lonely." He states the two best-known slogans at the officers' club bar at Little Creek were, "Sighted Sub . . . Glub, Glub!", a parody of a report from an American pilot who allegedly sent a message 'Sighted Sub, Sank Same'; and, "Ready—Aim—Abandon ship!" Daily postings of casualty lists, soon discontinued for obvious reasons, did nothing to dispel the feeling of impending doom. Even under the best of conditions, merchant ships at the outset sailed with pitifully inadequate armament, always outgunned by the enemy. A former newsman, Schofield has a great gift of description, as will be indicated by his appraisal of survival. "The chances of getting home alive were somewhat less than those of a jungle messenger taking a short cut through a river of crocodiles." He also painted an unforgettably poignant picture of his convoy passing two men adrift on a raft in the North Atlantic, 1,000 miles from land, waving forlornly as they faded slowly from sight, left behind because of security; "A convoy cannot stop. . . ."[30]

Lieutenant Commander Charles E. Odegaard, USNR (Ret.), president emeritus, University of Washington, relates a similar tale of "training." "By a letter dated 23 March 1942, the Navy responded notifying me that I had been appointed a Lieutenant (j.g.), D-V(S), deck, volunteer, special services, to rank from 5 March 1942. On 31 March 1942, orders were issued for me to proceed on the 14th of April to Boston and report for duty on the morning of 16 April 1942 at the Naval Training School (Local Defense), South Boston. At 0900, we were ordered to stand in a muster line, positioning ourselves in accordance with the alphabet. We were then informed that the typewriters which had been ordered for this Naval installation had not arrived and none were available. Therefore, our first task would be to write out longhand 25 copies of our orders, which covered three closely typed pages. It was a nervewracking, handwearying experience. . . . It turned out that there were two groups assembled in South Boston that day. One group was associated with local defense, that is, net tenders, small sub chasers, harbor defenses, etc. As for that group, it transpired that there was some touch of the sea about them, some prior experience on the water. Those of us who were not in the local defense group envied them their salty ways. The other group, the landlubbers, it turned out, were to see much more of the sea very quickly. It was the Armed Guard group. In the beginning, none of us knew what 'Armed Guard' meant. The favorite theory which spread among us was that we would be responsible for armed guards surrounding factories in which munitions were being manufactured. Our ego suffered badly for lack of the expectation of more appropriate Naval duty until we learned on the third day that our assignment was to be in charge of gun crews on merchant vessels. In retrospect, the Armed Guard group appeared to consist of a superior group of men, about 70 strong. Their ages centered around 35 to 40, a few somewhat older, and a few somewhat younger. The youngest in our group was Ensign Maddux, age 29, who was to die only a few months later after some 76 days on a raft in the South Atlantic, and only a few days before the several survivors aboard were rescued. All members of the group were college men with a rather heavy professional stamp. There were lawyers, architects, a few college teachers, a few businessmen, and bond salesmen. In view of the duty to which they were to be assigned, it was presumed that they needed to be men of stability, good judgment, and independence. We had four weeks of schoolroom training in South Boston. We were taught about gunnery, much of it irrelevant to the actual conditions we would encounter in the armament on merchant ships. We were taught a lot about Naval regulations, very little of which seemed to have much bearing upon the kind of duty aboard merchant vessels we would soon encounter. We did get some lectures about the merchant marine. A former Merchant Master, then serving in the Navy, gave us very bad advice about handling merchant officers and crew, including the message, 'Shoot the bastards!' After four weeks of training in Boston, we were ordered to duty in Chicago at the Naval armory located on the municipal pier. Thirty-five of our group of 70 were ordered to report there, the other 35 going to Little Creek, Virginia. There were enlisted men assigned to the Naval armory, and the officers were trained on the proceedings for handling the Mark IX 4-inch gun, which had been the destroyer gun in World War I. We drilled the gun crews in the handling of the equipment, and in the loading of guns, using dummy ammunition. In the fourth week, along with five or six others, I went aboard the USS *Dover* on Lake Michigan for a 4-day spell. This ship had once been called the USS *Wilmington,* and had been the flagship, many years before, of the Asiatic fleet. It was very flat-bottomed, and held the record for surviving an extreme roll in the course of a typhoon. It was, in fact, at the time we were aboard, the oldest ship in active commission in the United States Navy, and it certainly looked like it. Theoretically, each of us was allowed five rounds, but only had three; we also trained on a .30 caliber machine gun."[31] Dr. Odegaard's delightfully humorous experience with the "armament" he found on his first ship is related elsewhere.

Lieutenant Robert Ruark, USNR, possibly had the best credentials for being in the armed guard. Although a professional newsman, he had served a hitch in the U.S. Merchant Marine before the war, and so had no surprises when he went to sea in the "SS Rustpot" and sister ships. In a fascinating story on the armed guard in a May 1944 issue of the *Saturday Evening Post* entitled, "They Called 'Em Fish Food," he graphically described the lives of the valiant navy gun crews who thought, too often correctly, that an assignment to a merchantman was a sentence of death. Despite many close calls, Ruark survived the war to become an internationally known, best-selling author.[32]

While in the early stage of naval armed guard development, a "warm body" would suffice; a later member had to be in especially good physical condition, as there were no doctors aboard a merchant ship. Good vision, especially night vision, was a requisite, to enable spotting of enemy ships or aircraft. The ability to improvise and make repairs to faulty equipment, and boyhood hunting experience in "leading" targets were both assets to gunners, who had a new and more deadly type of bird to shoot at. One gun crew was composed entirely of "West (By God!) Virginians." They were an unruly bunch, and one or more was always on report, but as an admiring shipmate said, "They were the best gunners I have ever seen. It usually only took one shot to get range on a smoke pot, and the second was dead on."

If it appears from what has been said that the planning, organization, and training of the NAG service in its early stages might be considered a bit haphazard and more than a little inefficient, some unofficial and unpublished navy reports are in complete agreement. A navy officer ordered to prepare a history of the Armed Guard Center at Treasure Island obviously did not intend to make the navy his career. He wrote, "In spite of the many difficulties, misunderstandings, jealousies, rivalries and confusion" (and alleged stupidity of most people in Washington D.C.), "the Center does not appear to have had greater difficulties than other Centers in its basic mission. . . ." Such viewpoints are not new; undoubtedly Roman legionnaires in cold, wet encampments along the Rhine must have grouched, "There are two [expletive deleted] ways of doing things, the right way and the Legion way."[33]

Nevertheless, the "haphazard" training of AGs gave way

to a well-designed program based on previous mistakes or lessons learned the hard way. The *Training Review* of the U.S. Naval School, New Orleans, gives a clear picture of improvement in gunnery training, gun maintenance, and drills, and accuracy of firing. Later AG gun crews, with their merchant crew volunteers, were able to put up such a curtain of fire that submarines feared to surface, and so many enemy planes were destroyed that previously successful low-level air attacks were changed to higher level and less-accurate attack by enemy airmen of non-kamikaze frame of mind. Techniques designed to combat the slow, medium-level bombers of 1942 were totally inadequate against the suicidal kamikazes of 1945.

"Abandon ship" courses were begun, stressing celestial navigation, seamanship, operation of lifeboats and rafts, small-boat rigging, plotting of position, and setting course. What could be more important in a crowded lifeboat, seemingly a million miles from land? Training in aircraft recognition became a vital course, as it had been found, often tragically, that previous techniques had been too slow and inefficient, and "friendlies" had been shot down. Training in navigation, at first voluntary, became a 30-hour required course.[34]

In "Part B" of the war (1943–45), a flood of new, more comfortable, well-armed ships poured out of United States shipyards. They were manned by youthful, newly trained merchant crews and officers. With vastly improved antisubmarine (ASW) tactics and equipment and AA, assignments to the AG, formerly objects of horror to many, became highly desired. On more than one occasion, promotions to higher ratings were evaded, as they generally involved transfer to fleet duty above 2nd-class ratings.

Indicative of the development and improvement of NAG training was the comparison in the experiences of two communications assignees. Richard E. Williams, Mission, Kansas, reports, "I was a member of the Naval Armed Guard shipping out of New Orleans, La. I was a Radioman 2/c and I shipped out on a Dutch-flag freighter. The Center ran out of signalmen, so they gave me two and a half days of instruction in flag hoist and semaphore, and then shipped me out. Having been a Boy Scout helped out in remembering the semaphore signals."[35] William P. Watson, USNR, Pennington, New Jersey, says, "I was in Navy Communications School in Noroton Heights, Conn., in October 1942, and the week I was assigned to a merchant ship the cover story of a national magazine (I think it was *Life*) was, 'How to be Torpedoed and Live', and showed a large merchant ship with the stern high in the air and the bow deep in the water. Our instruction was slightly more than inadequate as none of our teachers had been in a convoy.

"A bright young Ensign Gilbert Clee, USNR, was given duty in the New York Port Director's Office; his assignment was to work with merchant ship captains and the Naval escort through the process of a convoy conference. . . . Ensign Clee saw quickly the need for better inter-ship communication and asked to go on a convoy as an observer. On return, he reported on the need for specific convoy communications training. He was eventually given approval of his idea, and his first class was our group from Noroton Heights. We were trained in flag hoists, convoy formation, flashing light, zigzagging, verbal talk procedure, HF radio and general convoy operations. This came from his own experience and the Merchant Ship Communications book, known as 'Mersigs,' which had been used by the British Admiralty in the early days of the war. Training was four–six weeks, and assignments were generally to larger ships such as troop carriers. On my ship, the *Sea Train Texas*, the Navy personnel consisted of a senior and junior gunnery officer with about 40 gun crew. As Commo officer, I had six signalmen and 3 Army radio operators. I spent all my time on the bridge with the Captain and deck officers; although most deck officers had not been to sea very long themselves, they were often contemptuous of some '30-day Navy wonders.'

"Ensign Clee, later promoted to Lt. (jg), was successful in getting the Navy to set up communications schools around the country similar to our original class, and after a number of convoy operations, I was reassigned to the West Coast to establish such training. Reception at first was cold, as most shipping lines and even high-ranking Navy personnel felt that training was unnecessary as few ships traveled in convoy in the Pacific. AG Gunnery officers were assigned to the class, and eventually deck officers of merchant ships were required to obtain a Certificate of Instruction from a Wartime Merchant Ship Communications School, which really boosted attendance. In one class we even had a non-English-speaking Russian captain, with interpreter.

"When we closed on V-J Day, our attendance figures totaled 10,000 men who had completed the course, better than half of whom were AG gunnery officers. Maybe a mutual knowledge of merchant ship communications was an ingredient to success of later wartime operations."[36]

The three primary AG training schools for much of the war were Little Creek, Virginia (later moved to Camp Shelton), Gulfport, Mississippi (after the training at Great Lakes Training Station was closed out), and San Diego, California. The first and largest was Little Creek/Shelton, and training programs developed there were subsequently adopted by the others. Little Creek trained 533 classes of officers and men, a grand total of 72,278. Opened in late 1941, it was converted to a separation center in August 1945. Gulfport opened on 1 September 1942, and BuPers estimates that 2,005 officers and 32,401 enlisted men were trained there. The AG School at San Diego was opened even before the repeal of the Neutrality Act; it trained 1,273 officers and 16,931 men according to BuPers.[37]

Gunnery schools to provide refresher training in new weapons were established in New York, New Orleans, San Francisco, and Seattle. New and larger ships, carrying expanded weapons systems, led to sophisticated training devices that almost simulated the "real thing."

There could be few better evaluators in the improvement in equipment and training than Lieutenant Robert Ruark, USNR, who wrote later: "There was a time when, if you had a ten-man gun crew, a 4-inch gun, and a couple of 50-caliber machine guns, you were considered a very lucky guy. Today a Liberty ship carries two dual-purpose, 3-inch guns, or a 4 or 5-inch gun aft, and a 3-inch gun forward, and eight 20mms, with explosive shells . . . the 20mm, probably more than any other single factor, has made aircraft attack on convoys highly impracticable. Sixty or eighty ships armed with Oerlikons and 3-inchers can toss up a screen of flak that a hummingbird couldn't get through." (No kamikazes at that time of writing.) [38]

Remarking on the increased manpower in gun crews and their later lengthy and advanced training, he said, "When the AG officer takes a ship today, his skull is bulging with fire control, and gunnery, seamanship, communications, navigation, convoy procedure, aircraft identification, first aid and simple surgery. . .", indeed a drastic change from the days of "fish food."

In an article written during the war, BM 1/c Warren Chapman wrote of the armament on his tanker, "I was fresh out of AG school at Great Lakes, and had eleven men under me. We had an old, heavy-caliber gun mounted aft, and two 30-cal machine guns, one aft and one forward on the bridge. We all knew that those guns wouldn't stop a U-boat any more than so many peashooters. For protection against torpedoes we had to rely on our ship's speed." It wasn't enough. Chapman's tanker was soon sunk by torpedo, the first of two sinkings on his first two voyages. [39]

Slowly, obsolete guns were replaced on merchant shipping with dual-purpose 5-inch 38s, which became the gunner's dream weapon and could shoot almost straight up. The .30- and .50-caliber machine guns were replaced by 20-mm Oerlikons, with tracers every fourth round. On the new ships pouring out of the yards, standard armament was one 5-inch gun, one 3-inch, and eight 20-mm Oerlikons, and by 1943, the standard AG gun crew had increased to one officer, a boatswain's mate or coxwain, two gunner's mates and nineteen seamen 1/c. Two signalmen and one radio operator raised the total navy crew to as many as twenty-seven, but they still had to rely on merchant-seamen volunteers to pass the ammunition and assist at the guns, and they often proved of invaluable assistance.

Possibly the biggest improvement in weaponry was the development of the 5-inch .38-cal gun. As one "grizzled" young gun captain reported, "It is an electric hydraulic operated gun. You have to call the engine room over the stern telephone and tell them to turn on the generator that furnishes power to operate the gun. It can be operated manually, but it is like steering an auto with power steering with a dead engine. The gun was a honey, dual-purpose, which meant it could be used against surface or air targets. It had a loading tray, the powderman would put the brass case of powder in the tray, then the shellman would lay the shell in the tray. The shellman would then hit a small lever by his left hand with a downward push. When the lever was pushed down, the spade would ram the shell and powder case into the gun, and as soon as the breech closed she was ready to fire on command from the gun captain.

"The gun operated smoothly and easily. It could be swung from port to starboard in just a few seconds, and the same was true of the elevations. It was hard to believe that we could elevate 88°, just two short of straight up."

The changes and improvement in armament were such that it almost seems incredible that Signalman Pete Burke, the commodore's signalman on the SS *John D. Archbold,* describing the ship's 1942 armament of one .30-cal machine gun on each side of the bridge, could ever write, "As the Bos'n put it, 'If we're ever attacked, with the arms we got, we might as well throw potatoes at them'." [40]

A navy report prepared by the Office of the CNO after the war lists the grand total of the armed guard service at 144,970, assigned from 7 December 1941 to 30 September 1945. Officers totaled 9,390, of which 8,587 were gunnery officers and 803 communications; enlisted personnel totaled 135,580, petty officers and seamen 119,811, and radiomen and signalmen 15,769. The naval armed guard reached its peak of 5,447 officers and 106,661 enlisted on 1 November 1944, for a total of 112,108. [41]

CHAPTER FOUR
THE "OTHER NAVY" AT SEA

The Armed Guard has met the enemy
oftener and on more widely divergent
fronts than any other branch of our
fighting forces.
—Lieutenant Robert Ruark, USNR [1]

Members of the NAG often regarded themselves as belonging to a completely different and unrecognized U.S. Navy. Their "navy" consisted of a small group of gunners, with perhaps a signalman or radioman or two, aboard a merchant ship of varying degrees of decrepitude, especially in the early days. Having enlisted in the navy, they undoubtedly had believed that they would be assigned to a spic-and-span battleship, a powerful cruiser, or a sleek destroyer, heading out at flank speed to engage the enemy. Many a jaw dropped when an AG first saw "his" ship, an old rust-bucket, filthy decks, gear rusty and in complete disorder, and quarters and food that could turn a stomach. One such vessel was the ship to which Lieutenant Charles E. Odegaard, USNR, reported, fresh out of gunnery school. The ship had been in service for years in the Gulf area and was overrun with rats and cockroaches, which welcomed him by promptly eating the leather sweatband in his brand new cap. He also was not favorably impressed when a rat ran over his chest in his bunk. After complaining, he did manage at a later date to persuade a port director to order the ship fumigated. The NAGs could not refuse to serve on a ship regardless of her destination, and seldom because of her condition, and their pay was the same whether en route to Murmansk or Hawaii.

Shipboard conditions, however, were not Odegaard's only problem. He reports, "When I went aboard the ship, gunners from the Navy were in the process of installing its armament. On the fantail they were placing a 4-inch gun, but not a Mark IX, on which we had been trained. It was a Mark VII, dating from 1898, and had obviously been used in the port side of an older Navy vessel. A portion of the arc was loose and wobbly, but either side was tight and stiff for lack of use. A warrant gunner with 25-years service told me he had never seen a Mark VII, 4-inch before. The gun crew consisted of six apprentice seamen, one seaman 2/c and a coxswain with seven years in the navy. One morning at dawn we set out for Lake Charles, La., and were ready to test fire the 4-inch gun. Imagine our reaction when we fired the gun and nothing happened. We attempted to fire eight times, with the same result. The merchant crew had already evidenced its confidence in the Navy gun crew by taking itself forward of the deckhouse. The coxswain and I heaved the shell over the side and then turned to the Oerlikons. Not one of them would fire. At this time the crew, who had been something less than hospitable and friendly, now had good reason to show their contempt for the Navy. . . . Finally a petty officer from another ship checked the correct seating of the gun barrels, after we arrived at Lake Charles. When we left Lake Charles we fired the 4-inch; she fired with a very satisfactory 'boom' and the spirits of the gun crew considerably improved. The Oerlikons also fired without a hitch, and the merchant crew began to show a friendlier attitude.

"It is a good thing everything worked, for we had to fire at a submarine which submerged, passed a number of hulls of sunken ships, or just a portion of the mast or part of the ship showing; others had turned turtle. We saw two ships torpedoed and sunk within minutes. There was something so final about seeing ships go down this way. . . ."[2]

Lieutenant Odegaard was not the only gunnery officer to find an antique weapon on board. One amazed officer found a monstrous 5-inch 50-bag gun mounted on the stern of his ship. It was only fired once, for the result was almost calamitous. The old relic's thunderous concussion knocked the gun crew in all directions, causing havoc with stanchions, broken glass on instruments, pipes blown from fittings, door panels demolished, and shattered glassware everywhere. The gun crew were surprised to find no broken bones.

Gunnery officer Ensign Hal Bondhus, USNR, Oxford, Ohio, was another "antique collector." He writes, "After a couple of weeks in San Francisco, I got assigned to a Liberty Ship—S.S. *David Bushnell.* The 5″ 50 gun had 1907 stamped on the breech. I learned later that it was obsolete in World War I. The inside of the barrel was so badly worn, that it resembled the markings on a coke bottle. Mechanisms for elevating and training the gun were so worn, that you would have to back them up several revolutions in order to get the gears to mesh. The azimuth scale had a midpoint of 50. It could be moved to 47 and to 52. It had a horizontal breech mechanism which came half-way open each time the gun was fired. They gave us two .30 caliber machine guns. The only mounts that could be fitted to them were the two that they sent along. They were the tripod mounts that are used in the field. Somehow, we didn't find a way to sink them into the steel decks. We did have five .20 mm caliber Oerlikons. When I would report into the Port Director's office, I would get all kinds of knowing looks, when I reported that the 5″ 50 gun was in bad condition. The secondary battery on the battleships were 5″ 51's. So, they would assume that a green Ensign just didn't know his terminology. I do not know how many times I was told that they had a Chief who knew everything that there was to know, and he would have the gun in ship shape in no time at all. I had Chiefs with years of experience who admitted that they had never seen a gun like mine. Also, there was never a single one of them who put a tool on the gun. They would scratch their heads and wish me luck."[5]

AG crews on merchant ships received continuing jibes from merchant mariners that they weren't in the "real" navy, and were ribbed for serving for such low pay. The feeling of isolation extended to many AG gunnery officers, and probably the best summation of the role of the NAG was made by Lieutenant Commander Beverley Britton, USNR, who served two years as a gunnery officer on merchant ships. In an article in *Proceedings,* published after the war by the U.S. Naval Institute, he referred to the naval armed guard as the "Navy's Stepchildren" and wrote, "It is not surprising that the AG quickly became known as the least-desired duty in the Navy. The AG was physically separated from his fellow Navymen, placed in a small group aboard a ship run by civilians. He was automatically excluded from the glamor, glory and common experience of those who serve aboard a warship. It isolated him from a feeling of 'belonging,' as well as being separated from the creature comforts which are an integral part of Navy ships—the services of a doctor, paymaster, mail clerk, ship's store, recreational facilities, movies, and the fixed, secure routine of a Navy vessel, which in spite of 'gripes' makes a sailor feel secure. But the most important thing taken from him, before he even had it, was the feeling of pride in 'his' ship.

"The AG officer at first fared little better. He was a military commander on a non-military ship. At the beginning, most had no naval experience and skimpy training. He was an unwelcome interloper to many skippers and ship's officers, and was resented when he tried to exercise his authority regarding security of the ship. Some were capable of developing harmonious relationships between Navy and Merchant Mariners, others fought bitter and continuing battles with merchant officers and crews.

"In addition to all the stress of operating aboard a civilian ship, he was pretty much of a 'stepchild' to the Navy. He didn't even have a typewriter to prepare his official reports, unless he borrowed one or supplied his own. But worst of all, the AG could be considered a 'dead-end' street as far as a Naval career was concerned. He was not only out of sight of the 'brass,' but pretty much out of mind, unless something bad happened. He had lost touch with Navy life, promotions were slow, and his experience aboard a civilian ship was not conducive to getting desirable duty in the fleet, or other assignment. A number of AGs did remain and make a career of the navy, but almost all invariably came to love armed guard service, and the old "SS Rustpot."[4]

Aside from antique or inadequate weaponry, one of the first hurdles an AG gunnery officer had to face after boarding his ship was to establish his authority regarding security and the defense of the ship, a division of authority greatly resented by many masters as well as merchant officers and crews. By law, the master was responsible for the navigation and safety of his ship, but in wartime the AG commander had exclusive responsibility for the ship's defense. A considerable number of masters considered this an infringement on their Jove-like power aboard ship, and made no secret of their opinions, not only of the regulation, but of the landlubbers with the shiny new stripes. The master was also required to make merchant seamen available to assist at the guns, either in actual operation or in handling ammunition. Most of the time this was not a problem, as there were many volunteers who accepted training and served bravely and effectively. However, in the early stages, there were occasions when merchant crews objected and had to be ordered to comply.

The reaction of an old-time skipper to the newly minted gunnery officer is quite understandable. Requiring an experienced master to entrust his ship, in an emergency, to a very young man whose sole nautical training consisted of a few weeks in a naval gunnery school and who may have never even seen a ship until assignment to the naval armed guard, was enough to fill him with horror. The gunnery officer often had to train his neophyte AG and MM gun crew with weapons he knew nothing about, a case of the blind leading the blind, unless he was lucky enough to have an experienced and capable petty officer such as Lieutenant Odegaard had in Coxswain Morin. He knew a lot more about the navy than the lieutenant, as Odegaard freely admits, ". . . and in his own subtle way was a good teacher," for him as well as the men. "He put in long hours doing his best to train the sailors in handling the equipment and to encourage their military demeanor; he obviously had pride in his Naval service." The net result of good training aboard ship was a well-knit and capable gun crew, able to put up a defense against submarines, aircraft, or sea raiders.

Before that happened, the young, inexperienced AG gun-crew commander found that his duties were incredibly complicated and surprising. Upon arrival at the port director's office, he was given the AG "Bible," the *Instructions for the Commanding Officer of Naval Armed Guard Crews Aboard Merchant Ships in Time of War*, intended to guide him through the uncertainty of his first command. He would quickly learn that it actually did not cover what would come and that his real education would come at sea. His *Instructions* gave an ominous hint, "There shall be no surrender and no abandoning ship, so long as the guns can be fought. . . . The Navy Department considers that as long as there remains a chance to save the ship, the Armed Guard shall remain thereon and take every opportunity that may present itself to destroy the submarine."

To their everlasting credit, many AG crews lived—and died—by those instructions, serving their guns until they could no longer be fired, or standing by their ship until decks were awash. There will be many descriptions of such heroism to follow.

In addition to the many duties specifically detailed, the AG officer also quickly found that he was to serve in new and strange capacities. He had to be a doctor when needed, a chaplain, a diplomat aboard ship and in foreign ports, a salesman and mediator in developing cooperation between his AG crew and merchant marine officers and seamen, an adviser to the love-lorn, a school teacher to his crew for them to obtain higher ratings, and lest we forget, often a companion to the skipper during "happy hour." Many became outstanding officers, respected by the "merchants" and loved by their men; others failed sometimes due to being overly impressed by their new authority or because of immaturity and poor judgment.

Lieutenant Gib Robinson, USNR, reports, "My time in the Navy with many young men, hardly more than boys, most of them away from home for the first time, was an experience I'll never forget. I was considerably older than they, and we got along splendidly, little or no disciplinary problems. I was a combination of father–big brother, and they became almost like my own kin. Fortunately, I have no bad memories of having lost any, in spite of being under attack many times."[5] On the other hand, a young but experienced gun captain reported on his difficulties with a new AG officer who obviously had a lot to learn. "I got crossways with the new Ensign, and stayed that way. We finally joined our convoy and were assigned our position. We hadn't seen the gunnery officer all day. Then he finally came out on the boat deck while we were getting in position. He was dressed in his dress blues, with white hat. The Second Mate said, 'Well, would you look at that!' About that time, the wind got that white hat and it sailed away to the deep six. The Ensign dashed back into his cabin and the next time we saw him he was in his sheepskin mackinaw with a hood. The Ensign was a brand new officer, fresh out of school. He replaced a very good gunnery officer who had been promoted to full Lieutenant and was relieved. The new man was a smart-alec type and he didn't hit it off with the merchant officers or with the AG petty officers. He wanted to know why everybody was carrying a knife on his belt. I told him that if you end up in the water, you will most likely need it. He said he didn't like the idea and we should quit wearing them. I said as long as we are at sea, I'll wear mine, and if you look around you, you'll see that all the merchant crew, including the officers, are wearing one, and if you don't have one, you'd better get one. . . . After some time, he apologized to me and reported that he had learned a lot, and wanted to let me know that he had gotten a good sheath knife." Obviously, the ensign had not noted a tip in *The Little Creek Blast* of 28 September 1942, "Always carry a sharp knife, and know where to find a water-tight flashlight, a rope belt with a hook for holding onto the side of a boat. Keep heavy clothing laid out—check lifeboat provisions often and always keep a small fishing tackle handy." These were practical tips that could and have saved lives.

There were ways in which good relations were cemented between the MM crews and AGs. Lieutenant Robert Ruark, USNR, reported, "Any sailor who has been through a couple of stiff air attacks loses any animosity he might have cher-

ished against the gun crew. I remember a snappish old engineer who had no use for the Navy and never missed an opportunity to get in a couple of cracks against us. A few weeks
and several attacks later, the old boy could be seen dashing
around the exposed flying bridge, in a perfect hail of flying
flak and falling bombs with a bucket of water for my gunners, the "Sea Scouts" he used to ridicule. When we finally
hit dock, after a mean run up the Adriatic, the merchant marine fell all over itself trying to buy drinks for my boys."
Ruark added that some beautiful jobs of auxiliary loading
and firing were done by merchant sailors when the navy
crew was inadequate in number or depleted by casualties.[6]

On the basis of experience, the navy replaced many of
the younger AG officers with older men of more experience
and maturity. A good example of what can be accomplished
is the story of Lieutenant Commander Leo Blackburn, USN
(Ret.), from Portsmouth, Ohio. As LCDR Blackburn puts it,
"As the AG Center's Assigning Officer at Brooklyn was assigning me to a ship, he mumbled, 'Trouble ship. Merchant
captain and officer hate each other's guts, and rush to the
Port Director at every port of call to blast each other. Have to
release the AG officer. Try to get along with the merchant
crew. AG officer says 1st Engineer worst troublemaker on
ship.' With these words ringing in my ears, my Navy gun
crew (none of whom I had ever seen before) and I were
driven to the ship, which was preparing to sail. It was an old
merchant ship, built in 1914. About a half-dozen carry-over
crew members met us at the gangway and helped us bring
our gear aboard. I thought it was very nice, they being real
sea dogs after one or two voyages, and we sailors going to
sea for the first time.

"I somewhat dreaded my first encounter with the merchant captain, officers and crew, but faced up to it quickly. I
found Captain Lindgren to be an old Swedish captain, and
after showing him great respect, asking a few questions
which showed I respected his age, knowledge and experience, he seemed to mellow, and got very friendly on a father-
son basis, and introduced me to his officers. I could see the 1st

Engineer looking at me rather disdainfully, and I planned then and there to cultivate him and make him a friend. After all, there was a good chance we'd be living together in the ship's close quarters for a year or so. Also, I had just read Dale Carnegie's *How to Win Friends and Influence People*, and here was my chance to try it out in a real-life and vital situation. Well, it turned out that we all soon became a harmonious Armed Guard-Merchant Marine group, gradually ironing out problems common to such living arrangements."[7]

AG officers had many other unofficial "duties" that they sometimes discharged in unofficial ways. Lieutenant Gib Robinson reports, "I always had more athletic equipment aboard for my crews than most other officers I visited with— how did I get it? Well, as is pretty generally known, the skipper could always purchase a case of Scotch when in England (for medicinal purposes I think it was), and due to the fact that I got along pretty well with my skippers, I usually had a few "fifths" on hand when we reached the States. It was very beneficial when it came to securing medicine balls, punching bags, baseball equipment, footballs, boxing gloves—and extra allotments of practice ammunition. Invariably at Navy Supply it was, 'Out of the question! We just can't furnish all the requests. AG crews don't normally get that type of equipment, or the quantity requested.' It was very interesting that when you casually mentioned to someone that you thought you might be able to help a little, and that you could possibly find some Scotch, if certain equipment could be located, it was not only found, but furnished promptly! I never failed to get everything I wanted, and my crews and the merchant crews loved their recreational equipment. Once we were tied up off a barren area of Scotland for two weeks, and the crews did a lot of rifle and hand-gun target shooting, played a lot of baseball, and we nearly filled our refrigerator storage with fine-eating fish filets. We built a raft, and put it in the water, and I made some simple spears from engineer's furnishings. Crewmen nearly fought to man the raft and spear the fish. I was proud that my crews kept the AG in good relationship with the Merchant Marine. I really enjoyed my AG duty. You were your own boss, so to speak, and whatever innovations you might try, the results were yours."[8]

Lieutenant Norman Alston, USNR, boarded his first ship, the SS *Thomas J. Rusk*, in Houston, Texas. The gun crew was made up of southern boys away from home for the first time, but it was not until they had been at sea for some time that the truth came out. One was a fifteen-year-old and another just sixteen. The fifteen-year-old had so badgered his parents that they finally consented for him to enlist along with his older brother. They hoped that the seventeen-year-old would be able to "care" for his younger brother. Luckily, the two boys were together, at least for the first year.

A night or two after leaving port, there was a knock at Lieutenant Alston's door. Looking out, he found two of the youngest and smallest of the crew. They were pale, visibly scared, and their knees actually knocked. "Suh," said one. "Can we-uns ask you a question, Suh?" Alston replied, "Indeed you may, but I reserve the right whether to answer." Whereupon one of them said, "Well Suh, it's this way, Suh, we boys, we-uns want to know. Is you a Yankee?" Alston reflected before answering, "I don't know what you consider a Yankee, but I was born and have lived all my life in the West. I'm a Westerner." At this the boys faces lit up with happiness and the older one said, "Oh! Thank you, Suh, thank you. We-uns is going to get along fine, just so you ain't a Yankee." And they did get along just fine. Alston found them to be a most cooperative and willing group, receptive to learning the routine of shipboard life and accepting the rather relaxed discipline of the armed guard. However, he notes that these southern boys did have one major complaint. While they continued to grow, as boys will, some right out of their pants, they repeatedly complained, "Suh, this here's a starvation ship." And then one night the chief steward broke out the blackeyed peas, the salt pork, and the grits. As the boys came from dinner, they inquired, "Lieutenant, did you ever taste such a fine meal?" War can indeed be hell (as some Yankee general said a while back), but it is especially hell if you are young and homesick and away from the familiar things of life.[9]

As the navy learned by experience, each AG gunnery officer was supplied with a medicine chest about as large as a steamer trunk. It contained aspirin, phenobarbital, laxatives, morphine syrettes, catgut sutures, splints, tourniquet bands, and sulfa drugs when they became available. While better prepared to deal with medical emergencies than before, with no doctors or even pharmacist's mates aboard most merchant vessels, there was probably not a single AG officer who was not secretly terrified about the possible need for him to perform an operation at sea, like in the movies. They did successfully handle many problems with injuries and illness aboard ship, which did wonders in increasing the regard of the merchant crews for the AG contingent. However, as was to be expected, there were times when nothing could be done. On one occasion several members of the gun crew and some merchant seamen were badly battered trying to effect repairs on deck during a vicious storm. One unfortunate seaman sustained a broken back, and there was little that could be done for him. The AG officer slung a bunk bed from the overhead and made him as comfortable as possible until they were close enough to New York for the commodore to signal for a Coast Guard vessel to pick up the injured man.

Among the many problems aboard ship faced by the AG officer, on occasion he also had to become an amateur psychiatrist, especially in dealing with problems of the love-lorn young. In one case, the malaise was cured by simply giving a flat-broke sailor the money to pay for a long-distance call to his girlfriend, with whom he had had a quarrel. It worked to perfection, and the happy young man promptly repaid the money.

Lieutenant Commander Charles Odegaard reported that he and his new gun crew got off to a poor start when the guns wouldn't fire, but he made up for it as an amateur doctor: "I first learned of the problem when a sailor came running to me to tell me that Koughn had passed out. Was it heat prostration or heat exhaustion? I had a suitcase full of emergency medical supplies, which fortunately included also a manual. I read through the manual trying to determine which was which, and finally made a diagnosis, and handled him, fortunately, in the right way, which brought him to. My stock went up as my fame as a medicine man spread. The following day a wiper in the heat of the engine room passed out, and an engineer officer came running to me asking that I come down to the engine room to determine what to do with the man. Again my treatment proved successful, so my stock in the merchant marine rose."[10]

As gun crews grew larger, AGs stood watches on the heavy guns (if any). Two men were on lookout duty at each 3-inch or larger gun. A normal (later in the war) twenty-four-man gun crew had men on watch at all times while at sea: two men at the stern gun, forward gun, and a petty officer and three men stationed in the vicinity of the bridge. The petty officer did not stand lookout duty. The three men in the vicinity of the bridge were to stand by and relieve the lookouts. The strain was such that no more than two hours of steady lookout duty for submarines or one hour steady lookout for aircraft was allowed before relief was supplied. Where aircraft attack was a possibility, half the gun crew were on watch. One man was ordered to be at each machine gun in such cases, but the merchant crew was supposed to furnish half the watch at the machine guns.

Normally, men were on watch for four hours, eight hours out of each twenty-four-hour period while at sea, but when attack was expected half the gun crews were on watch and half off watch. AGs went to General Quarters manning all guns for about an hour at dawn and sunset, when submarine or air attacks were most likely.

In between keeping their quarters and clothing in good shape, being on watch up to twelve hours a day, GQ twice a day, cleaning and lubricating guns and other tasks involved in maintaining navy equipment on board, plus training the merchant crews, the AG men did not have much time for doing any heavy reading, although they were encouraged to study for advancement when they could.

Other than manning the guns, the "Other Navy" earned the respect and appreciation of the merchant marine in many ways, one of which was fire fighting. As NAG training improved during the war and the need for instruction and training in fighting fire aboard merchant ships became more evident, a program of fire fighting was inaugurated. It proved so successful that a number of merchant marine masters wrote commendations on the performance of the AG crews. Typical is the letter from the master of the SS *Woodbridge N. Ferris,* Calmar Steamship Corporation, New York, NY, addressed to Capt. William Coakley, U.S. Naval Armed Guard Center, South Brooklyn, New York: "Dear Sir: As Master of the *S.S. Woodbridge N. Ferris,* I should like to take the opportunity of commending the U.S. Naval Armed Guard Crew attached to this ship for their splendid and most efficient action in controlling and putting out a fire which started on the pier to which we are tied. At 15:50 November 24, 1943, a fire of uncertain origin broke out at Pier #1, Erie Basin. The U.S. Naval Gun Crew aboard promptly broke out the fire hoses and eased off on the stern lines. These men manned the hoses and stood by until the fire was put out.

"It is my belief that without the prompt action of the U.S. Naval Gun Crew, the fire might have grown to very large proportions thereby causing considerable damage. These men are to be commended for their fine action. Sincerely, Henning Lind, Master, S.S. *Woodbridge N. Ferris.*"[11]

The navy training was so good and in practice proved so effective that many NAGs became fire fighters upon discharge, including C. A. Lloyd, who became a captain in the Raleigh, North Carolina, Fire Department.

Shakedown cruises of new ships were never particularly enjoyed by an AG gun captain, particularly if he noticed a red and white sign riveted to the gun mount saying that the gun had never been fired. An old hand as gun captain explains, "When our gun crew moved on board the *Bullfinch,* we spent several days moving ammo up from the magazine to the ready boxes for the 3″ 50 on the bow and the 5″ 38 on the stern. Before we put the shells in the ready boxes, we preset the fuse, and marked each row of shells with the fuse setting. The biggest job was the 20mm magazines. Each round had to have a thin coat of grease on it or the gun would jam. Each magazine held sixty rounds and each gun had two ready boxes with a magazine in each box. Each magazine had to have sixty pounds of tension. This was done with a crank, winding up the spring until 60 showed on the dial in the magazine. The shakedown run consisted of running at different speeds, making all kinds of turns, so that the shipyard engineers could see if everything was working properly. At a safe distance out we test-fired the new guns which had never been fired. This can be tricky, and since I was the gun captain I put my crew through loading drills for several days. We would load the gun and then clear the gun deck of everybody but me. After the gun deck was cleared, I would pull the trigger. The first time was always the worst because you didn't know if it was going to come apart, or fly off the mount. The last round was to be fired at 88 degrees, just two degrees from straight up. My regular position was directly behind the breech block. I believe it had a 20″ recoil and I had a back rest to keep from being blown off the gun deck." [12]

Discipline in AG crews aboard merchant vessels varied, generally depending on the attitude of the gunnery officer and petty officers, but was almost invariably relaxed in comparison with that on fleet ships. It could often be in accordance with the instructions of one gunnery officer who told his crew that unless certain people other than the merchant crew were around, to forget about saluting and "Yes, Sir— No, Sir." Dress aboard ship was also much different from dress in the fleet, and in the tropics often consisted of cut-off shorts, thongs, and a baseball cap. Food, especially on tankers, could be plentiful and excellent and readily available between watches.

Life aboard a merchant ship could be a horror or so pleasant that transfer to fleet duty held no charm. One gunner reported that after their arrival in New York his gunnery officer told them that they were going back to New Orleans and that he would have liked going with them but he was being sent to fleet duty. "He did not like the idea much, and I told him that this was the reason I stayed with my 3rd class PO rating. I didn't want any part of the Fleet, and you could bet that after you made a trip in the AG as 2nd class PO, they would pull you out for the fleet when you returned. I usually asked for the first ship out when I returned from leave."

Armed guards reporting back to AG centers after voyages were usually the center of attention of new men awaiting their first trip and were asked many questions as to "What is it really like?" Herb Norch of the Bronx, NY, recently back from the flaming Anzio beachhead, was wearing several area ribbons and battle stars, very impressive to the neophytes awaiting assignment. When asked what was the worst action he had ever seen, Norch thought a few minutes, as befits an old hand, and finally said, "The Staten Island Ferry—you can't believe what I've seen on that ferry!" Norch himself was taken in when on his first trip. As the ship was pulling out of New York harbor, a merchant seaman told him and other new AGs to be sure they had all their letters written as they would be dropped off at the Ambrose Light buoy. There followed a flurry of activity, with lots of letters being written, but there seemed to be considerable delay in getting to the postal drop-off. Whenever Norch would ask where Ambrose Light buoy was, he would be told, "It's a little farther out." He still had his letters when they dropped anchor in Liverpool.[13]

Humor, as always, relieves tension; however, even for veterans of many voyages, heading out into the North Atlantic was a sobering experience. As one gunner wrote in his diary, "You can't help but wonder every time you go out in the Atlantic, would you make it home again. There aren't many young ones making their first trip nowadays. We have a lot of Armed Guards in our crew that have been in all kinds of attacks; bombings, and submarines. We have two boys who had been torpedoed twice, and sunk both times, and one machine gunner that was credited with shooting down a Stuka dive bomber. I have made up a waterproof bundle which has a pair of dungarees, a long sleeve shirt, 4 packs of cigarettes, and a box of matches. This I sewed to my life jacket. We keep our life jackets nearby at all times. After we hit the open sea we cease taking our clothes off for a shower or to sleep. The first thing everyone wants after we have been at sea for some time is a good hot shower and a good night's sleep, without clothes or interruption. When in convoy, in fog, you can't see the ship in column next to you much of the time, so the fog horns kept blowing all night."

While many AGs had a comparatively tranquil existence on board merchant ships, and some never heard a shot fired in anger, others had horror piled upon horror—repeated sinkings, watching helplessly as buddies were caught by a flaming oil spill, on-lookers of atrocities as survivors of ships sunk by Japanese submarines were murdered in cold blood, and many other ghastly experiences. The navy inaugurated rest camps for war-worn veterans of AG service. One was at the converted Hotel College in Deland, Florida, an old rambling wooden hotel with spacious grounds and lush landscaping, a great place to relax and forget about the war for a while. The men there, according to Jim Bennett, SCPO, USN (Ret.), " . . . were convalescing from wounds, [were] survivors, or suffering exhaustion from prolonged exposure to combat conditions at sea." Bennett is now a successful freelance writer, largely on navy subjects. He reports that one teenage gunner was a survivor of three sinkings on one round trip, twice going across the Atlantic and once on return. He was still in shock from seeing shipmates dying before rescue and had daily sessions with a camp psychiatrist. Some men were "withdrawn" and others raised "cain." The commanding officer of the rest camp was "Jock" Sutherland, tough former football coach at the University of Pittsburgh. For those who got too carried away by the relaxed surroundings, Sutherland had a unique penalty duty. He had a pet monkey in a cage on the front lawn of the hotel. The monkey was filthy, as was the cage. Extra duty punishment involved cleaning the monkey's cage, a distasteful job to say the least. While the miscreant was cleaning the cage, his comrades would gather round and offer sympathy and encouragement, making monkey imitations—bending over, pushing out their upper lip with their tongue and scratching their ribs and grunting. The assignment apparently was not habit-forming. Without incriminating himself, Bennett accurately describes the job as "loathsome." The rest camp did a lot of good for the worn-out young men, as they took sightseeing trips, went fishing and horseback riding, or just rested and unwound. After a week or two of such R&R, they went back to the U-boats and Stukas, but the respite from the war worked wonders to relieve tension.[14]

Lest it be thought that the navy had a monopoly on AG duty on merchant ships, Raymond J. Roy, Acushnet, Massachusetts, advises that he too was an armed guard, but with the army. "I was in the Army before 7 December 1941, and after the attack on Pearl Harbor there was a great need for gunners to serve as Armed Guards. I served on two ships during the entire war, from January 1942–April 1945. The first was the S.S. *Thomas H. Barry,* and we sailed the South Pacific. At the time, the Navy was so short of personnel that we were called. We were taken off the *Barry* when replaced by Navy personnel. The second ship was the *Queen Mary,* which carried a division of 15,000 men at a time. I stayed on her until April 1945. Army Armed Guards manned a number of the largest liners in the world, including *Queen Elizabeth, Ile de France, Kungsholm, Aquitania, Empress of Australia,* plus many American-flag liners."[15]

Army personnel manned the guns on many ships as volunteers. A twenty-man detachment of the 5201st Engineer Construction Battalion was being transported to the Philippines aboard a Liberty ship, the SS *Benjamin Ide Wheeler,* for the invasion. After boarding, as PFC Russell Best wrote later, they were delighted to find that "instead of polishing GI cans or scrubbing down the decks each day en route, we were given instructions by the Navy Armed Guard crew in cleaning, greasing and care of the guns, as well as the operation of them, and the leading of targets. We came to accept the Navy crew with high regard for their cool courage and calm assurance, unflinching in the face of danger. Not only that, they were a most congenial group, taking a keen interest in our progress."

The training came in very handy for all, as upon arrival

at Leyte, even before dropping anchor, the ship was subjected to a continuing series of heavy air attacks. The army contingent stayed on General Quarters the whole time alongside the navy gun crew, shooting down several enemy aircraft and damaging others. Even after the army group was put ashore, they returned several times to visit their navy buddies and faced still more Japanese raids. The Port Command later reported that there were 118 raids (not alerts) during the week of 24–30 October 1944.[16]

Probably no other members of the naval armed guard had a more unique, if short, tour of duty than Gunner's Mate 2/c DeWitt Welch and others of a pick-up gun crew. While at the Brooklyn Armed Guard Center, Welch noted a group of civilians walking around and looking over the men, and one said, "We got 24, and we need one more seaman." Not having any idea what was going on, Welch was called over and told by the lieutenant to join the group, which had a signalman, coxswain, three gunner's mates and twenty seamen. Welch reports, "We were told we were a specially picked group, but never told what we were picked for. We didn't figure it was anything good because of special treatment we were receiving, such as weekend liberty. We were told to report back on Monday in fresh clothing and with fresh haircuts. On Monday, we were finally told what the assignment was all about. The government was going to make a film and we were part of the cast. A professional actor was to play the part of the gunnery officer. The film was to be made on a new Liberty ship, and was to include filming of loading, tearing-down and cleaning guns, gun drills, chow time, in our living quarters, and a scene of me unpacking my sea bag, stowing it in a locker and looking lovingly at a sexy pin-up girl, I know not whom, give her a big kiss and stick it up on the inside of "my" locker door.

"Then it was to sea for more filming, but on a real voyage on the SS *Worth*, carrying cargo to Puerto Rico. The weather kept getting hotter, but since the film was supposed to represent the North Atlantic, they had us wearing wool blues with life jackets, and we really sweated it out. The director would say that we are going to have an attack coming in on the port side, and that when we started firing we were to swing the gun around just as if we were tracking a plane. While the gunners were changing the magazines, the director would say that the next attack will be from another position. We would shoot up five or six magazines in about two hours, and get a 30-minute break. Then we had surface attacks in which we used our old WW I 4″50. We just plain shot up the world for about three days and never hit a thing, but sky and water. Getting out of those blues and life jackets after a hot day of shooting, cleaning up and getting a shower was the best part of our movie career. Finally we were finished with the film, the director and crew dropped off at Guantánamo to be flown back to New York, and our movie stardom came to an abrupt end. During all of our 'battles' the sea was very calm, but we soon had a taste of the real North Atlantic.[17]

Navy communications on shore do not always move as swiftly and efficiently as aboard ship, and to some AGs this often proved the case; they could be found in ports circling the globe and be moved elsewhere with little or no advance notice. It is no wonder why some communications never seemed to catch up. DeWitt Welch, erstwhile gunner's mate and movie star, was at NOLA awaiting discharge and became well acquainted with a fellow AG also pending discharge and transportation home. One day his friend was called to the personnel office, and didn't show up again for many hours. When DeWitt asked where he had been all day, the answer was that it was a long story. "He told me that when he had first enlisted, he had applied for a commission as, although he didn't have a degree, he had completed three years of college. They told him that if his application was approved, he would be notified. He had been in the Navy almost four years, and while they were checking his discharge records, they discovered that he had been awarded the commission over three years before. So, he said that he was not going to be discharged, and was going somewhere for further duty, and that he had been at the tailor's shop almost all day getting measured for an officer's uniform.

"When I asked his rank, he said he was a senior Lieutenant, and that the Payroll Office reported that it would be several days before they could finish figuring out how much money he had coming, but with his base pay, sea duty and other allowances, it would be a bundle." The next day a Pullman carload of AG veterans having been gathered together, DeWitt headed for Jacksonville, and out.[18]

Reflecting on his armed guard experience, Lieutenant Commander Norman Alston sums it up: "The boys did not get the carriers or battleships of their dreams, but they got something else from their time in the Armed Guard. They learned about the world and the people in it. They rode the subways of New York, transited the Canal, saw the villages of the Middle East, and the towns and cities of Brazil, Australia and other far-flung places. They grew up and became better men while the Navy was fulfilling its long-standing promise, "Join the Navy and See the World." [19]

Thomas Hedge, Hiwassee, Virginia, provides a perfect example; his travels made Ulysses look like a stay-at-home. His first voyage was aboard the famed SS *Virginia Dare,* from January–September 1943. On this trip he visited Cuba, Trinidad, South Africa, the Persian Gulf, Egypt, Argentina, and Brazil. This was followed by service on the SS *Alexander White,* with travel to Ireland, Scotland, and Russia (on the Murmansk run); then the SS *Jon Sedgewick* took him to England, North Africa, and southern France. In the SS *Franklin H. King* he went to the Admiralty Islands and the Philippines. Along the way, he gathered a lot of photographs, including one of him riding a camel at the Pyramids, and picked up a Bronze Star.[20]

CHAPTER FIVE
THE SHIPS THEY SAILED

Each with her own special memories . . .
—John Masefield, Sailor-Poet

Masefield was writing of the graceful sailing ships he had known in his youth. Certainly, each member of the naval armed guard has his own special memories, good or bad (and sometimes, endearingly both), of the ships that he served in. They ranged from near-derelict rust-buckets to luxury liners converted to wartime use as troop carriers. They included Hog Islanders of World War I vintage, "floating firecracker" tankers, thousands of "Ugly Ducklings," the famed Liberty ships that poured out of newly built shipyards to the amazement of both Allied and Axis powers, and the later, more-modern, bigger and faster Victory ships, which never seemed to capture the affection, and exasperation, felt for the Liberties.

The armed guards' ships served a multitude of uses: they primarily served as cargo carriers, but they included troop ships, PW ships, and many others. There were even mule transports, a seeming anachronism in the midst of the most sophisticated killing machinery the world had ever seen, but required in some areas.

At the end of December 1941, eleven U.S. ships carried armed guard crews, generally seven to eleven men, feebly armed with old light machine guns to protect lives and cargoes. By the end of 1942, there were armed guards aboard 1,000 merchantmen, eventually to become over 6,000. By the end of the war, merchant ships had become warships in reality, with well-trained AG gun crews capable of throwing a discouraging curtain of fire against attackers below or above the sea.[1]

To gain a clearer picture of what armed guard crews faced in the early days of U.S. participation in the war, it helps to look at the Hog Islanders, built at the Hog Island shipyards on the Delaware River south of Philadelphia. Numbering in the thousands, as part of the massive "Ships, Ships and More Ships!" building program of WW I, not one was produced in time to contribute to victory in that war, the first not being delivered until after the war, but they were laid down in sufficient numbers to knock the U.S. shipbuilding industry in the head for years. Many decrepit Hog Islanders were still serving in backwaters of the world when WW II came around and were among the first to receive AG crews. They had a strange-looking silhouette, but were relatively efficient. Fifty-eight were lost in WW II to submarines or other causes, including foundering.[2]

Tales of the Hog Islanders are particularly picturesque among the early AGs. One, who had observed a number of bigger and better ships in his convoy sunk by U-boats in the then-deadly Caribbean, wrote, "The reason they didn't sink us was because they thought we had already been hit and were sinking." Another veteran of Hog Islanders attributed his ship's survival to, "They didn't want to waste a torpedo— we'd sink soon anyway."

A former signalman reported, "While I have sailed on many types of ships, and under a number of foreign flags, the worst ship I ever sailed on was an old Hog Islander. It was my first AG vessel, and we didn't have a gunnery officer. The ship was in terrible condition mechanically and every other way. It had a motley crew which could charitably be called "scum," and the captain was an alcoholic who stocked his cabin with 14 cases of Scotch before leaving the U.S. for Ponce, Puerto Rico, and was seldom seen thereafter. The ship was a real rust-bucket, and could not do more than 5–6 knots. Fortunately, I had to be taken off the ship in Puerto Rico and hospitalized, and it left without me. Months later I ran into the Third Mate, who told me that the ship, carrying a load of bulk sugar, had foundered and sunk in a storm off Cape Hatteras on the return trip."[3]

Hog Islanders were not the only antiques pressed into WW II service. Gerald Sossaman, fresh off a farm in Mulberry, Arkansas, served as a gunner in the AG detachment

World War II Hog Islander rounding Cape Horn in 1943. (Courtesy of Q. M. Hunsaker)

aboard the SS *Virginian*. The *Virginian* had been built in happier days, in 1904, originally as a coal burner. It saw service in WW I, and although slow and arthritic, responded to the call to colors in WW II.[4] Joe Kushner of Houston, Texas, served as a gunner aboard a number of ships, one of which was the USAT *Edward Chambers*, built about 1900 and originally operated under the name *North Star*. "It was an old Great Lakes ore boat, about 350 feet long and deadly slow. We had as motley a crew as could be found—the captain was Norwegian, two mates were Yugoslavs, the bos'n was a Turk, and the crew included an Australian, a White Russian, and a guy of undesignated nationality who said he had deserted from the French Foreign Legion.

"We had armament of four 20 mm and a 3″ 50 cal on the stern. However, the ship was so slow that we were a sitting duck for a Japanese submarine that came along. It caused a great deal of damage, but we limped into port. Later off Panama we were hit by a torpedo and the ship exploded and went down immediately." Kushner went on to serve in several Liberties in the Pacific and Indian Oceans.[5]

Ed Krupski, Grand Island, Nebraska, reports that "after boot camp training at Great Lakes, I was sent to Gulfport, Mississippi, for gunnery training for AG duty. I was first assigned to a T-2 tanker, but was picked as a single replacement for the gun crew of the SS *Caloria*. She had been sunk in the English Channel in WW I, but had been raised after the war and converted into a tanker, used by Standard Fruit & Steamship to supply fuel for banana plantations in Central America. When WW II broke out, the U.S. government took her over, installed guns and assigned an AG crew under a Lt. (jg). We sailed in the Atlantic and Gulf of Mexico, mostly, and had daily reminders of the U-boat war when we saw the many masts of ships sunk by the Germans sticking out of the water. Our ship was so old that, when we had gunnery practice, all the light bulbs would break off at the sockets. We were firing a 4" 50, which was a very old gun to begin with. I am sure glad that we really didn't have to defend ourselves with it as we might have done more damage to ourselves than to an experienced sub surface gunnery crew.

"At first, being on a tanker with a strange crew was quite scary, but eventually you fit in with your new surroundings and your new crew. We always knew what we had to look out for with all that oil or gasoline, but you learn to live with danger. The most shaken I ever was was on my first night watch, on the fantail gun tub. It was dark and all the lights on the ship were turned off or blacked out. I had all my training about torpedoes dancing in my head when suddenly I saw two wakes coming right at us toward the stern. I just knew it was a pair of torpedoes, and we were only a half-day out of Corpus. Just as I was ready to ring GQ, I saw two porpoises jump out of the water. What a relief, but when you are new at the game all kinds of exciting things can occur.

"While the ship was an antique, it was good duty. We ate

well and the merchants treated us well also. The master was a Scotsman and a nice old man. I had dinner with him and his wife a couple of times when she would come to visit him in port in Galveston."[6]

Lieutenant Commander Leo Blackburn, USNR (Ret.), reports, "My first sea duty was aboard an old German merchant vessel which had been taken over by the U.S. Government, renamed MV *Blenheim,* and transferred to the American Merchant Marine. The *Blenheim* was assigned to Waterman Steamship Co., and her homeport was Hoboken, New Jersey. She had been built in 1914, in Hamburg, Germany, so when I first boarded her in October 1943, I could readily see I was on a unique ship.

"Her career was not, shall we say, trouble-free. It seemed that every stop the *Blenheim* made there was some kind of repair needed. Even at sea, things went wrong; non-working plumbing, fouled water supply, food contamination, false alarms going off, engine trouble, etc. Some wag suggested that the name be changed from MV *Blenheim* to 'Hitler's Secret Weapon.' He implied that Hitler had really let her be confiscated in order to slow the Allied war effort, in fact, Hitler had 'planted' it in the U.S. for that very purpose. On this, my first voyage, with a load of raw sugar, the *Blenheim* attracted more names, the kindest of which was 'Rust Bucket.' However, we did make Liverpool, unloaded and started back. On the return, we encountered the worst storm I have ever been in, by the third day, the convoy was scattered and we of the *Blenheim* were all alone, like a sitting duck, with nine 20 mm and a 4-inch cannon, and a 25-man gun crew, augmented with several merchant seamen volunteers. Day after day we plowed slowly through the stormy North Atlantic, pitching and rolling, making very little headway, wondering if we would ever see land again. Then we learned something.

"While in Liverpool, the ships' steward, instead of supplying the ship with food, had spent his time in bars and brothels, and after sobering up, informed us that a food shortage was imminent and rationing had better be considered. Abuse was heaped upon the steward, and several suggestions, including keelhauling, were seriously considered. Although this was bad enough, our principal problem was seasickness, and wondering if the old ship would hold together under all the North Atlantic battering. Then one day a merchant deck hand rushed to the bridge with some really bad news. "We are taking water, the port bow has been ruptured, and we'll never make it to Hoboken!' The captain and the merchant marine officers quickly checked the report, verified it, estimated the ship's list and degree of worsening, studied the charts, and the captain announced that he felt that we could make it to St. Johns, Newfoundland. We just barely made it. After the rough crossing, and [the crew] nearly starved, the old *Blenheim* stayed in drydock for about a month, getting patched up. By this time we were sure that she was truly Hitler's secret weapon. Eventually, temporary repairs were made and we made it back to Hoboken to finish off the job, after which we loaded up with lumber and started off to London. We were there for three weeks, met lots of people, saw the destruction, and could finally realize what the Londoners had been going through for years. We received orders to return to the U.S. on June 6th. We were ready to sail when a stevedore ran by yelling, 'The invasion is on!' The Navy AG crew unanimously signed a petition that our sailing be cancelled, and that *Blenheim* be assigned to take part in the invasion. However, all arrangements had been made and there was no changing plans now. So, reluctantly we sailed down the Thames and turned west. We all felt that this trip would be the *Blenheim*'s last, she was old, she was lame, she was tired, but we underestimated the old girl's stamina and toughness.

"After the war, I heard the continuation of her saga. With a new officer and almost new crew, she left Hoboken for her last wartime destination, Antwerp, Belgium. Feeling her way cautiously up the Scheldt River, she was attacked by a low-flying German plane. With AGs firing every gun she carried, a direct hit or a fusillade brought the plane down, to a mighty cheer from the Navy and Merchant Marines. The next day, the stack was decorated with the silhouette of the downed plane. Never again was she called, 'Hitler's Secret Weapon.' But her story was not over. Proceeding to the docks, the *Blenheim* was a target for the final dying gasp the Germans were making with the V-2 rocket bombs. One found its point of impact right beside the *Blenheim* and exploded, doing considerable damage, and wounding my replacement gunnery officer.

"Wherever the final resting place for the *Blenheim* is (I've never known) she can rest there proudly, knowing that old, battered and ridiculed, she rose to the occasion when the right time came, and she can take her place in the annals of naval warfare. As far as I know, the *Blenheim* was the only naval vessel to suffer damage from the V-2 rocket. Perhaps Hitler's spirit hurled one last thunderbolt in revenge for his 'Secret Weapon' shooting down his attacking plane."[7]

The SS *El Coston* was certainly one of the most unique ships and probably caused more questions among both friend and foe as to just what she was. Lieutenant Commander Carl E. Odegaard, USNR, reports on his experience in her: "On 19 September 1942, I detached from the *Margaret Lykes* and had to report to the SS *El Coston*. When my predecessor had disappeared over the side, I mustered the crew and gave them a rigorous personnel inspection. I would certainly not have known how to do this three months earlier. I had learned a good deal from watching Morin, the coxswain, operate on the *Margaret Lykes*. I had two voyages with that crew and no disciplinary troubles with them except for one replacement, a man who had had the experience of being aboard one ship which was torpedoed, only to be picked up by another ship which was also torpedoed and sunk. He did his work conscientiously, but as much as possible avoided going below deck. He persisted in sleeping topside in whatever covered area he could find in preference to his bunk below decks. By the end of the return trip from Iceland he looked terribly haggard. We sailed from Boston to New York on the inside passage, but again I found that he would not go below decks despite the fact that the

weather had turned bitterly cold. I concluded that he definitely should be assigned, for the time being at least, to
shore duty. I did not have very much time to arrange it, but I
succeeded in having him transferred to the sick bay in New
York, and a relief sent aboard for him. Upon my return later
to New York, I found out from a personnel officer that the
medical officer to whom the sailor had been sent had said all
that he suffered from was a yellow streak down his back, and
he refused to recommend the man for shore duty, so he had
been sent out to sea again. Meanwhile, a citation had arrived in New York for him, citing his very good conduct during the earlier torpedoings. What a hollow honor. I never
was able to learn anything of his subsequent history.

"The SS *El Coston* was an interesting ship. She was built
for the Panama Railroad line in the early 1920's for the run
from New York to Panama, and was called then the *Bienville*.
Still in the 1920's, however, the ship caught fire and was
badly burned. She was never rebuilt as a passenger ship.
She was converted into a freighter, and for many years she
was the fastest freighter carrying cargo along the east coast
of the United States. She was a strange appearing ship in the
sense that she had two stacks like many passenger ships, but
obviously lacked the superstructure associated with accommodations for passengers. By the time I went aboard the
ship, she had been placed under Panamanian registry and
renamed the *El Coston,* though she was actually managed
by the United States Lines. It was a common practice at that
time to place ships under Panamanian registry in order to
get around the requirement of U.S. law with reference to the
U.S. citizenship of members of the crew. The *El Coston* was
really an international ship. Seven languages were spoken
aboard. The captain and first mate were Norwegians, the
second mate was an Englishman, who had acquired an
American sweetheart, the third mate was Flemish, the chief
engineer was a Belgian, who had been chief engineer on
passenger ships which ran between the Lowlands and South
America. He had had two passenger ships torpedoed out
from under him in the earlier course of the war in Europe,

and of course could not return to Belgium, then occupied by Germany. His first engineer was Norwegian. The deck and engineering hands were of mixed nationalities, the stewards were all Chinese.

The spirit of the merchant crew was very much set by Captain Olsen, a superior person who made it a kind of Viking ship. The previous winter the *El Coston* had made a trip to Archangel. It had been frozen in there along with four other American ships. The Russians finally succeeded in getting an icebreaker into Archangel which could break ships away, but only three at a time. The three ships, including the *El Coston*, had orders to sail together to a rendezvous point near Murmansk where they were to meet up with a convoy which would head around the northern tip of Norway. At that point, the ships were vulnerable to attack from German planes. Captain Olsen allegedly lost the other two ships in the fog, and he therefore turned north into the Arctic sea ice, where, relying on the strength of the *El Coston*, he threaded his way through the floe ice as he headed westward. The *El Coston* was not detected by the Germans and finally, when west of Iceland, he turned south. The *El Coston* was detected in murky weather by an American destroyer. It is not surprising that the first reaction to this ship with its two stacks and strange configuration was that it was a German raider. The destroyer ordered her to stop and it fired a couple of shots across her bow.

"Following her return from Archangel, the *El Coston* made several runs to Iceland. She was based at Boston, the gathering point for supplies for Iceland. I was ordered to duty aboard the SS *El Coston*, in Boston, on 21 September 1942, and made two trips to Iceland in her, the first from New York to Reykjavik. It was stormy weather in the North Atlantic both times. There always seemed to be enough incidents to liven things up. On the first trip, on the second night out, in the morning, the rudder of the *El Coston* jammed. She was in position 32, that is to say, in the third column, the second ship in line. We had been running blacked out. As we swung to the right, we barely missed the SS *Chateau Thierry*.

Lights began to go on about us and whistles began blowing. It is a miracle that we didn't crash into another ship in the convoy. The *El Coston* fell back out of line while the engineers frantically worked to repair the steering mechanisms. It seemed very lonely to lie there seeing the other ships proceeding on without us. The steering gear was repaired and we had the speed to catch up with the convoy. The commodore prudently put us the last ship in line. I am sure the others all wanted to give us a wide berth.

"Captain Olsen, I think, had more faith in the speed of his ship than he did in the effectiveness of the screen. As sunset came on, he would keep watching the commodore's ship for a signal to us to proceed independently. At that point, he would be calling down to the chief engineer, repeatedly saying, 'Get those horses out of the stable, get that steam up.' As soon as the signal appeared, he would order full speed ahead; we pulled into place between the columns and then pulled ahead of the convoy, and finally, ahead of the escort, to be on our own for the remainder of the trip to Iceland, running at maximum speed. The next day we had another moment of excitement. The *El Coston* had nothing but a magnetic compass, which is very unreliable in those northern areas. Add to that the fog and the difficulty of getting navigational sights, and it was easy to be off-course. We had repeatedly requested the Navy to put radio direction-finder equipment and a gyrocompass on the ship, but to no avail. Of course we did not have radar and Loran was still far in the future. While running full speed in the fog the bow lookout fortunately reported the sound of surf ahead. At that moment, I happened to be in my cabin stretched out about to take a nap. I dashed to the bridge the moment I heard the propeller stop. We prayed that the ship would stop in time. It seemed forever before the bow began to swing and we began to slowly move backward and away from the rocks.

"On the second trip we headed into a storm of hurricane proportions which reached its maximum the second day after we left the convoy. A German sub pack had gotten into the convoy and we received signals from ships which had been with us before, indicating that they had been torpedoed. The captain with his passion for speed was driving the ship very hard. Rails were carried away, boats were smashed from their davits. Even with bunk boards, it was impossible to sleep; the ship was rolling 35° one way and 35° the other. For 24 hours we steamed ahead, yet virtually stood still, she seemed heavy in the head and responded more slowly. As soon as it was light enough to work one's hazardous way toward the bow, the boatswain discovered that the two decks of storerooms over Number 1 hold were entirely filled with sea water. There was no way to drain this water into the ship's bilges, from which it could have been pumped out. Then I made my one engineering contribution by suggesting a siphoning technique using a firehose, with one end pushed down into the water to be drained, and the other hung over the side of the ship. The siphon was induced by using the firehose to shoot water under pressure in the end of the hose submerged in the spaces to be drained. It took us almost 24 hours to complete the draining of those spaces. There was something heroic about the old *El Coston* tearing her heart out against those northern seas. The ship ran into storms which were very severe. She was covered with ice when she finally managed to limp into Reykjavik with her engines crippled. They finally succeeded in patching her up enough so that she could get back to New York for overhaul, but she had lost her speed and was condemned to convoy travel. She sailed for England on what was to be her last voyage. She collided in a storm with a Navy tanker, their bows were crushed. The *El Coston* had been set afire. She was ordered to head for Bermuda. The crew had to continue fighting the fire by putting more and more water into her, and before the ship could reach Bermuda, the water won by sinking the ship.

"In retrospect, I think these days aboard the *El Coston* were the days of the greatest continuous tension, the most arduous, and in a sense heroic of my war experience. There were ships being lost all around us. At each port we would find that old friends were gone."[8]

James Handy also served in the *El Coston* and remembers her fondly. He adds, "The crew of this ship was made up of so many different nationalities that the ship had to post crew orders in seven different languages, in order for everybody to understand them. One amusing incident that happened on our way back to the states that I vividly recall was a few days before we got to New York, somebody in the gun crew was kidding around and put up a real colorful bedspread on the flag staff on the stern of the ship and forgot about it. The flag staff on the stern could not be seen from the bridge and the ship's crew seldom went back there. Anyway, as we were nearing the lightship off New York, a Coast Guard cutter pulled alongside and challenged the captain to identify his flag. The captain replied 'Panamanian', and the cutter said, 'I have no flag listed like the one you are flying.' The captain sent one of the mates back to the stern to see what was going on and he came back with this colorful bedspread. Needless to say there were some red faces and some tall explaining to do to the Coast Guard."[9]

Tankers were not everybody's favorite assignment, as they were always prime targets. However, Walter Peters, signalman 1/c, now of El Paso, Texas, says, "I served on many types of ships, but tankers were my favorite ship. One I served on was a new ship which could make 28 knots, and we traveled alone, without convoy. It was good duty, but above all, was the food. We had a choice of ham, sausage or bacon every day, hot cakes, dry cereal, eggs any way, and at dinner we had steak, pork chops, chicken and a choice of vegetable. The ship had an enormous refrigerator with soft drinks, ice cream, which you could get any time. The compensations more than made up for the hazards of being on a tanker." However, while a nineteen-year-old boy's appetite has frequently been regarded with awe, spectacular photos of burning tankers and oil-covered survivors give some solid reason for some doubt about his judgment. (One hundred forty-two U.S. tankers were attacked and 102 lost from 7 December 1941–VJ-Day.)[10]

The war could not have been won if it weren't for the

tankers. One company alone had 135 ocean tankers in service, which delivered an astounding total of 665,000,000 barrels of oil and oil products for military use, plus deckloads of planes, PT boats, trucks, and other heavy equipment.[11]

Between 7 December 1941 and 30 June 1942, there were eighty-three tankers attacked and sixty lost; between 1 July 1942 and 30 June 1943, there were forty-one tankers attacked and twenty-nine lost, but losses were lessening. From 1 July 1943 and 30 June 1944, the U.S. only suffered ten tankers attacked, with nine lost, and between 1 July 1944 and VJ-Day, only eight tankers were attacked, with four being lost. One of the most important developments as regards tankers was that beginning in 1942, tankers in both Atlantic and Pacific convoys were equipped with spar decks, on which they carried airplanes and other bulky military equipment for campaigns in Asia, Africa, and Europe. In 1945, tankers of Standard Oil of New Jersey carried almost a thousand planes, an invaluable time-saver, as the use of spar decks enabled the complete plane to be placed on deck rather than being dismantled and being shipped as underdeck cargo on regular freighters. They could then be taken off and readied for flight in a minimum of time.

Much more favored over tankers by armed guards were former passenger liners that had been converted to troop transports. One of these was the USAT *President Grant.* Rosalio Martinez, El Paso, Texas, served in the *President Grant,* carrying the 12th Cavalry to Guadalcanal to relieve the 1st Marines. The transport traveled by herself because of her speed, but caused consternation when she was reported lost at sea because she was late in arriving and a Japanese submarine had been reported in her path. Martinez reported that accommodations and food were fine, and even better, the AG crew was able to arrange a swap of "shampoo for booze" with a group of nurses aboard who were having trouble washing their hair with saltwater; although not in accord with standard navy operating procedure, the agreement was eminently satisfactory as a morale builder to both sides.

The *President Grant* carried a navy AG crew of twenty-five, and her armament consisted of a 4″ on the stern, two 3″ 50s on the bridge, plus one on the bow, two 30-caliber air-cooled Lewis guns on the bridge, and four 50-caliber Lewis guns amidships. After departing Guadalcanal, the *President Grant* picked up survivors of the Australian cruiser HMAS *Canberra* and carried them to Sydney.

During the course of his thirty-six months of active AG sea duty, Martinez also served on a number of Liberty and Victory ships. He says that discipline was tighter on the *President Grant* than on Liberties or Victories, but not as strict as fleet duty. An orphan, Martinez had lied about his age and enlisted in the navy in January 1942 at age fifteen. To him, the armed guard was his home and his family.

Later assigned to the SS *Salinas Victory*, he found that she had much better quarters and armament than Liberty ships. The gun crew of twenty-one included a signalman and radio operator, and the *Salinas* carried a 5″ 38 on the stern, a 3″ 50 on the bow, and eight 20 mm, plus smoke pots and Hedgehogs. Like all gunners, Martinez loved his 5″ 38, far superior to early AG weapons; improved 20 mm, every fourth round a tracer, also inspired increased respect in enemy attackers.[12]

Of all possible AG assignments, probably the least favored would be a munitions ship. Upon reporting to a new ship being loaded and noting the red flag, a new crew member could make a remark considerably more forceful than "Oh! Oh!" At sea, in convoy, the AG crew was liable to feel, as one described it, "Like the bastard at the family reunion." Convoy commodores would often put the ammunition ships as far back on the tail as they could, as the other ships wanted as much space between them as possible. It could generally be said that in a convoy, the munitions ship, with a cargo of high explosives, was about as popular as Hester Prynne in Salem in the days of the "Scarlet Letter." One crew member said it was like carrying a huge sign "UNCLEAN!" Unfortunately, there was plenty of justification for others' fears of such neighbors.

After basic training as a signalman, and special training in MERSIGS (special convoy signaling), SM/3 Frank Belsito was assigned to the SS *James C. Cameron*, a Liberty ship so badly constructed that he insists she should have been declared uninsurable. She was also an ammunition ship, but Belsito says that the nastiest experiences on the ship were the constant series of breakdowns in the North Atlantic, during the kind of stormy sailing that was routine in that area. That bothered him more than being on an ammo ship, and he says, "In a way, that was convenient because it freed one from wearing Mae Wests and other paraphernalia on the theory that if you got hit, you'd never know it. I was probably wrong, but we never did get hit, although a ship to starboard did sink after it hit a mine in the St. George Channel."

Belsito was aboard the SS *Cameron* for a number of trips to the U.K., Italy, and France, "but never Murmansk, thank God!" An instructor in his signal school was sunk three times on that run and swore that he would accept a court-martial rather than brave it again. With the exception of the many breakdowns in undesirable areas, Belsito enjoyed his AG assignment. "The AG had certain advantages. The food was good, because the grievance committee of the merchant seamen aboard would file protests if it weren't. Discipline was comparatively lax, which made life pretty pleasant and informal. Quarters were probably better than in the fleet at that time, and for signalmen, who had to be close to the bridge, they were quite nice."[15]

Belsito's career in the AG came to an end when he was selected for V-7 and ultimately became a naval intelligence officer.

Although the raid at Bari was one of the worst disasters of the war in terms of ships and material lost, the *Paul Hamilton* produced a larger casualty list, to become the most costly Liberty ship disaster, in terms of human life, in all of World War II. The ship was making her fifth voyage, as part of a huge convoy, UGS38, when she was attacked by twenty-three German bombers near sunset on 20 April 1944. As was frequently the custom, in addition to her load of high explosives and bombs, the ship carried enough troops to bring the total on-board complement to 498 men. The bombers came in low; men on the bridge of the British tanker *Athelchief* looked down on one as it went by. Her gunners set it on fire, but it launched its torpedo less than 150 feet from the *Paul Hamilton.* A violent explosion threw debris and dense black smoke high in the air. When the smoke cleared, there was no sign of the ship. Not one of the 498 men survived.[14]

Several months later, in an amazing switch in the vagaries of war, another Liberty ship, the *Augustus Thomas,* carrying a cargo of ammunition and gasoline and 548 men in the Philippines, was hit and set on fire by a dive-bomber. Not a man was hurt.

More NAGs served aboard Liberty ships than on any other type of vessel in World War II, so it is appropriate to relate some basic facts about these sturdy workhorses that helped to win the war. They were big, useful, and they carried millions of tons of vital war supplies across the oceans of the world. They did the job they were designed for, but they were disparagingly referred to early on as "sea scows." They were based upon a nineteenth-century design of a British tramp steamer, adapted to meet modern needs. The simplicity of the Liberty-ship design, engines, and boilers made them economical and easy to build quickly as experience was gained. The American Society of Mechanical Engineers described them colorfully as ". . . an 1879 steamer sailing across the oceans of the world to 20th-century triumph." The reincarnation of the basic old tramp steamer came about almost accidentally. In September 1940, Britain was reeling under the catastrophic losses of its merchant shipping to German U-boats. A British Merchant Shipbuilding Mission visited the United States and contracted for sixty "Ocean-class" vessels, based on the old design, for use in the transatlantic run. American planners, with their own ideas for expanding the merchant fleet, had paid scant recognition to such outmoded designs, and were not interested, but the subsequent need for a vast and immediate shipbuilding program led them to go along, reluctantly, with the

"Ocean-class" vessels. [U.S. shipbuilders' experience in building these ships was invaluable as a learning experience in saving precious time for developing new designs and facilities.][15]

While examining the plans, ex-Secretary of the Navy, and then-President Franklin D. Roosevelt, a devotee of graceful ships, allowed that they would probably do the job, but disdainfully referred to them as "Ugly Ducklings," a name that stuck in the mind of the public. Admiral Emory Scott Land, chairman of the Maritime Commission felt that the term was too derogatory and proposed the more euphonious-sounding name, "Liberty ships," and as such they became well and favorably known in far-flung ports around globe.

In short order, Liberty ships began pouring out of eighteen shipyards, most started from scratch, along the East, West and Gulf coasts of the U.S. The Liberties could be likened to have been turned out by gigantic standardized cookie cutters. Dimensions almost invariably were 441′6″ in length, 57′ beam, deadweight tonnage of 10,428 tons. They were designed to carry over 9,000 tons of cargo, with a full load of fuel, but often carried much more—their holds filled and decks jammed with planes, tanks, trucks, railroad locomotives, and other huge and heavy equipment. In her five holds, a Liberty could carry 2,840 jeeps, 440 light tanks, plus ammunition, food, and other necessities for both military and civilian use. However, the Liberties had faults, some very serious. They were slow, sometimes excruciatingly so. Their top speed when new was about 11 knots, but speed usually dropped off with age and barnacles. It was "life in the slow lane" for the Liberties. But by far the most disturbing and dangerous shortcoming was the tendency of the welded hulls of the Liberty to split open and even break apart. Liberties were too rigid in mountainous seas, with the ship pitching and rolling violently; they could not bend with the waves, and many broke their backs.

The silhouette of a Liberty ship was easily recognizable. The superstructure was located amidships, which provided crews quarters and bridge. However, the AG gun crews were

Liberty ships under construction at the Fairfield Yards in Maryland. (Courtesy Bethlehem Steel Corporation)

accommodated in the after deckhouse, directly above the steering engine and below the 5″ gun, a sure guarantee for a rough or otherwise uncomfortable ride. Designated EC2-S-C1 by the Maritime Commission, indicating that it was an emergency-class vessel, the Liberties were originally conceived as being only a temporary expedient, with an expected service of five years or so. However, the "temporary expedient" roamed the seas for up to twenty years after the war, and one was reported still in Greek Isles service as late as 1985. Still another, given to the Russians during the war, turned up delivering military supplies to Cuba during the Cuban Missile Crisis of 1962.[16]

Construction techniques for the newly authorized Liberty ships aroused considerable controversy. Welding vs riveting was hotly contested, and traditional shipbuilders took a very dim view of neophyte Henry J. Kaiser's ideas of

The launching of the SS *Patrick Henry* at Fairfield Yard, Maryland, on 27 September 1941. The SS *Patrick Henry* was the first of 2,710 Liberty ships built during World War II. (Courtesy Bethlehem Steel Corporation)

mass-producing ships by using prefabrication methods. It was a case of where ignorance might be bliss, for neither Kaiser nor his top executives, and certainly none of his vast work force, had had enough experience in the field of ship-building to know what "couldn't" be done. It has been said of Henry J. Kaiser, major builder of roads, bridges, and dams, that it is questionable if he could design a rowboat, but he was a genius at prefabrication, and he became the Henry Ford of shipbuilding, by using mass-production techniques. Kaiser couldn't have cared less as to what was the "front" or the "rear" end of a ship. To the traditionalists of the Todd Corporation, a ship was to be "built," not "assembled," so the Todd-Kaiser early partnership dissolved to their mutual satisfaction.[17]

Liberty hulls, as developed by Kaiser, were all-welded, with only a few exceptions—a calculated risk. New yards were built from rock flats or swamps, and whole ship sections were prefabricated and assembled elsewhere, completely fitted, and delivered to the shipyard ready to be installed. Many of the reservations of the "traditional" shipbuilders proved justified. Kaiser-built ships appeared to be particularly susceptible to hull cracking, and at an early stage of the war, AG crews on the West Coast, who were assigned to the newly built Kaiser Liberties, referred to the ships as "floating coffins," and hated to serve in them. The Kaiser ships appeared especially vulnerable to frigid Arctic waters, but Liberty-ship hull fractures occurred in many other parts of the world and under many conditions. One wartime report indicated that 12 1/2 percent of all Liberties had weld defects, nearly 10 percent had developed cracks, and that one ship in thirty had sustained major hull fractures. Some of the West Coast-based AGs referred to the breaks as caused by "lipstick welding," a jibe at the thousands of women recruited to work as welders in the shipyards. They were better known to the American public as the famous "Rosie the Riveter."

Seemingly as a result of trial and error, corrections of faults in the Liberties were made, and weak spots in design strengthened. As a consequence, Liberties were frequently able to survive terrible punishment from the enemy as well as from the elements.

The results of the American genius for industrial organization of vast new projects, plus fast, unorthodox methods of ship construction, awed both Allies and Axis powers. At the request of the Maritime Commission, in 1941 Bethlehem Steel Corporation organized the Bethlehem-Fairfield Shipyard Inc., Baltimore, Maryland. In just nine months, the company built a sixteen-way shipyard and launched the SS *Patrick Henry*, the very first Liberty ship, and the first of 384 Liberties, 94 Victory ships and 30 LSTs (tank-landing ships) built at the Fairfield yard. At the peak of war production, the yard employed 47,000 workers.

The SS *Patrick Henry* was laid down on 30 April 1941, launched on 27 September, and was delivered on 30 December 1941, a remarkable performance at that time. However, other new yards cut production time regularly, with new records being set frequently. The ultimate record belongs to the SS *Robert E. Peary*, which was assembled and launched by Kaiser Yard #2, using the mass-production techniques of the automobile assembly lines, in the incredible time of four days and fifteen and one half hours, after the keel had been laid. That time was never equaled again. On 8 November 1942, the hull of the *Robert E. Peary* was assembled from 250-ton prefabricated sections, with engines in place. On the second day the upper deck was completed; on the third, the masts, derricks, and superstructure were installed, with final wiring, welding, and painting. On the fourth day plus fifteen hours, the *Peary* was launched. At last, ships were being built faster than they were getting sunk.[18]

The figure of 2,710 Liberty ships built is generally considered close, but the records vary. Of this number, over two hundred were lost, mostly by enemy action, fifty on their first (and last) voyage.[19]

The AG crew and the merchant seamen aboard the SS *James Bowie* were entitled to think a hex had been put on them. In addition to being ordered to go to Murmansk in February 1943, they ran into weather so bad that the mountainous seas and strong winds loosened the lifeboats and shifted the deck cargo. Their luck didn't change, and a few days later they heard a "loud jarring report," an eighteen-inch-wide split in the hull. Water poured into the engine room, and all pumps were pressed into use. Inspection then showed that the break extended from the main deck to the engine room. Emergency repairs were hastily made to attempt to hold the break. By this time, the convoy was out of sight and they were all alone in an unhospitable sea. They improvised a repair by welding a piece of steel over the worst part of the split and miraculously limped back to Loch Ewe for major repairs.

The Murmansk run was hard on ships as well as men. The SS *J. L. M. Curry* broke up and sank in a 40-knot gale, en route home after having fought her way in and used Sherman tanks carried as deck cargo for defense against air raids while waiting to unload. Finally heading back after several months in that frigid port, the *Curry* ran into such a severe gale that the hull cracked with a sound like gunfire, a common effect in hull cracking. The break continued, and the captain ordered the crew to abandon ship. The *Curry* was finally sunk by an escort HMS *St. Elston.*

The stockyards in Chicago were once widely recognized for "using everything but the squeal" of the animals they processed. The loaders of Liberty ships and tankers must have adopted the same policy, for they utilized every inch of space above and below deck. An AG gunner reports, "They would usually load the big stuff first and then fill in the small spaces with smaller cargo. When they were loading large pieces, they used a blueprint so as to keep the ship on an even keel. Most of the boxes were knocked-down trucks, aircraft engines, wings and other parts. Some of the cargo was jeeps, which were not crated. They also loaded a lot of bagged sulphur.

"The stevedores finally finished loading the holds, put the hatch covers in place, and the merchant seamen put the tarp covers on and battened them down. I thought we were ready to go to sea, but then comes a train of flat cars alongside the ship, loaded with huge crates, about 10' × 10' × 18', which were to be loaded on deck. They were all Caterpillars and bulldozers and other grading equipment. The deck was so full that to get from the stern to amidships, we had to go down a ladder to the dock, then walk up to the gangway. After everything was anchored down, a work gang of carpenters built a catwalk across the top of the cargo from the stern to the amidships boat deck, also a stairway from the main deck to the catwalk, and the same forward, so that we could now get to our guns. We were ready to sail, in more ways than one."

While the NAG served on ships of many flags and carried a variety of cargo, surely the SS *Big Foot Wallace* had one of the most unusual experiences of the war. In Calcutta, loading a full cargo for the U.S. consisting of tin ingots smuggled out of China, jute, burlap, dried cocoanut, rice, tea, and cinnamon, the *Big Foot Wallace* was about ready to sail when the captain was informed that he was to wait for the arrival of some deck cargo. The next morning the deck cargo arrived, three hundred Rhesus monkeys, en route to the U.S. Infantile Paralysis Foundation.

The monkeys were in cages about $3' \times 3' \times 6'$, and they were put in #5 hold, in two rows of six cages each. The monkeys' food—rice in husk and yams—was put on board, and the ship's bos'n, paid extra for looking after the monkeys, rigged a canvas shelter over them as protection from the sun and rain. All was made secure, and the *Wallace* cast off for its first stop, Colombo, Ceylon.

DeWitt Welch, gunner's mate, naval armed guard, picks up the story. "I was on the 4 to 8 watch, on the bridge with the Third Mate. The Mate told me to pass the word to my boys that if they saw a loose monkey to report it. He said he had been informed that there was a loose monkey running around. Now, these monkeys were wild, and you dare not try to catch one with your hands because they would bite like a raccoon. It was getting near daylight and time for the mate to wake up the captain. He liked to be on the bridge at daylight.

"The first streak of dawn had broken through, and by the time the mate and captain got on the bridge, I had spotted a monkey on the yardarm of # 1 mast, and after I had pointed him out, I saw two more. I went down to call the sunrise watch, 'Everybody on the gun decks.' The captain told a merchant seaman to go down and get the bos'n up and tell him to report to the bridge. By that time, I was back on the bridge. The captain told the mate and the bos'n to go and check the cages. It was getting lighter all the time. The mate came back on the bridge and told the captain that all the cages on the starboard side were open. That meant we had 150 wild monkeys running loose. By the time the sun peaked over the horizon, you could see monkeys everywhere.

"The captain was some more than mad, and he said that if he ever found out who let them out, that that man would never go to sea again, as long as he lived. The captain sent for the bos'n and told him to see what he could do about catching the monkeys. They tried hemming them up, but after two or three of the merchant seamen had been bitten, they decided they were going to have to do something different. The bos'n got some heavy twine and a couple of the old seamen knew how to weave fish nets, so they began working on the nets. A lot of the monkeys went back to the cages for food, then someone would slip in the tent and close the door.

"The way the word was passed that there was a monkey on the loose was that the radioman had gone to bed somewhere around midnight. His hatchway was latched open. He said he woke up and felt like someone was in the cabin with him. He got up and closed the hatchway and turned on the light, but found nothing, so he went back to bed. He woke up a second time with the same feeling, got up and checked again, but still nothing, so he went back to bed again. He said, the third time he woke up, he felt that hairy SOB in the bed with him, and he yelled and came out running. He went to the bridge and told the Second Mate. They went back and checked his cabin, but still nothing, so he closed the hatchway and went back to bed and finally got some sleep. By the time we were about four days out of Aden, we had caught a lot of the monkeys. Everybody in their off-time was trying to catch them. We were running pretty close to the Arabian coast and not too far from the African coast in the Red Sea. Somebody reported what looked like a very black cloud coming toward our port bow. The mate put the long glass on it and said it looked like millions of black locusts. In a few minutes, the ship was covered with them and we had to close all portholes and outside hatchways. The monkeys still on the loose began to catch and eat them. Nobody knew what to do, as no one had ever heard of such a thing. The crew was afraid that they would eat up the hawsers and other grip stored on deck, but the next morning, all of a sudden, they took off going towards Arabia.

"We were nearing Suez and had caught all the monkeys, except two. After clearing the Suez Canal, we got orders in Port Said to go to Oran, Algeria, and we arrived in a couple of days. We received orders to tie up beside another ship and wait for a convoy. Just before we left Oran, the last two monkeys went AWOL, they jumped over on the ship we were tied beside, and we saw the last of them. However, we still had the 298 others. Since the weather was getting very cool, the bos'n had to put a canvas wall around the sides of the monkey tent. He put some water buckets in there with large flood lights in them, and a cover for blackout because we were getting into U-boat waters.

"We made it to the States without incident, and arrived at Jacksonville where they unloaded the monkeys."

DeWitt indicated that he did not know whether he or the monkeys were the happiest to get off the ship. He doesn't know what happened to the monkeys, but he headed for Atlanta and home leave. It had been an interesting trip.[20]

The navy is still using monkeys to test anti-motion-sickness drugs, and apparently their dispositions have not improved any, as two handlers at a navy lab in Pensacola, Florida, were bitten recently and were in serious condition at time of writing.

CHAPTER SIX
GALLANT SHIPS,
GALLANT MEN

You will engage the enemy until your
guns can no longer be fired—until the
decks are awash and the guns are
going under. . . .
—Naval Armed Guard Instruction

And the young men of the naval armed guard, from all parts of the country and representing all walks of life, did just that. Most had never seen a body of water they couldn't throw a rock across. Many had never fired anything more deadly than a Daisy air rifle, received as a Christmas present. Their occupations included every conceivable type of activity—students, farmers, loggers, construction workers, clerks, salesmen, mechanics, truck drivers, and railroad gandy dancers. Their education ranged from being almost nonexistent to professional level— lawyers, engineers, accountants, newspapermen, college professors, and many others. The reader will meet them in these pages and may well be impressed by their honesty, simplicity, and above all, love of country. Most had one common denominator—they had never seen a real "live" ship before. In the early stages of the war, some received only the most elementary training and went to sea in ancient ships, required to face the enemy using ancient weapons. They manned their ships and they stuck to their guns, setting a tradition for those to come. Many died, others, more lucky, survived, but the records of the naval armed guard service are full of accounts of stirring heroism and performance of duty against incredible odds. The green, landlubber kids and their almost equally inexperienced officers compiled an imposing record of awards for outstanding performance; the men of the NAG service were awarded 5 Navy Crosses, 2 Legions of Merit, 75 Silver Stars, 54 Bronze Stars, and 24 Navy and Marine Corps Medals, over 8,000 individual citations, and over 36,000 combat and engagement stars. Seven AG officers were awarded the honor of having U.S. Navy ships named after them for conspicuous gallantry, all posthumously. Many others undoubtedly deserved the same recognition, but the fortunes of war prevented their stories from being recorded. Unfortunately also, the passage of years has led to the loss or destruction of many official documents that could add to the list of heroic actions, long-ignored and forgotten.[1]

Sharing their lives and their deaths were their shipmates, the officers and men of the merchant marine, who proved time and again that heroism and devotion to country are not restricted to any one body of men. They manned and maneuvered the ships under attack, passed ammunition and fought at the guns alongside often-understrength or incapacitated navy gun crews; 142 cadet/midshipmen gave their lives at sea, along with some 6,000 merchant seamen.[2]

The ships on which they sailed suffered terrible poundings from both the human enemy and the violence of the elements. While hundreds of ships deserved the honor, only nine merchant vessels were officially designated "Gallant Ships" by the U.S. Maritime Commission. The award was authorized by presidential executive order, to be presented to merchant ships for gallantry in action while under attack, or in marine disasters or other emergencies at sea. The nine ships so honored and the theaters of operation involved are:

SS *Samuel Parker* (Mediterranean)
SS *Cedar Mills* (Atlantic)
SS *William Moultrie* (North Russia)
SS *Adoniram Judson* (Philippines invasion)
SS *Marcus Daly* (Philippines invasion)
SS *Virginia Dare* (North Russia)
SS *Nathaniel Greene* (North Russia)

SS *Stephen Hopkins* (Indian Ocean)
SS *Stanvac Calcutta* (South Atlantic)[5]

By a remarkable coincidence all three ships listed above for the deadly Murmansk run were built by the same shipyard, North Carolina Shipbuilding Company, Wilmington, North Carolina, within a period of four months, March–June 1942. All of the ships were involved in heavy battle action except the *Cedar Mills,* which was honored for the rescue of a French destroyer serving as escort. She was wallowing helplessly in sinking condition in heavy seas; all personnel aboard and the ship itself were saved by the masterful handling and performance of the crew of the *Cedar Mills* who transferred most of the destroyer's crew and towed the ship for several days until relieved. Her citation reads, in part, ". . . the stark courage of her gallant crew in this heroic rescue caused her to be perpetuated as a Gallant Ship."[4]

The SS *William Moultrie, Virginia Dare,* and *Nathaniel Greene* were honored for getting their vital cargoes through to North Russia in spite of heavy and constant air and sea attacks; the SS *Samuel Parker* spent six months in the Mediterranean in 1943 transporting troops and war materiel to the battlefronts while under continuous attack that damaged her severely, as well as being damaged by burning fuel from exploding ships. Three of her crew, including Captain Elmer J. Stull, were awarded Merchant Marine Distinguished Service Medals for leadership and heroism in battle. The SS *Adoniram Judson* and *Marcus Daly* were among the first ships to arrive at Leyte during the initial invasion of the Philippines and underwent extensive attack.[5]

More detailed accounts of heroic actions against impossible odds by the SS *Stanvac Calcutta* and the SS *Stephen Hopkins* will be found in chapter 8, "The Sea Raiders."

Seven U.S. Navy ships have been named, posthumously, in honor of armed guard gunnery officers who displayed extraordinary heroism and devotion to duty. They are:

Destroyer Escort (DE) *John R. Borum* (for his service in SS *Brilliant*)

An Armed Guard gun crew at action stations. (National Archives)

DE *John J. Brennan* (for service in SS *Otho*)
DE *William R. Herzog* (for service in SS *Pan New York*)
DE *Hunter Marshall* (for service in SS *Merrimack*)
DE *Kenneth Willett* (for service in *Stephen Hopkins*)
Destroyer (DD) *Kay K. Vesole* (for service in SS *John Bascom*)
Transport *Patrick Walsh* (for service in SS *Patrick J. Hurley*)[6]

Unfortunately, full documentation of the heroism of many armed guards, including some of the seven listed above, is not available due to the passage of time, transfer of documents, a disastrous fire at the Records Center in St. Louis, and other causes. Nevertheless, the heroic story of Ensign Kay K. Vesole is available in great detail, and will serve to represent some of the others whose official files are incomplete and who cannot be given the full credit they deserve.

Ensign Kay K. Vesole, USNR, was born in Predboz, Poland, on 11 September 1913. Shortly thereafter, his family emigrated to the United States and settled in Iowa. He received a bachelor's degree in 1936 from the University of Iowa, and graduated from the Law School of the university in 1939. He was a practicing attorney when he was commissioned an ensign, U.S. Naval Reserve, on 19 October 1942. He attended navy training schools in Tucson and Boston, (Local Defense), and in February 1943 he was assigned to the Armed Guard School, Gulfport, Mississippi. On April 25 he was assigned to duty in command of the AG unit on the brand new Liberty ship, SS *John Bascom*, just completed at Panama City, Florida. On 2 December 1943, the *Bascom* was moored off the seawall at Bari, Italy, one of thirty freighters and tankers offloading or waiting to discharge supplies for the British 8th Army drive north, when a massive enemy air attack occurred. In twenty minutes, seventeen of the ships were sunk or damaged beyond repair, one of the worst disasters of the war.

The full story of the attack, which included hundreds of deaths caused by mustard gas carried on at least one ship, will be covered in a chapter on action in the Mediterranean, but the following will describe the heroic action of Ensign Vesole, which won him the Navy Cross, posthumously, and the naming of the destroyer, USS *Vesole* (DD878) in his honor.[7]

At the time, Bari was considered a quiet zone, but Ensign Vesole had trained his gun crew to be ready for anything, and they were at action stations when the attack began at 1945 hours. When parachute flares illuminated the harbor and planes were heard overhead, Vesole did not wait for the designated signal from shore batteries, and when Vesole observed to the master, "I think we have waited long enough," and the captain agreed, the *Bascom* was the first gun crew to fire. Three bombs hit the ship in the #1, #3, and #5 holds, causing fires to break out immediately. The gun crew, with many wounded, stayed at battle stations until the abandonship order was given. The citation accompanying the presentation of the Navy Cross gives the simple statement of Vesole's actions:

For extraordinary heroism as Commanding Officer of the United States Navy Armed Guard aboard the S.S. *JOHN BASCOM* when that vessel was bombed and sunk by enemy aircraft in the harbor of Bari, Italy, on the night of December 2, 1943. Weakened by loss of blood from an extensive wound over his heart and with his right arm helpless, Ensign Vesole valiantly remained in action, calmly proceeding from gun to gun, directing his crew and giving aid and encouragement to the injured. With the *JOHN BASCOM* fiercely ablaze and sinking, he conducted a party of his men below decks and super- vised the evacuation of wounded comrades to the only undamaged lifeboat, persistently manning an oar with his uninjured arm after being forced to occupy a seat in the boat, and upon reaching the seawall, immediately assisted in disembarking the men. Heroically disregard- ing his own desperate plight as wind and tide whipped the blaze along the jetty, he constantly risked his life to pull the wounded out of flaming, oil-covered waters and, although nearly overcome by smoke and fumes, assisted in the removal of casualties to a bomb shelter before the terrific explosion of a nearby ammunition ship inflicted injuries which later proved fatal. His exceptional forti- tude and self-sacrificing concern for others were in keeping with the highest traditions of the United States Naval Service. He gallantly gave his life for his country.

> For the President,
> /s/ James Forrestal
> Secretary of the Navy[8]

The *Bascom* carried a complement of forty-three crew members, a navy gun crew of twenty-eight, and one army security officer. Four of the crew were killed and twenty in- jured. All twenty-eight AGs were wounded, ten fatally. Nine

Winter gun practice for a NAG crew. The first shellman is shown loading a four-inch gun. (Courtesy Nimitz Library, U.S. Naval Academy)

AGs were awarded the Bronze Star, and all received Letters of Commendation, with authorization to wear the Commendation Ribbon. A navy report, listing the men who were awarded the Bronze Star Medal states: "They and the other eighteen, each of whom received a Letter of Commendation . . . disregarded their wounds to stick by their battle stations until every gun was out of action. Heavily bombed, the ship was ablaze and sinking. Only one lifeboat remained undamaged. Ensign Vesole, badly wounded, went below decks with Bishop, Goldstein, Ainsworth and Ruddiman, through fire and wreckage, to carry out the wounded and get blankets for them. Making way for others in the lifeboat, Anderson, Baker, Boyce, Ruddiman, Kelly and Behm swam to the jetty. There Ensign Vesole and Goldstein risked their lives further to pull injured men from the blazing, oil-covered water and carry them to a bomb shelter, while Kelly and William A. Kreimer, Signalman, Second Class, USNR, signalled with painfully burned hands to summon rescue boats for them. Explosion of an ammunition ship cut short these efforts, mortally wounding Ensign Vesole."[9]

Several months later, when survivors arrived at the Armed Guard Center, New Orleans, they were permitted to discuss the attack and report on Ensign Vesole's heroic death. The report of the interview, as carried in the *Daily Times,* Davenport, Iowa, gives a dramatic personal story of conscientiousness of duty and consideration of his men. The story relates how the eleven young men on occasion cried unashamedly as they described their commanding officer.

"We were the first ship to fire," said Bill Kreimer, signalman, from Cincinnati, "That's the way the 'old man' had us trained." Seaman Walter Ainsworth, Kansas City, reported, "Ensign Vesole was all over the ship, looking after his men and seeing that the guns were fought with 100% efficiency. He kept counting the men, spurring them on. It's hard to imagine how cool he was, and how much confidence we got from him."

"We took three direct hits, right down the middle of the ship," said Coxswain David Goldstein, Cleveland. "Mr. Vesole had just checked the stern gun and was going forward. He came reeling to the forward gun with his clothes blown off, and his right arm dangling useless, bleeding from the shoulder. The first thing he asked was whether anyone on the gun had been hurt!"

Warned that an ammunition ship nearby, burning fiercely, would go "up" any minute, Ensign Vesole went below to haul up the wounded. "The 'old man' was wonderful then," exclaimed Ainsworth. "The ensign wouldn't leave until he had checked every inch of the ship himself and had accounted for everyone. Then he insisted, with his bum arm, that he was going to swim ashore so that there would be more room in the boat for the wounded. We had to use physical force to put him in the boat, and even then he insisted in pulling an oar with his one good arm! He fished three or four injured men out of the water. Then as the flames moved closer, he got three men on the only stretcher, and insisted on helping to carry the wounded with his one good arm." "When the ammunition ship went up, the heat and concussion were terrible, and more flames were thrown across the oily water and the jetty," reported Seaman Bob Boyce, from Zanesville, ". . . but we had to grab the Ensign again to keep him from going into the fire. There just wasn't anything that could be done for the poor devils trapped in it." [10]

Ensign Vesole refused to leave the jetty until the last man had been removed to safety. The men also told of his self-lessness and devotion to his men at other times—how he got them out of personal difficulties, made friends with the merchant crew and taught them how to fire the guns, "broke out" cigarettes for them when they ran out; even in the hospital, and conscious only part of the time, he worried about replacing the men's pay cards. When he died, the over-worked British doctors, afraid of the effect it would have on the more seriously injured men, delayed telling them. Later it was said that he had two deathbed wishes—he wanted to get a crack at the Nazis in the daytime, and he wished he could see his baby. He never made it.

As the navy said, the young lawyer turned naval officer lived and died "in keeping with the highest traditions of the U.S. Naval Service." He is a worthy representative of all the other young men who gallantly served their country and may have died in obscurity.

Lieutenant (j.g.) John Randolph Borum could have been considered one of the "old men" of the NAG. Born in Norfolk, Virginia, 8 December 1907, he was almost thirty-five when he took the oath of office as a naval officer on 10 March 1942. He had previously enlisted in the army as a flying cadet and was honorably discharged in May 1934. After receiving his commission in the navy, he reported to the Naval Training School (Local Defense) in Boston, but was transferred to the Armed Guard School, Little Creek, on 15 May, and on 4 June

1942 he was assigned as officer-in-charge of an AG unit on the merchant vessel, SS *Brilliant.*

Within a very short time he had distinguished himself. The *Brilliant* was torpedoed off Newfoundland in November 1942 while in convoy. The explosion caused a roaring blaze and the "Abandon Ship" signal was quickly given. The crew and most of the ship's officers took to the lifeboats, but Borum and Third Mate J. C. Cameron, with a few crewmen still on board, decided they could put out the fire and save the ship, and that they did. They were able to get her underway again, and several days later, crawling along at 3 knots, on 24 November they brought the battered ship into St. John's. After a temporary patching up, a tug was called to tow her to Halifax for further repair. Unfortunately, the coolness and fortitude of Borum and his make-shift crew were in vain. On 20 January 1943, the *Brilliant* ran into a vicious Arctic gale that she had no strength left to withstand. The crippled ship fought well, but it was her last battle; she broke up and went down, taking the gallant Borum and Cameron with her.

Prior to his death, the Navy Board of Awards prepared a citation for Borum, which he never saw. The Letter of Commendation reads, "The Bureau is informed that while you were Officer-in-Charge of the Armed Guard Crew on board a U.S. merchantman, that ship was torpedoed and set on fire. In these circumstances you remained on board and assisted in extinguishing the fires and in bringing the ship, in a badly damaged condition, safely to port. For your courage, devotion to duty and your calm disregard of your own safety on this occasion, you are hereby commended."[11]

Lieutenant (j.g.) Kenneth Martin Willett, Sacramento, California, died in one of the most unique sea battles of World War II—a battle to the death between the German sea raider *Stier,* and the Liberty ship SS *Stephen Hopkins,* on her first and last voyage. Willett enlisted for four years in the U.S. Naval Reserve as an apprentice seaman, Class V-7, on 10 August 1940. After training in the Midshipman School he served on the USS *California* but was transferred to the Armed

Guard Center, Treasure Island, California, and in January 1942 was assigned to the SS *Stephen Hopkins*. The full story will be told in chapter 8, but his heroic actions earned him the Navy Cross, with the following citation.

"The Navy Cross has been awarded to Lieutenant (junior grade) Kenneth M. Willett, U.S.N.R., 23, of 708 Thirty-fifth Street, Sacramento, California.

"For extraordinary heroism and conspicuous courage as Commanding Officer of the United States Navy Armed Guard aboard a merchant vessel during action with unidentified enemy forces. In an attack launched by the enemy, and with no friendly ship in sight, Lieutenant (junior grade) Willett promptly manned his station at the 4-inch gun as the first shell struck, and opened fire on the most heavily armed of the two enemy raiders. Although seriously wounded in the stomach almost immediately, he kept up a sustained and rapid fire at close range, hitting his target along the waterline with most of the 35 shells fired. Because of his great personal valor and gallant spirit of self-sacrifice, he was able to maintain a determined and heroic defense of his ship until forced by a magazine explosion to cease his fire. Still refusing to give up, Lieutenant (junior grade) Willett, obviously weakened and suffering, went down on deck and was seen helping to cast loose the life rafts in a desperate effort to save the lives of others. His vessel was shelled repeatedly from stem to stern, but before she plunged stern first, wrecked and blazing into the sea, her guns had inflicted serious damage on both enemy raiders and caused the probable destruction of one of them."[12]

William Randolph Herzog, Troy, New York, took the oath of office as Lieutenant (j.g.), USNR, on 13 March 1942. Lieutenant Herzog had received an A.B. degree in 1932, and an L.L.B. degree from Harvard University in 1935. In April, he reported to the AG School, Section Base, Little Creek, Virginia, and on 1 May 1942 he was detached and reported to the AG Receiving Station, Brooklyn, New York, for active duty. He was assigned as officer-in-charge of the AG detachment on board the tanker SS *Pan New York*. The *Pan New York*, carrying a full load of 88,000 barrels of gasoline from

Galveston to the United Kingdom, was torpedoed by German sub *U-624* on 29 October 1942, while about 550 miles off Ireland in Convoy HX 21. The explosion blew blazing gasoline over most of the ship and surrounding waters. It was impossible to launch lifeboats or rafts. Of seventeen NAG, only one survived, as did twelve of the merchant crew.

Lieutenant Herzog was posthumously awarded the Navy and Marine Corps Awards, with the following citation:

"For heroic action as Officer-in-Charge of the United States Navy Armed Guard on board an American merchant vessel, when that vessel was torpedoed and sunk. With his ship ablaze and rocked by explosions, Lieutenant Herzog, trapped amidships with several of his gun crew, made courageous and determined efforts to free them by battering the jammed door with all the strength at his command. Stopping long enough to procure a gas mask for the radio operator who was able to escape through a porthole, Lieutenant Herzog, despite the suffocating smoke and fumes from burning gasoline and paint, made one last effort to force the door open by firing at it with his pistol, before falling unconscious to the deck. He gallantly gave up his life in the service of his country."[15]

Lieutenant (j.g.) Patrick J. Walsh's navy record, as furnished, is incomplete. He served on the SS *Patrick Hurley,* a 10,865-ton tanker of Sinclair Refining Co., a new tanker launched in November 1941. On 12 September 1942, while traveling alone in the Caribbean from Aruba to the U.K. with high-octane gasoline and diesel fuel, the *Hurley* was attacked by the *U-512* and was shelled rather than torpedoed. The eighteen-man AG crew under Lieutenant Walsh took to the guns and fought back, but the forward 3" gun was knocked out of action. The fight was continued, however, with the 4" gun aft and the 20-mm guns. The ship was ablaze from stem to stern when she had to be abandoned. Two lifeboats were launched, one with twenty-two men including four AGs, and one with twenty-three men, including ten AGs. The first lifeboat was picked up on 19 September, but the second was not picked up until 4 October 1942.

Lieutenant (j.g.) Walsh was one of four navy men who

went down with the ship. He directed the fight from his battle station on the bridge. Badly injured but remaining at his post though weak from loss of blood, Lieutenant (j.g.) Walsh was posthumously awarded the Purple Heart and Silver Star medals, for "displaying selfless gallantry in battle." [14]

Ensign John J. Brennan, Philadelphia, Pennsylvania, enlisted in the USNR on 14 June 1940. He was appointed a midshipman in the U.S. Naval Reserve on 10 August 1940. He was a member of the first class to attend the Midshipman's School, New York, and reported for duty aboard the USS *Quincy*, then with the Neutrality Patrol, on 29 November 1940. He was detached as an ensign, USNR, on 15 December 1941 to join AG Crew #34 at the AG Center, NYC, and on 31 December 1941 received his orders detailing him to command the AG unit of the merchantman SS *Otho*. On 3 April 1942, the *Otho* was torpedoed by the German sub *U-754* while en route alone from the African Gold Coast to Philadelphia with manganese ore and other cargo. The ship sank about ten minutes after the attack, and survivors took to the boats. Of the ten-man NAG crew, five navy men were lost, including Ensign Brennan. [15]

Ensign Hunter Marshall III, USNR, Charlotte, North Carolina, entered the U.S. Naval Reserve as an apprentice seaman on 12 July 1941. He graduated from the NR Midshipman's School, 16 January 1942. He reported to the AG School, Little Creek, Virginia, on 22 March 1942. On 10 April 1942 he was ordered to duty as AG officer-in-charge of the SS *Merrimack*, attached to the AG Center, South Brooklyn, NY. On 9 June 1942, the *Merrimack* was torpedoed by German sub *U-107* in the Caribbean Sea off the coast of Honduras, while en route from New Orleans to Cristobal, Canal Zone, with a cargo of military supplies. Of the forty-two merchant crewmen and nine AG, only nine crew and one AG survived. Ensign Marshall was awarded the Silver Star Medal, posthumously, with the following citation:

"For gallant and intrepid conduct as Commanding Officer of the United States Armed Guard aboard a U.S. Naval vessel on the occasion of the torpedoing of that vessel by an enemy submarine. Immediately following the explosion, the Armed Guard, under the resolute leadership of Ensign Marshall, promptly manned their guns and despite the hazards of further imminent torpedo attacks, remained at their battle stations until the forward part of the ship was awash and the order, 'Abandon Ship', was given. Because of his loyal and determined fighting spirit, Ensign Marshall was one of the last to leave the ship. His courage and exemplary devotion to duty were in keeping with the highest traditions of the United States Naval Service." [16]

There are so many others who fought heroically and died in obscurity. As a long-ago poet once wrote, "It is the pen that gives immortality to men. . . ." However, it is possible to record a few instances of heroic action "above and beyond." One such case is Lieutenant Kenneth Muir, USNR, who was commanding officer of a naval gun crew of ten aboard the Liberty SS *Nathaniel Hawthorne.* In November 1942, while en route from British Guiana carrying a cargo of 7,500 tons of vital bauxite, she was torpedoed by the *U-508* just north of Trinidad, the last leg of a long voyage home from the Persian Gulf. In rapid succession two torpedoes demolished the midships, and a third exploded the acetylene supply in a blast of flame and jagged fragments of shrapnel. The *Hawthorne* went down in less than two minutes; the last seen of Lieutenant Muir was of him driving a few of his crew from the blazing wreck. He went down with the ship, along with thirty merchant crew and six AGs. The story of Muir's last moments were told by one of the survivors, a merchant crewman. He said that Muir was clearly visible in the flames, "With one arm blown off, he stayed calm and pushed several men to the stern and ordered them to jump. He could have jumped, but he went back into the flames for more and went down with the ship and the rest of his crew." The navy awarded Muir the Navy Cross posthumously for extraordinary heroism. [17]

Our Navy of December 1943 reported on the heroic action of an AG crew on an unidentified ship (customary at that time). The twenty-man AG crew, under the command of Lieutenant Robert McIllwane of Lakeland, Florida, came under five attacks by waves of German torpedo planes, coming in from three directions, followed by high-level bombers. The dark camouflage of the attackers blended in with the darkening skies, making it difficult to draw a careful bead. The ship was badly damaged and was going down by the head when it finally made port, but the gun crew was credited with four planes downed and two probables. The gunners received high commendation from the ship's master and chief officer, and the navy followed, giving McIllwane a Silver Star and awarding individual letters of commendation to the entire gun crew.[18]

Another crew took a chance on being barbecued to save a tanker loaded with vital high-octane gas that was docked at an African port. Hit by bombs, blazing gasoline sprayed everywhere. Four members of the crew inched their way into the hold to ascertain damage and the possibilities of fighting the fire, while others, under the direction of Ensign H. P. Gilman, USNR, began heaving ammunition overboard and flooding the ammunition magazine. Thinking of their ship alone, they eventually brought the fire under control, saving the ship and half of the gasoline.

On 10 June 1943, the *Esso Gettysburg*, a newly built tanker, left Gulfport, Mississippi, with a cargo of 119,726 barrels of crude oil. She was armed with a 3″ gun on the bow, ten 20-mm guns, and a 4″ stern gun, all manned by a twenty-seven-man AG gun crew under the command of Ensign John S. Arnold II, USNR. She had previously made sixteen voyages, nine of which were to foreign areas, including North Africa. About 100 miles SE of Savannah, she was suddenly struck without warning by two torpedoes on the port side. Almost immediately the vessel burst into flames and settled by the stern. Heat and flames became so intense that it was impossible to launch the lifeboats. Making matters worse, the crew was forced to jump into shark-infested waters. Two of the survivors found a charred and gutted lifeboat that had drifted clear of the flames and later picked up six other men of the crew and seven navy gunners. They drifted for nineteen hours before being picked up. Thirty-seven crewmen and twenty AGs were lost, including the master and a number of officers of the ship.

Ensign Arnold was one of those saved. Just before the explosions he had been drilling the forward gun crew. When the first torpedo hit, he was sprayed with flaming oil, receiving serious burns on face, neck, and arms. Nevertheless, he directed the firing of the 3″ gun at the submarine until it was necessary to abandon ship. Ensign Arnold later was awarded the Navy Cross. The chief mate survived, finding a charred lifeboat that had three bodies in it; he made a full report of the torpedoing and its aftermath. In his report, he gave great credit to Ensign Arnold, "He was stoical and uncomplaining, waiting until daylight for treatment of his burns. When there was light enough, he asked me to cut some of the hanging flesh from his burns. I did this carefully and applied a dressing from the first-aid kit. I also applied it to two other men."[19]

Enlisted personnel of the naval armed guard received innumerable commendations, including the following:

James David Handy, seaman 2/c, V-6, USNR, on the torpedoing of his ship on 12 June 1942. "All survivors were high in their praise of the U.S. Navy gun crew. All members of the gun crew stayed at their positions until the gun would fire no longer and were the last to abandon ship."[20]

Edward Perry Rego, seaman first class, USNR, on his service aboard the SS *James Woodrow*, during action at Salerno, Italy, 11–17 September 1943. "In spite of the danger from falling bombs, shrapnel, and machine gun fire, the Navy Gun Crew remained at battle stations, day and night, savagely striking back at the enemy with a sustained and accurate barrage of shellfire which contributed to the destruction of four German planes. . . ."[21]

The following pages will record many instances of heroism of both naval armed guards and their shipmates of the merchant marine. Unfortunately, a great number were never recognized by commendations or awards, a situation that occurred often; papers get lost, observers or commanding officers become casualties or are reassigned, and pertinent supporting details are garbled or incomplete. In other cases, government bureaucracy thwarted justified citation and honors. The naval armed guard gun crew, under command of Ensign Edward Anderson, USNR, in the SS *Stanvac Calcutta*, received no recognition for their gallant fight against the heavily armed German raider *Stier*, which was followed by years of harsh treatment in Japanese military work camps. None of the navy crew was authorized a battle star for the engagement since the *Stanvac Calcutta* was not a navy ship, in spite of the fact that all were U.S. Navy men, on assignment by the navy, with instructions to do exactly what they did so gallantly.[22]

Another case of obvious injustice was the lack of recognition of the heroism of the cadet/midshipmen of the U.S. Merchant Marine. The cadets went to sea as part of the federal government's training program, on ships that were sent into combat areas, and made up part of gun crews of the naval armed guard. They were sworn members of the U.S. Naval Reserve, and were to obtain commission as an ensign, USNR, upon completion of training. Unfortunately, over 140 cadets were killed in action, and their families were advised that the navy would not grant them posthumous awards, apparently on grounds that they did not live to graduate. C/M Edwin O'Hara, who died in the epic battle of the SS *Stephen Hopkins* with the *Stier* (described elsewhere) would have been an ideal candidate for a Medal of Honor, but he and other cadet/midshipmen lost at sea were not considered eligible for the Purple Heart or even campaign medals.[23]

CHAPTER SEVEN
THE CONVOYS

*Those who cannot remember the past
are condemned to repeat it.*
—George Santayana

The convoy system, although generally credited with saving Great Britain in World War II, was not entirely blessed by Allied naval leaders early in that war. The hard lessons learned by both Britain and the U.S. in World War I had been forgotten between wars, and had to be learned over again at great cost. At the start of WW II, Britain was again caught short of ASW plans and materiel, notably escorts, and Churchill had to importune Roosevelt repeatedly for aid. After the U.S. entry into the war and the subsequent launching of intensive U-boat attacks with heavy losses along the East Coast, the British tried to convince Fleet Admiral Ernest J. King, CIC, U.S. Navy, to inaugurate a system of convoying along that coast.

Admiral King could never be considered as a role model of an avuncular figure. "He was so tough," said one dubious admirer, "that he shaved with a blow-torch." King strongly resisted all British pressure to establish a convoy system. He felt that a weakly escorted convoy was worse than none, and that the U.S. lacked adequate escorts because of its far-flung global commitments. With a decimated Pacific Fleet, he stated, "The plain fact is that we do not have the 'tools' to meet the enemy at all points he is threatening us." He was also hampered by the fact that the army air corps was less than enthusiastic in assisting the navy in offshore patrols, and by President Roosevelt's lack of priority support for construction of antisubmarine vessels. Mistakenly, as it now appears, in a meeting with the British Combined Chiefs of Staff, he raised the point that in his opinion "submarines can be stopped only by wiping out the building yards and basins—a matter which I have been pressing for with only moderate success." In this he followed the philosophy of a number of British naval authorities who felt earlier that protection of convoys was purely defensive in nature, and what was needed was a strong offense.[1] King pointed out that U.S. coastal lanes, including the Caribbean and Panama routes, totaled 7,000 miles in length and "to this must be added the ocean convoy system to Great Britain and Iceland (already in effect) and extensions which should be made to protect traffic to the east coast of South America, perhaps to the Cape of Good Hope, not to mention our Pacific commitments."[2]

A steady stream of senior representatives of the Royal Navy crossed the Atlantic in an endeavor to persuade King to change his mind, to no avail. British official reports include such descriptions of meetings with King as "stormy," "abominably rude," "quite impossible," "royal row," and other remarks decidedly not complimentary in nature. At one point Admiral Sir Andrew Cunningham, First Sea Lord, told Captain Stephen W. Roskill, RN, whimsically that things would go better if Roskill would "shoot Ernie King." The British were particularly upset because of the catastrophic losses of vital tankers along the United States East Coast. Roskill's view was that King had always wanted to deploy his full force and strength in the Pacific.[3]

The British had a good point. Losses along the East Coast had become disastrous. In the first three months of 1942, the Allies lost 128 ships to U-boat action, and in the Gulf, U-boats sank 41 ships, half of them tankers, prompting the British to cry that the sinkings were endangering the war effort. In April, King reluctantly agreed to start a "Bucket Brigade" as an experiment; 28 escorts were detailed to handle 120 ships per day along the East Coast. They would convoy up to 120 miles per day and anchor in safe harbors at night. The reductions of sinkings proved so dramatic that King finally agreed to a full interlocking convoy system, which was extended to the Caribbean and Gulf, and there were practically no losses at all in the last six months of the year. Before this happened, however, masts sticking out of the water or other remains of ships lost along the coast provided grim evidence that death could strike at any moment. AG lookouts strained

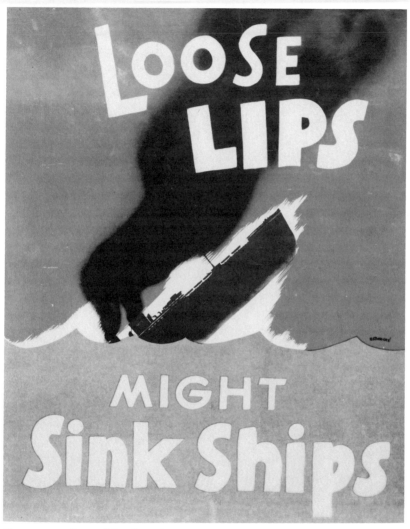

Posters such as this played a significant role in mobilizing citizens for wartime existence. (National Archives)

their eyes for a glimpse of a strange shape low in the water, or the phosphorescent wake of an approaching torpedo, many times too late. About one million tons of shipping were lost before convoying drove the U-boats south.[4]

It must be said that Admiral King was not overemphasizing the problem of lack of "tools" available for antisubmarine operations. Early on, the navy took over many pleasure craft and sent them off the coast with makeshift arms and untrained crews. Civilian aircraft that could not carry bombs were used for patrol work; fishing boats were pressed into service as volunteer lookouts. A few army bombers were relunctantly made available for patrol, but did little good as their time over target was so limited. Eventually, a fleet of slow-moving blimps was put into service and proved quite effective in patrolling the waters around convoys. Blimp protection was eventually extended as far south as Brazil.

With the increase in the number of escort vessels becoming available, the interlocking network system ultimately developed into a highly efficient operation on a regular schedule. Northbound convoys from New York operated on a five-day cycle to Halifax; southbound convoys for the Gulf and Caribbean ports operated on a ten-day cycle. A ship could join or leave the convoy at any point along the route. While a big success, the East Coast interlocking convoy system was just a minor segment of the massive movement of convoys across the Atlantic, carrying supplies and war materiel to North Russia, the British Isles, North Africa, the Mediterranean, the Persian Gulf, and onward to India and other far-flung locations.[5]

As the convoy system from the United States developed, ships were gathered at ports such as New York or Halifax, and shortly before departure, a convoy conference was held. All masters of merchant vessels, usually accompanied by their NAG gunnery officers, were in attendance and the convoy commander (always called commodore, and often an experienced merchant captain) and escort commander were introduced. The convoy plan was laid out, each ship identified by name and number and given coded call letters, position in column formation, route, destination, special emergency tactics, and signals. Distance between ships was generally about 500 feet fore and aft and 1,000 feet abeam, but such instructions often proved purely theoretical. The commodore's flag was carried aboard a merchant ship at the head of the center column, and he was in command of the convoy unless attacked, when the escort commander took over and could recommend change of course.

Convoy conferences could be pretty grim affairs, particularly in the early days when the destination was revealed. One AG gunnery officer reported later that he felt it was only one step to death. Unless they were lucky enough to have a rescue ship to the rear, they knew what their fate would be if they were hit and left behind. The AGs well remembered what they had heard in training; never expect another ship to stop and pick them up, nor could they stop their ship for others. For the safety of the many, the convoy must pass by survivors in the sea.

With a polyglot combination of flags and languages spoken by the officers of the varied nationalities of the ships represented, proper understanding of communications and response to orders was imperative. Garbled communications could wreak havoc if a commodore's orders to make a sharp turn to port were interpreted as a sharp turn to starboard. For this reason, AG signalmen were placed aboard many ships, and a special group served on the commodore's staff. In the Caribbean, the communications staff consisted of one signalman 2/c, two signalmen 1/c, and one radioman 1/c. Out of New York, with larger convoys, the staff consisted of a communications officer, three signalmen, and two radiomen. Signalman Pete Burke of Philadelphia reports, "All communications to and from the Commodore were handled by us. Most convoy maneuvers, course changes and general orders were accomplished by flag hoists. Specific instructions to individual ships were usually sent by blinker light, all by daylight; very seldom were any lights shown at night. The most difficult form of communication was to or from an aircraft or blimp. Compared with the sophistication of equipment today, our procedures were pretty crude, but we got the job done."[6]

Signalmen considered their jobs "good duty." Quarters were generally good, close to the bridge, and if they were assigned to a flag officer and not to a particular ship, when the convoy reached destination they were taken off and sent to base for several days and not required to make the typical fast turn-around of loading and unloading tankers.

Radiomen were also vital elements in maintaining communications. While most U.S. merchant ships had their own radio operators who were senior to navy radiomen who might be assigned to the ship, many navy men were assigned to foreign-flag ships to ensure accuracy of communications because of the use of different systems. Jim Bennett of Los Angeles reports that he graduated in the top ten of his class in radio training and was ready to challenge the seven seas in a battlewagon, or at least a heavy cruiser. To his horror, he was assigned to the NAG, which, like many others, he had never heard of. "Here they've spent all this time and money to make me a radio operator, and now I'm going to be guarding a damn building, . . ." was his reaction. However, he was quickly sent to the communications pool at Noroton Heights, Connecticut, for a crash course in signalman training. One day while discussing the duties of a radioman during battle, the question was raised to the chief signalman, who had seen plenty of action, as to how long the operator was expected to stay at his post in the radio shack when the ship is sinking. "Until the water is up to your chin, and the barracuda are nibbling at your ass," was the grim reply.[7]

Bennett had an unusual and unpleasant experience on one convoy. The commodore's flag had to be transferred from the *Esso Concord* to the British freighter *Empire Stalwart,* an old coal burner. The operation involved the transfer of heavy radio and other communications gear, and it took place by lifeboat, during a submarine alert, in a heavy mid-Atlantic sea. "Cargo booms were used to load and unload the weighty objects while the lighter stuff was hand carried on board the *Stalwart* via the Jacob's ladder. Naturally, under those adverse conditions, we were beat up and bruised by the turbulent sea." However, they were extremely lucky; while they were transferring equipment from one ship to another, the escort carrier USS *Block Island* was torpedoed and sunk while scouting ahead of the *Stalwart.*

Sometimes life could be very pleasant. Walter Peters of El Paso says, "I was a signalman on the staff of a commodore, and made a number of trips with him to the West Indies. He was a retired Navy Commander, recalled to duty, and having served in the Far East for a number of years, he considered himself a gourmet. On each trip he put his flag on a different foreign-flag ship so that he could sample the cuisine. The worst was a British ship, where the food was abominable, and the best was a French ship, where the food was not only good, but wine was served at every meal. The Commodore had forbidden us to sample the supply, but we found our way."[8]

Life was not always so easy, as excerpts from a signalman's log indicate, involving messages from another convoy commodore to his charges: "Some ships showed navigation lights last night. This practice is strictly against orders, and you are endangering the whole convoy. Severe action will be taken if you do not comply."

"Funeral will be held tomorrow for Lt. Col. Logan (a British flyer who had been flying an observation plane. He failed to land on a small converted carrier and plunged into the sea). Half-mast ensign from 0830–0930."

"To all lead ships of columns. Take efforts in keeping stationed. There are subs between here and Kola. Keep proper station."

"The Arctic has knocked us about this time. A storm has spread the convoy all over the Arctic Ocean, but under the hand of Providence, we survived three gales, a hurricane of snow and the darkness with surprisingly little damage. I admire your guts for sticking together so well and I send congratulations to you all. I hope that I will sail with you again."

The incredible logistics of organizing a massive convoy can be illustrated by a log kept by Ken Cauble, Portland, Oregon. In 1943–44, Cauble served as gunner in numerous convoys to the Caribbean aboard the tanker MS *Spidolene*, convoys running from eighteen to thirty ships, with four to seven escorts. Transferred to the new Liberty SS *Raymond Clapper*, he served in a dozen or so convoys to Europe. His log indicates that on 3 July 1944, the *Clapper* was in a convoy

of fifteen ships that left New York; by 6 July, the convoy had
increased in size to 120 ships, with 12 escorts and 3 escort
carriers. In early August, a convoy started with twenty ships
and one escort, and was quickly joined by sixty ships, plus
fifteen escorts and aircraft carriers. The efficient meshing of
so many ships, cargoes, and destinations seems almost impossible, but only occasionally did things go awry. On 12 December 1944, a fifty-four-ship convoy that included the *Clapper* was caught in a raging storm and broke apart, with
three-quarters of the ships missing. Two days later, most of
the convoy was located and reassembled, but sixteen ships
were lost, some of which may have made port on their own.[9]

In the latter days of the war, the logistics involved in
organizing a major convoy increased with the ever-growing
numbers of ships involved. Convoys could have up to 200
ships, stretching for miles across and beyond both horizons.
A convoy could be the maritime equivalent of a vast railroad
marshalling yard, with each ship representing a boxcar
brought in from widely distributed origins and placed in
position so that it could be dropped off at a given point to
proceed to its final destination, without disrupting the convoy as a whole. A North Atlantic convoy would have ships
bound for North Russia lined up on the port side, so they
could peel off and leave the convoy without problem. Ships
destined for North Africa or the Mediterranean would be
placed to starboard, and the central section would continue
ahead to the United Kingdom. It was a masterpiece of organization, but, of course, was always subject to Murphy's Law.
Storms could break up a convoy beyond recovery, with each
straggler traveling alone or perhaps finding and joining other
refugees. Weather or reported wolfpacks ahead could force
a convoy far off course, making it difficult for aerial escorts
to locate it. Reckoning of position in bad weather could pose
a problem for stragglers, or any ships sailing alone, as three
ship's officers could reach three different conclusions as to
where they were.

In all the well-organized confusion of convoys, the high-
level decisions of who went where, carrying what, ships
pulling out to head for the frigid Arctic or the blazing Per-

sian Gulf, the scurrying about of escorts tossing depth charges day and night, the small groups of AGs on the many ships went about their daily duties. Lookouts scanned the sea to the horizon, gunners sharpened their skills with drills. General Quarters was held daily at the principal danger hours of sunrise and sunset. When the alarm gongs rang, gun crews leaped to stations, merchant volunteers jumped to jobs as ammo handlers or took places at guns, and signalmen translated flag hoists, "Enemy subs at hand," "Emergency turn 45 degrees to starboard," "Need immediate medical aid," or the cheerier message from the commodore, "One enemy sub destroyed."

All too frequently they would observe, at a distance or nearby, the results of a direct hit on a fellow voyager, perhaps a brilliant burst of flame followed by a billowing cloud of dirty smoke and concussion reflecting the death of a ship and crew. Sometimes, if the victim were close enough, a grim shower of remnants of the ship and her company would fall on their own decks.

Early convoys were very vulnerable as they spread over a vast area of sea with limited escort and little or no air cover. A forty-five-ship convoy, made up of nine columns, would cover more than 20 square miles. There were not enough escorts at the time to sweep ahead or provide sufficient close cover, and they were easy pickings for the wolfpacks, which usually made a combined attack at night from a position forward of the convoy. Daring submariners, notably Otto Kretschmer, Dönitz's top ace, would frequently surface in the middle of a convoy, selecting tankers to light up the area and provide a better choice of targets. Surface attacks were carried out only at night, because of the low visibility of the attackers. The wolfpacks took a heavy toll of merchant shipping in convoy until mid-1943, when they were driven back. However, before this time they destroyed Convoy PQ 17 to North Russia, and decimated Convoys HX 229 and SC 122, to be described elsewhere.

One of the deepest concerns shared by both officers and men aboard merchant ships, particularly in North Atlantic service, was the possibility of the vessel breaking down, a quite common occurrence. Louis Ritter, a gunner from Far Rockaway, New York, was on two ships that had such mishaps, and because of the standing order not to stop, they were left behind. He reports, "An escort ship, usually a destroyer or corvette, would stay with you for a while. If you couldn't get the engines going, the escort would send a code message over the blinker lights wishing you well. She would then take off after the convoy, which would be on or beyond the horizon. Being left behind, we really felt a sense of helplessness. In the North Atlantic, infested with U-boats, we were sitting ducks for any that found us. Luckily, on the ships on which I served, nothing happened, and we were eventually able to get underway." [10]

As sophisticated aerial and surface defenses were developed and expanded, the gaps in air cover in the North Atlantic were closed by carriers, long-range bombers, and additional escorts. U-boat losses increased to the point where they exceeded their successes. The size of convoys and their escorts became so large that U-boats were unable to penetrate the defenses and survive the constant barrage of depth charges dropped by destroyers and other escorts and the bombs dropped from above.

Not all skippers appreciated the "protection" of the convoy and its escorts. Reasons for disliking convoys were many and varied. Some of the older masters whose ships had good speed and could outrun submarines would become almost choleric by having to reduce speed to that of the slowest and possibly most-decrepit ship in the convoy. Some hated to obey the orders of commodores, many taken off the shelf and not always having the best judgment or performance. Entire convoys sometimes blundered into minefields, as did Convoys KS-520 and PQ-13. After her officers took a vote that reflected a lack of confidence in the commodore of one badly battered convoy (HX 229), the SS *Matthew Luckenbach* deliberately took off on her own after the convoy had been hit by German wolfpacks. It was not too sound a decision, as the *Luckenbach* was torpedoed and sunk as she traveled alone at high speed ahead of the beleaguered convoy. [11]

One of the greatest fears of all skippers in convoy was collision. Zigzagging on a pitch-black night, or in bad weather, with ships all around who were equally blind and running without lights or were lost in fog, sleet, snow, or mountainous seas, was a nerve-wracking and often fatal experience. A spark could lead to the annihilation of an ammo ship and nearby vessels. In an instant a tanker could be converted into a pillar of flame that would illuminate all vessels in the vicinity. Even in good weather, malfunctioning steering equipment could send a ship out of control, veering insanely through the rows of ships on either side.

One skipper who preferred traveling all alone was the master of the SS *Henry George,* in which Grady Railsback of Cranfills Gap, Texas, was serving his first trip as an AG gunner. She took him around the world, and after sixty days without seeing land or another ship, in the Indian Ocean a tanker was sighted in the distance. Apparently feeling that the neighborhood was getting too crowded, the skipper, an old Norwegian who obviously disliked company, even in the middle of the ocean, immediately ordered a change of course that would get him out of all the "traffic."

While proceeding across the Indian Ocean alone, the *Henry George* ran into a storm so violent that it broke a couple of beams, and after her arrival in Suez, a welding team had to be flown in to repair the damage. Finally repaired, the *Henry George,* empty and riding high, set out for home via Capetown, Rio de Janeiro, and Trinidad, where she picked up a load of bauxite. Then to the captain's vast distaste, the *Henry George* had to join a convoy of some thirty ships heading for the Gulf of Mexico. A German wolf-pack of about six U-boats was waiting for them, and the ensuing action resulted in nine ships hit and three sunk before the *Henry George* made it to Mobile. One torpedo missed the *George* by fifty feet. Grady's report on the captain's unvarnished opinion of masters ahead who went too slow, masters behind who went too fast, and idiots alongside who didn't know how to drive straight is best left to the imagination.[12]

Nevertheless, with all due respect for the doughty old-timers, it was the convoys that eventually ended the U-boat threat and ensured Allied victory. On 9 May 1945, aboard the new Liberty ship SS *Robert H. Harrison,* Ken Cauble was on the last Allied convoy from the United States to Europe. It consisted of forty-five ships and four escorts, and the *Harrison* was the first American ship to arrive in Holland in seven years.

CHAPTER EIGHT
THE SEA RAIDERS

*. . . an exploit which equals anything in
John Paul Jones' experiences . . . one of
the few cases in naval history where a
lightly armed ship was able to sink by
gunfire a vessel with virtually the armament of a cruiser. (Battle of the SS*
Stephen Hopkins *and the German surface raider* Stier*)*
—U.S. Navy Historical Report[1]

While members of the German Naval High Command, like the British between wars, either forgot or ignored how close U-boats came to bringing Great Britain to her knees in World War I,
they did not forget the early tactic of using surface sea raiders to harass Allied and neutral shipping. The best known of
the World War I raiders was the legendary Count Felix von
Luckner, the "Happy Corsair," made famous after the war
by American author and lecturer Lowell Thomas. Von Luckner never captured many ships or had any appreciable effect
on the war, but his flamboyant gallantry and courtesies extended to his "guests," as he called his prisoners, and his
daring and imaginative exploits elicited reluctant admiration even from his enemies. When the quarters on his ship
became too crowded with prisoners, he captured the French
bark *Cambronne* and transferred his prisoners to her.
Having the foresight to cut back her masts to preclude the
possibility of too much speed in reaching port, he bade his
"guests" bon voyage to Rio.[2]

The most-feared German surface raider in World War I
was the cruiser *Emden,* which created havoc with Allied
shipping in the Indian Ocean until finally caught and sunk
by HMS *Sydney.*[3] The raider *Wolf,* under the command of
Captain Karl August Nerger, also had a remarkable record,

steaming a distance of three times around the world while sinking 300,000 tons of enemy shipping and laying a half-dozen minefields. She brought several hundred prisoners back through the British blockade and tied up a large number of British ships in search of her. Nerger operated successfully from 30 November 1916 through 1918.[4]

In an obvious attempt to emulate the successes of World War I, the German Naval High Command dispatched surface raiders again, as early as March 1940. During the period of German-Soviet rapprochement, Hitler received material aid from the Soviets. The famed raider *Atlantis* (Ship #16), a former 7,860-ton motor ship of the Hansa Line, was disguised as the Soviet auxiliary cruiser *Kim,* and German naval uniforms were altered to appear Russian. The raider *Komet* (Ship #45) was assisted through the Northwest Passage by two Soviet icebreakers, appropriately named *Lenin* and *Stalin.* After further assistance by the icebreaker *Kagonovich,* the *Komet* broke through and entered the Pacific via the Bering Strait. The raiders carried dummy funnels, false derricks and deckhouses, and heavy concealed armament, and they were quite successful, sinking nearly one-half-million tons of Allied shipping by the end of 1941 alone before they were finally driven from the seas.

While one aim of the raiders was to inflict harm from both a strategic and economic point of view, the principal purpose was to force the enemy to form convoys, even in remote waters and to stretch his naval forces thin, diverting them from home waters. Instructions were given masters to prolong the life of the raider as long as possible; they were to move periodically into new areas, suspend operations for a period of time and then to emerge as a completely different ship in appearance and "nationality." Keeping the enemy in suspense was vital, and strict orders were given to avoid action with naval forces or convoys. They accounted for 133 ships, totalling 829,644 tons before their usefulness was ended.[5]

As far as is known, only two of the ten disguised German surface raiders in World War II were actively engaged against

A portrayal of Cadet/Midshipman Edwin O'Hara firing "the last shot" of the SS *Stephen Hopkins* in her epic battle to the death with the German raider *Stier*. (Courtesy American Merchant Marine Museum Foundation, Kings Point, New York)

American vessels—the *Stier* (Ship #23) and the *Michel* (Ship #28), operating in the central and South Atlantic, Indian Ocean, and the Pacific. A navy report dated shortly after the war states that the number of U.S. merchant ships lost to raiders is not definitely known, as "several ships went out independently and were never heard of again. They may have been torpedoed, have suffered marine casualty or gone down before the heavy guns of armed surface raiders." Six merchant ships carrying AG gun crews are known to have encountered enemy raiders, and all were sunk, but at least two, the *Stanvac Calcutta* and *Stephen Hopkins*, fought back gallantly. The battle of the *Stephen Hopkins* and the raider *Stier* "ranks with the greatest ship actions of all time. . . ." Both the *Stanvac Calcutta* and *Stephen Hopkins* were designated "Gallant Ships." While losses in ships and men due to raiders were infinitesimal compared with those of the Battle of the Atlantic, the ordeal of survivors turned over as prisoners to the Japanese was barbaric.[6]

In spite of early success, the logistical difficulties of replenishing the raiders' supplies by sea plus losses as they were tracked down ultimately proved insurmountable. A number of raiders successfully returned to Germany, but the *Atlantis* (Ship #16), *Pinguin* (Ship #33), and *Komoran* (Ship #41) were eventually caught and sunk by British naval units. Nevertheless, the *Atlantis* operated successfully from 31 March 1940 through 22 November 1941, capturing or sinking twenty-two ships totaling over 145,000 tons before being sunk by HMS *Devonshire.* The track of the *Atlantis* is little short of amazing, covering vast areas of the South Atlantic, Indian Ocean, and South Pacific. The *Stier* sank the *Stanvac Calcutta* and the SS *Stephen Hopkins,* the latter after an epic battle to the death that sent both to the bottom. The *Michel* (Ship #29) sank the SS *William C. Humphrey,* the MV *American Leader,* plus several others.

The Texaco tanker SS *Connecticut* was the first American-flag ship attacked by a German raider, on 27 April 1942 in the South Atlantic. A motor torpedo boat from the *Michel* scored a hit, and twenty-four merchant crew and the entire eleven-man NAG detachment were killed in the attack. The Liberty SS *George W. Clymer* was also attacked in the South Atlantic on 7 June 1942, while broken down at sea. Her distress message was intercepted by the *Michel,* which promptly sent in a motor torpedo boat to attack. One seaman was killed, and thirty-eight merchant crew and twelve NAG survivors were taken aboard the *Michel.* The MS *Sawokla* was shelled and torpedoed by the *Michel* on 29 November 1942 off Madagascar; sixteen merchant crewmen, including the master, and four AGs were killed, and thirty seamen and nine AGs taken prisoner. When they were taken aboard, Captain Helmut von Ruckteschell commented on the tenacity of *Sawolka*'s gunners, who, when their main gun was knocked out, continued fighting with antiaircraft guns. According to the record, survivors were picked from the water and the wounded received excellent care from the ship's doctor, who was subsequently lost when the *Michel* was later sunk.[7]

The SS *William F. Humphrey* encountered an unidentified raider on 16 July 1942 while en route from Capetown to Trinidad. The raider fired once and stopped. When the *Humphrey* answered her fire, the enemy ship opened up with all guns, including her machine guns. A shell hit the *Humphrey*'s gun deck, and the old 5" 51 stern gun could no longer be fired. According to a navy report, "A fighting coxswain named Jennings Jack Bennett, in charge of the five-man AG crew, was hit in both legs and one arm while loading a second round, but continued loading and pointing the gun until it was knocked out of action. He then threw life preservers in the water and proceeded amidships to throw confidential papers overboard. . . . He was hit by shrapnel, but managed to free himself and roll into the water and swim to a life-raft. . . . For seven days he lay in a lifeboat to which he was transferred, with many wounds, including shrapnel in his stomach, before survivors were rescued by a Norwegian ship. For his heroic conduct, Bennett was awarded the Silver Star."[8]

The MS *American Leader*, a C-1 type freighter carrying essential wartime raw materials and general cargo, was about 1,000 miles west of Capetown, bound for Punta Arenas and the Pacific, and thence through the Panama Canal to the U.S. East Coast, when she was unfortunate enough to encounter the heavily armed *Michel*. On 10 September 1942, the 4 to 8 morning watch picked up a ship that was assumed to be a friendly vessel on a reciprocal course for Capetown. Everything seemed normal until the other vessel made an "end run," eventually positioning itself ahead of the *American Leader*. Then after dark, at about 2000, using a new tactic she came down on the *Leader*. She began attacking without warning and gave the *Leader* a pounding as she came along the starboard side. The *Leader*'s helmsman put the wheel hard left and the *Michel* came across the wake and up the port side, holding that position and firing at will, including two torpedoes. It was no contest. The *Leader's* armament consisted of a single 4″ 50 mounted on the stern, two .50-caliber machine guns on the deckhouse, and two .30-cal Lewis guns also aft. The *Leader* settled by the stern and went down in about twenty-five minutes. The *Leader* had a complement of forty-nine merchant crew and a nine-man NAG gun crew; ten of the merchant crew and one AG were killed in the attack. Shortly after the *Leader* went to the bottom, the *Michel* returned and picked up forty-seven survivors from the water, including most of the gun crew.

George W. Duffy, a Massachusetts Maritime Academy graduate, was third officer on the *Leader,* and he recounts the story of what occurred following the sinking of his ship. "The skipper of the raider, Captain Hellmuth [*sic*] von Ruckteschell, was a rather Jekyll-and-Hyde type of man. When he went into action he was utterly ruthless, but afterwards he reverted to the personality of the clergyman's son, which he was. We were told immediately that our treatment would depend upon our conduct. . . . They were strict with us, understandably so, but we ate the same food, and in the same quantity as the German crew. We had a loudspeaker in our quarters, usually carrying German radio broadcasts. When the raider was not in company with another German ship, we were allowed an hour's exercise morning and afternoon. The *Michel* generally was supplied by blockade runners; we were with the raider *Stier* on one occasion and the tanker *Uckermark* twice. She was the former *Altmark* of Graf Spee fame, and was 'running' from France to Japan. In October, we were transferred to the *Uckermark*, whose skipper was Captain von Zwatowski [*sic*], whom we called 'von Zed.' He knew what we were experiencing as he had been a prisoner of the British in New Zealand in World War I. He was in the same camp as the well-known Count Felix von Luckner, who recruited him for an escape attempt. A small boat was built in the camp, and a number of seamen escaped with von Luckner and 'von Zed.' They eluded capture for some fourteen days, but never got out of sight of land. 'Von

Zed' was easy on us, we were free to leave our quarters and go onto the foredeck from sunrise to sunset. He saw to it that we had bundles of reading material and had no objection to our attempts to get a latitude at noon. (We were survivors off several ships, and had two Captains, a Chief Officer, two Second Officers and two Third Officers who pooled their talents in this.)

"Two days after we were sunk, the *Michel* caught the British *Empire Dawn;* twenty-two survivors were picked up by the *Michel*'s torpedo boat. We also had a number of men from other ships, including two badly wounded men from the SS *William F. Humphrey.* Most were transferred to the *Uckermark,* except one too serious to be moved. On 2 November, the *Uckermark* anchored just outside of Batavia, where we were turned over to the Japanese, who had been there since March. We were put on Japanese work parties, but when the *Michel* came into Batavia we were able to talk with our old acquaintances. The *Michel* then went on to Singapore where she dropped her latest prisoners, and thence to Japan."[9]

Many survivors of the work camps in Java and Sumatra were eventually sent to Japan, after having lost 500-plus men building the "Death Railway" across Sumatra. There was little food, no medicine to speak of, forced labor sometimes as long as fourteen to fifteen hours per day. Duffy reports that treatment by the Germans was "fair, but strict," but the Japanese "basically did not care if we lived or died." He adds, "The greatest atrocity was transporting prisoners in unmarked Japanese ships. Of the *American Leader*'s fifty-eight-man crew, including the navy gun crew, eleven were lost in the *Michel* action, thirteen lost aboard the *Tomohaku Maru* when she was torpedoed by USS *Tang* on 26 June 1944, and four more lost on the Junyo Maru on 8 September when she was sunk. The 'Death Railway' on Sumatra claimed two of the *Leader*'s crew. Of the Navy gun crew, a young sailor named Ragland [other details are unknown] was killed at the 4″ gun, and the four lost on the *Tomohaku Maru* were D. Behrendt, Yeoman 3/c, A. Mlodzik, Seaman

2/c, H. Myers, Seaman 2/c and C. Mogenson, Seaman 2/c. Ensign W. Dryer, commander of the Navy gun crew, was lost on the *Junyo Maru.* Only three men of the Navy gun crew survived the war."

The tough young Duffy survived the *Michel* and a series of labor camps, including thirteen months building the "Death Railway," and was repatriated in September 1945, after totaling 1,108 days as a prisoner of war of both enemy countries.

The SS *Stanvac Calcutta* was a one-year-old, 10,170-ton Socony Vacuum Company tanker, commanded by Captain Gustav O. Karlsson, and she carried a crew of forty-two, plus a nine-man navy armed guard crew. Her armament consisted of one out-dated 4″ 50-caliber naval rifle on the stern and one obsolete 3″ 23-caliber antiaircraft gun on the bow. The forward gun was manned by a volunteer merchant marine gun crew trained by Ensign Edward L. Anderson, Beaufort, South Carolina, commander of the armed guard unit, as he did not have enough navy gunners to operate them both. The gun captain on the forward gun was Hartswohl E. Sarrazin, a former navy man from La Place, Louisiana.

Ensign Anderson, later to become lieutenant commander, was unique in his qualifications as an AG gunnery officer compared with so many others who were hastily trained and sent to sea with equally inexperienced gun crews. He had received training at the U.S. Naval Academy in a special Gunnery Officers Ordnance course, for possible use on merchant ships, shortly after being commissioned there in a reserve officers class in May 1941. He was assigned to the USS *Mizar* (AF12) as assistant gunnery officer, but when the navy sent a request for officers, preferably with gunnery experience, for the naval AG, he volunteered. He was first assigned to Little Creek to train gun crews, but received orders to report to the SS *La Perla,* a small banana boat. Upon reporting, he found she still did not have guns or a gun crew, and was then ordered to go aboard the *Stanvac Calcutta* as her gunnery officer. An old 4″ 50-caliber gun was available, but there was no one to mount it, although the ship was

NAG crew aboard the Liberty ship SS *William J. Worth* at firing practice in September 1943. (Courtesy Nimitz Library, U.S. Naval Academy)

loaded and ready to sail. In desperation, the port director asked Anderson to mount the gun, as he had assisted in mounting new guns on the *Mizar*. Anderson agreed to try and credits the "unstinting help" of the *Calcutta*'s chief engineer in completing the job. Navy ordnance men finally showed up, checked and approved the mounting, and the *Stanvac Calcutta* was able to get underway for her rendezvous with destiny.

After making several voyages without incident, the *Stanvac Calcutta* departed Montevideo on 29 May, light, bound for Caripito, Venezuela. On a premonition, Ensign Anderson had a number of additional rounds for the after gun brought up on deck and lashed down by the ready box. They were soon to be needed. At approximately 1010 hours on 6 June

1942, about 500 miles east of Pernambuco, Brazil, a ship was sighted coming out of a rain squall off the port bow. She came down the port side, fired a warning shot, and signaled for the *Calcutta* to stop engines. Instead, according to previous arrangements made between Captain Gustav O. Karlsson and Ensign Anderson, the captain began to swing the ship to bring the after gun to bear. The gun crews had been at action stations since the unknown ship was first reported and were tracking her. Anderson gave an initial range estimate of 3,500 yards, and ordered open fire. The first round was over, but the *Calcutta*'s fifth round knocked out one of the port guns of the raider, which was firing four-gun broadsides and scoring hits. Captain Karlsson, several others on the bridge, and the radio operator, who was trying to get out word that the ship was under attack by a German raider, were killed. The success in knocking out one of the raider's guns had given Anderson some encouragement, but shell fragments from the raider hit the sight bar, shattering the pointer's scope, knocking the trainer's scope out of alignment, nicking the breech plug, and wounding one man in the face. The gun crew continued to fire, without sights, trying to lay the gun "à la John Paul Jones" but without success, for seventeen rounds, until they ran out of ammunition on deck.

The forward gun was in continuous action, despite a number of misfires due to the age of the ammunition. Sarrazin kept the gun crew in action until the signal to abandon ship was given, but two of his gun crew were killed and three wounded. By this time, the *Stanvac Calcutta* was listing heavily to port, and the ammo lashed on deck had been spent. Ensign Anderson ordered two loaders to get more from the magazine, but a torpedo struck with a tremendous explosion and the ship began to list even faster; the port rail was almost in the water and the gun could not be elevated enough to bring it to bear on the raider. Anderson and one member of the gun crew tried to free a lifeboat and a raft that was stuck in its chute, but Anderson was struck in the back by a shell fragment. He found his legs paralyzed but slid down the canting deck, took one last look around, saw no one alive, and slid into a heavy oil slick. Feeling had returned, but one leg was broken. He swam to the second officer, who was wounded and having trouble keeping his head above water. Anderson tried to tow him to a nearby raft but upon looking back found he was dead, with oily water washing over unseeing eyes.

There were a number of wounded men on the raft, several seriously. Anderson started to break out the raft's first-aid kit, but noticed that the raider had lowered boats to pick up survivors; of thirty-seven picked up, fourteen were wounded. They then learned that the raider was the *Stier* (Ship #23), formerly the MV *Cairo*. The wounded overflowed the sick bay, and one soon died aboard the ship. He was buried at sea with proper honors. Also aboard were the crew of the British SS *Gemstone,* sunk without a fight a few days previously. On 12 June, the *Stier* rendezvoused with the tanker *Charlotte Schliemann* to reprovision and transfer all the unwounded and less seriously injured prisoners. On 2 August, 102 prisoners were brought aboard the tanker from another raider, the *Michel* (Ship #29). These included men from the SS *William F. Humphrey,* SS *Gloucester Castle* (British), SS *Patella* (British), SS *Lyle Park* (British) and the SS *Aramis* (Norwegian). Later, six more men, all wounded, were brought aboard from the *Michel.* A few days later twenty-three additional men from the SS *Dalhousie* (British) were brought in by the *Stier.* The *Schliemann* was now heavily overcrowded with prisoners and running short of food, clothing, and blankets. It was considered too dangerous to run the British blockade to return to Europe, so she headed for the Far East, via the Indian Ocean. On 28 September, she dropped anchor at Singapore and turned over fifty prisoners to the Japanese, then continued to Japan, after taking on some thirty Germans who had been prisoners of the British. On 6 November, the last group of 158 prisoners was turned over to Japanese military. Ensign Anderson, being the only military officer in the group, was put in charge and ordered to march them through the streets of

Yokohama for transport to Osaka #1, a military work camp in that city. He saw only one of his gun crew briefly, J. C. Muldrow, seaman 2/c who had been injured in the attack on their ship. Three years later, on 9 September 1945, Anderson was transferred to Yokohama where he underwent medical treatment until being released to fly to hospitals in Guam, Hawaii, and the U.S., finally returning to sea duty after months-long recuperation from his experience as a POW.[10]

Anderson has nothing but praise for the navy and merchant marine gunners who fought their guns to the last. Among the many singled out for heroic action was AG T. P. Cox, seaman 2/c, who had no hot-shell gloves and was severely burned on both forearms and across his chest, but continued at his station until later wounded. Anderson also reports that the German doctor on Raider #23 was very competent and "worked tirelessly in treating the wounded."

In reviewing the *Calcutta's* battle with the *Stier,* Anderson compares the *Stier's* heavy armament, manned by experienced German Navy personnel, with the "inadequate" equipment on the *Stanvac Calcutta.* However, he adds, "We did have that inspirational phrase on our orders, 'There shall be no surrender, and no abandoning ship as long as the guns can be fought,' and so it was."

In comparison with other AG-crewed American ships that were encountered and destroyed by German surface raiders, the story of the epic battle of the Liberty ship SS *Stephen Hopkins* and the raider *Stier* and its consort *Tannenfels* is well known. It has been written about in many articles and books, and the *Hopkins* was awarded the honor of being named a "Gallant Ship." However, no account of the history of the NAG could fail to refer to the battle, a throwback to the early days of naval warfare, ship vs ship, slugging it out in action worthy of the descriptive genius of a Joseph Conrad. The outcome could never have been in doubt: the *Hopkins* was out-numbered, out-gunned, and out-manned, but she fought with a fury that aroused the admiration and high praise of both German Vice Admiral Friedrich Hoge, and Captain Stephen R. Roskill, RN, in his official history of the war at sea. Captain Horst Gerlach, master of the *Stier,* stated at a hearing on the loss of his ship that the battle had been with a "10,000-ton auxiliary cruiser."[11]

The Liberty *Stephen Hopkins,* launched at the Kaiser shipyard at Richmond, California, on 14 April 1942, sailed from San Francisco on her first, and last, voyage. Two quirks of fate combined to place her in the path of the heavily armed *Stier* and *Tannenfels.* In Australia, the *Hopkins* was substituted for another Liberty, the SS *Robert P. Harper,* which originally had been ordered to carry a load of grain to South Africa, but had suffered a mishap at sea. En route, the *Hopkins* encountered two severe storms with winds of Force 9 and Force 11, which caused great damage and drove her far off course. When she belatedly limped into port, considerable time was lost in making her seaworthy and repairing her guns. Finally, on 18 September, she weighed anchor and headed home, on a trip that would have taken her around the world. Several days out of Capetown she received a radio warning of a German raider in the area; she kept a sharp lookout, but fog and rain hampered visibility, to the point that prevented both American and German ships from sighting each other until the mist suddenly lifted and they found themselves almost upon each other. The *Stier* immediately signaled, "Stop at Once." The *Hopkins* was having nothing of it, and turned hard to port to bring her main gun to bear.

The battle was on. It would have been "no contest" except for the bravery and determination of the small group of navy gunners and the equally gallant members of the merchant crew. The odds against the *Hopkins* were impossible. She had only one old 4″ gun aft, salvaged from World War I, two 37-mm antiaircraft guns, and six machine guns. The *Stier* carried six 5.9″ guns, directed by sophisticated fire-control apparatus, and a variety of rapid-firing guns, plus torpedoes. The *Tannenfels* also carried one 5.9″ gun, plus antiaircraft 30-mm and 50-mm machine guns, which poured unrelenting fire into the *Hopkins.*

Aboard the *Hopkins,* gun crews raced to their stations, assisted by well-trained volunteer merchant crew members, including two cadet midshipmen, C/M Edwin O'Hara, who supervised ammunition loading, and C/M Arthur Chamberlin, Jr., who served as spotter. Intense enemy machine-gun fire and shrapnel from shells swept the deck of the *Hopkins.* Ensign Kenneth Willett, commanding officer of the armed guard gun crew, was fatally wounded but continued to direct the fire of the 4″ gun, although bleeding profusely from a number of wounds, until all of his gun crew were killed. Second Mate Joseph Lyman, in charge of the 37-mm guns, hit the *Stier* repeatedly at close range, inflicting casualties, but the enemy fire was intense. He and a number of forward gunners were hit and the guns knocked out of action. The *Stephen Hopkins* was hit repeatedly by the heavy guns of the *Stier,* doing great damage, including knocking out her rudder. Willett's 4-inch returned the favor by landing several hits on the *Stier*'s waterline and hitting the *Stier*'s rudder. The *Hopkins*' radio shack was blown away while the operator was still trying to get out "under attack" signals, the engine room was ablaze, guns silenced, the ship sinking. It was the end, and Captain Paul Buck reluctantly approved the signal to abandon ship.

Cadet O'Hara had been working feverishly to service the 4-inch gun, until the ammunition locker was destroyed. He then climbed to the wrecked gun platform where he found its gun crew all dead or dying. To his amazement, incredibly, the gun standard had survived, and five rounds were still available. O'Hara had studied the operations of the gun crew and knew what to do. All by himself he rammed one round after another into the breech, fired, and miraculously scored five direct hits on the *Stier* before a return salvo aimed directly at him wounded him fatally. He died at his gun, but he had inflicted mortal damage as well on the raider.

In the meantime, Cadet Chamberlin, serving as a gun spotter, left his post after his guns had been silenced. His close friend, Wallace Breck, a navy gunner, saw him with Captain Buck just before the ship went under. Chamberlin apparently waited too long to abandon ship; he went over the stern and was apparently sucked to his death. As the ship went down, a number of survivors in the water were gathered together by Second Engineer George Cronk, who had made his way to a lifeboat. Although not a navigator, and with no instruments, Cronk succeeded in bringing fifteen survivors into a small fishing port in Brazil after an arduous voyage of thirty-one days. Cronk kept a log of the lifeboat's long voyage, which in his understated way gives a vivid picture of the ordeal. Four men died and were given burial at sea. Five naval armed guards survived; Wallace Breck had had to have a piece of shrapnel dug out of his shoulder without anesthesia. The other navy survivors were Virgil Bullock, Ted Barnes, Moses Barker, and Paul Boyer, all seamen 2/c.[12]

Breck later visited the family of Cadet Chamberlin; he and Arthur were close friends, and Chamberlin had given him instructions in navigation and seamanship. Breck became so interested that, in spite of his ordeal, after the war he enrolled in the Merchant Marine Academy at Kings Point and eventually received his master's papers.

Of the merchant crew of forty-one and the fifteen-man NAG unit, forty-one were lost, including Captain Buck. A Liberty ship was named in honor of Captain Paul Buck, and a destroyer escort for Ensign Willett; the *Stephen Hopkins* was designated a "Gallant Ship," one of only nine so honored. A painting of Cadet O'Hara firing the last shot of the *Stephen Hopkins* hangs in a place of honor at the U.S. Merchant Marine Academy at Kings Point.

The *Stier* had sustained such heavy damage that it had to be scuttled and the *Tannenfels* took off her 325 survivors. The battle was brief; it only lasted about fifteen minutes before the *Stephen Hopkins* went down with her dead, but that battle will live long in the annals of Kings Point, the U.S. Merchant Marine, and the U.S. Naval Armed Guard.

CHAPTER NINE
OTHER HAZARDS

They died on rusty old freighters,
jarred apart by a torpedo, on a tanker
in an inferno of flames, they choked to
death or were incinerated in oil-
covered waters, they starved to death
or died of thirst on rafts in the tropics
or of cold or exposure in lifeboats in the
Arctic. . .
—*All Hands,* November 1945

The above, from a wartime story on the naval armed guard service, is quite true, but they also died in a wide variety of mishaps unrelated to enemy action. It might be thought that after evading or surviving enemy air attack, buzz bombs, mines, surface raiders, or torpedo boats, one might feel reasonably secure about getting home in one piece. However, in the globe-girdling odyssey of merchantmen carrying armed guard crews, there was a bewildering assortment of possible troubles, ranging from the dangerous-but-survived, to the absolutely catastrophic.

Into the first category could fall such problems as the malfunctioning of items such as navigational equipment, which could cause embarrassment, at least, or lead to loss of the ship by grounding. Also included would be mechanical breakdown at sea, alone in a vast, empty expanse of water, at the mercy of weather or any lurking submarine. A common problem was the cracking of Liberty-ship hulls, which might be repaired after harrowing experience. Damage, possibly fatal to a vessel, could occur from huge icebergs drifting silently into ship lanes from the frigid Arctic, or from frogmen attaching mines to the hulls of ships at anchor in the warm Mediterranean ports. However, collision at sea was a common, ever-feared and often deadly event, particularly if tank-

ers, munitions ships, or transports were involved. During
World War II, collisions proved terribly costly to the Allies in
lives, ships, and essential cargoes. Collisions can happen almost anywhere, even under favorable weather conditions,
but they were most frequent in convoy, where weather or
malfunction put a ship out of control.

One of the most spectacular collisions of the war involved
the tanker MS *J. H. Senior* (Panamanian flag, but carrying a
NAG gun crew of twenty-seven), and the SS *J. Pinckney Henderson.* Both ships were gutted by fire, and only nine men of
both ships survived. Prior to the collision, the *J. H. Senior*
had made forty-nine voyages and delivered over 5,000,000
barrels of oil. On this occasion, she was carrying high-octane
aviation gas, and the *Henderson* was carrying an equally vol-
atile cargo, 10,000 tons of cotton, magnesium, glycerine,
wax, oil, and other combustibles. Only five men of the forty-
five-man merchant crew and the twenty-seven-man AG
crew serving in the *Senior* were able to come out of that inferno alive. The only AG to survive was Walter A. Gawlik,
seaman 1/c. One of the five merchant survivors was Messman Karl O. Ruud. In Ruud's report to his company he states
that "the flames were like a torch, and burning oil had spread
on the water to 100 feet from the vessel's side. I swam underwater away from the flames, coming to the surface only to
breathe. I was severely burned about the face and hands, but
continued swimming around in the water. Later one of the
lifeboats passed by with Navy gunner Gawlik and oiler Wihlborg in it. Wihlborg pulled me in, along with Junior Engineer Frank Freundlich and Second Engineer Harry Sondergaard. The other lifeboats were destroyed in the flaming
oil around the ship. Our boat was burning, but Gawlik and
Wihlborg managed to put the fire out before it ignited the
gasoline cans stored for the outboard motor. . . ."[1]

The survivors were picked up by a hospital ship and put
into a British hospital. Ruud was under treatment for two
months. Incredibly, the *Senior* was salvaged, after having
been described by an Imperial Oil Company representative
at St. John's as "one of the worst we have seen"; she appar-

ently was never repaired. The aircraft being carried as deck cargo were reduced to molten metal.

The brand new Liberty ship SS *John Morgan* was outbound from Baltimore on her maiden voyage 1 June 1943, carrying a cargo of explosives, when she veered suddenly and rammed her bow into the tanker SS *Montana,* inbound. The resulting explosions were so tremendous that they snuffed out the lives of 83 of the 150 men aboard the two ships, and wreckage and debris were hurtled through the air and showered the decks of a Coast Guard ship a quarter-mile distant. According to an Associated Press delayed dispatch, sixty-five of the sixty-eight men aboard the *Morgan* perished in the blasts, the only survivors being three members of the AG crew out of the twenty-three-man detachment. Eighteen of the tanker's complement, including ten AGs, were lost in the flaming inferno that followed the collision and destroyed her lifeboats before they could be launched. One of the survivors was a deck cadet in the tanker's wheelhouse when the freighter struck; he was knocked down, which probably saved his life as a sheet of flame swept through the wheelhouse while he was on the floor. He reported, "The captain, first, second and third mates, six Navy gunners and two signalmen were in the wheelhouse. I believe they were all lost, they must have swallowed the flame." While the collision occurred in pre-dawn darkness, no reason has been given for the sudden veering off course of the *Morgan.*[2]

Another serious collision involving a freighter and a tanker occurred in Convoy CU-15 on 26 February 1944. The tanker SS *Murfreesboro* was rammed by the SS *El Coston,* whose steering mechanism broke down. The tanker was carrying 130,000 barrels of gasoline and burned for hours; twenty-nine crew members and sixteen members of the navy gun crew were lost. The *El Coston* flew the Panamanian flag and carried a navy gun crew, but no casualty figures were announced. Many of the dead from the tanker died in the flaming waters, but some survivors were able to swim under the oil until they were clear. Almost unbelievably, the *Murfreesboro* was salvaged and returned to service.[3]

Convoy CU-15 wasn't the only convoy to have problems. Thirteen more armed guards and twenty crewmen were lost when the new tanker SS *Mihiel* collided with another tanker, SS *Nashbulk,* in Convoy CU-65 in the Atlantic.[4]

DeWitt Welch, gunner's mate 2/c, was a member of the sixty-five-man NAG gun crew on the USAT *Uruguay,* a converted luxury liner that formerly ran between the United States and South America. Carrying 5,000 troops, the *Uruguay* was in a large convoy of up to ninety ships. The whole convoy had orders to make a starboard turn at 0130 hours: the night was pitch black with poor visibility. Welch reports, "Everybody made the turn except the Navy tanker in position on the starboard side to the rear, and she hit us square on the beam. The general alarm went off, sparks were flying and we thought we were going to blow up at any minute. Orders were given to prepare to abandon ship, but in the morning, the engineers figured the ship could stay afloat about 76 hours. The convoy had left us except for the tanker which was following us, bow smashed. We had eight dead aboard and 24 missing with the gash in our side measuring 65 feet high and 75 feet in length. We could make no more than five knots, but arrived in Bermuda in 72 hours and the ship was settled in shallow waters where the troops were disembarked. Repair crews worked around the clock for five weeks before we were taken back to Hampton Roads for major repair. Her next voyage was to Australia, and thankfully was less eventful."[5]

Ed Quin was a signalman on the new Liberty, SS *Frederick L. Dau.* He reports another unusual collision: "Our maiden voyage was in convoy to Newfoundland, where fog was so heavy that we could not see ahead although there was blue sky directly overhead. Suddenly a vessel came up fast from behind, pulled away just in time and disappeared but just as suddenly, reappeared, crossing the *Dau*'s bow. Although the *Dau* was only making three knots, we rammed the mystery ship at the #3 hold and wiped out 40 feet of the *Dau*'s bow above the waterline. Emergency repairs involved putting plate in the bow and limping into Liverpool, where British workers welded what was left with railroad track, and the *Dau* was sent back to Brooklyn for major repair." Quin next found himself aboard the SS *Henry Villard* en route to Archangel, even today an unappealing port for cruise ships.[6]

A major maritime disaster was narrowly averted on 2 October 1942 when the British *Queen Mary*, carrying some 15,000 American troops, rammed the British cruiser escort, HMS *Curacoa*. Steaming at 31 knots or more off the coast of Scotland, the *Queen* smashed into the smaller ship, splitting her amidships. Private 1st Class Ray Roy, Acushnet, Massachusetts, one of the ninety army gunners aboard the *Queen*, reports, "The *Curacoa* had been patrolling in advance of the *Queen*, pursuing a zigzag course when she was hit; the ship went down within minutes, with a loss of 338 men aboard. There were no injuries and only slight damage to the bow of the huge *Queen*." The American troops aboard the *Queen*, however, were extremely lucky: the *Curacoa* was carrying a load of depth charges on her stern that could have exploded with terrible results if she had not been rammed amidships. The army AGs were part of the 1034th Army Transport Service Coast Artillery; Roy had formerly been in the army national guard, in New Bedford, Massachusetts.

According to other army gunners, John Steinbeck, world-famed author but then a war correspondent, was aboard the *Queen Mary* that day and observed the whole disaster. The accident was reportedly kept secret for years. In a newspaper account much later, one army gunner was quoted as saying that they were ordered not to talk about it, and Steinbeck was asked not to write about it. A month or so after the incident, a story appeared in the press stating that "the Admiralty had lost a ship." That was it.[7]

In common with mariners since time immemorial, one of the major hazards of the sea has been the elements, and the NAG experienced its fury in many parts of the globe. While the North Atlantic and the Barents Sea in the Arctic could probably claim the record for the most continuous display of bad temper, the Pacific could also show its teeth. Joseph Conrad, master of description of the many moods of

The end of the SS *Byron D. Benson,* after being torpedoed off the coast of North Carolina on 4 April 1942. (National Archives)

the sea, wrote of a typhoon, "It was something formidable and swift, like the sudden smashing of a vial of wrath. It seemed to explode all around the ship with an overpowering concussion and a rush of great waters. . . ."

Few personnel on naval or merchant ships in the South China Sea will ever forget the typhoon of 18 December 1944, so vicious that three U.S. Navy ships were lost and many others of all types damaged. The wind and seas had all ships, regardless of size, in their grip; the barometer fell below 27, and ships rolled as much as 70 degrees, seeming to lie on their sides, shuddering under the onslaught of the gigantic seas. The typhoon of '44 was said to be the worst ever experienced by the U.S. Navy in its history, but it was not the only one.[8] On 9–10 October 1945, Bob Heitzinger, AG radioman 3/c, Woodenville, Washington, was aboard the SS *Alcoa Puritan* off Okinawa, when another typhoon hit. At his station he heard SOS distress calls for assistance from a number of ships in the area. The details in his log are clear evidence of the power and danger of a typhoon:

0422 KVSA Aground off CSINA Point. Require immediate assistance.

0631 KVBA *William Ralston* aground near Berth Baker 124. Please send boat to stand by. Master.

0730 KYAG Aground on reef south of Berth Baker 172. Not sure of breaking up.

0736 KVSA Aground off China Saki Point. Have stopped engines. Unable to get off. Pounding badly. Visibility Zero. Require immediate assistance.

0744 KHRJ Aground.

0814 KHRJ Aground Buckner Bay. Position unknown.

0946 KHGU Have lost steerage way. Approximate position . . . Flooded number three four and five holds.

1152 KVBA We have no anchors. Will beach. (Rest of message lost).

1250 KFYZ Engine lost steerage. Deck cargo shifted. Hove to approximate position . . . Drifting westerly toward Okinawa. Be on lookout for U.S. man overboard. Master.

1306 KISX Approximate position . . . We have lost steerage way. Ship unmanageable. Drifting ashore into Okinawa.

1325 ANOL To all ships. Heard cries of men adrift in approximate position . . . Unable to locate. Am continuing search and will stand by until daylight. Strong NW winds. Heavy swells. Master.

1513 ANOL To all ships. Picked up a lot of wreckage. Also life raft. No one aboard. Will continue search. Would like someone here to help at daylight. Master.

1757 ANOL Found one body. Am stopping to pick up for identification. Master.

2031 ANMK Picked up two survivors from *LSM 15*.

After the typhoon had subsided, other messages from various ships included sighting horned mine, "suspicious vessel," and enemy submarine, plus a report of man overboard.

Heitzinger's *Alcoa Puritan* was a lucky ship. She not only got through the typhoon with minimum damage, but had previously survived an attack by a German sub, in which she was damaged severely by both shellfire and torpedoes but was repaired and got back into action.[9]

Whether known as typhoons (Pacific), hurricanes (South Atlantic/Caribbean) or tropical cyclones (Indian Ocean/Arabian Sea), such storms are still remembered vividly by many AGs and others who lived through them. According to scientists, the release of latent heat from condensation of water vapor can provide as much energy as the detonation of 400 20-megaton hydrogen bombs.

AG Irving C. Brownell, now of Deerfield Beach, Florida, was on two Liberties that were damaged in collisions, and went through one hurricane in the Atlantic and two typhoons in the Pacific. He says, "Each storm is different, with many variables to consider . . . anyway, whatever you may call them, wherever they may occur, they are nature's way of showing who's boss."[10]

It did not take a hurricane or typhoon to wreck a ship; many broke in two in heavy storms, including the Liberty SS *William H. Welch.* She was off Loch Ewe, Scotland, when gigantic waves broke her back. There were only twelve survivors out of a complement of forty-two crew members and twelve AGs, plus three passengers.[11]

One of the most unique and awesome hazards of the sea is a "rogue wave," a peculiar freak of nature that can come out of nowhere, with no warning, and severely damage or capsize even large ships. PFC Raymond Roy, an army armed guard on the *Queen Mary,* then used as a troop transport, describes an incident that occurred in December 1942, which could have become the world's greatest and most horrible marine disaster. Carrying 15,000 American troops jammed into every inch of space, the huge liner, 81,237 tons and over 1,000 feet in length, was struck on the starboard side without warning by a gigantic rogue wave. The ship heeled over to a degree that her upper decks were awash and she was in imminent danger of capsizing. It was estimated that her safety depended on no more than five degrees, and Roy, at his station on A deck, felt that she would never be able to recover, but she slowly fought her way back and he began to breathe again. But he says that he will never forget the experience when she almost turned over and took 15,000 men with her.

Roy says he had just finished his watch on his 20-mm gun and was heading for his cabin on the promenade deck forward. He was using "A" deck because the promenade deck had so many troops that they were lying from bulkhead to bulkhead. "As I was walking, I removed my parka, pistol, and lifebelt and was carrying them when the ship started to rise and roll to port, so that I couldn't walk. I was actually laying [*sic*] on my side against the bulkhead. I figured that was it, she was not going to be able to come back. I could hear the dishes and pans below in the galley sliding around and crashing; as the ship slowly righted herself and started to careen to starboard, members of my gun crew came sliding from their cabins through the doorways along with so much water that I knew the portholes had broken. It was quite scary for some minutes before she regained position. On the return trip one of our gunners died in his sleep; he was deadly afraid of ships and water and we all thought he had never recovered from the fright of almost rolling over."[12]

The *Queen Mary* was so fast that Roy reports traveling in convoy only once; on all other trips she traveled alone. He served aboard her from 8 December 1942 through April 1945.

Certainly, Mike Molinari will never forget one voyage as a gunner aboard the T-2 tanker SS *Esso Philadelphia*, on a return trip from Freetown, West Africa, in the summer of 1945. They ran into a hurricane and lost their lifeboats. Tons of water poured into the bow via the chain locker, as the anchor had caused the metal to break away at the hawsepipes. They then lost power as the valves blew on the three-piston diesel engine. "We were in the trough of the seas, rolling back and forth like a cork, completely at the mercy of the sea. It appeared that the ship was about to sink, but we had nothing but our life jackets, so all we could do was stay with the ship and pray. We could watch the bow go under, shudder, and come up more slowly each time. The pumps wouldn't work because of no power. The only thing that kept us up was the air above the water ballast in the tanks. The Engineer finally got one piston working and we got three knots out of the engine to keep the bow into the wind, and we also got the pumps working so that we could limp in. We had been sending SOS messages with no response, but when we eventually got back to the entrance to New York harbor, the Coast Guard called and asked if we needed assistance. The captain fired off some unkind remarks to the effect of 'Where were you when we needed help—we'll make it to dock.' By this time the bow was really low in the water, and when we cut the power the ship settled slowly by the bow at the dock."

In one of the strange coincidences of war, Molinari's father was working as a guard at the dock and observed the ship settle. He didn't know his son was aboard, and when Molinari got off the ship and they met and embraced, the first question his father asked was "How the hell did you make it back in that?" [13]

Mechanical breakdowns at sea often required a high degree of engineering skill and ingenuity to effect repair and get the vessel in motion again, regardless of how slowly. While few AGs aboard merchant ships might ever have seen an albatross or perhaps heard of Coleridge's *Ancient Mariner*, on many occasions they were indeed ". . . as idle as a painted ship, upon a painted ocean." They were not only at the mercy of the sea, but to make matters worse, they often ran almost out of food, carefully budgeted for a shorter time at sea. Glen Kittleman, Oakville, Washington, was a gunner aboard the new tanker SS *Brookfield*, out of Portland, Oregon. She was a fast ship of 20 knots, clean, and with a very good merchant and AG crew. The food was far above average until his last trip aboard her. The *Brookfield* left Lima, Peru, on 13 October 1943. "After a few days we hit a storm that did everything but break us in two, and I'm sure that every man on the ship was as scared as I. The waves looked like Mt. Rainier. After fighting the storm, with the screw out of the water more than in, the propellor shaft froze to the thrust bearing; it is no fun to be aboard a large tanker carrying a full load of high-test gasoline on the high seas with no power. After some time, the crew would get the shaft free only to have it freeze up again. They finally put rags on the bearing and ran sea water on it to keep it cool, then we could travel about four knots. . . . After two weeks we were out of the storm, but a sitting duck for any Japanese sub, and by this time our food supply was down to a bowl of barley soup which had more weevils than barley. . . . The only thing that kept me going was fruit cocktail, and for years later, I couldn't look at a bowl of fruit cocktail. We arrived in Sydney on 10 November, almost too weak to carry our gear to the dock and one gunner's mate passed out. They took all of us to sick bay to recover." [14]

Halfway around the world, another ship was having similar problems. An AG gunnery officer reports, "After 72 hours dead in the water, in the middle of a wolfpack area, we got underway at three knots. . . . Our meat storage and fresh food went bad and canned goods were gone, but we did have some coffee and flour. We couldn't get replenishment of supplies in England, so we were on a short and odd diet before we got home. In New York, I went to a good restaurant and ordered a huge meal, but all I could eat was a dish of celery, plus a lot of milk."

Off the Panama Canal, the *Esso Richmond* had some bad moments on 9 June 1944 when the log showed, "8:25 A.M.— Engine stopped. No steam owing to water in fuel. 8:37—Ship drifting into minefield." Fortunately, tugs arrived in time to assist the vessel back into the channel.

One of the major concerns of both merchant seamen and AGs was the type and loading of cargo. Improper loading could cause any number of unpleasant results, such as when a Sherman tank being carried in the hold of a Liberty ship broke loose and did its best to escape by driving a hole through the hull. Armed guards assisted the crew in the dangerous job of securing the tank before it succeeded. Ammunition was usually handled very carefully; first the stevedores put a number of bags of cement on the bottom, and then placed boxes of ammunition or cases of bombs atop the cement. Then would come such items as 55-gallon barrels of oil. It was all done according to the book, except that on the SS *Alexander H. Stephens,* making a periodic supply run to Anzio beachhead, stevedores loaded a number of tanks atop a cargo of shells and hand grenades, without securing them. All hands aged markedly as the tanks began to move back and forth over the ammo when the ship hit rough weather.

Al Gonzales of Santa Rita, New Mexico, reports that on one ship in which he served as an AG gunner, a load of big canisters of mustard gas was being transported to Pearl Harbor in case of need. A meeting of the crew and the NAG was held that night, and they were told, "When you go to bed, to the head, the shower, take your gas mask with you!" An alarm sounding meant that there was a gas leak so, "Get your masks on quick! And put your gas masks under your pillow at night." Gonzales says that his gas mask was his best friend for the duration of the trip, never out of his reach. Gonzales also served on two ammunition ships in a row. While there was no advance notice, when he observed a red security flag flying high, denoting loading of ammo or high-octane fuel, his immediate reaction was, "Oh-Oh, here we go." [15]

While aboard the SS *Joshua L. Chamberlain,* loading in San Francisco, an AG gunner observed the stevedores moving at a snail's pace. He was moved to ask loudly, "Don't union rules let you load any faster?" "Not with what we're loading," was the response, and he learned that the cargo was nitroglycerine, in small bottles that had to be put in a place where the temperature could be maintained at a certain level, and strapped down tightly so that they could not move. The young gunner reports that he immediately went to the armed guard lieutenant and requested permission for leave to go into town. "What for?" was the reply, and the prudent gunner answered, "Sir, don't you see what we're loading?"

Munitions ships were never too popular as neighbors, at sea or at dockside. The explosions of munitions ships, including the SS *Mary Luckenbach* that disappeared in sec-

onds in a towering pillar of smoke and debris, are well remembered as a horror by those who observed the sight.
However, the ultimate in such hazard remains the explosion
at Port Chicago, California, 17 July 1944. The Liberty ship SS
E. A. Bryan and the SS *Quinault Victory* were loading munitions at the Mare Island Navy Yard, about 35 miles from San
Francisco. Suddenly, a deafening explosion leveled the entire area; the 10,000 tons of explosive cargo aboard the *Bryan*
were set off by an unknown cause, and the explosion also
detonated the munitions being loaded aboard the *Victory.*
Both ships disintegrated in a blinding flash, and debris was
scattered for miles around. The piers and building installations of Port Chicago were almost completely wiped out, and
windows were broken over a space of 50 miles. The town of
Port Chicago itself, a mile away, was almost obliterated, and
the two ships, a dock, an ammunition train, plus two Coast
Guard boats just vanished. Over 300 lives were lost, with
many more injured. All the crews of both ships were killed,
with the miraculous exception of eleven AGs who were on
liberty from the *Bryan* at the time. One of these was George
Diller, Sr., of New York. The cost of the explosion was estimated in the millions, but nothing could equal the cost of
lives, snuffed out in an instant.[16]

An almost incredible story of narrow escape from death
is told by Willie Achee, Abita Springs, Louisiana, Bob Garner
of Oklahoma City, and Durard Solsbury, Lohan, Texas. They
were AG gunners aboard the SS *Mormactern.* The ship was
being loaded with munitions at Port Chicago and was almost
fully loaded when orders were received to pull away from
the only dock at the port to permit what they believe was the
SS *Quinault Victory* to come in and begin loading. The *Mormactern* was to complete loading by barge at a point near
San Francisco. She was about one and one-half hours out of
Port Chicago when the explosion occurred where they had
been docked. Solsbury was on leave at the time of the explosion, and he was horrified that his ship had been lost, but
finally was informed that she was safe at San Francisco where
he rejoined her. The three men had not met for forty-three

years when they were reunited at an AG veterans' reunion; it was a joyous occasion for the three, who still marvel at their good luck.

Deck loading was also observed carefully and with caution, especially if railroad locomotives were included. They were not only extremely heavy and hard to balance, but gave every indication of making a ship top-heavy, a most hazardous situation in mountainous seas. There was always the danger of their breaking loose and creating havoc aboard. John J. Pohl, Pittsburgh, Pennsylvania, was a member of the AG crew on the SS *Irving McDowell*, part of a large convoy heading for Murmansk, with locomotives on deck. The weather in the North Atlantic was so bad that the ship was taking water in the engine room, and it was decided that she would never make it to North Russia. After losing two steam engines overboard, and with the *McDowell* listing dangerously to port, she was ordered out of the convoy and directed to Antwerp, where there were cranes large enough to unload the locomotives. Right after arrival, however, buzz bombs began to come in, and the *McDowell* was ordered again to move, this time to Oran, where large cranes were also available. Alone again, the ship made it to North Africa and unloaded her unwelcome cargo of locomotives, tanks, and 500-pound bombs, to the relief of one and all.[17] Rick Whalen, Hyattsville, Maryland, AG gunner on the SS *William H. Moody*, also reports difficulty with heavy deck cargo. En route to India, near Gibraltar heavy equipment broke loose on deck and caused considerable damage. "We had water, water everywhere inside the ship." The *Moody* continued to Port Said where the AG crew was taken off and reassigned as the *Moody* was ordered back to the States for repair.[18]

With no doctor or pharmacist's mate aboard a merchant ship, a medical emergency could be frightening. Eugene Meadows, Waynesboro, Virginia, signalman aboard the SS *Henry Wynkoop*, reports on one case that almost had a tragic ending. The *Wynkoop* left Greenock, Scotland, on the day after Christmas 1944 for Murmansk. "Before arriving, one of the AG gunners had an acute attack of appendicitis. The only doctor in the convoy was on the Commodore's ship, quite a distance away from us and they would not risk endangering the convoy by transferring him. We were barely able to keep the man alive by communicating daily with the doctor via flashing light, as we had to maintain radio silence. We couldn't use the light in the darkness for fear of being sighted by the enemy, and we only had about an hour of semi-daylight in which to do this. I was given the duty of sending, by red lens small light, the medical data to the Commodore's ship, pulse, temperature, and received pre-scribed treatments, such as, sulfa drug dosages, etc. The purser acted as pharmacist's mate in administering the treatment. The man was removed from the ship immediately upon arrival and was operated upon in their hospital. He was told that if he had been one day later, he would not have made it to port alive.[19]

A tragic event occurred aboard another vessel. A young third mate, on his first voyage to Murmansk, began to announce on the return voyage that "enemy spies" were aboard, and that it was his duty to catch them. When he started wearing a pistol and saying he was about to catch the "spies," the captain had him put under constant guard, and he was removed from the ship on reaching port. As he was being taken off the ship, he said that he was going to get a medal from the FBI.

Cases of mental breakdown were not uncommon, particularly among those who had suffered several sinkings and had lost friends in tragic circumstances, such as blazing oil. They became "torpedo happy," and had to be taken off the ship, perhaps to be sent to the scoffingly termed "rubber room," but with the deep concern and sympathy of ship-mates who well understood how a mind can finally snap. It is no wonder that this occurred because survivors' descriptions of shipmates in the water, faces charred beyond recognition, can do nothing but fill one with horror. In just one such possible case, the SS *Jacksonville* was torpedoed, fire broke out immediately enveloping the vessel, and there were just two survivors, a merchant seaman and a navy AG, out of a merchant crew of forty-nine and an AG crew of twenty-nine.[20]

Undercover German intelligence agents operated in many areas, and one of the most unique operations was a secret radio transmitter located aboard a German freighter, the MS *Ehrenfels*. She had been interned along with a number of other Axis ships in Marmagoa Harbor in the Portuguese colony of Goa on the Indian Ocean, taken over by India in 1961. Information on sailing times of Allied merchant vessels was passed on by a German spy living in Goa, and in turn relayed to the *U-181*. At least three ships were subsequently sunk by the *U-181*, including the SS *Alcoa Pathfinder* and the SS *Excello*. None of the twenty-man NAG gun crew aboard the *Pathfinder* were killed, but four crewmen and the radio operator were lost. One navy man was killed on the *Excello* in the explosion following the torpedoing; the first engineer died in a lifeboat after swallowing too much fuel oil.[21]

There was heavy German intelligence activity in neutral Argentina, which had a large and prosperous German colony. After much postwar research, Lieutenant Commander Harold J. McCormick, USNR, AG commanding officer of the Liberty SS *William Gaston,* which was torpedoed after being trailed by an Argentine-flag vessel, found much information on the German intelligence activities. They included at least nine clandestine shortwave radio stations in and around Buenos Aires, which sent nightly dispatches regarding Allied ship movements and other information of significance. It has also been reported that enemy agents also moved navigational markers in the Strait of Magellan, luring ships onto the rocks and forcing Allied shipping to travel around always-tempestuous Cape Horn.

Allied merchant ships entering or leaving the Mediterranean were also subjects of attention to German agents. "Neutral" Spain and Portugal were hotbeds of intrigue and espionage, and German agents were able to pass-on vital information about shipping to attackers lying in wait. On occasion, blacked-out convoys were trailed by brightly lighted "fishing boats," which also relayed information on size, course, and the defense of convoys. Enemy agents observed the departure of Convoy MKS-9 from Gibraltar, which consisted of twenty-three freighters, eleven transports, and nine escorts. It was located by German aerial reconnaissance and was attacked by several U-boats with considerable success. *U-107* fired a salvo of six torpedoes and all of them hit, a remarkable performance. Nazi agents in Algeciras also photographed Allied naval vessels with telephoto lenses and were able to detect new defensive equipment.[22]

One of the most unusual incidents in the war in the Pacific could be called, "The Case of Mistaken Identity." The SS *Dominican Victory* was returning to a rear base after discharging cargo at an advanced base. En route at night, she was challenged by an American escort vessel, which misunderstood the identification and opened fire on the *Victory*, in the belief that she was a Japanese raider. The *Victory*, in turn, presumed she was being attacked by a Japanese warship, and opened her engines to full speed, zigzagging her course at 90-degrees angles to avoid the attacker's fire. Pursuit continued for over a half-hour, while the *Victory* sent out an SOS signal, picked up first in Australia and then in Honolulu. Her identity was confirmed and the attacker notified to cease fire, whereupon the *Dominican Victory* proceeded to base. The incident was reported on arrival by crew members. The presumption was made that the mistake was caused by the speed of the *Victory* being miscalculated by the American naval vessel, leading to the belief that she was a fast warship. No reference was made to the undoubtedly red faces on the American warship.[23]

Health and sanitation conditions were often a hazard in many areas, ranging from bubonic plague in Africa to poisonous water snakes found along beaches in India. Courting local belles was the equivalent of playing Russian roulette, but personnel of one merchant ship in India discovered that ship's linen was a highly valuable medium of exchange, and the ship returned almost wiped out of supplies.

During World War II, over thirty American merchant

ships sailed into oblivion, never to be heard of again, lost with all hands. Fourteen carried NAG gun crews and involved the loss of 271 armed guards. The fate of the SS *La-Salle,* carrying munitions and with an armed guard gun crew headed by Lieutenant (j.g.) Carl Zeidler, former mayor of Milwaukee, was uncovered in a postwar search of German Navy records. She was "atomized" when struck by a torpedo launched by the *U-159* (Witte) while en route to Capetown, South Africa. (See chapter 21 for more details.)

CHAPTER TEN
RELATIONS WITH THE
MERCHANT MARINE

They that go down to the sea in ships,
That do business in great waters. . . .
—Psalm 107:23–24

Possibly no other American industry has been subject to as much consistent "boom and bust" as the United States Merchant Marine and its sister industry, shipbuilding. Our early history is replete with the exploits of the Yankee Clippers, whose unfamiliar new colors were found increasingly in ports throughout the seven seas. They were legendary for their speed, efficiency, and beauty. At one time the American merchant marine carried as much as 77 percent of our products and contributed mightily to the development and wealth of the new nation. However, by the time of the Civil War, British-developed ships of iron and steel and the forces of economics were driving vessels of wood and sail slowly, but inexorably, from the high seas. Beauty of design, under a cloud of sails, could not compete with the brute power of steamships, and by 1869 the era of commercial sailing ships had almost come to an end.[1] The decline of the American merchant marine accelerated, and in World War I we had to rely largely on foreign-flag or confiscated German ships to carry our arms and even our troops to the battle fields of Europe.[2]

The belated post–World War I arrival of some 2,000 Hog Islanders proved a disaster for both the merchant marine and the shipbuilding industry. In WW I, Todd Shipyards Corporation had made a great contribution to the Allied victory in building and repairing ships and returning them promptly to service. After the war, the entire U.S. shipbuilding industry tried to convince the nation's policymakers that the rebuilt merchant marine should be kept in a healthy state for peacetime trade and future emergencies. However, as Todd president John T. Gilbride reported, "This proved a hopeless task. 'The war to end all wars had been won,' it was said, 'why should we stay in readiness for another?' A familiar theme."[3]

During the depression years of the 1930s, American shipbuilding virtually disappeared, and existing yards were reduced to fighting for whatever repair work was available. Todd, which can trace its history to 1835, almost had to fold. Its big Tacoma yard had to be closed, and overall employment was cut back from 17,000 to about 2,000.[4]

By 1935 we were carrying only about one-third of what we produced, which in retrospect looks great. To improve the situation, however, in 1936 Congress passed the Bland Act, which created the United States Maritime Commission and authorized a program for constructing fifty ships a year. This was designed not only to carry a larger portion of American imports and exports, but to provide auxiliary service to the armed forces in times of emergency. The outbreak of war in Europe in September 1939 was to give the still-depression-wracked American shipbuilding industry a major shot in the arm. The British order for the sixty "Ocean Victories" was not only a financial windfall, but it enabled American shipbuilders to gear up for the soon-to-come need for a tremendously expanded shipping capacity, with its concomitant invigorated merchant marine. At the time of Pearl Harbor, the American merchant marine had about 60,000 men by various estimates. By the end of the war, to man the flood of new ships pouring out of the many new shipyards, the number of merchant seamen had grown to over 250,000.

When the United States entered the war, all American merchant ships were requisitioned by the government. The War Shipping Agency (WSA) as established to serve as the operating end of the Maritime Commission, and Admiral Emory S. Land served as administrator of both. Old ships, many little better than derelicts, were rescued from death by rust, towed out of obscure backwaters, hastily refitted, and put into service. Many of these were the "pig boats," the World War I Hog Islanders; comparatively sturdy, the passage of years and neglect led a number to be lost by foundering. While the WSA, established 7 February 1942, was authorized to control all merchant shipping and personnel, the actual operational details were handled by private shipping companies, some of which handled as many as eighty-five ships, under contract with WSA, which ultimately controlled the largest fleet the world had ever seen.

The policy of placing U.S. Navy gunners on merchant vessels was completely different from the system on British merchantmen. The armed guards aboard British ships were called DEMS (after the Defensively Equipped Merchant Ship program). As in World War I, the British depended largely upon merchant seamen to man the guns on merchant vessels. In Britain, all merchant seamen were registered under the Universal Conscription Act of 1940, placed in seamen pools, and paid both afloat and ashore. They were completely under the control of the Ministry of Shipping; they went wherever and whenever they were sent and were required to take gunnery training while ashore. The master was in complete command of the "defence" of the ship. Royal Navy personnel formed only a small percentage of the officers and men assigned, and only on larger transports. When assigned to a gunnery station, a British seaman received only one shilling a day extra. American signalmen attached to a commodore's staff and assigned to a British ship were often shocked, and sometimes horrified, by the living and sanitary conditions and quality of food.[5]

In contrast, American seamen were paid off at the end of each voyage and were on their own until they signed on for another voyage, following limited time and refusals. They could not be required to take essential training in defense of ships; U.S. Navy personnel were thus supplied to merchant ships to man all key defense positions, with assistance from the merchant crew, usually volunteers, who passed ammunition and served as loaders or gunners if the navy crew was undermanned or had suffered casualties. The defense of the ship was the NAG officer's responsibility rather than the master's, as was the case on British ships. The AG detachment frequently numbered less than ten in the early stages, but increased to an average of twenty-seven, as new, larger, and better-armed merchant ships were put into service.

American maritime unions were very strong and had no intention of giving up hard-won working conditions and other benefits while steamship operators were allegedly reaping high profits from the war. Joseph Curran, tough president of the National Maritime Union (NMU) strongly attacked a 1943 WSA program to train 75,000 new seamen to man the new ships coming out of the yards, claiming it was a plot to "flood the industry with thousands of non-union-minded personnel." Rear Admiral Samuel E. Morison, USN, has reported on considerable friction between the navy and the maritime unions, but does credit Curran and the union with efforts to rid the union of drunkards and troublemakers. A WSA report of clashes aboard ships says that the principal causes were about what could be expected—clashes of personality, intransigence, incompetence, and negligence.[6]

It is quite possible that one ship's merchant crew who had resisted orders to darken ship might have had a change of mind shortly thereafter, for the ship was torpedoed, a hatch door was jammed shut by explosions, and a tank on deck broke loose. The ship was sinking fast, but the AG crew remained at their guns until they had to jump into the water. They swam in oil, blessedly not afire, until they were pulled into a lifeboat. In another ship, a recalcitrant smoker had a sudden change of heart after mysteriously being hit on the head by a piece of 2 × 4 that had fallen out of nowhere.

It would indeed be a remarkable world if, within any group of men gathered together, regardless of age, background, education, or personality, there were no differences or friction. So, it would be unrealistic to report that a situation of full cooperation toward the common goal of winning the war prevailed on armed merchant ships. Friction there was on many, particularly in the early days of the assignment of AG gun crews. To many of the green kids who boarded the old ships available at the time, it was the equivalent of Daniel entering the lion's den. By no stretch of the imagination could the usual prewar merchant seaman be considered an exemplary role model. They were a polyglot group of many nations, with an equally wide assortment of reasons for going to sea. A former merchant seaman turned exceptional author stated that the merchant marine attracted the adventurer, the homeless, the restless, and included the emotionally unstable, alcoholics, or just plain hard cases who loved trouble. Many were tough characters, termed "performers," veterans of bitter union-organizing strife, and more familiar with bars, brothels, and brawls than in cultural pursuit in worldwide ports. They jeered at the "Sea Scouts," who had never been on, or perhaps even seen, a ship before. They also resented sharing quarters with newcomers who had to be jammed into already cramped space. They laughed at the discipline and low pay of the navy gun crews and the "landlubbers" who commanded them. On the other hand, a favorite jibe of the AGs was, "There are only three kinds of time aboard ship: sack time, coffee time and overtime." There were also some unkind references to "high-paid draft dodgers."[7]

A respected spokesman for the merchant marine has said that many AGs were undesirables who had been shipped out by the navy to the merchant fleet for disciplinary reasons. A number of gunnery officers, in certain cases, might agree, but such would be an exception. One AG gunnery officer who had some hard cases in his gun crew, thinking of his teaching days in college remarked wistfully, "You can't flunk a sailor overboard." However, he soon got his "problem children" straightened out.[8]

Even within gun crews there could be friction, mostly good-natured ribbing of each other, and such things as drawing a line down AG quarters and announcing, "Yankees on that side, Rebs over here." North vs South did become a real problem on one ship; all of the merchant officers and crew were from the South, the navy gun crew, with the exception of the gunnery officer, were pure Brooklyn. There was so much friction that the gunnery officer finally requested that the gun crew be replaced. On another ship, however, the gun crew was also from Brooklyn, and the AG officer reported with a grin that upon return from a long voyage the whole crew of the ship was speaking "Brooklynese."

Rear Admiral Samuel E. Morison, in his monumental fifteen-volume history of the navy in World War II, said that at an early stage of operations of the naval armed guard, trouble or friction aboard merchant ships was reported by some thirty percent of NAG gunnery officers. Needling included such things as, "If you're really in the Navy why aren't you on a Navy ship?" Answers could be unprintable. A naval intelligence officer was ordered to go aboard a ship in Buenos Aires to investigate many complaints by the AG officer of harrassment of his men by the merchant crew. Excerpts from his report follow: "At approximately 2400, the third mate, who had been released from the brig to go ashore and file a complaint against the captain and the ship, came aboard very drunk. He had been confined to the brig for 1) having absented himself from the ship for four days while on a drunk and 2) having threatened to kill the captain. Previous to this, he had been first mate, but had been reduced to third for his conduct. . . . The Navy officer's comments on the merchant seamen after the voyage included, 'constant complaints, undependable, refusal to obey orders, no respect for their officers, staying ashore, coming aboard drunk, desertion, and fighting.' Also, in Buenos Aires, three seaman were brought aboard who had deserted ship in Montevideo." He adds, "The merchant crew is constantly, 'riding' the Navy crew; telling them they are suckers for working for such small pay, that they don't have to obey their officer, as he is not a 'real' Navy man, but just another civilian drafted into service. On this ship, there is no practical way of segregating the two areas, as the mess room must serve for both crews." To add insult to injury, the investigating officer reported that someone stole his new watch while he was taking a shower, his last day aboard the ship.[9]

As is to be expected, things worked both ways. A third

officer on one ship, a well-trained graduate of a marine nautical school, followed by two years of training at sea, reports, "My dismay knew no bounds, when in April 1942, the Navy assigned a gun crew of seven seamen, a third-class petty officer, commanded by a '90-day Wonder' Ensign. Somehow or other, in his brief career, he had gotten the idea that he was to command, not only the gun crew, but the whole ship! He came to the bridge, at sea, and criticized the captain's handling of the vessel. Not only was the captain a long-time master of a large passenger ship, he was also a Commander, USNR, and the chief officer was, as well, a commissioned Naval Reservist. Even after forty-five years, I find it unbelievable." [10]

Lieutenant Robert Ruark, USNR, the author, wrote in an article late in the war that the navy had made a serious mistake in the AG's infancy by assigning immature gun crew commanders, but that the problem had been caught and the typical gunnery officer then was in his mid-thirties, married, had executive experience, and had one and one-half or two full stripes. [11]

Lieutenant Commander Beverley Britton, USNR, in a postwar article written for the U.S. Naval Institute *Proceedings,* referred to the fact that many "old salts" resented it strongly when told when to darken ship, not to smoke on deck, when not to dump garbage, or when they could or couldn't use the ship's radio. Some masters objected to having a group of men aboard over whom they didn't have complete control. In turn, navy personnel often resented what they considered petty grievances, exorbitant union demands, arguments over "jurisdiction," and overtime. In fact, a number of merchant seamen were subjected to the Articles of War for recalcitrance and removed from ships, in various ports, by U.S. Army authorities. The relationship between the ship's master and the AG gunnery officer might determine the fate of the ship, or at the very least decide whether or not it was going to be a "happy ship." [12]

Fortunately, the difficulties were usually worked out, especially after the first engagement with the enemy, in which the "merchants" assisted at the guns and worked together with navy gunners, frequently working the guns themselves when there were not enough navy gunners or if they had become incapacitated. Such action soon welded them into an effective fighting team, with heroism common on both sides. As one "merchant" wrote, "They may have been rookies when they joined the ship at Pier 4, Hoboken, but when the ship passed through the first lock of the Mersey River at Liverpool, they were combat veterans; they had survived a battle of fourteen days—as a merchant sailor, I say to the U.S. Naval Armed Guard, Well Done!"

The master of the SS *Stanvac Calcutta* provided outstanding cooperation with the navy crew, as reported by Lieutenant Commander Edward L. Anderson, USNR, Beaufort, South Carolina, then ensign in command of the small navy gun crew aboard. "I, of course, was aware of some of the problems encountered by other AG detachments, and was determined to reduce friction to a minimum while carrying out my orders. Fortunately, Captain Gustav O. Karlsson recognized the potential for trouble and made my task much easier. His treatment of me as a man with a job to do rather than a 22-year-old Navy upstart helped tremendously. . . . We went over my orders, and Captain Karlsson said that he had no problem with them. . . . Minor problems that developed between merchant crew and the AG were easily worked out and our overall relations were excellent." Captain Karlsson's complete cooperation was evidenced in the engagement between the *Stanvac Calcutta* and the German raider *Stier,* in which the captain lost his life while maneuvering his ship to fight the enemy.[15]

Wells Bain, Fair Oaks, California, a 1944 graduate of Kings Point, reports on a master of a different nature: "The captain was a mean SOB, an old Dane, who called the AG gunnery officer, a corporate attorney in civilian life, a 'draft dodger.' I thought the Ensign was going to punch him in the nose, but he controlled himself, merely telling the captain that he was a 'goddam liar.' The AG crew was a bunch of nice kids from Iowa (the AG must have recruited every farm boy in the state). They were very well-behaved, had the worst quarters on the ship but never complained. However, they had had no training in lifeboat drills, and got into a bad way while trying to lower a boat. Some ablebodied seamen took it upon themselves to go to their aid to avoid injury. With the exception of the captain, we had no problems. The merchant crew and the AG got along well."[14]

There were always some hard-bitten old skippers, and one, reported to be a man of few words, mostly cuss-words, had many unkind comments on the "amateurs" he had to sail with, "Dummies, dummies everywhere. Even in the Navy. I hope they don't sink us by mistake."

Not all "dummies" were in the AG crews. Some masters were not competent due to age, alcoholism, or inexperience in open-ocean sailing. A master with papers for commanding a 600' ore boat on the Great Lakes might experience problems, navigational or otherwise, operating in a vast ocean. Commander Edward Ellsberg, USN, gave a vivid example in a book in which he described a voyage to the Persian Gulf aboard the "SS Pigs Knuckle," so-called because it was served so often by order of the skipper, a fancier of the delicacy. The ship carried 380 passengers, mostly construction technicians for building docks, warehouses, and transportation facilities to handle the flood of lend-lease materiel destined for Russia via the southern route. Ellsberg recounts that the skipper had always been engaged in Atlantic coastal service and insisted on following his old route, close in, suicidal in such waters in February 1942. Commander Ellsberg states, "Our safety had to depend solely on our ability to avoid attack, or on our AG crew in case we failed in avoidance." He almost had a heart attack when he noted that the ship was traveling down the coast with its running lights on! Considerable effort was required to "convince" the skipper to cut off the lights. The master had a distrust, not uncommon among merchant officers of the day according to Ellsberg, of all naval officers as not really being practical seamen.[15]

Fortunately, "horror stories" were the exception rather

than the rule, particularly as the war wore on and the older ships that were first in service and their "old salt" crews were whittled down by enemy action and other causes. Thousands of ships came out of the yards, and to man them the merchant marine had to be greatly expanded. To accomplish this, training schools for both officers and men were established. Most of these trainees were as "green" as the AG aboard the vessels, and closer to the same age and interests. Some of the new masters were almost as young as their crews, a number receiving their papers while still in their twenties, then becoming naval reservists. As a result, a much closer personal relationship between crews was developed, and complaints of friction steadily diminished. This was particularly true of relationships developed between the AGs and the Kings Point cadet/midshipmen, who were assigned to freighters or tankers for six months sea duty as deck or engine cadets. The C/Ms of the merchant marine served at sea in combat areas the world over, and a total of 142 cadets and 70 graduates were killed in action when their ships were torpedoed, bombed, or sunk by collision, or foundered or exploded from unknown causes. Seven midshipmen were awarded the merchant marine's highest decoration for conspicuous gallantry and devotion to duty. Of the ships covered in this account, cadet/midshipmen were lost on the SS *Harry Luckenbach* (4), the *Jonathan Sturges* (4), the *William C. Gorgas* (4), the *Timothy Pickering* (3), the *La Salle* (2), the *Esso Gettysburg* (2), and the *J. Pinckney Henderson* (2), plus Cadets Edwin O'Hara and Arthur Chamberlin lost in the heroic fight between the SS *Stephen Hopkins* and the German raider *Stier*. C/M George Miller was lost in the sinking of the SS *Wade Hampton*, en route to Murmansk. C/M Jim Hoffman, who survived the sinking, wrote a glowing report of the heroism of the AG commanding officer, Ensign Kendall Cramm, USNR, and of the skipper of HMS *Verain*, a British corvette, who risked his ship by not dropping dreaded depth charges while so many survivors were in the water, and succeeded in saving them all.[16]

There are many examples in navy and merchant marine

files of expressions of appreciation for extraordinary services rendered or excellent relations between NAG crews
and their merchant counterparts. Such is a letter from Lieutenant Fred U. Sisson, USNR, to Mr. B. B. Howard, General
Manager of Marine Operations, Standard Oil Co. of New
Jersey, dated 28 September 1945: "It has been my pleasant
duty to be Commanding Officer of the Armed Guard unit
aboard your ship, the SS *Esso Richmond,* during the past few
months. I cannot say enough about the complete cooperation and cheerful helpfulness of Captain W. F. Besse, his
mates and engineers. Now that the war is over and won, and
the Armed Guard is being removed, may I say for my crew
and for myself, Good sailing, Godspeed. . . ."[17]

Many AG officers became close to the masters of their
ships, and one reports that they were on such good terms
that the captain and his wife would often take him to dinner
with them in port. Another says that his skipper frequently
would invite him for a couple of drinks before dinner. "It
might have been a Navy no-no, but it sure helped friendly
relations."

A sad example of sacrifice for one another occurred
when the SS *Timothy Pickering* took a direct hit in Sicily
while carrying a load of aviation gas and bombs. Second
Mate George Alther lost his life going to the assistance of the
NAG gunnery officer. They were among twenty-two crew
members, eight NAGs, and over one hundred British soldiers
lost on the *Pickering.*

Fifteen-year old Harry Koch, now of Phoenix, Arizona,
ran away from an orphanage, lied about his age, and enlisted in the merchant marine. He was assigned as mess
boy to the AG detachment on board his ship and promptly
"adopted" them. He volunteered to man the guns, but was so
small and light that he could not handle the heavy shells, but
finally was permitted to work out on the 20-mm guns, which
thrilled him. He considers the AG crew as the only family he
ever had in his early years; they trained him how to box, to
defend himself, and when he was older and bigger, he enlisted in the marines, and the scrawny kid made sergeant

before he became twenty. He proudly wore four merchant marine awards below his marine corps award.[18]

Frank Davis of Durango, Colorado, a former merchant mariner, reports that on a number of ships on which he served, when the crew got paid off, "tarpaulin musters" were held to distribute funds to the AG crews whose pay had not caught up with them.[19] Walter Peters, AG signalman on a variety of ships, confirms this, saying that after a months-long voyage that took his ship around the world, pay-off day came, and the merchant crew drew a bundle of cash. They got together and contributed to a "kitty" for the armed guards, who were drawing their comparatively small monthly pay. Peters says his share of the merchant seaman fund was over $300, a fortune for a boy of nineteen at the time.[20]

Comparative pay of merchant crews and navy gun crews has been a long-lingering bone of contention. One former navy gunnery officer says, "The Filipino mess boy made more money than I did as a gunnery officer—he got paid $170 per month, plus $125 bonus for each Atlantic crossing, plus $5 daily for being in a combat area, plus overtime for Saturdays and Sundays." The rebuttal from a merchant marine spokesman says that it should be remembered that a merchant seaman's pay stopped when his ship went down, the navy's did not; the merchant seaman's pay ceased when he became a prisoner of war, and the navy's did not; and the merchant seaman was not paid while on vacation, the navy man was. A detailed comparison of wages was also offered to prove that pay basically was in balance. Whatever the merits of each argument, the question is moot. At time of writing a decision was reached by a federal judge that ended a long legal battle by merchant seaman and entitled them to full Veteran's Administration benefits, including use of VA hospitals, certain medical and disability benefits, and payment of burial costs. There can be no question that armed guards and merchant seamen faced the same hazards aboard merchant ships; over 6,000 merchant seamen lost their lives, and several hundred were taken by the Axis powers and treated as prisoners of war. And as this account demonstrates, there is no question that great heroism was displayed by many seamen in engagements with the enemy. In actuality, the new benefits have been reported as being largely symbolic for most, "A flag and a headstone in a military cemetery."

While it was standard procedure on merchant vessels for members of the merchant crew to be trained to operate the guns, training often went both ways. Warm friendships developed, and one former AG reported that as a nineteen-year-old kid he came to idolize an old bos'n, a master seaman who taught him a lot about deck seamanship that he never forgot. Other AG "landlubbers" formed such an affection for the sea that they remained with it. Wallace Breck, a gunner aboard the ill-fated SS *Stephen Hopkins,* was given instruction in seamanship and navigation by C/M Arthur Chamberlin, Jr., one of the two cadets who lost their lives on the *Hopkins.* After the war, Breck went to Kings Point, graduated, and eventually received his master's papers. He had previously visited Chamberlin's family to tell them the details of Arthur's death; it was a great relief to them to know that he did not suffer long.[21]

Heroism also went both ways, on many occasions. Charles Richardson, able seaman on the *Esso Bolivar,* received the Merchant Marine Distinguished Service Medal for heroism above and beyond the call of duty: "On duty with the Navy gun crew, while his ship was under heavy submarine attack, he undertook the rescue of two severely wounded Navy members of the crew when the abandon ship order was given. Although himself wounded in the back by a shell fragment, he got both men in the water, placed one on his back and had the other grasp him around the neck. In this manner, he was swimming toward a lifeboat when sharks attacked, and he was obliged to defend himself and his companions by slashing out with a knife. A shark pulled the wounded man off his back and this man was lost, but he succeeded in getting the second wounded man and himself into the lifeboat. He suffered hand lacerations while fighting off the sharks."[22] Richardson was but one of many merchant seamen who received awards for heroism. Aboard the *Esso Baton Rouge,* AB Russell Wirth saved the lives of seven men, including an AG who was burned over one-third of his body and was blinded by oil.[23]

There have been many commendations from former AGs regarding the "professionalism" of merchant crews, and scores of pictures of hideously damaged merchant ships that made it to port with makeshift repairs by the crew underscores the point. A tribute by Lieutenant Commander Gib Robinson, USNR, gives a graphic example: "In the winter of 1943, we were about 300 miles off the coast of Ireland, at early daylight, trying to reform convoy as we had been zigzagging the evening before because of submarine attacks. The sea was very rough, wind quite high, foggy with rain and mist. Suddenly, a Panamanian ship, the SS *Santa Maria,* came out of nowhere on our starboard side and rammed us at midships, at the exact location of my cabin. I rushed out on deck and found myself about eight feet from the bow of the *Santa Maria.* There was quite a bit of confusion for a few moments, but she backed out and cleared us. We were taking on water quite rapidly and were dead in the water. Although our engine room was taking on water, our pumps were holding their own and there was no serious damage to the engines. We tried to make some headway, but by doing so the water inflow increased and was more than our pumps could handle, so we went dead in the water again.

"It was then that I learned a lot about sea-going vessels and the men who sail them. Where it all came from I can't tell to this day, but timbers aboard were cut and filled into our damaged hull on the inside. They were temporarily secured, and bunks and whatever were packed into the gaping hole in the hull. There was some sand and cement aboard, and the crew patched that hole up, and we were able to crawl into Southhampton."[24]

CHAPTER ELEVEN
HELL BELOW ZERO:
THE MURMANSK RUN

I have today found the defense of the
Union of Soviet Socialist Republics vital
to the defense of the United States. . . .
—President Franklin D. Roosevelt,
   7 Nov 1941[1]

The above directive to Edward R. Stettinius, Director, Office of Lend-Lease Administration, received a hostile reception in the Congress and from the American public, but U.S. Navy records indicate that on 6 December 1941, the SS *Larranga* departed Boston harbor on a voyage that would ultimately lead to Murmansk. The naval AG gun crew on board got its first taste of action on Christmas Eve, when it fired three rounds at a surfaced submarine before joining British Convoy PQ-8. She arrived in Murmansk on 19 January and made it back to New York on 20 April. The urgent need for vital war supplies by Russia was such that it was considered necessary to send a number of succeeding vessels out without "being delayed for armament," but even those armed carried only a few .30- or .50-caliber machine guns.[2]

The first few convoys had comparatively little difficulty with weather or enemy attack, mines being the principal hazards. With Convoy PQ-13, however, heavy enemy action was encountered, and three of ten American ships in the convoy were sunk; from then on enemy opposition became steadily worse, and casualties of men and ships increased greatly.

What was the dreaded "Murmansk run?" It was one of only two practical deep-water routes available to carry vital supplies to Russia, in order to keep it in the war. It involved a

4,500-mile voyage from New York, through the dangerous waters of the North Atlantic and Barents Sea to the north Russian ports of Murmansk, Molotovsk, and Archangel, the latter two in the White Sea. It was the preferred route because the other terminated in rickety ports in the Persian Gulf, soon hopelessly overcrowded and under-equipped. Vessels had to wait weeks, and sometimes months, in blistering heat to unload their cargoes, and the antique railroad and so-called roads to Russia could not begin to handle the flood of munitions, materiel, food, and other supplies coming in from around the world.

The Murmansk run was made via Reykjavik, Iceland, or Loch Ewe, Scotland, each over 1,500 miles distant. As more ships and supplies were sent to Russia, the Germans massed U-boat wolfpacks, aircraft in strategic bases along the route, and surface raiders operating out of newly invaded Norway to harass shipping with continuing attacks. The Murmansk run was rivaled in hazard and losses only by the supply run to Malta, until the tide of war turned. And no man who survived the Murmansk run will ever forget the combination of enemy attack and the elements, the sheer nightmare of which could prove almost as much a menace as the enemy and represented physical torture for both man and ship.

In the pre-dawn darkness of the Brooklyn Armed Guard Center, men awaiting shipping out could hear the insistent call, "Now hear this! Now hear this! All men listed for the [whatever ship they were assigned to] will report to Gate 1 at 0700." Gunner's Mate 2/c John Sheridan of Stamford, Connecticut, dropped out of his hammock, groped for his shoes and other personal items. He was scheduled to go out on the Liberty SS *Owen Wister*, one of a number of ships called. Destination was unknown, but not long in being learned; on the call board a notice ordered "All hands report to Supply for Arctic gear." That could mean only one thing, the Murmansk run, a three-month trip if all went well, but with more than a high degree of uncertainty as to a safe return. Death was a constant companion on the Murmansk run; if foul weather did not crack a ship's hull or capsize her, there was a good chance that collision, mines, U-boats, enemy aircraft, or surface raiders would do her in. A man exposed for just minutes in the frigid waters stood little or no chance of survival. Those in lifeboats suffered terribly from exposure and frostbite, and many lost limbs as a result of their ordeal.[3]

The next step was to pick up several pairs of thick sox, heavy thermal "longjohns," face mask, and other foul-weather gear. GM Sheridan checked the list of men assigned to the *Owen Wister* for familiar names, shipmates in previous AG crews. Then it was the usual "hurry up and wait" as the new crew sat on their seabags awaiting transport to their ship.

As an old-timer, a veteran of several voyages, Sheridan was pleased to note that the *Owen Wister* was of riveted construction, with less chance of plates cracking at the welds. He checked the guns and gun tub on the bridge. The *Wister* was a quite-new Liberty and was well armed, a world of difference from the peashooters with which early AG crews went to sea. It had a 5″ 38, which could spit out shells in a hurry, and a 3″ 50, eight 20-mm, firing a 60-shell magazine in seconds, with a tracer every fourth round. In addition to the AG gunnery officer, the crew had a bos'n and two gunner's mates to train the mostly green gun crew.

Their first duties were to clean the guns, paint the gun tubs, and hold frequent gun drills and General Alarms to check response. Then came the loading of ammunition in the ship's magazine. After loading hold cargo, six railroad locomotives were hoisted aboard as deck cargo, plus a number of tanks. The locomotives were not regarded too happily as they always made a ship appear top-heavy, and it was a case of, "God help us if they break loose in heavy seas."

The ship's master and the AG lieutenant returned from the convoy conference, and the *Wister* was towed from the pier, to drop anchor in the Hudson and await the formation of her convoy. The ship was ready to sail and become a small part of a great war, the Battle of the Atlantic and the Murmansk run.

Iced up on the Murmansk run. (National Archives)

If a ship were going out in January, the crew could expect about four hours of daylight per day, gradually increasing to about 20 hours in May; during June, July, and August there were virtually twenty-four hours of daylight, with the sun low in the horizon, a suicidal period for transit as was learned by ill-fated Convoy PQ-17. During the winter months, ships would get coated with tons of ice, which had to be chipped away, and steam hoses had to be used to thaw out the guns. The most dangerous part of the run was between Bear Island and Murmansk, as pack ice could force convoys south within range of German aircraft, strung out in many bases along the Norwegian coast. The Germans basically used five types of aircraft to attack shipping: Dorniers (high-level bombers), Heinkels (torpedo bombers that attacked at close to wave-top level), Stukas (dive-bombers that came in near-vertical attacks), Focke-Wulf 200s (that could be used as bombers, but were also valuable in long-distance reconnaissance), and Blohm-Voss bombers.

Visibility was reduced as ships moved north, fog frequently cutting it to 100 feet or less, and the danger of collision was great. Watches were doubled, and each ship blew her call letters constantly on her horn. The situation was especially dangerous when munitions ships were in the convoy. As they moved into bad weather, the seas would pick up and waves 30 feet or more would crash over the bow, tons of water sweeping the deck. Lines were strung from midship to bow and stern to which the men attached lifelines to keep from being washed over the side. Life rafts and lifeboats were often swept away. Snow brought its own problems, filling up the gun tubs, and trying to climb ladders with wet, heavy clothing became a real problem. On the bridge, wet face masks would freeze to the skin and a man's nose would freeze shut, forcing him to breathe through his mouth. However, while the elements were merciless at times, on other occasions they were friends; submarines had equally bad visibility, and enemy planes, while heard above, could not find the ships.

A cold, miserable John Sheridan remarked to the gunnery officer that he hoped the next trip would be to South America, but the officer grinned and said, "Do you think they would spend all that money getting this ship insulated the way it is? Guess again." (The *Wister* had a four-inch layer of insulation around cabin, bridge, and exposed pipes.) He was right, they made a second trip to Murmansk.

Although he wouldn't have appreciated being so informed at the time, Sheridan was lucky; the naval armed guard had learned much, the hard way, in earlier voyages. The SS *Dunboyne*, with Gun Crew #1E, under Ensign Rufus Brinn, USNR, had been scheduled to make the first NAG run to Murmansk, but was delayed by a variety of circumstances. However, she did make the run early in January 1942, via Halifax to Archangel. Ensign Brinn's voyage report, made upon return, was so good that Captain William J. Coakley, commanding officer, Armed Guard Center, Brooklyn, wrote:

"This report contains much valuable information, suggestions and recommendations and Ensign Brinn is to be commended for a very complete and comprehensive report. . . ."[4]

The *Dunboyne* was part of Convoy PG-13, heavily attacked by "submarines, aircraft, four surface raiders and four enemy destroyers," a number of which were sunk by escort vessels. While in Murmansk, the *Dunboyne* ". . . sustained 110 air alarms and 54 bombing attacks. The eleven-man gun crew of 1E shot down two enemy planes, helped bring down another, put one rear gunner out of business and hit several others . . ." according to Ensign Brinn's voyage report. All of the gun crew were recommended for awards for meritorious service by the vice chief of naval operations. The *Dunboyne* had a charmed life, lasting out the entire war.

The SS *Yaka*, built in 1920, was another of the early arrivals and had a lengthy stay in Murmansk to repair damage sustained en route from weather and over 150 air raids. The *Yaka* was one of only two ships in Convoy PQ-14 that carried NAG crews, one member being George T. Smith, now Justice of the Georgia Supreme Court. The *Yaka*'s luck ran out on 18 November 1942 while steaming in convoy ONS-144 from Iceland to Halifax, Nova Scotia. All of her merchant crew of forty-one and the eleven-man AG crew were picked up by HMS *Vervain*, which later also rescued all survivors in the water from the SS *Wade Hampton*.[5]

Having survived the sinking of his tanker on his first voyage, Warren Chapman, BM 1/c, was pleased to note that his second tanker was much better armed and had a larger AG gun crew, under command of a lieutenant (j.g.), and it was proceeding in convoy. No one on the Murmansk run, however, ever felt peace of mind, coming or going.

"On the fourteenth day, in mountainous seas, the ship was rocked by a major explosion, a torpedo apparently fired at random, as visibility was near zero for both U-boats and gun crews. Flames licked up from amidship, and a second, even worse explosion followed the first as the oil in the hit compartments went up." Chapman wrote later, "As I clung to the gun at the after battle station, I saw the whole bow of our ship turn and rise on a big swell, a good twenty yards from where it ought to be. We'd been broken in half!

"On the separated bow were the AG lieutenant, and all of the ship's officers, except the engineer. That left me in charge of the remaining Navy men, and him in charge of a piece of the ship. We immediately checked the bulkheads to see how long our half-ship could stay afloat. Things did not look good. A British corvette came up but could not get close enough, for fear of collision, and the waves were much too high for us to attempt to get off. Besides the water is so cold that if you are in the water for just a few minutes your arms and legs are so badly frozen that you risk amputation, if you survive.

"Just before dark we got a real turn. Out of the mist, dead ahead, coming straight for our piece of a ship was a huge object, the bow of our own ship. After a few moments of heart-stop, the hulk slid off into the midst. It was never seen again. Our part held together until morning when we realized we would have to take the chance of leaving. We let down our one life raft, put eight men in it and watched nervously as they tried to paddle to the corvette. We thought they were gone three times, but the corvette pulled up and hauled them, half dead, on deck. The rest of us put on our life-saving suits and went over the side. Fortunately, the corvette was able to close in on us and pull us aboard. I didn't think I would ever thaw out, in spite of dry clothes, blankets and rum.

"The corvette sank what was left of our ship as she was a menace to navigation, and got us back to a base in the British Isles. I came back to the states on a former luxury liner."[6] Upon Chapman's return he was promoted in rank. (Records are not available to indicate if Chapman survived the war.)

Lieutenant (j.g.) Irving Kaplan of El Cerrito, California, was AG commanding officer on the SS *Woodbridge N. Ferris.* He reports: "I well remember the convoy conference held at

Loch Ewe on 12 January 1944. It was a very sober one, we knew that we were heading into the jaws of the enemy as well as the vile weather that went with it. We ran into trouble soon after we left Scotland; Ship #61, dead-ahead of us was torpedoed. She listed to starboard and was hissing steam and being abandoned as we passed her close to her starboard side and moved up to position #61. At the same time, two other ships to our port were torpedoed and were seen smoking and sinking. The convoy maintained the same course, and it is estimated that 100 depth charges were discharged, but the submarine pack continued to attack persistently from all sides. At 1010 on 26 January flag hoist indicated enemy aircraft approaching, but they circled around out of our range, obviously reporting our position and course. The weather was another problem. The sun rose weakly, skirted briefly along the horizon; then those long nights, with constant action. I watched many men abandoning ship—what a lonely way to die in that vast waste area. There was frustration at not being able to see the enemy, flares didn't seem to help much, even though we were heavily armed, a 3-inch 50 dual-purpose gun in the bow, 5-inch double-purpose gun aft, and eight 20mm spaced around the ship. It was bitter cold and the mount on the bow gun froze, torches were applied to free it, ice was everywhere; each man who came off watch reported to me and was given a stiff hooker of Scotch whisky as I had managed to pick up a few bottles of Johnny Walker before sailing. During the brief daylight hours we watched carefully as we passed alongside floating mines." [7]

Kaplan's voyage report indicates that the *Ferris* arrived alongside the pier at Molotovsk at 1530 on 29 January. He adds, "My first exposure to Russia was not a good one. An arrogant chap came aboard to check us out. When he got to my cabin, he insisted on going through everything. I made it clear that the contents of my cabin were restricted U.S. Navy material and were none of his business. I let him know I could escort him off this ship. When he left he posted a guard at our gangway.

"While anchored in Kola Inlet, we dragged anchor one night during a storm and damaged a screw. Russian divers repaired what they could, but on the return voyage we had engine trouble and became a dreaded straggler. The rest of the convoy continued on its way. The engine is the heart and pulse of a ship and when it stops, one's heart and pulse misses a few beats too."

The convoy was kept under continuing attack, and Kaplan noted in his voyage report that some 300 depth charges were dropped. Ship #31 was torpedoed and drifting out of command. "Some hands were taking to the boats, but she was still afloat as she dropped below the horizon." The *Ferris* made it back safely, and Kaplan completed his tour of duty in the NAG in North Africa, Sicily, and Italy.

SMC Joseph E. Hecht, Reeders, Pennsylvania, was aboard the SS *Hugh Williamson* when she reached Reykjavik, Iceland. After a prolonged stay of six weeks, during which no liberty was allowed, "the crisis of my life came about." After the destruction of Convoy PQ-17, convoys during the long hours of daylight in the Arctic were cancelled, but someone in the British Admiralty got the idea that by sending single vessels through the strong German blockade, perhaps some ships could get through. It was "common knowledge" among the merchant fleet personnel in Iceland that convoys were being demolished as rapidly as they were sent. So, by the British plan, at the end of the first week of November, "All assigned vessels should be on their dangerous errand." The admiral chose eleven ships; the sailing date for each ship was to exceed the other by twenty-four hours. In that way, he figured, these ships would not arouse suspicion, and therefore some would reach destination. In an isolated fjord, somewhere in Iceland, these eleven vessels awaited their marked missions. Each vessel moved out according to pre-arranged plan, the *Williamson* being the seventh ship to leave so mysteriously.

"After arriving into the Greenland area, we were getting into Arctic weather, but to date it had treated us mighty fine, going only as low as 33 below zero. At this point we just drifted along as our magnetic compasses were off and we were lost. The next morning, the #8 ship (British) overtook us. We checked our position and resumed speed and soon out-distanced the old ship, a coal-burner. Later that night we received a distress call from her saying she was being attacked by a submarine. We could hear the explosions, and orders were to run for it. Somehow, we escaped. The next morning we were picked up by a Focke-Wulf four-engine; seeing we were alone, he came in for the attack immediately, but we beat him off after part of his load of bombs missed the ship by a mere fraction, causing loosened plates, taking on some water and knocking out the after-steering. Other planes were sighted, but we made the White Sea and felt comparatively safe. However, en route to the dock at Molotovsk with a Russian pilot, we rammed a Russian ship alongside the pier. The Russians wanted us to pay for the damage; we were thankful that our ammo didn't go up. We moved on to Murmansk and starting Christmas afternoon, we had fourteen straight days of bombings, almost enough to put me in a straitjacket.

"On the return trip, we were part of a fifteen-ship convoy, escorted by the British. The American ships were the SS *Richard Alvey, Johnny Walker, Meanticut, Camp Fire,* and the *Williamson,* plus four Brits and six Russians. We arrived at Loch Ewe and joined a 64-ship convoy to the United States; two British ships collided one day out of New York. When we finally arrived at Philadelphia on 12 February 1943, I was skin-and-bones and felt about ten years older.

"Of the original eleven ships sailing independently to Russia, each supposedly 100 miles apart, five were lost, one turned back, three were bombed and only two had no problems. The *Williamson,* although bombed, was the last ship to get through. The SS *William Clark* was the only American ship lost, although three others were damaged."[8]

After the disaster of PQ-17, no effort was made to restore convoys to North Russia for several months, until darkness offered more protection. The original Liberty ship, SS *Patrick Henry,* was one of the forty merchantmen that left Loch

The last trip of the gallant SS *Patrick Henry,* under tow to the scrap yard. (Courtesy Bethlehem Steel Corporation)

Ewe on 2 September 1942. PQ-18's escort was the heaviest ever assigned to a convoy—a cruiser, twenty-nine destroyers, an escort carrier, five armed trawlers, and three rescue ships, the best-armed and defended convoy to this time. The convoy was sighted 11 September, and the battle began on 13 September, between Jan Mayen Island and Spitzbergen. The first wave of enemy aircraft came in with about fifty planes, and the attack went on for days, wave after wave of bombers. Of the convoy of forty merchant vessels, twenty-three were American, and eight of the thirteen ships lost were American, including the SS *Mary Luckenbach,* a munitions ship carrying 1,000 tons of TNT. She was torpedoed on 14 September by German aircraft and disintegrated in a huge explosion, taking at least one enemy aircraft with her and raining debris on ships nearby, including the SS *Na-*

thaniel Greene, wounding a number of men on deck. There were no survivors of the forty-eight-man merchant crew and sixteen NAGs.

Louis Vigh, Toledo, Ohio, was a gunner aboard the Liberty SS *John Penn,* carrying tanks. He reports: "I was on a 20-mm gun on the starboard side, and things were relatively quiet when all of a sudden all hell broke loose. Over the horizon came all kinds of German torpedo planes and high-level bombers. The sky was filled with tracer fire, and ships were burning all around. The SS *Mary Luckenbach* was off our starboard, I saw her, and then she was gone, just a cloud of smoke. I could not believe my eyes, but just then I heard a thud, we had taken a torpedo amidship. The captain sounded 'Abandon Ship,' so I jumped out of the gun tub and landed below on my rear end. I raced for the lifeboat which was already overcrowded. I was the last one to slide down the lifeline; the seas were heavy with oil, and our oars bent back like bamboo poles when we tried to row. Finally a British destroyer picked us up, although there were German subs all around us. HMS *Eskimo* was also towing another destroyer that had been hit by a torpedo. The seas were running high, and she commenced to take on water, but they took the crew off before she sank. The *Eskimo* kept dropping depth charges for about an hour, before heading for the British naval base at Scapa Flow, and we were eventually brought back to the U.S. on the *Queen Elizabeth.* We were torpedoed on September 13, 1942, and I spent my birthday on the *Eskimo* in the Barents Sea. It's one birthday I'll always remember. When we arrived back at the Brooklyn AG Center, we were awarded a citation for downing an enemy plane."[9]

During the convoy battle, the armed guard gun crews were credited with downing twenty-eight enemy planes—the SS *Nathaniel Green* with eight, *Virginia Dare* with seven, *William Moultrie* with five. German losses were never officially totaled, but are believed to have been at least forty planes. This fierce battle is often referred to as the turning point in the battle of supply to North Russia; the Germans

A convoy forming up in Iceland in World War II. (National Archives)

were never as aggressive after this fight. American losses, in addition to the *Mary Luckenbach,* were the SS *Oliver Ellsworth, Kentucky, Oregonian, Wacosta, John Penn, Africander,* and the *MacBeth,* sailing under the Panamanian flag.[10]

While the effort to reach Russia and deliver their cargoes of vital war supplies was always dangerous and frequently fatal, many vessels that survived the inbound passage and heavy air attacks in port, were lost on the return voyage. The Esso tanker SS *Paul H. Harwood* had to unload hurriedly in Murmansk and try to catch up with Convoy RA-64, which had left two days earlier, but soon found that that convoy was no guarantee of safe passage. A Norwegian vessel, two ships ahead of the *Harwood,* was torpedoed, followed by the SS *Horace Gray* immediately ahead. Shortly thereafter, the SS *Thomas Scott* went down; HMS *Onslaught* pulled along-

A ship burning after being hit by an enemy plane while on the Murmansk run. (Navy Department, National Archives)

side and took off the forty-two-man merchant crew, twenty-seven NAGs and forty Norwegian refugees, with no loss of life. Soon to follow was the SS *Henry Bacon,* a straggler traveling alone. However, the worst disaster of the convoy occurred to the British corvette, HMS *Bluebell.* Chief Engineer Peck of the *Paul H. Harwood* reports: "About 3 P.M. of 17 February, we heard an explosion astern. One of the British destroyers following us was hit, apparently in her magazine. She was only a few cable lengths from us. A steam cloud rose about 300 feet in the air and when it gradually settled down there was nothing left of the vessel. Other destroyers headed for the vicinity of the attack, but only one man was saved. After this grim disaster, the convoy assumed close formation and headed north until the time came to turn west." After reloading in Scotland, the *Harwood* returned to Murmansk.[11]

Certainly one of the most dramatic stories of the Murmansk run was that of the Liberty SS *Henry Bacon,* in Convoy RA-64. Having made it safely to Murmansk and survived enemy attacks, she was on return to Scotland in ballast. However, she carried as passengers a number of Norwegian refugees, evacuated from the island of Soroya by the British. They were distributed among several ships in the convoy. Badly damaged in a gale and with steering impaired, the *Bacon* lost the convoy and was traveling alone when she was attacked by over twenty Heinkel bombers. The *Bacon* fought back gallantly and downed five enemy planes and detonated several torpedoes before a torpedo put her in sinking condition, and the ship had to be abandoned. The story is picked up in the words of ex-Able Seaman William L. Phillips, HMS *Opportune,* dispatched from the main convoy when the *Bacon* reported being under attack: "Most of the lifeboats and life-saving gear had been damaged by the severe storms. The one lifeboat that was serviceable was allocated to the civilians aboard, plus a few men to handle the boat. Most of the crew and the U.S. AGs opted to take their chance on whatever they could hold onto. When we arrived in the area, debris was everywhere. Survivors were in the water, some clinging to boards and anything that floated. We drew down the scramble nets and I climbed down to assist the exhausted survivors. I was handed a bundle, and struggled aboard thinking it was a bundle of belongings until I heard a cry. I opened the bundle and there was a baby's face looking at me. I held the child until the other civilians were rescued. We also rescued some of the crew and a number of U.S. AGs; two other destroyers also rescued some crew and Navy men. Two of the Armed Guards we picked up were Norman Croteau, Fall River, Mass., and Lewis Walker, address unknown, who had been blown overboard. We picked up a couple more AGs, who had been knocked about pretty badly, and they were ministered to, but I do not know the results or their names.

"The rescue had to be carried out quickly, as it was known that U-boat packs were in the vicinity, and it didn't matter in a periscope if you were on an errand of mercy. When there was no more possibility of finding any other survivors, we rejoined the convoy. The experience highlighted the bravery and self-sacrifice of both crew and Armed Guards in insisting that the Norwegian civilians should have use of the lifeboat, and indeed all these were saved, whilst several AGs and crew members perished. We left Norman

Croteau at the Faroe Islands for hospital treatment and proceeded to Gourock, where the other survivors were landed."[12]

Ironically, QP-13, which had escaped destruction because of the movement eastbound of heavily laden PQ-17, subsequently had troubles of its own. In dense fog and storm, it blundered into one of the Allies own minefields in the Denmark Strait off Iceland and lost five merchant ships and a minesweeper. One of the ships lost on the return trip of QP-13 was the SS *Massmar,* which in turn was carrying survivors of the SS *Alamar,* sunk eastbound in PQ-16. This represented two sinkings in one trip to Russia for the thirty-six-man merchant crew and nine navy gunners on the *Alamar;* sadly, the captain and twenty-two crewmen were lost when the *Massmar* struck a mine on return. Other vessels lost were the SS *John Randolph* and SS *Heffron,* which was also carrying survivors of four ships previously lost. However, only one man was lost on the two ships. The disaster of QP-13 was said to have happened because the convoy escort commander was unable to get a good fix on the position of the convoy as it was about to enter mined waters because of the foul weather conditions.[13]

Luckier was the SS *J. H. Latrobe,* a Liberty that had become unmanageable in terrible weather. She was drifting into a minefield when HMS *Opportune,* which had rescued survivors of the *Henry Bacon,* again lived up to her name. Able Seaman Len Phillips reports: "Our skipper, Commander J. Lee Barber, decided to help and we managed to work ourselves into a position where we could attach a tow, then facing the full fury of the relentless storm we managed to get the sinking *Latrobe* into Seydisfjördur, Iceland. For this heroic effort in saving the *Latrobe,* our skipper received a special commendation from the Commander-in-Chief, Home Fleet. At the time, we were being harrassed by U-boats that had already sunk the merchant ships SS *Puerto Rican* and the SS *Richard Bland.* For our effort we received prize money and as an Able Seaman, I received one pound, eight shillings, in today's currency about U.S. $2.00."[14]

Certainly one of the most unlucky ships that ever made

the Murmansk run was the Liberty ship SS *Richard Bland.* Originally scheduled for PQ-17, she ran into fog and struck a large ice floe off Iceland, staving in her forepeak and taking on water rapidly in #1 hold. Down by the head and still in heavy fog, she then ran aground. Finally pulled off by two British vessels, she was towed into Reykjavik for temporary repairs after discharging cargo. She then sailed to Loch Ewe for another try at getting cargo to Murmansk. This time she made it, but underwent thirty-five days of heavy air attack. She headed home in Convoy RA-53, along with the equally unlucky Liberty *J. L. M. Curry,* which split her hull in two in a vicious storm. On 5 March, the *Bland* was hit by a torpedo from the *U-255,* which had wreaked such havoc with PQ-17. The SS *Executive* on her starboard side was also hit and sunk, but the *Bland* was able to keep afloat, although losing the convoy. She was attacked by twelve Heinkel 111s, but sustained no direct hits and was able to rejoin the convoy. Then came a heavy gale, winds Force 5–8; the bridge steering went out; she had to be managed from the after-steering platform and lost the convoy again. To add insult to injury, she next ran into heavy drift ice. After finally emerging safely from the ice pack, she was torpedoed again twice, once more by the *U-255.* The main gun could not be used because the ship was listing badly and wallowing in heavy seas, and at least one 20-mm jammed. Lieutenant William A. Carter, a passenger, and Ensign E. S. Neely, commander of the navy gun crew, were on the bridge when the third torpedo struck and were surrounded by flame, but were able to jump into the water and make it to a heavily overloaded lifeboat. Although the third officer and third assistant engineer held onto Ensign Neely as long as they could, they could not get him into the lifeboat, and he was lost.

After the twenty-seven men in the lifeboat were rescued, Lieutenant Carter wrote the voyage report in lieu of Ensign Neely, in which he praised him highly for his conduct and coolness under fire. Carter also wrote a special recommendation for recognition of the heroism of two other members of the AG crew, Wayne Baker, BM2/c, USN, and Herbert A.

Petersen, SM2/c, USNR. Excerpts from his report follow: "Subject men distinguished themselves by their exceptional heroism and absolute disregard for their own personal safety. . . . Two boats had been lost and there was not sufficient boat space to accommodate the remaining members of the crew. A third torpedo hit was received which set the ship afire and broke her in half. At this time, Baker and Petersen were standing by the boats. Both men assisted in lowering the after boat when the falls were deserted by the men whose duty it was to lower them. They still did not embark although the vessel was sinking rapidly and they were enveloped in flames. They attempted to clear the forward boat which was hanging in the water by one davit. Only when they were unable to do this did they give thought to saving themselves. Petersen was able to jump into the lifeboat which had 27 men in it already and had only a few inches of freeboard. Baker realized this situation, and in spite of the entreaties of the men in the boat he refused to jump. Instead, he drew his sheath knife and helped cut the tangle of lines which enabled the boat to get clear of the ship before she sank. Baker went down with the ship, preferring to sacrifice his own life rather than risk swamping the boat and costing the lives of 27 other men. I was among the men whose lives were saved by Baker's magnificent self-sacrifice."[15]

The lifeboat with the twenty-seven men was later picked up by HMS *Impulsive,* and another destroyer picked up two more boats with four men each. Carter's voyage report ends, "A total of 35 men from a crew of 68 were saved. Twelve of the men saved were members of the Armed Guard, fifteen AG are missing."

Even in the midst of the most dangerous supply run of the war, there could be found some elements of humor. In Convoy PQ-18, the steward in the SS *Charles McAllister* thought that the gun crews, who had been at GQ for some time, needed some hot coffee. He carried a coffee pot, and a messman carried a tray of cups. When making his rounds someone yelled, "Sub!" and the steward reacted quickly; he threw the coffee, pot and all, over the side so that he could pitch in and pass ammo. Not to be outdone, the messman threw his cups overboard. According to a report, the steward later had to be told what he had done.

Ernie Sanders, Princeton, Kentucky, sent a clipping from the *Stars and Stripes* of 15 February 1943, dateline Londonderry, North Ireland. It described a detachment of NAGs stationed there: "There are a score or more sailors here who are waiting anxiously for their ship to come in . . . any ship will do so long as it carries a four-inch dual purpose gun, or a brace of .50 caliber machine guns, just for their personal use." Sanders adds, "We were in an AG pool waiting to go aboard merchant ships on the Murmansk Run as replacements for sick or injured. Most of them had already made the run and the general comment about the story was, what a crock—the only ship we want to see is one going Stateside!"[16]

Jim Blalock, a farm boy from Mississippi, joined the armed guard as a gunner. Aboard the SS *Willard Hall*, he quickly found himself in unfamiliar climes. In Loch Ewe, Scotland, the *Willard Hall* joined a convoy to Murmansk. The cold reached 70 below and, "Spit froze before it hit the deck and bounced." Pack ice was a serious problem, and at one time the ship hit ice and shuddered violently. It was necessary for escorts to break up the ice with depth charges. Blalock had frozen his feet some years earlier, and huge blisters broke out on his feet and burst, with others forming. The medic had only APC pills and Epsom Salts, but came up with an idea to rub fish oil on his feet regularly, and it worked fine. Not surprisingly, Blalock didn't care much for the weather, and he says, "I prayed, Oh! Lord, if you get me out of this cold weather, I'll never ask you for a thing again." However, finally getting out of Archangel after several weeks, and delayed by running aground because the Soviets would not indicate the depth of the river, the *Willard Hall* was later assigned to the Persian Gulf run. Here the weather was so blisteringly hot that Blalock prayed again. "Oh! Lord, I was a big liar. Please get me out of here!"[17]

The price paid to deliver the goods was a heavy one, for

both Great Britain and the United States. Winston Churchill wrote that in the whole war ninety-one merchant ships were lost on the Murmansk run, and of about four million tons of cargo dispatched from the United States and England, an eighth was lost. The British Merchant Navy lost 829 lives, and the Royal Navy lost two cruisers and seventeen other warships in which 1,840 officers and men died. U.S. Navy records indicate 347 merchant ships were dispatched to North Russia through 26 April 1945, and "about one out of three were lost in the early stages."[18]

CHAPTER TWELVE
THE PQ-17 DISASTER

*The Russian convoy is and always has
been an unsound operation of war.*
—Rear Admiral L. H. K. Hamilton, RN[1]

Of the hundreds of convoys in all theaters of operation in World War II, none endured greater disaster
than that which befell Convoy PQ-17, Iceland–
Archangel/Murmansk.

In the summer of 1942, Russia was reeling before the onslaught of Hitler's Great Summer Offensive; the situation on
the Eastern Front was precarious in the extreme. Convoy
PQ-17, heavily laden with strategic materiel, largely explosives and high-octane gasoline, was dispatched to assist the
Soviets. PQ-17 was a large mixed convoy, consisting of thirty-
three American, British, Dutch, Russian, and Panamanian-
flag merchant ships, three rescue ships, a fleet oiler, and an
unusually large Anglo-American escort. There were twenty-
two American merchantmen in the convoy, including six
brand-new Liberty ships fresh out of the yards. Several U.S.
ships had been to Murmansk before, and their crews and
naval armed guards aboard were well aware of the hazards
that lay ahead, but their worst forebodings could not have
matched the reality of the nightmare to come.

Under command of Commodore J. C. K. Dowding, RNR,
the convoy, which had been gathering for weeks, set out
from Hvalfjord, Iceland, on 27 June 1942. Dowding's flag was
aboard the SS *River Afton*. It was midsummer, a suicidal sea-
son for the voyage, as in those latitudes summer days are so
long that there is no protective darkness. The major com-
pensating factor was that there were actually more combat
ships protecting this convoy than there were merchant ships
to protect.

The immediate close escort consisted of six destroyers,

two antiaircraft ships, two submarines, and eleven smaller craft. Also in close support were two British and two American cruisers, with three destroyers, under command of Rear Admiral L. H. K. Hamilton, RN. Not part of the escort force, but as a further protective measure, nine British and two Soviet submarines were stationed off the coast of Norway to either intercept and attack the powerful German battleship *Tirpitz* and her consort of cruisers and destroyers, should they leave their port in Norway, or at least to give the convoy warning of their departure.

The distant covering force, under Admiral Sir John Tovey, commander-in-chief, British Home Fleet, aboard HMS *Duke of York,* had two battleships, including the USS *Washington,* three cruisers, a flotilla of fourteen destroyers, and the aircraft carrier HMS *Victorious.* Admiral Tovey's force took position between Iceland and Bear Island to provide protection for convoys in northern waters, and possibly trap an attacking German surface force.[2]

Convoys to North Russia (1941–45) were always under British command, but of many flags, and on occasion included U.S. Navy ships as escorts. PQ-17's escort force included the cruisers USS *Wichita* and *Tuscaloosa,* and destroyers USS *Wainwright* and *Rowan.* Security of the convoy appeared overwhelming.

PQ-17 and close escorts headed northeast from Iceland. Official German records of a conference between Grand-Admiral Raeder and Hitler (15 June 1942) indicate that the German Admiralty was well aware of the sailing date and composition of the convoy and planned an attack by using a strong surface force, consisting of the *Tirpitz,* several heavy cruisers, destroyers, plus smaller craft, U-boats, and aircraft. The operation was given the code name "Rösselsprung" (Knight's Gambit).[3]

Always, the most dangerous part of the Murmansk run was between Bear Island and Murmansk. PQ-17's track was to take it along the western and northern coasts of Iceland, east of Jan Mayen Island, past Bear Island, and then south to Kola Inlet and the mouth of the White Sea. Its misfortunes

Convoy PQ-17 forming in Iceland. The ship in the foreground is believed to be the SS *Troubadour.* (Courtesy C. A. Lloyd)

began early; in the Strait of Denmark the convoy encountered heavy fog and ice floes. The Liberty ship SS *Richard Bland* and two tankers were so damaged by running aground, or by ice, that they had to turn back. They were the lucky ones, but only temporarily for the *Bland.*

Coincidentally, on 26 June, QP-13 had set out westward from Archangel. It picked up some additional ships at Murmansk, almost at the same time that PQ-17 headed east. It comprised thirty-five merchant ships, traveling empty, with a comparatively small escort. Normally it would have been an attractive target, an easy opportunity to wipe out badly needed Allied shipping and experienced crews. Although spotted by German air reconnaissance in the Barents Sea on 30 June, it was not molested; the principal target of German operations was to be heavily laden PQ-17. The distant covering force, under Admiral Tovey, was directed to provide protection for QP-13 in the vicinity of Bear Island, and after dropping QP-13, was to cover PQ-17.[4]

On 1 July, PQ-17 was sighted by U-boats #255 and #408,

about 60 nautical miles east of Jan Mayen. Two additional U-boats were dispatched at once to shadow the convoy, and six more U-boats were directed to form a partial line farther east. The *Tirpitz* and supporting units were alerted to move out of bases in Norway to intercept the convoy.

PQ-17 encountered pack ice just north of Bear Island, which forced it to move within 300 miles of German air bases, easy range for the enemy. Air attacks began on 1 July but, fortunately for the convoy, were unsuccessful because of bad weather and poor visibility. Initial submarine attacks were also frustrated by escort destroyers.

While the close and distant escorts were of formidable strength, the armament aboard the merchant ships was puny indeed. Only three of the ships carried 3″ guns, the others had nothing but .30- and .50-caliber machine guns, totally ineffective against the armament of attacking planes or U-boats. On 3 July, convoys QP-13 and PQ-17 passed, just out of sight of each other, in the Barents Sea; QP-13 was still unmolested, but PQ-17 was about to enter the channel to Hell. The *Tirpitz*, the heavy cruiser *Admiral Hipper*, destroyers, and torpedo boats of Force I, under Admiral Schniewind, left base in Trondheim for northern Norway, and the beginning of Operation Rösselsprung. Force II, including the battlecruisers *Admiral Scheer* and *Lutzow* and several destroyers, left Narvik, to join Force I at Altafjord, Norway, near the North Cape.

The German ship movements were observed by British air reconnaissance and immediately reported to the Admiralty. Additional cruisers and destroyers were dispatched to reinforce Tovey's distant covering force; it appeared that the long-awaited trap for the *Tirpitz* was about to be sprung. However, the German force picked up a British radio signal reporting its position and course, proving that it had been spotted. Upon Hitler's strict orders following the loss of the battleship *Bismarck*, the *Tirpitz* was not to be exposed to danger, especially from aircraft carriers. The squadron was ordered to turn about and return to base.[5]

Unaware of the most recent developments, the British

Admiralty expected the *Tirpitz* and her supporting units to attack PQ-17 with overwhelming force, against which Hamilton's cruisers would be to no avail. Even though the *Tirpitz* was never seen, and never came anywhere near PQ-17, the very threat of her was such that on the evening of 4 July, the Admiralty sent a series of urgent "Immediate" signals to Hamilton, by direct order of Admiral Sir Dudley Pound, First Sea Lord:

"Cruiser force withdraw to westward at high speed"— (2111 hours)

"Owing to threat from surface ships, convoy is to disperse and proceed to Russian ports"—(2123 hours)

"Convoy is to scatter"—(2136 hours)[6]

The orders left Admiral Hamilton no alternative, and he reluctantly gave orders to withdraw. Although the destroyer screen was not so ordered, the commander of the destroyer force pulled out to support the cruisers, and a number of smaller units also left the convoy.

For two days after having been spotted, convoy PQ-17 was lucky; dense fog covered its position. However, on the morning of the fourth of July, the fog lifted, and the convoy's tragic ordeal began. Heavy air attack commenced, first by Heinkel 111K torpedo planes, followed by bombing by some twenty-five long-range Focke-Wulfs. Four ships were hit, but able to keep in convoy. Late in the day, eluding a hail of fire, a single Heinkel 115 launched a torpedo that hit the new Liberty ship SS *Christopher Newport* in her engine room, and she was abandoned to her fate.

Naval armed guard gunner Hugh Wright, manning his .30-cal Browning, attempted to explode the torpedo before it hit his ship. The official report states, "Realizing the complete uselessness of his .30 caliber, Wright kept firing until the torpedo passed out of sight. . . ." He hit the torpedo several times, but the bullets bounced off. When the torpedo exploded, Wright was blown off the flying bridge, down two decks to the boat deck, knocking him unconscious. He was hauled off by shipmates. Of the twelve-man armed guard crew, none were killed, but three crewmen were lost. The

Christopher Newport was finished off by the guns of an escort.[7]

About three hours later, the SS *William Hooper,* another of the new Liberty ships, was hit in the engine room, despite evasive maneuvering. Captain Edward L. Graves later reported that the ship was hit by a torpedo from a Junkers 88, and it wrecked the starboard boiler. The explosion blew the engine up through the stack. The naval armed guard, under lieutenant (j.g.) Brian Welch, remained at their positions, and Welch reported that the two after gunners continued to fire at the plane after the ship was hit. Welch attempted to get to his cabin to destroy classified papers, but smoke and flame in the passageway prevented that. He then waited until he saw his men off the ship before climbing into a boat.[8]

Picked up by the rescue ship HMRS *Rathlin,* he observed a British destroyer shelling the *William Hooper* from close by. Welch warned the captain of the *Rathlin* that the *Hooper* was carrying several hundred tons of ammunition, and a signal was sent to the destroyer to pull away. The coup de grace was delivered to the *William Hooper* by U-boat #334. Of the forty-four crewmen and sixteen naval armed guards, three crewmen in the engine room were killed in the explosion; survivors were taken to Archangel by the *Rathlin.*

At about the same time, the British freighter *Navarino* was sunk, and the Soviet tanker *Azerbaijan* was hit by torpedo bombers, but the tanker stayed afloat, burning fiercely, and eventually reached port. Three Heinkel 111s were shot down, one by SS *Washington*'s gunners.

Action, while heavy, did not turn catastrophic until the bewildered merchantmen observed the high-speed departure of their escort; the feelings of the men aboard the almost-defenseless convoy can well be imagined. The next day, 5 July, turned out to be what one German officer later referred to as a "shooting gallery." Now sailing singly, or in small groups, fourteen ships went down under merciless attack by planes and U-boats, easy prey for the far-flung searchers.

The day's losses included seven U.S.-flag ships, the *Wash-*

ington, Pan Kraft, Peter Kerr, Fairfield City, Carlton, Daniel Morgan (another of the new Liberties), and *Honomu.* There was no loss of life on the *Washington* or *Peter Kerr,* but the unlucky *Fairfield City* lost eight crewmen and nine armed guards. The *Pan Kraft* had two killed and eleven seriously wounded, the *Carlton* had three killed and thirty-four taken prisoner, and the *Daniel Morgan,* four killed. After twenty-three days in an open boat in the Barents Sea, only four of fifteen men in the #2 lifeboat of *Honomu* were found alive when picked up by a German submarine; nineteen others had been picked up off rafts by a U-boat ten days earlier.

Non–U.S. ships lost during the ghastly day included the rescue ship *Zaafaram, Earlston, Empire Byron,* fleet tanker *Aldersdale,* the Dutch SS *Paulus Potter,* and the *River Afton,* carrying Commodore Dowding's flag. He was picked up from a raft and taken to Murmansk.

Seventeen-year old Kenneth E. Clasen, now of Middletown, New York, was one of the ten-man navy gun crew aboard the 1919 freighter SS *Pan Kraft,* carrying a load of aircraft parts and a deck load of bombers. After the convoy was ordered to scatter, *Pan Kraft* veered north and hugged the ice pack, but it was spotted by seven JU-88 dive-bombers, and was vigorously attacked. In spite of a good defense, the ship was hit by three bombs, one of which ruptured the steam and oil lines. When the order to abandon ship was given, Clasen found himself in a 25-foot lifeboat with fourteen others. He picks up the story:

"After a couple of hours, we were picked up by a British corvette, HMS *Lotus.* We were taken to Novaya Zemlya, but on the way, the captain picked up still more survivors from a couple of other ships that were sunk. He wasn't supposed to do this, but the captain was a former merchant mariner, and he decided to disobey orders and take a chance.

"Once onboard the corvette, they gave us all a good shot of British rum. After only catnapping for five days, coupled with the rum, I went out like the lights. I was put in a bunk right under a 4-inch AA gun and when some German planes came in, they opened fire. I knew nothing about it at all, and when I woke up they told me I had slept right through an air raid.

"Later in Archangel, the Navy men were transferred to a schoolhouse where we slept on straw. I couldn't eat the fish they gave us, only black bread, dried oats and barley. I lost about 50 pounds. I had no shoes and it took weeks before I could obtain a pair of boots from the Russians, although there were piles of them offloaded from our ships, rotting there. The treatment we got from the Russians was nothing I would want to discuss openly. At best, they didn't want any part of us, nor we of them."[9]

Clasen and the others were "stuck" in Russia until the end of August. At that time they were taken to Murmansk by a British destroyer for further transfer to the USS *Philadelphia*, a light cruiser that took them to Iceland, where they were again transferred to the USS *Tuscaloosa*, which brought them back to Norfolk on 10 September 1942.

The *Daniel Morgan* put up a particularly dogged fight to get her cargo through. She zigzagged, hid in fog banks, and fought off repeated air attacks. One of only three U.S. ships with a 3″ gun, she drove off a number of dive-bombers. Lieutenant (j.g.) Morton E. Wolfson, USNR, armed guard officer, reported that her steady barrage directed at a patrol plane diverted it from checking the course of several other merchantmen, which were able to find protection in a fog bank. Later, attacked by five Junkers 88s, the *Morgan* shot down two.[10]

After the initial attacks on Convoy PQ-17 on 4 July, the convoy reformed, and at 1800 hours all ships were given orders to scatter fanwise and proceed to Archangel. The *Morgan* stood off on a SE'ly course intending to make the Novaya Zemlya coast and then go SSW. Lieutenant Wolfson's report indicates that on the morning of 5 July, a group of ships were sighted, including an AA ship, a destroyer, corvette, and three merchant vessels. It was decided that the *Morgan* should join their company. "Upon joining, the naval escort left, ordering us to maintain course. At 1500, the fog lifted and the *Fairfield City* was observed on parallel course.

Six JU-88s attacked her, and we tried to divert the attack but were unsuccessful. A stick of bombs landed on her flying bridge, and four lifeboats were able to get away before she went down. The gun crews were beginning to show signs of exhaustion and eyestrain, having been at quarters for over 28 hours."

There was an interval of about fifteen minutes before the next attack—not a lot of time, but it gave the *Morgan*'s crew a chance to reload before the JU-88s returned to inflict more pain on an already battle-weary convoy. Upon their return, it became obvious that they meant business. The *Morgan* took several hits. The ship was settling aft and had lost control of her rudder. The 3-inch gun jammed and was impossible to clear. The lifeboats were lowered without order, leaving half of the merchant crew and most of the gun crew aboard. The captain maneuvered to where the boats were located and all remaining hands abandoned ship. She was then struck by two torpedoes. A submarine surfaced and asked her name, tonnage, and cargo. She was carrying steel, explosives, and tanks, but Captain George T. Sullivan replied, "General cargo—food and leather." The submarine commander said, "I don't believe you," but as one sailor to another, he gave course and distance to the nearest land.

"At 2200, the Soviet tanker *Donbass* was sighted and we were invited to come aboard. The master agreed to our gun crew manning the forward 3" 50 gun. Two members of the gun crew, S. Trahan and S. Bourg, had to be hospitalized for exposure." The *Donbass* was soon attacked by an enemy plane, but the AG gun crew was able to force it off-target and hit the plane in the engine, causing it to depart at reduced speed. Two others attacked and scored near-misses. During the attack, the aft 3-inch 50 gun, manned by the Russian crew, failed to fire once. The forward gun crew went aft to effect repair and found that the defect was due to lack of lubrication. "On 8 July, the *Donbass* arrived at Iokana; the NAG gun crew had been at their stations continuously until this time." Lieutenant Wolfson recommended advancement in rating for the entire gun crew. In his report, he states,

"These men were at quarters from the first attack on the 2nd of July, until abandoning the *Daniel Morgan* on 5 July, at 1730, and from 0900 on the morning of the 8th . . . all hands volunteered to man the guns of the *Donbass* and fought valiantly during all engagements with the enemy. . . ." He then adds, "Without the splendid cooperation of Captain George T. Sullivan, master of the *Daniel Morgan,* in furnishing men, providing food at the guns, etc., the fine work shown by the crew would not have been possible. Many drills were held and all members of the merchant crew were assigned to battle stations." Of the forty-one members of the merchant crew, seven were lost; all of the twenty-eight-man AG gun crew survived. A Soviet official personally appeared to thank the gun crew for helping to bring the *Donbass* in safely.

Air and U-boat attacks on the surviving ships of PQ-17 were incessant. The *Pan Atlantic,* carrying a load of explosives, was hit by two bombs and blew to pieces. She sank in three minutes, and eighteen crewmen and seven navy men were lost. Radioman Third Class William H. Shayer, Jr., survived, and reported that gunnery officer Ensign Charles Carroll, USNR, stayed at the guns, was wounded, and went down before he could be rescued.

On 6 July, the *U-255,* which had made the original sighting of PQ-17, sank the new Liberty ship SS *John Witherspoon,* the second torpedo breaking her in two. The submarine surfaced and asked for the master; the U-boat commander offered food and water, and gave direction to the nearest land. The next day, the SS *Alcoa Ranger,* which had been fitted out with two World War I-vintage .45-cal AA guns prior to joining PQ-17, was torpedoed by the *U-255.* Radio operator William L. Smith reported that the submarine surfaced, asked about name, destination, and cargo, and inquired if survivors had sufficient food and water in the boats, and gave directions to land. The boats rigged sail, and made it to Novaya Zemlya, where they were picked up by the *Empire Tide* and eventually brought to Archangel, along with many other survivors. There were no casualties aboard the *Alcoa*

Ranger, although Smith had to be hospitalized in Archangel, where he described conditions as "deplorable." [11]

The SS *Washington* was so badly damaged by an air attack lasting twenty-two hours that she could not be steered, and the pumps could not handle the water pouring in from the wounds in her side. Forty-six survivors, including eleven naval armed guards, made it into two boats, without casualties. Within a few hours the SS *Olapana* came to their rescue, but they declined to be picked up on the grounds that the *Olapana*, carrying high-test gasoline, was a most-likely target herself. Unfortunately, they proved right, for on 8 July, the *Olapana* was attacked by nine Junkers and subsequently sunk by the *U-255*, which seemed to be all over the area. The submarine again surfaced, and the commander inquired if the survivors had enough food and water, and gave course to land, before shelling and sending the *Olapana* to the bottom. In this action, three crewmen were killed in the engine room, and one crewman and a navy gunner were blown over the side by the original explosion.

The survivors of the *Washington* suffered terribly in the small boats, fighting biting cold, wind, snow, and ice before finally making it to Novaya Zemlya. On this inhospitable shore, the *Washington*'s armed guard officer, who had kept his Colt .45, shot a seagull and they made "seagull soup." With still-able survivors from the *Paulus Potter*, they caught some ducks and made soup for over one hundred men who had made it to shore from the convoy. Many were so badly frostbitten that they could not walk, including ten men of the *Washington*'s naval unit.

Survivors in a number of boats kept rowing down the coast of Novaya Zemlya, a 500-mile island off the Russian mainland. It is split by Matochkin Strait, into which a number of ships took refuge. They came upon the SS *Winston-Salem*, hard aground, and got their first real meal in ten days and a blessed chance to rest and get warm. Later, coming upon the *Empire Tide*, they put those in bad condition aboard and again took to the boats. The small British ship then had over 240 survivors aboard, and food was almost exhausted. The *Empire Tide* reached Archangel on 24 July, where many survivors were hospitalized.

In the tragic saga of PQ-17, the exploits of a rusting old freighter, the Panamanian-flag *Troubadour,* provided one heroic success. The *Troubadour* was one of many Panamanian-flag vessels, operating under War Shipping Administration control, and with U.S. Naval Armed Guards. She carried a 4″ gun and four .30-cal Browning machine guns.

In his highly detailed book, *The Destruction of PQ-17,* David Irving has some extremely adverse remarks about the seventeen-nation merchant crew of the *Troubadour,* who mutinied in Reykjavik, were put in the hold for fifty hours, and imprisoned in Archangel by the Russians for trouble over women. The voyage report of the AG commanding officer, Ensign Howard E. Carraway, gives some details: "Throughout the voyage to Reykjavik, there had been continuous friction between the ship's officers and the ship's crew. While at anchor, on 20 June, about twenty members of the crew refused to turn-to. . . . the Port Director's Office gave the master instructions to call on the AGs for assistance in handling the situation, if necessary. On the ship, striking members of the crew were given an opportunity to turn-to. Twelve men who refused to do so were ordered locked below by the master. This was done by the AGs and an armed watch was placed over the prisoners. On the morning of 22 June, an agreement was reached and they were released by the master's orders."

The ship was short on ammunition on departure, and after a discussion with the master and chief officer, Carraway checked the suitability of using for defense the 37-mm guns of two U.S. Army tanks, carried as deck cargo. They were made ready and manned, ammunition was broken out of the hold, the guns were test-fired, and a two-man crew assigned General Quarters in each. It was a good decision because shortly thereafter, the ship was attacked by Blohm and Voss torpedo bombers, but the attack was beaten off by the help of the tank guns. The next attack was by twelve to fifteen torpedo planes and at least one salvo from the 37-mm tank guns scored a hit on one plane in her mid-section, causing her to turn away and vanish in the clouds, but her flight was unsteady and smoke was seen coming from her engine. Carraway was manning a .30-caliber Browning and fired at a torpedo that actually circled the ship twice. Carraway reported, "This time, I opened fire directly at the torpedo in an effort to sink it. After about 75 rounds were fired directly at it, it stopped, turned up on end, and sank from sight, tail first." [12]

After the convoy was ordered to scatter, the *Troubadour, Ironclad,* and *Silver Sword* headed to the southern edge of the ice fields and turned east, staying close to the ice. Distress messages from other ships of the convoy were heard steadily. At the suggestion of the skipper of the trawler, HMT *Ayrshire,* the ships were requested to break out white paint and paint the starboard sides. This allowed ships to blend in with the surrounding area, thus giving them a better chance of success. "The AG crew was 'turned to' to aid with this task, which took about five hours, and the ships were turned starboard sides to the sea. The maneuver was completely successful for the ships were not seen by the patrolling aircraft and ultimately made port safely on 25 July." Carraway's report ends, "During the afternoon of July 25, the ship was tied up at a dock in Molotovsk, USSR. Upon reaching port, the tank guns were thoroughly cleaned and made ready for discharge."

Trouble with the crew continued in port, and Carraway reports, "On 3 August 1942, the master handed me a list of names and members of the crew and requested that as they returned to the ship, they be placed in confinement and held until further notice. This was done and an armed guard was placed over them and they were kept under watch under conditions prescribed by the master until USSR officials removed them from the ship."

The *Troubadour*'s troubles were not yet over. After departing from Archangel on 13 September, the *Troubadour* constantly began to drop from position in the convoy, the problems attributed to the poor quality of Russian coal. Two members of the AG crew volunteered to go below to help keep up steam, one to work as fireman and one to pass coal. With the ship traveling alone, they were recalled to deck to resume lookout duty. Carraway reported, "A torpedo passed not more than six feet astern of our ship. A moment later, I sighted the track of a periscope and gave order to open fire. But the gun misfired and after several attempts to fire, both by electricity and percussion, I cleared the gun platform but for one member of the gun crew and myself. The gun was unloaded and the shell thrown over the side. When the gun was reloaded, the periscope was gone. We arrived at Reykjavik on 27 September."

Elsewhere, however, the news was all bad. The SS *Carlton*, which had narrowly escaped the torpedo that hit the *Christopher Newport*, ran out of luck and was struck by a torpedo amidships, below the waterline. The ship, carrying 50,000 barrels of fuel oil, tanks, and explosives, began to sink rapidly, and the master ordered the crew to abandon ship before the cargo of TNT exploded. Thirty-two crewmen and eleven naval armed guards took to the boats or rafts. Eighteen of the merchant crew and eight of the navy gun crew were picked up by German planes, and seventeen men in the #4 lifeboat made it to the Norwegian shore and were taken prisoner on 24 July. Prior to their being taken prisoners, on 13 July the *U-376* came alongside, and the commander offered medical aid, and gave them a compass, charts, position and course, and distance to the nearest land. He also gave them biscuits, cigarettes, water, and blankets.[15]

Two other members of the convoy almost made it to safety. The SS *Hoosier* and the Panamanian-flag *El Capitan* struggled to within 50 miles of the White Sea before they went down on 10 July. The *Hoosier* carried a crew of thirty-eight, an armed guard unit of twelve, plus nineteen survivors from the *John Witherspoon*. She was seriously damaged by bombers, but appeared capable of being towed to port. However, the towline had to be dropped because the *U-255* was closing in, and she was finished off by an escort.

Meanwhile, the SS *Samuel Chase* had been taking a beat-

ing from the air. Lieutenant (j.g.) John E. Sexton, USNR, reported her harrowing experience. The ship was so badly
damaged that the crew was ordered to abandon ship, thinking she was sinking. However, seeing her still afloat, the
crew and armed guard reboarded and held to course, finally
reaching Archangel on 11 July. Sexton reported watching
the *Peter Kerr* undergoing attack by seven torpedo planes
and sinking after three direct hits, her .30- and .50-cal machine guns firing to the end. Fortunately, only one man was
lost, thirty-seven crewmen and armed guards being picked
up by a Soviet ship and taken to Murmansk. Of the six
brand-new Liberties that had set out from Iceland with
PQ-17, only the *Samuel Chase* and the *Benjamin Harrison*
made it safely to port.[14]

The detailed voyage report of Lieutenant (j.g.) John E.
Sexton, Erdenheim, Pennsylvania, commanding officer of
armed guard unit #256, adds some details to previous reports: "The fire power of the convoy, including the one AA
British ship, was so ineffective that some German planes actually flew down the columns between ships." He added,
"The armament on the *Samuel Chase* consisted of a 4" 50 surface gun that was useless and never used, plus two .30-cal and
two .50-cal machine guns, with ball ammunition, which was
ineffective against armor of German planes. . . . Throughout
5 July, the air was filled with distress calls from a minimum
of eleven ships experiencing air and submarine attacks."

A radio log submitted by GM 3/c Robert H. Wolff, Key-
stone Heights, Florida, on communication between the
Samuel Chase and a British antiaircraft ship is as follows:

"AA Ship: Are you transmitting on R.D.F. If so, observe silence.

SS Chase: We are not transmitting. Can we accompany you?

AA Ship: If you are listening on R.D.F., can you hear
transmission?

SS Chase: What frequency?

AA Ship: 39 Meg.

SS Chase: Unable to listen on that wave. Where is base?

AA Ship: I am proceeding to make nearest point on coast of Novaya Zemlya before altering to southward. Suggest you do the same at utmost speed. *Tirpitz* and *Hipper* and six destroyers steering sixty from North Cape, twenty-two knots. What ship?

SS Chase: *Samuel Chase* Number 91. We can do twelve knots, can we accompany you?

AA Ship: My course and speed—102 degrees—14 knots.

SS Chase: Can you notify me when submarines are in vicinity?

AA Ship: Were you intercepted by subs or aircraft?

SS Chase: Both, can you give us your position?

AA Ship: My position—lat 75.40 north long 47.25 east dead reckoning. No reliable observation. Advise you to hide in some bay in Novaya Zemlya, but watch for uncharted rocks.

SS Chase: Had to go hard right to avoid AA Ship who swerved suddenly to starboard.

AA Ship: Decided to enter Matochkin Strait, western entrance lat. 72.01 north and I think you had better do the same. Course 150 true. Shall go right inside the strait and anchor. I think you should do the same.

SS Chase: Thank you.

End of Transmission."[15]

After being picked up and brought to Archangel, Commodore Dowding set out for Novaya Zemlya to locate the remnants of PQ-17. He brought back the *Benjamin Harrison, Silver Sword,* the damaged *Azerbaijan, Ironclad,* and the redoubtable *Troubadour* on 24 July. The last straggler, the *Winston-Salem,* arrived at Molotovsk on 28 July.

Of the thirty-three merchant ships that had left Iceland in PQ-17, three had turned back, thirteen, plus one rescue ship, had been sunk by aircraft, and ten were sunk by U-boats. Of the twenty-two American merchantmen carrying naval armed guards, fourteen were lost. Versus the twenty-four ships, totaling 143,977 tons, that were lost, German losses were only a handful of aircraft in over 200 sorties. The loss of cargo to PQ-17 was calamitous as well—3,350 vehicles, 430 tanks, 210 aircraft, and 99,316 tons of desperately needed war equipment and supplies.[16]

There is no accurate figure of total casualties available. The number of open boats and rafts on the Barents sea, after the demolishment of PQ-17, was over fifty. Captain S. B. Frankel, USN, reported 1,300 survivors were estimated to have reached Russia, including 500 from U.S. vessels. These numbers also included the U.S. Armed Guards aboard the merchantmen. The toll taken by exposure and frostbite was ghastly. Gangrene cost many survivors' limbs; one young American seaman lost both legs and all his fingers, except his right thumb and a couple of stubs on his left. Such mutilation was not uncommon, and the stench of gangrene in the hospital was vividly described by Radio Operator Smith of the *Alcoa Ranger.* He reported, "We had many men aboard on return with loss of both arms and some with loss of one and even some with loss of both legs." Some 400 American survivors were taken from the Kola Inlet to Scotland aboard the USS *Tuscaloosa* and several destroyers.[17]

The horrendous ordeal of PQ-17 shocked the British Admiralty, and all convoys to Russia were suspended for several months until early darkness could provide some protection. The suspension of convoys was made over the bitter objection of Josef Stalin, who considered the action a deliberate betrayal. Stalin refused to believe that there had been thirty-three ships in PQ-17; there were, he said, "No more than fifteen." In quite obvious reprisal, he soon ordered the British Naval Hospital at Varenga to close and the personnel to return home.[18]

Churchill was aghast at such action and wrote, "I should be glad if you would look into the matter yourself. Terrible cases of mutilation through frostbite are now arriving back here, and I have to consider constantly the morale of merchant seamen who have hitherto gone so willingly to man the merchant ships to Russia. The British hospital unit was sent simply to help, and implied no reflection on Russian arrangements under the pressure of air bombardment, etc. It is hard on men in a hospital not to have nurses who speak their own language. At any rate, I hope you will give me some solid reason which I can give should the matter be raised in Parliament, as it very likely will be."[19]

His request was brushed off rudely in a reply from V. M. Molotov, who referred only to ". . . the real state of affairs, particularly in regard to certain irregularities in the actions of respective British authorities."

In writing about the fate of PQ-17 in his epic account of the Second World War, Churchill referred to the decision of Admiral Pound to order the withdrawal of the cruiser escort of the convoy. He wrote, "If the *Tirpitz* and her consorts were approaching the escort cruisers and the convoy, it was right to order the cruisers to withdraw, as otherwise they would have been a useless sacrifice, and the best hope of the merchant ships lay in dispersal." He then speculated, "Admiral Pound would probably not have sent such vehement orders, if only our own British warships had been concerned. But the idea that our first large joint Anglo-American operation under British command should involve the destruction of two United States cruisers as well as our own may well have disturbed the poise with which he was accustomed to deal with such heart-shaking decisions."[20]

Churchill added, sometime after, in the light of later knowledge, that "The decision to scatter was precipitate, and the destroyer withdrawal was certainly a mistake. All risks should have been taken in defence of the merchant ships."

Rear Admiral W. D. Wright, USN, aboard the USS *Wichita,* was bitter about the loss of the convoy and blamed the British. After the arrival of the escort cruisers in Scapa Flow following withdrawal, Admiral Sir John Tovey boarded the *Wichita,* and with all hands at their stations, Admiral Tovey made a public apology for the fate of the merchant seamen in the abandoned convoy.[21]

As it is impossible to put a monetary value on the cost of lives, ships, and cargoes lost in PQ-17, a mere listing of ships lost gives no indication of the human suffering or the grisly manner in which hundreds of men perished, in flaming oil, icy water, or of exposure in open boats or rafts, as well as those who had to spend the rest of their lives with one or more of their limbs missing. Nor does it portray the harrowing conditions of constant stress and complete exhaustion under which they fought in their gallant efforts to get their cargoes through. Churchill wrote that the ordeal of Convoy PQ-17 was ". . . one of the most melancholy naval episodes in the whole of the war." Truer words have never been spoken.[22]

Much has been written about the tragedy of PQ-17, but perhaps the best commentary on it was by Lieutenant (j.g.) John E. Sexton, USNR, of the *Samuel Chase.* "Some events remain with us forever. I don't think I will ever forget the moment we were told to scatter. When we saw the signal from the Commodore and checked the signal book for its meaning, the captain and other officers on the bridge could not believe it. How could they desert us? It was a feeling of utter hopelessness. 'Scatter,' but where, what course, return to the west or press on eastward? We had been at GQ for almost 24 hours, and it took some doing to collect ourselves. I have also heard about the [bitter] feelings of the men on the escort vessels."

Sexton was awarded a Medal of Commendation for his action, and the naval armed guard gun crew was honored for devotion to duty and for courage in the face of enemy fire.

Captain Reinhart Reche, CO of the *U-255* later wrote, "A surplus of intelligence induced the Admiralty in London to withdraw the covering forces too early which led to the sinking of twenty-four ships, with no U-boats lost."[23]

Two of the battered survivors of PQ-17 that reached Archangel were lost soon after. The SS *Silver Sword* was torpedoed by the *U-255* on the return trip in QP-14 and was sunk by an escort in the Greenland Sea on 20 September

1942; the SS *Benjamin Harrison* was torpedoed off Casablanca while in a New York–North Africa convoy. Ironically, the coup de grace was delivered by the *USS Rowan,* one of the destroyer-covering force of PQ-17; the *Rowan* was also lost a short time later. The *Silver Sword* was carrying fifteen survivors of the SS *Honomu* and *Peter Kerr* when she was lost.

CHAPTER THIRTEEN
STRANDED IN RUSSIA:
THE FORGOTTEN CONVOY

Murmansk is a bleak place . . . reception as cold as the weather.
—Nicholas Montserrat, *The Cruel Sea*

Murmansk was indeed a bleak place, and life was not made any more attractive to the armed guards and their merchant shipmates by the heavy and continuous German air raids. Murmansk lies above the Arctic Circle, only 1,400 miles from the North Pole, and besides subzero cold it offers a six-week-long polar night. Conversely, at the height of summer, the midnight sun shines dimly through the night, low in the sky. Located on the Kola Gulf of the Barents Sea, Murmansk became the major port for delivery of lend-lease supplies, then transported by rail to the fronts to the south. Thanks to the moderating influence of the Gulf Stream, it is ice-free. Archangel, on the White Sea, was the second-most important port for delivery of war supplies, but Dvina Gulf would freeze over making it difficult to reach, so a new deep-water port was built at Molotovsk, and many ships on the Murmansk run would unload there. Much farther from German air bases, Archangel and Molotovsk did not take the battering that Murmansk underwent from enemy air attack.

When the weary and often badly injured or frost-bitten convoy survivors finally made it to port, they might have justifiably felt that they would be welcomed, along with the precious cargo they carried. However, they soon found that such was not the case. Gunner's Mate John Sheridan remembers his experience: ". . . Upon arrival in Murmansk, a Soviet officer came aboard and talked to the captain and the AG officer. He gave them a set of orders for the Americans.

When posted, Sheridan says that he and his mates wondered if this was a friendly nation. They quickly learned; there were only two places Americans could go, everything else was out of bounds. The two were the International Club and the Intourist Hotel. There was to be no contact with women, they were to speak only to hotel employees. The Americans were to be back on their ships by 10:00 P.M.; anyone on shore after that would be arrested and out of their ship's jurisdiction. No drunkenness was to be tolerated. There was to be no trade with civilians; it was a serious offense and could mean a jail term. If anyone got into trouble ashore, their AG officer could not help them.

As Sheridan's crew put it, "God, what a place this is!" It didn't improve as time went by. At the Intourist Hotel an upstairs room was supposed to be a restaurant for seamen from various ships, but only tea, vodka, and a hunk of black bread was available. They found that a Russian soldier on guard at their ship spoke some English, and when no one was observing, he delighted in smoking an American cigarette and talking until others showed up. He would never accept a pack of cigarettes, as he said he would be searched upon return from duty and it would be a serious offense.

Sheridan and the crew of the SS *Owen Wister* were lucky, they were only there three weeks the first time, but other ships had long delays unloading and getting away.[1]

Ed Quin served as a radioman aboard the Liberty SS *Henry Villard,* which arrived in Archangel in 1944. His convoy was one of the lucky ones; it never lost a ship, although it had a big scare out of Norway when the German *Scharnhorst* came out, guns blazing. Radio silence of the convoy was abruptly broken—"Disperse!" Quin reports: "The convoy had British corvettes as escort to the tip of Bear Island, when it met Soviet escorts, but communications left much to be desired. The Soviets never did tell us the depth of the Dvina River outside of Archangel, so we promptly went aground at the mouth of the river. It was not until the ship was unloaded that it popped up out of the ice and we backed down the river. We spent three months in Archangel and lived at the Intourist Hotel. There was no heat, and while the hotel had an excellent dining room, there was no food. We were told, "Don't go into town, or don't go anywhere without your guide, but our favorite pastime was to split up as soon as we got outside, and he couldn't follow everybody. We would go into the black market and barter or sell everything except the clothes on our backs. The guide, an elderly man, had lived for some years in New York City and had worked as a photographer; he would forget anything for Lucky Strikes.

"The weather was 40° below, and the stevedores worked twelve hours straight with only one bowl of borscht all day. Many of them were crippled war vets, minus a hand or an arm. There were also some husky women unloading cargo.

"We had a glimpse of Soviet justice, fast and final. As the cargo in crates was being unloaded, a net gave way and two crates crashed on the dock, splitting open. Inside were "long-johns." The spilled goods were quickly picked up and put back in crates and lids nailed down. At the end of the shift the workers were lined up at the end of the dock, and the Soviet Army guards checked them physically. One man was found to have stuffed a pair of long-johns inside his jacket. He was quickly marched to the end of the dock and shot immediately in front of everybody, including us.

"There was one movie house in town, with no heat and no seats, but it was warmer than anyplace else as bodies warmed it up a trifle."[2]

Eugene D. Meadows, at eighteen, was fresh out of convoy signal school when he was assigned to the SS *Henry Wynkoop* and found himself in Murmansk. "Upon arrival we were given a list of restrictions from the Russians, to abide by while we were in port. Our lieutenant advised us that if we got into trouble we were strictly on our own because the Navy would be unable to help us. Among these restrictions were that we could not have anything to do with Russian women nor could we do any trading with the Russian people. We saw no attractive women, so that was no problem, but we did want to bring some mementos back with us so we heard we could trade candy and cigarettes for knives, made from metal of German aircraft shot down over Murmansk. So, a shipmate and I left the ship one evening with pockets stuffed with candy bars and cigarettes. A boy about 14 indicated he had some knives, but as he was about to give them to us he was grabbed by two men with guns. They beat him up and told us we were under arrest. During that walk I could think of nothing else but having to spend the rest of my life in the Siberian salt mines. However, just before we got to the police station, they stopped and searched us and confiscated all our candy and cigarettes and ordered us to go. To this day I wonder what would really have happened to us if those Russian policemen had not become greedy."[3]

Art MacLaren, Mesa, Arizona, was a cadet/midshipman when he was assigned to the SS *Thomas Hartley* for her second trip to Russia. When he saw the Cyrillic marking on the cargo, he had no doubts as to where they were going. The rousing film, "Action in the North Atlantic," starring Humphrey Bogart, was popular at the time and did nothing to reduce concern. However, as the *Scharnhorst* had been sunk on the previous convoy, they traveled along the Norwegian coast route rather than go via Iceland. They were observed often by enemy planes, but did not sustain any serious attacks. He adds, "During our trip north we daily became heavier as ice formed and piled up until the decks were filled to the top of the hatches, ice was in the rigging, and the entire convoy took on an eerie appearance. Airplanes, tanks, and other deck cargo blended into a fantasy land. On arrival, steam was turned on deck to assist in loosening the ice, and the Russians brought a considerable number of people on board to clear the ice the old-fashioned way, by chipping. There were several members of the crew who professed to be of Communist-bent and were ecstatic at the prospect of being in Russia. Their first shock was to find they were denied shore leave as the Commissar stated the Russians did not want any 'opportunists' around." Other veterans of the run have confirmed that Communist agitators made no converts among those who were on the Murmansk run.

MacLaren added that Murmansk was so desolate that one

would expect that the bars would do a land-office business, but the limited funds allowed each member of the crew and the potency of the 200-proof vodka, plus the difficulty of navigating back to the ship in 25-below weather, put a decided chill on the social scene.[4]

World War I had its "Lost Battalion" in the Argonne Forest; World War II had its "Forgotten Convoy," seemingly lost in North Russian ports for up to eight months in 1943. The "Forgotten Convoy" is another strange story of the Murmansk run, certainly never to be forgotten by any of the members of the naval armed guard or their merchant marine shipmates who were aboard any of the eight ships involved. Certain memories are unprintable, but the general feeling was very well summed up in a few lines from a poem written by an AG in Murmansk after several months:

> In this forlorn place, for the best part of a year
>   Yet no sign of departure seems to draw near.
> Are we forgotten? Don't they know we exist?
>   Or are we marked "missing" in the casualty list?
> Why can't we leave here? Doesn't anyone know?
>   Can't hold out much longer, our stores have run low.
> Where is that damned convoy, why doesn't it come?
>   Let someone relieve us, so we can go home!

The eight ships that made up the Forgotten Convoy were the steamships *Artigas, Beaconhill, Bering, City of Omaha, Israel Putnam, Francis Scott Key, Mobile City,* and the *Thomas Hartley.* The tanker *Beaconhill* departed New York on 4 January 1943 and did not return until 3 December, but even so it beat the *Israel Putnam,* which did not get back until after Christmas. The *Thomas Hartley* also left New York in January and soon had a foretaste of what was to come. AG gunner Hilary Makowski of Pittsburgh describes the trip over. "We left New York for Scotland in a convoy of about thirty ships. The weather seemed pretty rough, compared with Three Rivers in Pittsburgh, but I thought it was supposed to be that way. Crossing the Atlantic was a battle, it took 16 days on a zig-zag course. At night star-shells would light the sky. A German sub appeared in the middle of the convoy, and was visible, but I couldn't shoot the 5-inch 51 since, in line with the sub, was a tanker and the AG officer said to hold. It was a rough trip, with ships being sunk all around us.

"On 15 February after regrouping in Scotland we set sail for Murmansk. The weather was terrible. Each day as we sailed, the waves were higher than the masts, when we were on top of a wave all you could see of the ships on your port or starboard sides was about a foot of their masts, and when we were in the pits, all they could see of us was the same. Depth charges were dropped constantly by the destroyers and cruisers protecting us. One of our ships was damaged in an air raid."[5]

On 26 February the main convoy divided, one group going to Murmansk, the other headed for Archangel. An AG on the tanker *Beaconhill* reported that the White Sea was frozen solid and was littered with seals and their pups. The convoy was met by a Russian icebreaker that led the ships to Molotovsk, the deep seaport for Archangel, about 30 miles to the west. Port facilities were still being built at time of arrival and it took ten days to unload the *Beaconhill,* following which it was ordered to carry a cargo of fuel oil to Murmansk. The *Beaconhill* then began a shuttle service of eight months in which it gained the name "Murmansk Ferry Boat." Murmansk was bombed almost constantly, but because of the added distance, Molotovsk was hit infrequently and was much safer for tankers. After the ice broke in the Dvina River, tankers were sent to Archangel, and Molotovsk was used for other vessels.[6]

The SS *Thomas Hartley* had a hard time of it in Murmansk; it was one air raid after another, the record showing 169 in a ninety-day period. John Mitchell, a gunner from Jeanette, Pennsylvania, kept a diary of the entire trip, excerpts of which reflect the action and complete exhaustion of the navy gun crew as a result of the attacks, which continued days on end and for hours at a time:

"2 March—We were the first ship to sail from the USA to

Murmansk that arrived safely with PT boats on our deck. Forty others were sunk or damaged beyond repair.

"3 March—Two air raids, but weather not good, so they were dropping incendiaries and one dropped into one of our life boats; smothered it before it burned the boat up.

"5 March—All quiet, snow storm.

"6 March—Our first big attack at the docks. They came in waves and gave us Hell. Started at 7:00 P.M. and ended at 9:00 P.M. Worse than 25 February because it was at night and there was nothing we could do. Hit an English ship and the Arctic Hotel, fires all over Murmansk. Hit ammo dump 100 yards from our ship.

"7 March—It is snowing and also my birthday, but didn't seem like any I had before.

"8 March—Skies full of hell-dropping planes. They kept coming over steady for seven hours, except for 32 minutes. All so damn tired we slept with our helmets and clothes on. What a night.

"9 March—Nearly all cargo discharged. No raids, bad weather. Thank God.

"10 March—At noon nine dive-bombers gave us plenty to think about, and they sure can give a man plenty to think about.

"11 March—First air raid around 9:30 A.M., got another plane. They kept us going all the rest of the day and all night till 6: A.M. the next morning.

"14 March—More raids, shot down three. We are so tired of staying up night and day. Almost discharged, starting to take on chrome ore for ballast.

"16 March—Two raids, bombed the docks right at our ship, left a hole 20 feet around and plenty deep, air full of debris. Flying bridge hit with pieces of logs.

"21 March—No planes, skies overcast with snow and clouds.

"25 March—Bad news, we have to go back into docks to load more chrome ore.

"26 March—Back in the hell-hole at same berth. If we stay here a week without being hit and sunk at dock we will be damn lucky. Sleeping with clothes and helmets on ready for battle station at any time.

"30 March—Away from docks, planes still try to get us but we are always ready for them and have more of a chance here. Have 17 hours of daylight now, Northern Lights beautiful to see.

"2 April—Waiting for convoy to come in so we can start home. Big snowstorm so no raids. Thank God for this weather.

"3 April—Beautiful and sky full of planes coming after us as no more ships at dock. Started at 8:30 P.M. and kept it up till 2:00 A.M. plus dropping floating mines into the river. Ship trembled from stem to stern.

"4 April—Back again, one of the floating mines hit the *Artigas* and they are towing her in to patch up the hole in her hull. Really had two close ones, one bomb hit ten feet off our port beam and one off the stern. Blew all the glass out of the gauge indicators in the engine room, knocked all lights out and men down, even turned the deck plates and bowed them. Kept coming till 1:25 A.M.

"5 April 1943—Well we had so many raids today I don't see how we can go on much longer without sleep or food. Captain asked for a new anchorage where it isn't so hot with dive-bombers.

"7 April—New anchorage so everyone got a bit of rest. Thank God.

"12 April—Just one month ago we were catching Hell at the docks. Now we are sure getting low on food, no fruit, butter all spoiled, eggs not fit to eat. Enough of canned milk for two weeks, but worst of all is that our ammo is almost gone and no place to get anything at all.

"28 April—Arrived Molotovsk, nice here because jerries don't bomb here as it is too far.

"4 July—First Christmas I ever had on the 4th of July for got a package, chewing gum and shaving cream from home.

"11 July—Second Christmas, 41 letters from home, January 1–April 28.

"22 July—Food very low, only one fair meal in five days.

"30 October—We are leaving for Murmansk tomorrow and that is what we have been waiting for for such a long time. Homeward Bound!

"3 November—Picked up our escort, we are in "coffin corner." Can make it back by 15 December if all goes well.

"15 December—Sixty-five miles out of New York. A long trip but over now, the Statute of Liberty will look awfully good to us."[7]

Hilary Makowski also served on the *Thomas Hartley* as gunner and vividly recalls the air raids and the 300 General Alarms. He reports that the navy gun crew and the merchant marines assisted in unloading the ship so it could get away from the dock. "We received a Letter of Commendation, but Hell, we just wanted to move out to a better location in the Kola River. However, we discovered quickly that it was just as bad. It was in 'Stuka Bend,' and every time we turned around we had a Stuka diving at us.

"Somebody had a brainstorm and decided to send us down to the White Sea, to Molotovsk. The move was said to be for our safety, but they forgot to send us any edibles, and we almost starved. I only had a 32-inch waist before, but I had so much belt left over that I had to tie a knot in it. We stayed in Molotovsk for five months, wondering what was going on. It was an awful bore, we all took turns arguing or fighting with each other. We made baseballs out of our sox, gloves from the asbestos gloves we used for our 20mm gun barrels, baseball bats were turned in the engine room from the 4 × 4s that we found on the docks.

"The Russians used convicts to unload ships. These people were so skinny from lack of food that it is a wonder they could do anything at all; they only got a piece of black bread and about four ounces of potato soup, once a day. We would give them left-overs from our meals when we had food, and they would stuff anything we gave them in their coat pockets including mashed potatoes. While in Molotovsk we had garbage trucks haul away the trash and garbage. One day a prisoner stepped out of line and grabbed a hand-ful of coffee grounds and jammed them into his mouth. For

Certificate of the "Forgotten Convoy of North Russia." (Courtesy of several members of the convoy)

that received a bayonet in the stomach. One ex-soldier told me that he got three–five years for getting drunk and throwing a stone through a window."

The only bright spot of his stay in Russia was one day when Makowski was in the Intourist dining room. "A guy from the *Francis Scott Key* came in and hollered, 'Is there anybody here from Pittsburgh?' I hollered back 'Hey, Hunky!', which was what we called him back home. He lived about three blocks from me in Pittsburgh."

He adds, "When we finally reached the Clyde River, tugs tied up and sent up sides of beef and a lot of other food. We were so close to starving that the doctors held us in quarantine, checked us out, and gave us pills to take before we ate, so that we would not vomit the food; it was too rich for our stomachs as we had eaten so poorly for six months . . . We had crossed the Arctic Circle on 27 February 1943 outbound, and did not get back to the States until the end of November—truly the Forgotten Convoy."[8]

Various ships of the Forgotten Convoy had other problems, but the food problem was universal. Max Jones, Apex, North Carolina, said, "We had fried Spam for breakfast, cold Spam for lunch, and Spam steak for dinner," but he added that "we were better off than the inhabitants of Molotovsk. They lived in a community building, one family to a room, and all cooked off the same stove, grass soup was a regular item in their diet. There was a prison nearby and the prisoners were used to unload ships; they would sneak into our quarters anytime they could searching for cigarette butts or any scrap of food." Jones was a navy gunner aboard the *Israel Putnam*, which broke its propeller in the ice and sat in dry dock for a lengthy period for repairs.[9] The SS *Artigas* was damaged by a bomb but was lucky. She had originally been scheduled to go to Russia in disastrous Convoy PQ-17, but drew 29 feet and had to be diverted to Scotland to unload some cargo, as the maximum draft in Soviet ports was 25 feet. Bob Layman of Augusta, Maine, served in the *City of Omaha* and reported that after forty-plus years he still dislikes anything Russian. However, he and the other NAGs of the Forgotten Convoy are proud of the certificate they received, acknowledging each as a member of the "Society of the Forgotten Convoy of North Russia, 64°35′N, 39°50′S." The certificate, signed by Commander S. B. Frankel, Assistant U.S. Naval Attaché, Archangel-Murmansk U.S.S.R. (later Rear Admiral) reads: ". . . did suffer—months confinement in North Russia, that he did shiver through the Arctic winter, and bask in the rays of the Midnight Sun . . ." The hand-drawn certificate listed the names of all ships of the Forgotten Convoy and had a slogan in the form of a scroll, "LEST WE FORGET." No one in that convoy ever will.[10]

There were a number of official reasons given for the long stay in Russia, including a shortage of escort vessels for the return voyage, the desire of naval authorities to wait until later in the year when darkness would provide more cover, and others, but it is still a question.

All veterans of the Murmansk run are in agreement that Russia was a grim and cheerless place, and nothing could be worse than being there at Christmas time. Signalman C. A. "Pete" Burke reports that spirits were even lower than usual as his crew sat around on Christmas Eve, until the subject of a Christmas party was discussed. Suggestions flew and were discarded; trees were available, but to cut one would immediately land the cutter in jail and incite an international incident. However, ideas were put into action, and a tree was produced as beautiful as any bunch of sailors could produce on Christmas Eve in Murmansk. "Our tree didn't have the scent of pine or spruce because it was the handle of a large deck swab. The carpenter drilled holes in it, so wires and coathangers immediately turned into branches. The skeleton tree was mounted and placed in the middle of the mess table, where strange ornaments began to pile up in preparation for the formal trimming. Yellow papers, once wrapped around oranges became Christmas balls, tin foil from the galley became tinsel, and the ship's machinist cut out a brass star for the top of the tree. Other improvised ornaments grew rapidly; our spirits soared and by 11:00 P.M. we were ready to put it all together.

"Security watch was at a minimum in port, so most of the gun crew were able to participate. The captain chipped in with a bottle of bourbon and one blended whisky, which went into a large 'punchbowl', a galley pot, along with cans of grapefruit juice, orange juice and pineapple juice,—plus a gallon of local moonshine, and this kept the party going until the tree was finally trimmed.

"We knew it was made of a mop handle and some wire, it was trimmed with bits of paper and junk, and it lacked the aroma of a real yuletide tree . . . but it was beautiful." [11]

CHAPTER FOURTEEN
BATTLE OF THE ATLANTIC

*The only thing that really frightened
me during the war was the U-boat peril
. . . the Admiralty shared these fears.*
—Winston S. Churchill

Churchill's fears were well-founded, for once again
Great Britain was brought to the verge of defeat by
German underseas warfare. Providentially, once
more Germany succeeded in "snatching defeat
from the jaws of victory." Admiral Karl Dönitz, "evil genius"
to some, but masterful tactician even to his adversaries, had
been denied the tools to do the job by an obtuse German
Naval High Command and a fanatical Adolph Hitler. Ignoring the lessons of how close U-boat warfare had come to
bringing victory in World War I, and obsessed by the glamor
of his small but deadly surface fleet, Hitler had given short
shrift to the requests of the U-boat service. It ranked a poor
fourth in priority to the army, *Luftwaffe,* and the new surface fleet of which he was so proud. Germany's battleships
and "pocket battleships" were incredibly powerful, coldly
beautiful machines of war, a masterwork of naval engineering, but in the end they were basically to prove a massive
waste of time, material and manpower.[2]

After the U.S. entry into the war, American merchant
ships and their NAG gun crews took a tremendous pounding
from *Luftwaffe* attacks on the North Russian run and in the
Mediterranean, but in the Battle of the Atlantic, the longest
struggle of the war, U-boat wolfpacks were their deadliest
foe. And it was the solitary U-boat, prowling the Seven Seas,
that was the principal cause of the loss of hundreds of vessels and lives in far-flung waters, along the U.S. East Coast,
Gulf of Mexico, the Caribbean, South Atlantic, Indian Ocean,
Arabian Sea, and elsewhere. According to a report prepared

for the Navy Department, about eight times as many merchant vessels were sunk by submarines as by aircraft.[3]

Innovator and director of the strategy of German underseas warfare was Admiral Karl Dönitz. Following traditional training in surface ships of the German Navy before WW I, he was assigned as a junior officer on the *U-39* and later given command of his own submarine, the *U-68*. It sank during a dive, and Dönitz and most of his crew were rescued by a British ship and became prisoners of war. During his imprisonment Dönitz developed the original idea of "wolf-packs," a strategy of coordinated attack by groups of U-boats to overcome the defenses of an escorted convoy. In World War II the new tactic soon justified his firm conviction that it would prove a decisive factor in a war at sea in the future.

Following release from the British POW camps, he returned home and made a seemingly surprising decision to remain in service in the tiny 15,000-man navy allowed Germany under terms of the Versailles Treaty. After service in torpedo boats, he was transferred into covert planning for a new submarine force, and in 1935 was given command of submarine operations by Adolph Hitler, following Great Britain's agreement to permit Germany to build a limited number of small submarines. At the time the German Naval High Command was proceeding full speed ahead with the development of Hitler's prized new surface fleet. Dönitz disagreed completely with the emphasis on surface vessels, believing the country's leaders had learned nothing from the experience of WW I, but his repeated requests for more U-boats were summarily dismissed.

Upon the outbreak of war in September 1939, the U-boat service possessed a total of forty-six boats ready for action, of which only twenty-two were suitable for service in the Atlantic. Dönitz later wrote in his memoirs, "A continentally minded government and High Command [proved] incapable of grasping the idea that U-boats could decide the issue of war."[4] In 1940 only two U-boats per month were being produced, later increased to six per month. Even so, their rate of success was so high that the British could not understand why a major expansion of production of U-boats did not quickly occur; Churchill expected it and later wrote, "The U-boat peril was our worst enemy. It would have been wise for the Germans to stake all on it."[5]

Dönitz had many other problems; at first "at least 30%" of torpedoes did not detonate, or detonated at the wrong place, which was eventually traced to a faulty magnetic head and corrected. Goering's *Luftwaffe* refused to cooperate in providing aerial reconnaissance until forced to do so. For a time U-boat availability actually declined, as a number of boats were diverted to Norway by Hitler's order, and high hull numbers assigned to newly built U-boats were used to conceal weakness. Dönitz kept asking for more boats—he believed that 100 U-boats could do more damage than all the battlecruisers ever built—but he recommended 300 boats "for successful operations." As usual, he was ignored by the Naval High Command.[6]

In 1939 Dönitz told Hitler that production of U-boats under current low priority could not even cover anticipated losses, but he could not convince him to upgrade his priorities.

While Germany was making its to-be-fatal mistakes, the British Admiralty could not be accorded much higher marks for judgment. Incredibly, also ignoring the lessons of WW I learned at such high cost, British officialdom again pooh-poohed the threat of submarine warfare. They placed complete faith in ASDIC, a revolutionary range-finding device that reportedly could perform miracles. It could not only detect a submerged submarine, but could reveal its position. A transmitter would send out impulses on a selected bearing, a receiver would pick up the impulses when they struck an object, and they were then reflected. ASDIC had a "ping" that clearly identified itself to listeners, operators, and submarines alike. Its main drawback at the time was its inability to pick up a surfaced submarine, and it had other "bugs" that were ultimately corrected, and it became increasingly effective and feared by the enemy as the war progressed. However, taking advantage of its early faults, Dönitz countered by instructing U-boats to attack at night on the surface, at which they became highly successful. With its newly developed "all-seeing underwater eye" and its overwhelming superiority in surface forces, plus its huge merchant marine, Britain felt that there would be no need for a convoy system nor, naturally, any need for convoy escorts. So, Britain entered the war without basic protection for its merchant fleet and learned a hard lesson, at very high cost, once again.

The Battle of the Atlantic, which lasted from September 1939 to May 1945, was to be the longest and costliest battle of the war in terms of lives lost, shipping damaged or sunk, and vital cargoes lost. It was marked by the highest heroism and sacrifice on the part of the men engaged, and by scientific genius in the development of new and esoteric weaponry on both sides, which became a key element in a "chess-match" of worldwide scope. Move and countermove would gain some temporary advantage for one side or the other, to be negated or overcome by even more advanced technology and strategy on the part of the opponent. It was a battle in which intelligence, developed by faceless behind-the-scenes technicians, played a crucial role and was largely responsible for ultimate success in achieving victory. The Battle of the Atlantic was perceived clearly by both Britain's "Former Naval Person" (Churchill) and submarine-warfare genius Dönitz as being the key to the winning of the war.

Churchill wrote later, "The Battle of the Atlantic was the dominating factor all through the war, never for one moment could we forget that everything happening elsewhere on land, at sea, or in the air depended ultimately on its outcome."[7]

In ignoring the critical lesson of WW I, that shipping losses had been cut by 80 percent by the belated adoption of a convoy system, the Admiralty watched shipping losses skyrocket as vessels were forced to travel alone; in one early month forty-one merchant ships were sunk. It was not until 1943 that a really effective system of convoying was established, but the battle had nearly been lost. In 1942 Dönitz be-

Grand Admiral Karl Dönitz with officers and men of the Kriegsmarine. (National Archives)

lieved that for offensive operations against the main enemy
(Britain), Germany had only one effective weapon—the
U-boat, adding that after three and one-half years Germany
had brought Britain to the verge of defeat in the Battle of the
Atlantic with only half the number of U-boats he had always
demanded. The undersea war also had some unexpected results in far-distant Allied strategy. "Operation Torch," the invasion of North Africa, was thrown so far off schedule that
the invasion had to be postponed a number of times.[8]

At an early stage of the war, Dönitz had hopes for assistance from the Italian Navy in pushing his newly developed
wolfpack tactics, and twenty-seven Italian submarines actually came to Bordeaux. However, it was soon found that the
results did not match his hoped-for potential; Italian reconnaissance reports were often erroneous, and the Italian subs
frequently failed to show up for general attacks. Moreover,
Italian submarines were poorly designed, with a long, high

conning tower that was conspicuous in appearance compared with the low silhouette of U-boats. With an eye apparently for comfort rather than battle-effectiveness, the
conning towers were enclosed, protecting crew from the
elements, but hindering operations. Dönitz soon brought
Italian "cooperation" to an end, with the dry observation
that Italian submarines did better operating alone than in
groups.[9]

The long-drawn-out Battle of the Atlantic was not only a
struggle between surface ships, submarines, and aircraft,
with floating mines or fixed minefields as additional hazards; it was a constant battle of wits. Early on, Germany developed magnetic mines, very successful for some time; the
British countered with "degaussing," wiping out a ship's
magnetism, and throughout the war each side continued to
develop sophisticated tools of warfare that had to be overcome by its opponent. However, the unknown and unrecognized code-breakers were key players in the game of wits,
and the battle was fought fiercely in the code rooms of
Germany's *B-Dienst* (observation service) and Britains's
Bletchley Park cryptanalysis laboratories. As early as 1930,
B-Dienst began cracking British naval codes and could read
naval traffic. Many in the U.S. who lived during the war will
remember wartime posters warning, "Loose Lips Sink
Ships!" and similar slogans. *B-Dienst* did not have to rely on
loose lips; by intercepting British, and later American, communications, it could forecast the origin, departure, and
route of convoys, as well as track the location of ships traveling alone. It was a tremendous advantage and resulted in a
horrendous loss of vital shipping. At that time Great Britain
could not penetrate the highly sophisticated and complicated German codes. Nevertheless, working from a carefully
planned program, Britain first captured a German weather
ship, with its super-secret Enigma coding machine and code
books. Again, with specific aim in mind, it succeeded in forcing a submarine, the *U-110,* to the surface and captured the
Enigma machine and highly classified U-boat code books
before the submarine sank. No announcement was ever

made of these events to preclude German knowledge of the loss of such vital secrets; it was to be presumed that the *U-110,* like many others, had been lost with all hands when it failed to report to headquarters. With such information and equipment on hand, the British cryptanalysis center at Bletchley Park was soon able to retaliate by intercepting and deciphering German submarine communications.[10]

This coup was one of the most significant developments of the Battle of the Atlantic. Knowing the location of individual U-boats and wolfpacks lying in wait for convoys, British Special Intelligence was able to change the course of the convoys and divert them around the U-boats, leading to a serious drop in tonnage sunk. Dönitz countered by throwing more submarines into the Atlantic, in patrol lines to serve as spotters and alert other U-boats when a convoy was sighted. Dönitz began to suspect that his communications were being intercepted, but was assured by the High Command that such was "out of the question," the codes being far too complicated to be susceptible, so he continued to send communications on convoys to his wolfpacks. Even though German codes were changed regularly, with their Enigmas the British soon broke the new codes. Timeliness was of the essence, otherwise the messages would have been as outdated as a week-old newspaper. British success was eventually to lead to disaster for Dönitz and his U-boats, but long before disaster struck, from July to October 1941, the German U-boat force enjoyed such a degree of success that it was termed the "Happy Time"; in three months U-boats sank one million tons of shipping. Six U-boats averaged 9,000 tons per day, the highest success rate of the war, but the end was in sight. The loss of Germany's three top U-boat aces, Kretschmer, Prien, and Schepke, in early 1941 marked the end of "Happy Time," but by the end of the year, even with evasive routing of convoys, the loss rate of Allied shipping exceeded seven million tons.

Experienced U-boat commanders were not caught napping by chance; being able to listen in on the heavy "chatter" between U-boats and their frequent reports to Admiral

The North Atlantic in a good mood. (National Archives)

U-boats while surfaced charging their batteries, the British were able to almost fix the exact position of the individual boats and direct convoy escorts or aircraft to the scene, catching them unaware. The development of "Huff-Duff," (High Frequency Direction Finding) was a major breakthrough in convoy defense, as was the increasing number of escorts, including "baby flattops" and long-range Liberator bombers. This serious and increasing problem led Dönitz to develop a mechanism whereby U-boats could charge their batteries while submerged and avoid the danger of being attacked on surface. The device, called "Schnorkel," was a scientific achievement, but it was so long being developed and installed that most U-boats still had to rely on charging batteries on the surface; Schnorkels did not get into service until early 1944, after a heavy loss of U-boats.

While the chances of survival for navy and merchant

crews aboard torpedoed munitions carriers were virtually nil, survival being invariably miraculous, those aboard standard merchant ships often went through terrible ordeals. Part of Convoy ON-166, the SS *Jonathan Sturges,* returning in ballast, was struck without warning on 23 February 1943. Ensign G. B. Watkins, USNR, in command of the AG crew, reported that en route outbound the rudder had jammed and the ship was unable to turn to port. After being corrected, the *Sturges* caught up with the convoy and ultimately made Liverpool after shipping so much water in a violent storm that shells were covered with water in one magazine and almost covered in another. On the return voyage her luck ran out, and she again became a straggler. A survivor's statement contained in a navy memorandum for file dated 7 April 1943 stated that she was struck by two torpedoes almost simultaneously in #1 and #2 holds, and the ship began to sink rapidly, apparently having broken her back. The ship was immediately abandoned upon order of her master, and all survivors were taken aboard two serviceable lifeboats, nineteen in one and seventeen in the other. After being afloat for three days, one met up with a lifeboat from the *Madoera* with only three survivors aboard, so the load was evened up. Those survivors were picked up by the USS *Belknap* and landed at Argentia, Newfoundland, on 14 March 1943. The other boat, carrying the master, was last seen steering a southwest course. When the boat was picked up forty-one days later, only five men of the original seventeen were still alive—three AGs and two merchant seamen. Over forty years later the three navy survivors had an emotional meeting at an armed guard reunion.[11]

The convoy itself had sustained heavy losses; of the forty-six ships in the convoy, fourteen were sunk.

It was into this maelstrom of merciless warfare, plot, and counterplot, that the ill-trained, poorly armed, and inexperienced recruits of the naval armed guard service were sent into action in the early days of U.S. participation in the war. While the global chess match was going on far away, they stood watches, manned their guns, and frequently never saw the enemy that hit them. The first voyage of many was also their last, and many others became survivors their first day at sea, their ships being sunk just off New York harbor. At the Brooklyn Armed Guard Center recruits met "veterans" who may have sailed that morning. All were eager to hear the "real story" of what it was like, and none of the tales they heard were conducive to peace of mind or an expectation of great longevity, unfortunately often all too true. It was not only U-boats that posed peril; the weather in the North Atlantic was usually bad and often worse. Winds howled night and day, huge waves crashed over the bow, lookouts and gunners were drenched by cold rain or stung by sleet, and ships rolled and pitched wildly, making it almost impossible to eat or rest. Visibility was often at or near zero, and collisions were common.

Eastbound convoys sailed into water infested with wolf-packs; the area between Iceland and Greenland became well and unfavorably known as "Torpedo Alley," and Churchill once described the Western Approaches as a veritable graveyard of ships. After such a voyage, landfall would seem to have come as a welcome relief, but it usually meant more submarines, enemy bombers, floating mines, high-speed E boats, particularly effective in the cramped, overcrowded English channel, and air raids and buzz bombs in London.

An entry in a diary kept by John Mitchell, AG gunner aboard the SS *Thomas Hartley,* gives an indication of the ordeal ships and men went through: "28 January—Fifth day of storm, getting even worse and also a blizzard to top things off. Everything covered with ice, taking seas over the flying bridge, up to the top of the stack and down inside the engine room. Two port side lifeboats smashed to pieces and washed away. Couldn't keep fire in galley stove for cooking, but dishes broken, lots of boys sick and can't eat, but you couldn't keep a plate on the table. Stood watch soaking wet, with ice freezing on clothes. Have to sleep in clothes except for sheepskin coats and rubber overalls. General alarm at 12:30, one Liberty sunk, another afire. We could hardly stand on ice-covered decks." The next day he wrote, "Storm easing off. Nice weather for subs. Lost #85 and straggler #45."[12]

Tankers, with their vital cargoes, were always priority targets for U-boats in wolfpacks or operating separately. The Esso fleet of tankers comprised over 130 vessels engaged in supplying vital petroleum products and high-octane gasoline in almost all oceans, and the North Atlantic was one of their major runs, with consequent hazards. The *Esso Baton Rouge* had the dubious distinction of being one of the few tankers torpedoed twice, commanded by the same captain on both occasions. She was torpedoed first on 8 April 1942 and sustained a twenty-five-foot hole in the ship's side, which flooded the engine room. Towed into port, she was repaired and returned to service. She wasn't so lucky the second time; traveling in convoy from Milford Haven to Curaçao with about thirty-two other tankers and freighters on 13 February 1943, a number of ships about her were torpedoed and sunk before a torpedo caught her on the starboard side aft, in way of the bunker fuel tank. A sheet of flame rose high in the air from the burning fuel oil, debris was scattered about, all the vessel's lights went out, and she began to settle by the stern. The *Esso Baton Rouge* carried a merchant crew of forty-three officers and men and a navy gun crew of twenty-five. Fortunately, only two merchant seamen and one AG were lost.[13]

Another ship of the Esso fleet, the Panamanian tanker SS *H. H. Rogers,* carrying a merchant crew of forty-seven and a navy gun crew of twenty-six under Lieutenant (j.g.) Edward W. Houghton, was torpedoed in convoy about 600 miles west of the Irish coast. The explosion resulted in water getting into the fuel, extinguishing the fires and flooding the engine room and fire room; realizing the ship was doomed, the master ordered "abandon ship" and all hands were later rescued.

The story of the MS *Esso Williamsburg* did not have such a happy ending. In September 1942, on her way from Aruba to Iceland with a cargo of navy fuel, the *Esso Williamsburg* disappeared in the North Atlantic, and all hands were lost. She was manned by a merchant crew of forty-two officers and men and a navy AG unit of eighteen, headed by Coxwain Fred J. Kindl. No circumstances of her sinking or the fate of the men aboard ever became known.[14]

One of the most melancholy sights of the war at sea was the sad debris of sunken and unknown ships. George Prestmo, of Mt. Vernon, Washington, recalls that on a return trip from Liverpool via Iceland, "For an entire day we went through a mass of debris floating in the ocean, lifeboats, rafts, trunks, clothes, shoes, but not a sign of life. Although I was in the AG from start to finish, and all around the world, the scene shook me more than any time I had been to sea. Apparently several ships had been sunk, leaving nothing but pieces of debris, floating in a silent sea. Occasionally a body would be seen in its bright jacket, head down in the oily water, amid the jetsam; other ships passed through similar results of sinking, a grim reminder to men on board that they might be next."[15]

Prestmo also recounts the sad position of not being able to help when nearby ships went down. "The hardest part was that when you were in convoy you couldn't stop to help. Christmastime of 1942, coming out of the Irish Sea, our convoy was nailed by a wolfpack. They moved in and started picking off the slower tankers, and they went up like flares in the night. You could see them in the distance burning for a long time, and you knew there were men on those ships including AGs." On the same voyage, they carried three American sailors who were survivors of the Murmansk run. "We lost our convoy the first day out of Ireland because of a storm. We followed smoke in the distance for a day and a half, shooting at and blowing up floating mines. When we caught up with the convoy, we found that it was the wrong one, in fact it was going in the wrong direction (to Russia), so we got out fast, undoubtedly to the great relief of the three survivors."

Another tragic ordeal was undergone by the Liberty ship SS *William C. Gorgas* en route to Liverpool in Convoy

HX-228 with a cargo consisting of TNT, food, steel, and a deck load of landing craft. On 10 March 1943 she was hit twice by two different German submarines, one torpedo hitting the #1 hold that contained the TNT. The attack was not merely a coincidence. In his memoirs, Admiral Dönitz said that on 9 March 1943, *B-Dienst* gave him the precise location of eastbound Convoy HX-228, 300 miles west of where he had deployed a U-boat group, so he immediately ordered a move to intercept, 120 miles to the north. But this was one of the few times that he guessed wrong. He figured the convoy would take evasive action, and "There I made a mistake." The next day the convoy sailed right past the southern end of the patrol line. "Had I not moved the boats, the convoy would have run straight into their midst. This shows how chess moves of this kind can often fail and how thinking ahead can sometimes be dangerous. It is possible that my British opponent guessed what my next move would be and therefore allowed the convoy to proceed on its old course. He too was thinking ahead . . ."[16]

The men of the AG crew and their merchant shipmates aboard the *Gorgas* could have no idea that they were pawns in a deadly chess match, but when their ship was lost, they began a nightmarish experience. Fifty-one men took to lifeboats and rafts; the master, Captain T. C. Ellis took charge of personally handling the searchlight while boats were being lowered and was the last to leave the ship. He was seen floating in a life ring, suffering from exposure. A seaman asked if Ellis would take his place on a raft, but the gallant captain replied, "No, son, keep your place." Shortly thereafter, he slipped through the life ring and was lost.[17]

Survivors must have thought they were safe after being picked up by HMS *Harvester* on 11 March, but they had only six hours of comfort until the *Harvester* was hit by two torpedoes and sank. A U.S. Navy memorandum dated 30 April, reporting on the double sinking, stated that the *Harvester* was attacked while she was hove to disabled, after being damaged and losing part of her screw earlier when she rammed the *U-144*. The submarine was subsequently sunk by the French corvette *Aconit*, which forced it to the surface with depth charges and destroyed it by gunfire, taking a number of German prisoners. The *Aconit* then picked up the survivors of the *Harvester* and the *Gorgas.* Only twelve of the original *Gorgas* survivors including five AGS, were saved out of sixty-seven men aboard; of the *Harvester*'s crew of 196, only 53 survived. Among those lost was the commander of the *Harvester,* Captain A. A. Tait, senior officer of the group of British, Polish, and Free French escorts.

Seaman First Class Edmund P. Rego, Somerset, Massachusetts, was one of the five navy survivors of the *William C. Gorgas.* He says, "Although the sinking of the *Gorgas* and *Harvester* occurred more than forty-four years ago, the events are deeply etched in my mind. I served ten long months in the Armed Guard before being sent to destroyer duty for a rest." He then went on to finish twenty years in the navy. However, before he got his "rest" he received a personal citation from the acting chief of Naval Personnel for outstanding service against enemy aircraft while aboard the SS *James Woodrow,* at Salerno, Italy, in September 1943.[18]

Sometimes a stricken ship seemed eager to take revenge on its tormentor. The same evening that the *Gorgas* was sunk, the *U-757* sank the Norwegian freighter SS *Brant County,* which was blown to pieces in a violent explosion, so much so that a rain of debris landed on the submarine and put it out of action until repairs were made. The *U-221* also hit a munitions ship, which disintegrated in flames and a dense cloud of smoke. The commander of the *U-221,* Korvetten Kapitän Trojer, reported, "Hundreds of steel plates flew like sheets of paper through the air. Heavy debris crashed against my periscope, which became difficult to turn, and then went completely black, while heavy fragments of debris continued to shower down on us. I tried to lower my periscope to clean the lens, but it came down only about five feet and then stuck."[19]

The spectacular end of the *Brant County* was described by Convoy Commander Dodd. "The ship fired two white rockets, burst into flames, the fire was like an inferno and lit everything in sight like daylight. I could see the whole convoy and escorts ahead on both wings. She blew up at 0415 with a tremendous explosion throwing debris hundreds of feet in the air."

A report that gives an indication of efficient German intelligence was made by survivors of the SS *James W. Denver*, a brand new Liberty ship on her maiden voyage. Broken down by engine trouble, she had to stop to effect repairs. At the time, she was carrying a full cargo of war supplies, including twelve P-38 fighter planes, and was about 250 miles southwest of the Canary Islands. Suddenly she was hit by two torpedoes and was immediately abandoned, her starboard side under water and her screw ten feet out of the water. All but two of the crew, and the navy gun crew, made it into lifeboats, one boat carrying eighteen engineers and the armed guard gunners. Nobody aboard that boat knew anything about small-boat seamanship, but their principal concern at first was the loss of their ship "without ever firing a shot from those beautiful new guns." According to the report, "The second night adrift, a sub came up under them, stranding the lifeboat on her stern." A German officer asked them where they came from. "Brooklyn!" was the reply. The officer laughed and in English said, "That's where baseball come from." He then asked the name of their ship, and since it was stenciled on the lifeboat equipment, they had no hesitation in telling him. "Well, well," the officer said, "you are from one of the new Liberty ships." One of his crew handed them a carton of cigarettes, the officer shouted a course for them to steer, and the U-boat moved off.[20]

Twenty-three days later, after living on four crackers and two ounces of water per day, fighting heavy seas, and once coming so close to a pod of seven whales that they could have hit them with a stone, they were picked up by a fishing vessel 30 miles off the West African coast and returned via Lisbon. The second boat carrying the captain made land two days later, and the survivors were picked up by a patrol boat. The crew of the *Denver* were lucky; only two men were lost out of a complement of forty-two merchant seamen, twenty-six NAGs and one army security officer.

German *B-Dienst* had been highly successful in reading messages from Commander-in-Chief Western Approaches directing convoys out of danger areas, even including a "U-boat Situation Report" on the location of U-boats. In March 1943 it deciphered two messages: the New York Port Director's sailing telegram and the commodore's report giving position, course, speed, and identification of stragglers of Convoy SC-122.[21]

The intelligence gathered from those two messages led to the greatest convoy battle of the war in the Atlantic, which occurred in a four-day period, 16–20 March 1943. While there were many such struggles, the extended battle between U-boats and Convoys SC-122 and HX-229 is generally recognized by experts as being the most crucial, and was loudly proclaimed by the Germans as their most significant convoy victory.

Convoy SC-122 departed New York, running somewhat ahead of Convoy HX-229. SC-122 consisted mostly of Allied ships, only four freighters and two LSTs being American flag out of the fifty-two ships in the convoy. Convoy HX-229 was so massive that it was split into two parts, one traveling to the north, the other following the track of SC-122. The section on the southern track had fifteen American ships out of thirty-eight, the others being British (sixteen), Dutch (three), Norwegian (two), and Panamanian (two). Only six of the American ships and one Panamanian, also carrying an AG gun crew, made it safely to port. One, the brand new Liberty ship, SS *Stephen C. Foster*, developed cracks in the welding in extremely bad weather and was sent back to St. Johns for repair before the battle started. The six that did make the voyage successfully were the steamers *Kofresi, Margaret Lykes, Pan Rhode Island, Jean, Gulf Disc,* and the *Daniel Webster*, lost a few months later.

The SS *William Eustis* took a torpedo hit on the port side, and the ship immediately began to settle at the stern. There was no time to send a distress signal, and the attack was not even noticed by the escorts until smoke began pouring out of her. Survivors, including the AG gun crew, were picked up by HMS *Volunteer*, a difficult feat because many men were

A depth charge explodes during the Battle of the Atlantic. (National Archives)

swimming and were widely dispersed. The Liberty SS *James C. Oglethorpe* was torpedoed on her maiden voyage, and fire broke out in the #1 hold, but she managed to stay afloat. Twenty-five men were put in the boats, but the captain and thirty men stayed with her, trying to get up steam and keep her going, until she was torpedoed again. A load of planes, tractors, and trucks went down with her, along with thirty-one members of the merchant crew, eleven NAG, and two naval passengers. The *Walter Q. Gresham,* carrying 9,000 tons of foodstuffs, was torpedoed on the port side, and the screw was torn off by the explosion. The master ordered abandon ship, but two boats capsized in the stormy seas with a heavy loss of life—twenty-two crew members and five navy gunners. The loss of life would have been higher except for an unidentified AG who swam from an overcrowded lifeboat to an empty one and helped transfer ten men to it.[22]

History as presented by noted scholars can be classics of research on facts, names, dates, places, and statistics of battles long forgotten. But such marvels of research often overlook the human touch, the details of the experience of those who lived through horror or died in it. The story of Convoys HX-229 and SC-122 has been told many times by writers whose work is beyond reproach in presenting details of the big picture. However, the story of the Stilinovich brothers adds a moving dimension as to just what it was like to the ordinary participant.

Bill and Joe Stilinovich, respectively eighteen and twenty-one, from the small northern mining town of Hibbing, Minnesota, enlisted together in the navy on 17 November 1942. Old photos in their dress blues show that they were so alike that they could be twins, and they were often taken for such. They took boot training at Great Lakes, were assigned to the same barracks, and their bunks were next to each other. After a happy home leave of seven days, they reported together to the Armed Guard Center, Brooklyn, New York, the same as thousands of other boys leaving their families under similar circumstances. It was hard parting from their mother, they knew the tears would come, but what they didn't know was that one was never to return. At the AG Center, Joe was assigned as a member of the AG gun crew on the SS *Harry Luckenbach,* and Bill as gunner on the SS *Irenee DuPont.* Both ships were assigned to Convoy HX-229. When it was time to go aboard ship, Joe shook his younger brother's hand and said, "Wherever we're going, I'll see you when we get there."

Their ships were in adjacent columns, a short distance apart. They soon entered dangerous waters, and depth charge after depth charge vibrated the ships. Suddenly,

early on St. Patrick's Day, the *Luckenbach* was hit by two torpedoes, resulting in a tremendous explosion and huge columns of smoke and flame. She sank in a matter of minutes.
Bill, horrified, could think only that his brother had been
killed in the explosion. He did not know that three boats had
been able to get safely away from the burning ship. Here,
Bill picks up the story, with simple eloquence: "There was a
short spell of quiet. I got relieved at my 20mm gun to go and
get some coffee. Then the first torpedo hit us with a shattering roar. I started running for the main deck hatchway and
the second torpedo hit. The deck shook under my feet. The
'abandon ship' order was given . . . I made my way to my assigned raft. The ship was beginning to settle.

"Ensign Frank Pilling, USNR, and four or five men tried
to break the raft loose, but it would not release. Crew members were jumping off the ship. I got into a lifeboat with
about twenty men, the bow line was released and it capsized. Men were falling out all around me. It dove into the
sea and filled with water. Cries for help were heard all over
the ocean. I remember screaming to one voice I thought I
recognized, R. J. Tresek of Akron, with whom I had gone to
boot camp. 'Over here! Over here!' I yelled, but we had lost
the oars and all survival gear and we could not get to them.
The heavy seas were pushing us up against the hull of the
ship. One AG had broken his leg and was in great pain. The
current finally pushed us away and we got clear of the ship. I
could still hear the cries for help. There were nine of us left
in the lifeboat. There were little red lights bobbing in the
water everywhere. These lights were pinned to our life jackets and could be seen a long way off. Two other ships were
hit, both British. The tanker *Southern Prince* caught fire and
lit up the night. She was aflame from stem to stern. Ammunition for her guns was blowing up.

"Destroyers were making dashes at high speed dropping
charge after charge. We drifted next to a ship that was still in
the water and someone yelled down that they would get us
on board. It was the SS *Tekoa*, picking up survivors on the
starboard side, but we drifted to port. From the three ships
there must have been 200 men in the water at the same time.

We drifted away and when day broke there were no ships around us. It was a strange feeling in that water-filled boat about 400 miles off the coast of Cape Farewell, Greenland. I thought of Joe and wondered if he might have lived. I knew we couldn't last long in that cold water. Suddenly we saw the mast of a ship, it was the British destroyer HMS *Mansfield.* It had gotten orders to go back and make one more search of the area. They had a hard time getting to us. They shot line after line. We finally got one of the lines and they pulled us in. A net was dropped over the side. The deep swells would take us even with the rail of the ship, then we would drop down and the lifeboat would slam against the side of the ship. I knew, with the oil smeared on me and making a grab at that oil-soaked net my chances were not too good. If you missed you would either be caught between the lifeboat and the ship or swept way. A British sailor yelled that he was coming down. He tied a rope around my waist. I remember laying on the deck not feeling too good as they were getting the heavy foul weather gear off of me. Lieutenant Commander Hill of the *Mansfield* asked me my name and how old I was. I told him and he said, 'you are now a veteran.' One sailor got picked up after us, but he died a few minutes later. He was buried at sea. The *Mansfield* trying to get to us, was in great danger, lying still in the water, as there were many subs still in the area . . . The *Dupont* was still afloat in the morning and in spite of firing shells and a depth charge she continued afloat, until a German sub was reported to have sunk her."

Bill did not know until after the war that the three boats had gotten away from the *Luckenbach* and were spotted at various times by at least four British vessels. He says the attacks by the submarines were severe, and because of confusion between the escorts, the three boats with survivors were never picked up and were never heard of again. "I guess you can only imagine what their feelings were with rescue so near and being left behind. I will always wonder if Joe was in one of those lifeboats. All eighty men on the *Luckenbach* were lost, including twenty-six Armed Guards. We lost seven crew, five AGS and one passenger on the *DuPont.*"

Taken to a hospital in England, Bill remembers being evacuated during an air raid and placed next to a big tree. "I remember this so clearly because it was my nineteenth birthday, and I was realizing how lucky I was to see it." Bill was sent home on a three-week leave, "but it wasn't the same. I was asked many times, 'Where is Joe?' I couldn't say the answer was 'somewhere at sea.'" It was harder to leave this time, as his brother Carl was fighting in the Pacific, and his brother John had been badly wounded in Belgium. On his next ship, the SS *George Leonard,* the first night at sea he says he, "got a second life jacket and hung it at the head of my bunk just in case I misplaced one of them. I guess I was a little on edge."

In retrospect, Bill says, "It was a long thirty-eight months since I enlisted. There were many AGS who would not be going home . . . heroes who did not get medals, like R. J. Tresek, Ohio, M. E. Stringer, Indiana, H. H. Schwinn, Maryland, G. E. Woods, Washington, R. A. Topel, Illinois, A. C., Jackson, North Carolina, and Ray Don E. Taylor, Massachusetts, just a few of the AGs on the *Irenee DuPont* and the *Harry Luckenbach* that I knew. Their names and my brother Joe's are inscribed on the wall of the missing at the American Cemetery and Memorial, Cambridge, England, with many other Armed Guards." [23]

Although not ordinarily a drinking man, on every St. Patrick's Day, Bill visits a little bar in Hibbing that he and Joe used to frequent and has a drink to Joe . . . somewhere in the Atlantic.

The SS *Mathew Luckenbach* represented a different story. With ships going down all around her, and reportedly after a meeting between captain and crew, the *Mathew Luckenbach* took off on her own, perhaps relying on her greater speed of 13 knots, and contrary to orders of the convoy commodore to return to position. She pulled ahead rapidly, but traveling alone she made an easy target and was torpedoed and settled by the stern. When next observed by the remnants of the convoy, she was still afloat, but three boats and two rafts filled with survivors were subsequently picked up. [24] The Panamanian SS *Granville,* under charter to

Standing the night watch in the North Atlantic. Twelve ships of this convoy are visible. (Courtesy John A. Driscoll)

the U.S. Army, was hit by a torpedo that blew a twenty-five-square-meter hole in her side. The captain tried to keep her afloat, to no avail. The lifeboats were smashed, but the crew and AG took to rafts. Also lost were the American-flag, *Hugh Williamson* and the *Walter Q. Gresham.* Weather probably played a major part in preventing a greater loss of ships, men, and cargoes because even the U-boats had problems of visibility.

According to Lieutenant Herbert Werner, the *U-230* had been ordered to break off pursuit of SC-121 and take position in a new patrol to intercept another convoy expected from Halifax. Some forty U-boats were deployed throughout an 80,000-square-mile area, and on 16 March one boat reported contact with SC-122. The entire group was given orders to proceed immediately to a given point and they found what they thought was SC-122, but was actually HX-229 following so close behind that they did not realize it. They believed HX-229 was still on the northern route. Werner reports that he fired a salvo of five torpedoes and heard the rumble of three heavy explosions. Shortly thereafter, out of torpedoes, low on fuel, and short of food, the *U-230* headed for home port.[25]

The battle of Convoys SC-122 and HX-229 was regarded by Admiral Dönitz as the biggest success of the war in a convoy battle; thirty-eight U-boats were deployed and a claimed thirty-two ships, totaling 186,000 tons, destroyed, plus a destroyer claimed sunk and nine other ships hit. The claim was exaggerated, but Dönitz did have grounds for elation; in the first ten days of March, forty-one Allied ships of 229,949 tons were sunk, followed in the second ten days by forty-four ships of 228,000 tons. Even worse for the Allies at the time, 68 percent of the ships had been torpedoed in convoy, at a cost of only six U-boats. In addition, the wild storms through the month had seriously damaged a number of escorts, which had to be laid up for repairs.[26]

The apparent cold-blooded abandonment of survivors in lifeboats or in the water, red lights blinking, by convoy escorts was anything but true. It represented an agonizing dilemma for the escort commander and obedience of orders by his escort captains, in cases where there were no rescue ships to pick up survivors. In his book, "The Naval War Against Hitler," Captain Donald MacIntyre, RN, experienced escort commander, gives a poignant statement by a fellow escort commander as to what it cost him to leave such men behind. He explains that the first priority of the commander is to search for the attacker. If an escort left her place, it would open a gap through which more attacks could be made and more ships and men lost. Only after the search for the enemy was concluded could escorts return to look for survivors, often too late. The reporting officer said that it preyed on his mind constantly, until the next attack when he again had to devote all of his attention to a search for the attacker and protection of the convoy.

Although Dönitz did not realize it then, the big convoy battle was the high-water mark of German underseas warfare. Although he had been brilliantly served by *B-Dienst*, which had "provided timely and accurate information" on the whereabouts of convoys, the gap in the air war in the North Atlantic, once the "Black Pit," was steadily decreasing. The growing and increasingly effective Allied air cover of the area and the ability of Huff-Duff (radar) to pinpoint the location of U-boats were such that Allied planes frequently arrived over the area before U-boats could submerge after sending the required transmissions to Admiral U-boats. Even though the Naval High Command refused to believe that U-boat transmissions were the cause of heavily increased losses, some individual commanders did, and took the precaution of not transmitting as often as ordered. U-boat losses in May 1943 alone in the North Atlantic were forty-seven, more than the number of ships sunk; in July thirty-seven U-boats were sunk and thirty damaged. Radar had robbed the U-boats of their power to fight on the surface, and in late 1943, Dönitz could only admit, "We have lost the Battle of the Atlantic." He added, "All we could hope to do was to maintain the efficiency of our U-boats, to sustain the morale of their crews, and to use them as economically as possible and to best possible advantage." Although he finally realized that his obligatory U-boat reports were giving the Allies the tip-off as to their location, and ordered transmissions shut down, it was too late; Dönitz had to pull his dwindling force out of the area, and with rare exception his submarines were no longer of much effect, with losses exceeding victories.[27]

The Admiralty Monthly Anti-Submarine Report for April 1943 stated:

Historians of this war are likely to single out the months of April and May 1943 as the critical period during which strength began to ebb away from the German U-boat offensive . . . for the first time U-boats failed to press home attacks on convoys when favourably placed to do so.

Dönitz had long fought for a completely "new" submarine, and a revolutionary new type of U-boat was developed that was bigger, faster, and stronger than the standard submarine. The Walter subs were designed to travel at 19 knots underwater and remain submerged for sixty hours, far superior to the standard. They could dive to 1,000 feet, safe from depth charging. He had tried repeatedly to convince Hitler to give him the necessary priorities for the new submarine, but it was not until after the complete collapse of the effectiveness of Hitler's prized Grand Fleet, and the steady attrition of the once-vaunted *Luftwaffe*, that Dönitz was given authorization and priorities for development and production. By then it was too late; the submarine was beset by technical problems and delays in getting components to the assembly place. It was built in eight large sections in scattered factories, and Germany's transportation system, ravaged by Allied bombings, was not able to cope. The first Walter boat was not delivered until June 1944; a few models received sea trials, but it never became operational.

In 1943, furious over his surface fleet's lack of accomplishment, Hitler replaced Grand Admiral Eric Raeder, navy chief, with Dönitz, but there was little he could do; the Allied noose was steadily tightening. Upon Hitler's death by suicide in his bunker in devastated Berlin on 30 April 1945, Dönitz found that he had been named as Hitler's successor. The military situation was catastrophic. Dönitz's main effort was to save as many men on the Eastern Front as possible by mass evacuation, at heavy cost. On 5 May 1945 he ordered his U-boat commanders to surrender their boats to the Allies, and slowly the surfaced U-boats, flying the black flag of surrender, began pulling into Allied ports. Defiantly, some 217 U-boat commanders scuttled their boats rather than surrender, but on 8 May World War II in Europe officially came to an end, and with it the end of the Third Reich, which was supposed to have lasted for a "thousand years." It was the long-awaited VE-Day. However, it was not until 28 May that the U.S. Navy and the British Admiralty issued the statement, "Effective this date . . . no further trade convoys will be sailed. Merchant ships by night will burn full navigational lights at full brilliancy and need not darken ship." It was a strange sight for men who had been at sea for years in a blackout.

Estimates of Allied ship losses and tonnage vary; but a generally acceptable figure is somewhat over 2,200 ships, totaling around 14,000,000 tons, over half of which represented British losses. Figures tabulated by HM Stationery Office, and published in British Official History, *War at Sea* (vols. 1–3), furnish a dramatic picture of the significance of the Battle of the Atlantic. "British, Allied and Neutral Merchant Ship Losses" from all causes, in worldwide Axis operations are as follows:[29]

Year	Total Losses (tons)	Atlantic TO Percentage of Total
1939	755,392	99.9
1940	3,991,641	91.6
1941	4,328,558	76.1
1942	7,790,697	79.0
1943	1,218,219	37.2
1944	530,510	63.9
1945	437,015	83.9

While reports of losses of Allied ships, both in the Battle of the Atlantic and in the war as a whole vary, in an appendix to his memoirs Admiral Dönitz listed merchant ships sunk by U-boats as follows:

Atlantic/Indian Ocean ... 2,449
Arctic Command 99
Mediterranean 113
Baltic 18
Black Sea 26
Total   2,705

Reported losses of U-boats, 1939–1945, also vary widely, but Dönitz lists a total of 753 lost; 630 lost at sea, of which 603 were from enemy action, and 123 lost in port, mostly by air attack and mines.[30]

CHAPTER FIFTEEN
THE "YANKEE TURKEY SHOOT"

Reports from the coastal waters indi-
cate that the U-boat campaign there
will be successful for much longer than
anticipated. . .
—Admiral Karl Dönitz, War Diary,
    17 January 1942[1]

Dönitz was wrong in only one respect; the success of the U-boat campaign off America's shores was much more of a victory than he possibly could have dreamed. Operation *Paukenschlag* ("Drum-roll") opened on America's front door on New Year's Day 1942, literally with a bang. The Panamanian tanker SS *Nor-vess* was torpedoed off Montauk Point, and then the action moved southward. U-boat commanders found the great sky-line of New York brilliantly lighted, as usual, moving one to remark in bewilderment, "My God, don't they know there's a war on!" Originally using only five Type-IX U-boats, carry-ing fourteen torpedoes each, submarine commanders were told to concentrate on large ships, with tankers given pri-ority of attack. It was like shooting fish in a barrel. Bright lights along the entire East Coast provided perfect targets for the marauders by silhouetting passing ships, and it was over three long and costly months before a coastal dim-out ordered by federal authorities became effective, over the op-position of some local business and civic promotion inter-ests. The British tanker *San Demetrio* was torpedoed and sunk on 16 March 1942, en route from Baltimore, and survi-vors commented on the enemy's audacity in operating so close to Norfolk, one of our greatest naval and air bases, which was "lit up like a Christmas tree!"[2]

The standard tactic of U-boats at the time was to rest on the bottom during the day and to surface after dark to select their victims. In one two-week period, twenty-five ships, of which 70 percent were tankers, went down. In September 1945 a navy report stated that during the war, in the 5th Naval District alone, seventy-nine vessels were sunk or damaged, sixty-six of which went down off Maryland, Virginia, and the part of North Carolina spanning Cape Hatteras, Cape Lookout, and Onslow Bay—an area that gained the unenviable distinction of being named "Torpedo Junction." Thirty-five of the ships were tankers, northbound and heavily laden. The total cost in the 5th Naval District was 843 lives lost and 520,914 tons of vital shipping sunk or damaged, of which 425,850 tons were lost.[3]

U-boats were also active laying mines in coastal waters and off harbors. Lieutenant Herbert Werner, executive officer of the *U-230*, has described one mission in July 1942 in which they laid mines in Chesapeake Bay, off Norfolk. To their immense surprise, they attracted absolutely no attention and were able to leave with no problems. Mines were also laid off Jacksonville and elsewhere, and even the huge port of New York was closed for two days in November 1942 because of mines. On 15 June 1942, crowds at Virginia Beach were able to see a lot of action offshore. The tankers SS *Robert Tuttle, Esso Augusta,* and a British trawler escort struck mines. Those on shore observed the spectacular sight of escorts dropping depth charges, with planes and blimps joining in. The *Tuttle* and the trawler sank, but the *Esso Augusta* was able to make Hampton Roads and was towed to Baltimore for repair.[4]

During the first six months of Operation *Paukenschlag,* more than two million tons of Allied shipping were sent to the bottom. The toll probably would have been much higher but for the fact that U-boats often ran out of torpedoes and had to return home for replenishment and supplies. The returning submariners were greeted as heroes, with champagne, flowers, and decorations for their successes. The reason for their success can be readily understood: merchant ships, most unarmed, had to travel alone—easy pickings for lurking submarines. Even when the tankers had an armed guard gun crew, in the early days these crews often consisted of as few as five men, under command of a low-ranking petty officer, or even a seaman 1/c. A review of AG units aboard Standard Oil (N.J.) tankers at that time reveals that none carried gunnery officers of higher grade than coxswain or gunner's mate 3/c.[5] Improvisation also played a part in the early days; with no defense at the time, resourceful Captain James Poche, master of the *Esso Baton Rouge,* built "gun" platforms fore and aft and added dummy guns, a 3-inch on the fantail and a 4-inch forward. He painted them regulation gray, and maintained a "gun watch" during the day to discourage a potential attacker from surfacing to use its deck guns. The ruse proved successful for a while, but the *Baton Rouge* gained the dubious distinction of being torpedoed twice during the war. In the last instance, four crewmen were seriously burned from flaming oil, but none of the twenty-five-man AG gun crew was killed or injured.

As has been related elsewhere, the British were vehemently upset by the lack of a convoy system; in referring to the heavy losses along the East Coast and later the Caribbean, Churchill wrote that "the protection afforded by the U.S. Navy was hopelessly inadequate." There were not enough escort vessels, the army air force had no training in ASW warfare, and the navy had no effective means of carrying it out.[6] The "protection" afforded early convoys was not impressive. The minesweeper *YMS-20* was diverted from duty in New York harbor and given command of a thirty-ship convoy from New York to the Delaware River. The two other escorts were 83-foot Coast Guard picket boats with no armament. No ships were lost or damaged by enemy attack, however, and probably the highlight of the war for the newly minted ensign commanding *YMS-20* was his moment of glory attending the convoy conference in the port captain's office in his capacity as ranking officer of the escort force.[7] After the success of the "partial convoy" system, a full convoy system was adopted in June 1942, and there were almost no sinkings along the East Coast in the third and fourth quarters of the year; from August-November some 1,400 ships were convoyed, with the loss of only eleven. The days of the "Yankee Turkey Shoot," so-called by U-boat commanders, were over, but before they ended, Henry Rehse, an engineer on the *U-511*, recalls observing tourists frolicking in the surf off Miami Beach, and the U-boat crew even taking swims in warm waters near an offshore lighthouse. He reported that the *U-511* traveled on the surface about five miles off Fort Lauderdale, her crew enjoying the warm sun as they headed south, but was never spotted.[8]

Before the happy days of near-zero sinkings arrived, the Esso Fleet of Standard Oil (N.J.) and other tanker operators were hard hit, and on 26 February, Esso's SS *R.P. Resor* sustained a major disaster with heavy loss of life. Carrying a cargo of 78,729 barrels of fuel oil to Fall River, Massachusetts, from Houston, with a crew of forty-one officers and men and a nine-man AG unit, she was torpedoed at night while traveling alone. She quickly became ablaze from the bridge aft and had her back broken by two explosions. Of the entire complement of fifty men, only two survived, seaman John J. Forsdal and navy coxswain Daniel Hey. Oil floating on the water was afire, and they had to struggle hard to get away before being picked up by a Coast Guard picket boat. The commander of the boat reported Forsdal was so coated with thick congealed oil that "we had to cut his clothes and jacket off with knives. They were so weighted with oil that we couldn't get him aboard, even his mouth was filled with a blob of oil." It took four men to pull Hey aboard; he was so coated with oil that he was three times his normal weight. The *Resor* burned for two days before she capsized and sank, so near the coast that the huge pall of smoke could be seen by people on shore.[9]

When the *Esso Augusta* hit the mine off Virginia Beach, she was carrying 120,429 barrels of oil consigned to the United Kingdom. The rudder and stern post had been blown off, there were holes in the hull, all auxiliary machinery foundations were cracked or shattered, electrical communi-

The sinking of the SS *R. P. Resor* after being torpedoed off the New Jersey coast on 28 February 1942. There were only two survivors. (Courtesy C. A. Lloyd)

cations were disrupted and fuel and steam lines broken; however, almost miraculously, there was only one injury, to a navy gunner, and repairs were completed on 7 November, after which she returned to service.[10]

Esso's MS *T.A. Moffett, Jr.*, was torpedoed and shelled in the Florida Straits; the five-man navy gun crew survived as did all of the merchant crew, but the master, Captain Mahoney, lost his life trying to launch the #2 lifeboat. Navy gunner Peter Oppacich had an almost unbelievable escape. He had been washed overboard after remaining at the gun with his crew until the ship listed too much for the gun to be effective. He could not swim, but was able to keep afloat until the next day when he was fished out of the water by a Coast Guard vessel.[11] On 29 March the SS *Esso Manhattan* was heading south to Curaçao when she experienced an explosion, believed to be a mine, that literally broke the back of the ship apart at midships. Incredibly, neither section sank, and there were no casualties among the forty-eight officers and men and the twenty-five-man navy gun crew. The master instructed the navy signalman to send an SOS and ordered the vessel abandoned. Fortunately, there was a Coast Guard cutter only a short distance away that picked up survivors; the two sections of the ship were rejoined and she returned to service.[12]

The new large *Esso Baltimore* was even luckier; she was only a few hundred feet ahead of the 1918 SS *Liberator* when the latter was torpedoed and sunk on 19 March 1942. In view of Dönitz's order, it can only be assumed that the torpedo was aimed at the *Baltimore* and missed.[13] Another lucky ship was the Liberty, SS *George Ade*. She was not only torpedoed on her maiden voyage, about 85 miles south of Cape Lookout, disabling her propeller and wrecking the navy gun-crew quarters, but was almost driven ashore in a hurricane two days later. However, she weathered both blows and was towed to Norfolk, with no casualties among her forty-man crew and twenty-seven navy gunners. For Captain T. C. Selness, it was his third torpedoing along the Atlantic coast in two years; from then he sailed in the Pacific.[14]

During the U-boat blitz along the East Coast in 1942, there were many losses and few victories. One of the latter was during one of the early convoys from the Chesapeake Bay area to Key West in July. Convoy KS-520, consisting of nineteen ships, was attacked by one or more submarines off Cape Hatteras. Several ships were sunk, damaged, or drifted into a minefield. The SS *Chilore*, SS *J. A. Mowinkel*, carrying the commodore's flag, and the SS *Bluefields* were hit by a submarine's spread; confusion reigned, not alleviated when the *U-576* surfaced in the middle of the convoy, about one hundred yards astern of the SS *Unicoi*. The *Unicoi's* quick-witted AG officer, Ensign M. K. Ames, USNR, immediately brought his 5-inch stern gun to bear on the U-boat and sent a shell squarely into the conning tower. Planes and escorts joined in and straddled the U-boat with charges, and shortly

The SS *Esso Boston* burns after being torpedoed off St. Martin, an island in the West Indies. (Courtesy C. A. Lloyd)

thereafter bits of wreckage and oil surfaced. The destruction of the U-boat was confirmed. Dönitz was still far ahead on points, but the loss of the *U-576* was prophetic of a trend that was to continue until his U-boats were driven out of the eastern seaboard campaign or destroyed.[15]

Even in the midst of sudden death, broken ships, and flaming seas, there are occasional moments remembered with a smile. Frank Davis, forty-four-year veteran of the merchant marine, reports he sailed tankers on the East Coast–Gulf run until about July 1942, without convoy or arms. "Aboard the SS *Sinclair Opaline* I served as a volunteer with the Armed Guard gun crew. Off Frying Pan Shoals, along the Carolinas coast, I was off-duty, sleeping on the boatdeck alongside of the stack, when I was awakened at sunrise by a tremendous explosion and I thought the old *Opaline* had got it. About twenty feet from me was this 5-inch 85 vintage 1898 gun which was firing away, getting off several rounds. Though there was a surface haze, clearly visible were two green can (wreck) buoys about 200 yards on the starboard quarter. The targets might have been harmless, but the shooting was good, I believe both sank. Why was the gun crew so trigger-happy? During the past

The end of the Mexican tanker *Portero del Llano*. (National Archives)

few months over 100 ships, mostly tankers, had been zapped on the east coast, possibly some that night. We were running alone, and all hands slept in their clothes with the Mae West always within arm's reach. No wonder they were nervous."[16]

While today the sea off the Virginia-Carolinas shore looks beautiful and peaceful, it is the graveyard of uncounted ships that have gone down in both war and peace.

When defenses tightened along the East Coast, Dönitz ordered his U-boats to move into the Gulf of Mexico, where they found another happy hunting ground. The Gulf had been undisturbed for months although it carried a large volume of tankers and freighters. The peace was rudely broken in early May 1942, and the toll of the Gulf Sea Frontier during that month alone was forty-one ships, all sailing unescorted. The *U-507* accounted for five sinkings in a matter of just a few days. A favorite tactic of U-boats was to lie just off the two passes of the Mississippi and wait for their victims to arrive.

The *U-106* had an unpleasant surprise on 26 May 1942

when it selected the SS *Atenas* as an easy target, and instead ran into a hornet's nest, with the hornets ready and willing to fight. Shortly after clearing the passes of the Mississippi, the vessel sighted a periscope. The master ordered a change of course to bring the stern gun into position to fire, and the gun crew scored a number of hits, one exploding on top of the periscope. The submarine submerged but soon reappeared and attacked the *Atenas* with shell fire, hitting it seven times. The stubborn thirteen-man AG gun crew fought back with such force and accuracy that the sub had to crash-dive and did not resume the fight. After patching up her wounds, the *Atenas* continued her voyage, landing general cargo safely at Cristobal. There were no casualties among the merchant crew, AG unit, or passengers.[17]

Unfortunately, not all ships were lucky enough to be forewarned of an attack and able to take defensive measures. In places the shallow Gulf resembled a sunken forest, the masts of lost ships standing clear, like lifeless trees above the water.

The SS *Benjamin Brewster* anchored for the night about 38 miles from Southwest Pass. She was carrying 70,578 barrels of aviation gasoline when she was struck by two torpedoes. She immediately burst into flames and sank in less than three minutes in 37 feet of water. Fire surrounded the wreck for nine days, until the cargo finally burned itself out. Twenty-four crewmen and one AG, Michael Domonkos, lost their lives, but the other four AGs survived, having been picked up after swimming for several hours. A burning lifeboat had been found and some survivors boarded it and put out the fire, later picking up the navy gunners. On an earlier voyage the *Benjamin Brewster* had rescued nineteen survivors of the SS *Gulfoil*, "so thickly covered with oil that it took an entire barrel of kerosene to get it off."[18]

As defenses were beefed up along the Eastern seaboard, a new tactic was developed. Slow-moving blimps were employed to patrol the waters in steamship lanes to scout for possible submarines in the path of ships sailing alone or in convoy. The blimps did not offer much in the line of grace or beauty, but they were a most welcome sight to the men on the freighters and tankers that had taken such a beating from U-boats. The blimps replaced the PBYs, which in turn had replaced ineffective army air force bombers. The PBY was a big improvement, but they could remain over a convoy usually no more than a couple of hours, whereas a blimp could stay with it for six to sixteen hours. The Type-K blimp was used for convoy duty; its speed could be 65–70 mph, but cruising speed over a convoy was about 30 mph. They cruised at an altitude of about 500 feet, moved forward and to the rear of the convoy, and covered about 30 degrees to port and starboard. They were equipped with ASG radar, which had a 90-mile radius, even at night. Blimps proved so successful that they were eventually used along the East Coast (bases in Massachusetts, New Jersey, North Carolina, Georgia, and Florida), in the Caribbean (bases at Guantánamo and Trinidad), and in the South Atlantic as far south as Rio de Janeiro. Particular coverage was given to the vitally important bauxite convoys out of Dutch Guyana, which would be handed off to blimps from the next base north.[19]

Blimps were armed with one 50-caliber machine gun in the turret and four depth charges, two on either side, set at 25–75 feet. They were not meant to attack, but a fight-to-the-death between a blimp and a U-boat was fought off the coast of Florida on 18 July 1943. While blimps had successfully patrolled thousands of miles of ocean and advised convoys of possible U-boats, there had never been a real confrontation between a blimp and a U-boat and a submarine kill. On 18 July 1943, Lieutenant N. G. Grills, USNR, commander of airship K-34, sighted a U-boat·off the coast of Florida. He attempted to maneuver his ship so that he could drop a depth charge, but before he could get into position the Germans had manned their guns and began pouring fire into the airship. Their target was so big and slow that they could not miss. Because of the use of helium in the envelope the airship did not explode, but the shells tore the envelope to the degree that the ship lost altitude. Grills attempted to get above the U-boat and did succeed in getting in position to drop depth charges, but nothing happened, the release gear had jammed. The blimp slowly settled into the sea and the U-boat sailed away, to be sunk soon thereafter by a British aircraft as she tried to return to base.[20]

Certainly, being aboard any ship that is hit and set ablaze has to be a traumatic experience, but trying to swim away from blazing oil-covered water, weighed down by oil-soaked clothing, has to be one of the most terrifying experiences of a lifetime. In May 1942 James D. Handy, S1/c, Eden, N.C., was assigned to the SS *Cities Service Toledo* as a member of a nine-man AG gun crew. Things didn't go well from the start; the *Toledo* was equipped with an old 5″ 51 bag gun on the stern gun deck and two tripod-mounted .30-caliber Colt machine guns mounted on the wings of the bridge. None of the AG crew had ever seen the guns before or had any instruction in them, and it took some time and a lot of experimenting to figure out what the powder sample bottles that came aboard with the ammunition were for. Leaving the little port of Aransas Pass, Texas, loaded with oil, they got hit the second night out. The torpedo hit the starboard side near the bridge, and the ship immediately began to list. The gun crew's S1/c gun captain trained it to starboard and the gun crew waited for a shot when the sub surfaced to give the ship the coup de grace with its deck gun, as was customary to save torpedoes. The ship continued to list, to the point where the gun was at almost extreme elevation to remain on horizon. The gunners observed a light believed to be on the conning tower and could hear the sub's diesels, and were able to get off three shots before the gun recoiled on the deck and broke the gears. A second torpedo hit the ship, which threw fire several hundred feet in all directions; the gun crew was ordered to abandon ship and they jumped over the side while the screw was still turning in the air. Handy was the last man off and jumped into the black crude oil pouring out of the ship.

"It seemed like I would never get back to the surface," he reports, "and when I did and wiped the oil from my eyes so I could see a little, I was real near the fire. I swam to a lifeboat which held Haddad, another AG, but we found the oars were smashed and we couldn't get away from the ship. We hit the water to try to swim away, but after what seemed an hour we were only able to stay about 10–15 feet ahead of the burning oil. Finally the wind or the current changed and we were able to make a little progress but we were real sick from swallowing oil and salt water. Haddad and I got separated, and I never saw him again. After the sun came up my eyes burned so bad from the oil that I had to keep them closed most of the time. I was within hearing of some of the rest of the crew, but couldn't get to them. I was getting quite a bit concerned as my life jacket was getting pretty well water-logged and didn't hold me up nearly as well as it did at first, and I knew I might be spending quite a bit more time in the water. A while later a tanker, the SS *Gulf King*, came by and picked up the other guys in the water and also pulled me on deck. I fully expected to be abandoning this ship too, as it was not armed and we passed several other ships that had got torpedoed and were still burning. I got me a new life jacket and slept on deck that night waiting for the next tor-pedo to hit, but nothing happened and we were put ashore at a coast guard station and went by bus to the Naval Station at Burwood, Louisiana. We had lost ten or eleven of the ship's crew and four AGs, Devault, Haddad, Hardin, and Harris.

"Then I had one of the most unpleasant experiences in my life. Since I was the senior member left with the gun crew I had to go to Morgan City to assist the captain of the ship in identifying bodies brought in from the Gulf from sev-eral sunken ships. There were 40–50 bodies laid out, and the stench was unbelievable. You did the best you could, I identified some of the merchant crew as I knew them better than the Captain did. . . One after-effect of the torpedoing other than being a little jumpy the next time at sea, was that if I'd smell burning, even an auto burning oil real bad, it would almost make me sick at the stomach, but I finally got over it."[21]

Also sunk off Southwest Pass was the SS *R.W. Gallagher,* torpedoed on 13 July 1942. Nine crew members were lost, but thirty-one crewmen and twelve AGs under GM3/c John Nibouar were rescued, several with severe burns.[22]

Ironically, Admiral Karl Dönitz could be credited with developing a philosophy that over forty years later would become a "buzz-word" in American economics, "cost-effectiveness." In the global sea battles he directed, Dönitz sought to achieve optimum benefit at minimum cost. As one theater of operations after another became too costly in terms of losses of U-boats in relation to number of Allied merchant ship sinkings, he moved his forces into new areas as yet ineffectively defended. So it was that, as U.S. defenses along the Eastern Seaboard tightened, he moved into the Gulf and the Caribbean, which were wide open to aggressive U-boat attacks. Sea traffic in the Caribbean was particularly heavy in strategic targets—tankers and bauxite carriers. In a matter of weeks after moving into the Caribbean, losses of Allied shipping became catastrophic. The Caribbean Coastal Frontier, with HQ in San Juan, Puerto Rico, had a protective assignment that must be called "Mission Impossible." It covered a vast area, from Cuba to Brazil, but had the slenderest of assets. In June 1942, forty-eight ships were lost in the Caribbean and its approaches. The narrow Windward Passage between Cuba and Haiti was a favorite hunting ground for U-boats. They would rest on the bottom during daylight hours and then rise at night to choose their targets. Losses continued to mount as Dönitz sent in more and larger U-boats, supported by "milch-cow" supply submarines. This enabled them to perform longer missions, and U-boat tactics became so brazen that they even attacked land refineries and storage areas, torpedoing tankers at anchor in harbors. The *U-161* gained notoriety for sailing directly into an anchorage and torpedoing two ships before departing, "nonchalantly, fully surfaced and displaying his running lights."[23]

The commander repeated this audacious procedure by attacking ships in harbor at St. Lucia and Puerto Limón, Costa Rica. His sister ship, the *U-162,* sank nine ships on its first patrol and seven on its second, three of which were vital tankers. Sinkings in the Caribbean Sea Frontier in 1942 amounted to 318 ships, a total of 1,362,278 tons. At one point, Churchill wrote Harry Hopkins, Roosevelt's special emissary, that he was deeply concerned about the loss of tankers in the Caribbean Sea, stating that in little over two months in the Caribbean some sixty tankers had been sunk, and others were overdue.[24]

With their priority set on tankers in hope of crippling the Allied war effort, U-boats in the Caribbean had a field day in 1942. The Esso fleet, including the tankers of the Panama Transport Company that flew the Panamian flag, all with armed guard crews, sustained heavy losses, a partial list of which follows.

MS *Penelope,* traveling alone from Trinidad with a crew of mainly Dutch, Norwegians, and Danes, plus an AG crew of ten, was hit by two torpedoes on March 13 and went down, blazing fiercely, within fifteen minutes. The only man lost was Stout R. Cheyne, a navy gunner who was on lookout in the crow's nest when the ship was hit and could not get away in time. The MS *Heinrich v. Riedemann* went down on April 16 off Trinidad, followed by the MS *Harry G. Seidel,* on April 27.[25] The *Seidel* carried a 4-inch gun mounted aft, and (two) 30-caliber machine guns, one on each side of the bridge, and had six AG gunners, all of whom survived. The U-boat surfaced and an officer inquired in good English if the survivors needed anything. The SS *Esso Houston* went down off Barbados on March 12. The sub commander offered assistance and returned about ten minutes later to inform the master that one of the lifeboats with three men in it was in a sinking condition and gave its location. All hands were picked up safely. The sub officer asked if the lifeboats had a compass or if survivors needed food, water, or medicine. One AG, John O. Person, was lost, and another had a miraculous escape. At daylight the men in one boat noticed a stick with a rag on it in the distance. The master took a look through his glasses and they went over and picked up navy gunner Sydney A. Winn, covered with oil, but very happy.[26] The Panamanian-flag MS *Arriaga* went down off Colombia on June 23, the AG remaining at their station, over their knees in water, firing at the sub until it submerged after a near miss. The submarine surfaced, and the commander asked if there were any injured men among the survivors. One AG had an injured back and was suffering from oil in his eyes, and he was treated in the submarine by its doctor. He was helped back to the lifeboat, and the sub commander gave the survivors five packs of cigarettes and course and distance to the nearest shore. The submarine had a black clove or ace of clubs painted on the conning tower and became well known in the Caribbean for the consideration shown survivors under similar circumstances.[27]

The first week in June was a bad one for the tanker fleet. The SS *M.F. Elliott* was sunk on June 3, the *L.J. Drake* was last seen on June 4 and disappeared without a trace with all hands, including the six-man AG crew under Cox. Velton L. Deazmond. The *C.O. Stillman* was destroyed off Aruba on June 5 and the *Franklin K. Lane* was lost on June 8. The *Elliot* sank in six minutes after being torpedoed off Trinidad, with a loss of thirteen crew members; the seven AGs survived. The ranking navy gunner was Seaman 1/c Otto H. Weiss, Jr. The sub surfaced, and several survivors, slimy with oil, were picked up from the water and taken aboard where they were cleaned up, given some rum, hot tea, and bread and cheese. They were aboard the sub for about three hours, and were given a dinghy, four gallons of water in petrol cans and a day's ration of hardtack. The commander wished them well and told them to row 6 miles south where they should find their comrades, "if not keep heading south and you will reach land." They missed their shipmates, but were picked up by a Brazilian tanker and taken to Santos.[28]

The SS *Franklin K. Lane,* in convoy, was hit on June 8, and the torpedo broke her back and set her afire. Burning oil spread over the water, and it was imperative to abandon ship immediately. The master, chief mate, and radio operator were apparently killed in the explosion. The six AGs under Coxswain Charles J. Bass survived along with thirty-one crewmen. The *Esso Aruba* was torpedoed in convoy off

Guantánamo, Cuba, on August 23, and went down along with three other vessels, including the Dutch tanker *Rotterdam* and the British tanker *San Fabian.* The thirteen-man AG crew of the *Esso Aruba,* under S1/c Harry Bronstein, all survived. Several subs were involved in the action, which lasted almost two hours in bright moonlight.

The Panamanian MS *Leda* was another tanker lost off Trinidad. She was the fourth victim of a convoy attacked about 90 miles northwest of Trinidad, two of the others being the Dutch freighter *Chr. J. Kampmann* and the Norwegian tanker *Thorshavet,* plus an unidentified American-flag ore carrier. The eight-man AG, under Coxswain Leonard D. Delaney, all survived, but the *Leda's* master was lost. A happier story was the encounter of the SS *Frederick R. Kellogg* with a U-boat on 5 December 1942 about 50 miles from Aruba. A periscope was sighted, and Ensign Elmer C. Brewton, USNR, gunnery officer, and his seven man AG crew took immediate action. His report to CNO stated that: "Our 16th round knocked the periscope off. . . a black puff of smoke and explosion of projectile was seen as the shell hit the water line of the periscope. About four feet of periscope was seen to topple over and roll backwards. Noticed churning of water or bubbles rising to the surface and bursting for fifty or more feet, astern of the sub and perpendicular to the line of fire. The seventeenth round was a hit with rapid fire; explosion seen at water's edge. . . the eighteenth round was fired immediately and it ricocheted. We fired the nineteenth round into the bubbles or churning still present. Sub believed to be sunk."[29]

Ensign Brewton added, "Due credit must be given our captain, who did a splendid job of maneuvering the ship and keeping the sub dead astern. The captain and the first mate gave 100% cooperation in helping to make the engagement a success. Some members of the merchant crew helped in passing the ammo from the magazine to the gun platform." The 4-inch gun was the only gun on the ship.

Ernie Sanders, Princeton, Kentucky, was gunner in the AG crew on the MV *Brunswick,* an old, decrepit pre–World

War I tanker under the Panamanian flag. On the third night out, in the Windward Passage, the most dangerous part of the trip, Sanders was on watch. "A small Dutch freighter was crowding us, barely fifty-sixty feet away. A torpedo hit her in the starboard side and blew out through the port side. We watched the crew try and launch lifeboats, but they couldn't make it, in three minutes all was gone." [30]

On the return voyage, the *Brunswick* again entered the Windward Passage, a favorite place for U-boats as there wasn't any room for maneuver. "We had to stay in line, and in a sudden attack they sank four tankers." Sanders's next trip was no less eventful. "At night a sub surfaced in the Windward Passage and shot tracers in the air. This drew the escort to one spot; the diversion worked—attacks began, and soon seven tankers were in flames. An awesome sight. They were all around us, but our old tub was not touched."

Lieutenant Commander Paul B. Kincade, USN, (Ret.) of San Diego, was a commodore's signalman on numerous convoys in the Caribbean. All told, he served on ten ships, five Panamanian-flag, one British, one Norwegian, one Dutch, and only two American-flag. One of the Americans was the new Liberty ship SS *Thomas Sumter.* It had been ordered to go to the U.S.S.R., but the welding parted and it had to return to New York for repairs. Once out of the yards it was assigned to Caribbean duty, and Kincade was aboard when the *Sumter,* riding high, had two torpedoes pass under it. Shortly thereafter, with the crew on lookout, two more torpedoes were seen and the alarm sounded. Fortunately, to everyone's relief the "torpedoes" were dolphins that approached the ship in a pair and then veered off. Kincade wonders if the dolphins might have said to each other, "I'll bet we scared the hell out of them, lets go find another ship." [31]

Kincade says the best ship he ever served on was a Norwegian freighter, MV *Trondanger,* built in 1932 out of Bergen. It was a combination passenger-cargo ship, 9,800 tons, and "it was so clean you could eat off the decks." It had beautiful furnishings, including the passenger cabins assigned to the American signalman, which even had a shower in the room. The food was superb, and the crew was more than hospitable. However, Kincade says that it was a sad ship. The Norwegians had been away from home for over three years and had no idea what had happened to their families under German occupation. In the evenings the crew would gather and play songs of their homeland, and Kincade says that it was a very poignant experience. He will always remember spending his eighteenth birthday on the ship. Signalmen often had a lonely time on foreign ships. As Kincade explains it, "The signalman had to contend with ship's crews who often spoke no English, with the exception of the captain and senior mates, with horrible food, (both quantity and quality), and often abominable living quarters. Usually we were the only American aboard, and with no relief, spent long hours on the bridge and on call when not there."

Kincade served on a Panamanian-flag bauxite carrier, the SS *Olambala*. It was an old 2,600-ton ore carrier, "not worth a torpedo," but he made two trips on her and became very fond of the old ship. It sank shortly after he left her in a gun battle with a German raider. Before his last trip on the *Olambala*, Kincade and two signalmen buddies were in Trinidad awaiting orders. One said he had a premonition that he would not make it home, but Kincade tried to cheer him up by pointing out that he had been assigned to the fine, clean Dutch freighter, *Suriname*, while he was still going to be aboard the old slow *Olambala*. The convoy sailed from Trinidad on Friday, 11 September 1942. All went well until 13 September when the convoy was hit by a German wolf-pack, lying in wait in the dangerous Windward Passage. Explosions were seen at night, and the next morning nothing was seen of the *Suriname*, which was lost with all hands.

Being torpedoed and having to swim through heavy oil, even if not afire, adrift in an overcrowded lifeboat, or bobbing at the mercy of the seas on a raft, hoping for days or weeks that you might be discovered, could never be described as anything but a nightmare. Many died, but even survivors will carry the memory through a lifetime. One who will not forget, after over forty years of pain, is Ed Knopf, AG gunner, originally of Milwaukee, but now living in Oregon City, Oregon. When his ship, the Hog Islander SS *Tachira,* was torpedoed by a U-boat in the Caribbean on 12 July 1942, Knopf was knocked unconscious by the blast. He was pulled from the water and dragged onto a raft by shipmates, along with AG gunner Jimmy Laney, also injured seriously.[32]

After four days and five nights, during which both were transferred to an overloaded lifeboat and sheltered from the sun under a canvas overhang, the lifeboat drifted close to shore at Cozumel Island, Mexico. Some survivors were in good enough shape to swim ashore, but Knopf and Laney had to be aided by young Mexican swimmers. Knopf had three fractures of the pelvis and other injuries and was paralyzed from the waist down; Laney had two broken legs, which were turning blue. Medical aid was called and a local doctor put Knopf in a body cast from his chest to his ankles. Since there was no hospital available, he used a shoemaker's last to lift Knopf so that the cast could be applied. There were no beds, so the injured were placed on a mat on the floor. Several days later Knopf was horrified to see hundreds of ants crawling into a hole in his cast. No one could speak English, and he knew nothing of Spanish, so the problem was not understood until later after he had been transferred to a hospital in New Orleans. There, in agony, he attempted to cut the cast off with a pair of scissors forgotten by a nurse. When the doctor was called, he berated him and opened the cast, then he exclaimed, "Oh, my God! Why didn't you tell someone?" Knopf tried to explain that he had been trying to do so for two weeks.

Knopf was eventually given a medical discharge, but after several operations, including amputations, he learned that his problems were not over; the navy had not only lost his Purple Heart and other medals to which he was entitled, but had said in a letter dated 1 April 1948 that he "did not participate in actual combat." It was not until February 1949 that he received an apology for the "administrative error" and was given the Purple Heart, plus five other medals to which he was entitled. He had lost track of his friend and shipmate Jimmy Laney, but was informed much later that Laney had lost both legs and one arm because of the delay in obtaining adequate medical care.

The heavy losses of merchant ships along the U.S. East Coast alone were covered in a Navy Department press release of 16 September 1945, "Summary of Merchant Ships Hit by Enemy Action in the 5th ND, World War II." This report listed sixty-six ships sunk, totaling 425,850 tons, and thirteen damaged of 95,064 tons, with loss of life reported at 843.

An ironic footnote to the "Yankee Turkey Shoot" was the strange death of Lieutenant Commander Wolfgang Luth (*U-181*), reported to have been the most decorated officer of the *Kriegsmarine.* He sank forty-three ships in fourteen patrols, and recorded the longest patrol in submarine history up to that time. He was active in Operation *Paukenschlag,* along with Captain Reinhard Hardegen (*U-123*). Luth survived the war at sea, but was shot and killed by a German sentry on shore in 1945, when he reportedly gave the wrong password. Hardegen later refuted this story, stating that Luth was so deep in thought when leaving Dönitz's headquarters that he didn't hear the question of the sentry. Hardegen then was on the staff of Admiral Dönitz, and actually heard the shot, but did not know until the next day that "it was my crewmate and friend Luth."[35]

CHAPTER SIXTEEN
THE MEDITERRANEAN

Mare Nostrum . . . Our Sea

Mare Nostrum" to the Romans, "British Lake" to Britons, to the naval armed guards and their merchant mariners, the Mediterranean Sea was more simply known as "The Med," and will be referred to as such frequently in the following account of the war in the Mediterranean.

Domination of the Mediterranean Sea, the long, narrow inland body of water that stretches from the Atlantic to the Dardanelles and is surrounded by Europe, Asia, and North Africa, has been contested from antiquity. It has been fought over by Greeks, Phoenicians, Persians, Romans, Carthaginians, Ottomans, and others over the centuries. However, nothing in its long history of conflict could approach the intensity of the continuous violent combat of World War II. While the Med is some 2,400 miles long, Europe and Africa are never more than 850 miles apart, and much closer at a number of points, the tiny island of Malta being the most strategic. Malta is equidistant from Gibraltar and Crete, Sicily is 90 miles to the north, and Tripoli in North Africa is little more than 200 miles to the south. Malta is the key to the Med, as it lies athwart both the east-west and north-south lines of communication and commerce. Great Britain ousted the French in 1800 and developed the island into a fortress dominating the trade routes. The completion of the Suez Canal in 1869 increased its importance as a key link in the road to the fabled riches of the East.

In World War II Malta was a bone in the throat of the Axis powers, a serious threat to the supply lines of Axis forces in North Africa. They agreed that Malta had to be immobilized or captured. Under air attack both day and night, Malta became the most heavily bombed place on earth, but stubbornly held out and even struck back when reinforcements of British Spitfires were delivered, taking a heavy toll of attackers. However, aerial attack was so constant that Malta was virtually isolated. In one four-month period only four ships carrying supplies and war material were able to make port. The narrow configuration of the Med made it possible for the Axis to completely surround it with air bases in Europe and North Africa. They were able to seize air control over the sea in January 1942, and it was quickly learned by the British that the system of convoys proving so successful elsewhere was not working in attempts to relieve Malta. Convoys were easily spotted by Axis aerial reconnaissance, with heavy and continuous attacks following. Ernle Bradford, a navigation officer on a British destroyer in 1943, reported that one convoy from Alexandria was almost completely wiped out, and another was forced to turn back even before reaching the halfway point because too many merchantmen had been lost to make it worthwhile to proceed any further and the escorts had run out of AA ammunition. A small but significant amount of vital necessities were brought in by submarine.[1]

The configuration of the Med led to the development of a new type of naval warfare, in which planes were more important than battleships. Since practically no target was inaccessible to attack, new dive-bombing tactics were perfected here by both sides, as was the use of torpedo planes. With the signing of a full military alliance with Italy in May 1939 and a Soviet-German non-aggression pact (August 1939), Hitler felt secure from the possibility of a two-front war and felt confident that the large and formidable Italian Navy developed by Il Duce would be able to take care of the Med. The new Italian fleet did look dashing on maneuvers; it was fast, powerful in balance, including some 100 submarines, and heavily gunned. However, defense of the fleet had been sacrificed for speed, proving to be a fatal error.

The loss of the powerful French fleet following the fall of France was a major blow to Britain's expectations of action in the Med. Ironically, the first major engagement in the

Med was not Britain versus the Axis, but Britain versus the immobilized French fleet in North Africa, to deny its possible use by Hitler. The French fleet was knocked out for good, at heavy cost in ships and men.

Success followed success for the Axis at first. The Italian campaign in North Africa went very well for a time, until it stalled and eventually collapsed. Germany had to reinforce its dubious ally with the famed Afrika Korps under Rommel, which was highly successful for months. However, the difficulty of keeping lines of supply open under heavy Allied attack eventually doomed its campaign. Meanwhile, the British were having supply troubles of their own. Heavy losses of convoys in the western Med led to a change of route, much slower, but a lot safer. Allied shipping was forced to follow the centuries-old route of renowned Portuguese navigator Vasco da Gama, who pioneered the journey by sea around the continent of Africa, via the Cape of Good Hope, up the east coast of Africa and across the Indian Ocean to India. Allied supply ships went down and around the Cape and cleared through the Suez Canal to deliver their supplies to Egypt, a voyage of some 12,000 miles. Many American merchantmen delivering supplies for the Russians followed the route to the Persian Gulf, via the Arabian Sea.

It did not take long for the British fleet and aircraft to dispose of the Italian fleet as a viable force. An occasional Italian submarine met with some success, but the most effective naval weapon used by the Italians was frogmen, who did more damage than the rest of the navy combined. These special assault forces, comprising flimsy one-way E-boats carrying torpedoes, one and two-man torpedoes, and strong individual swimmers who affixed heavy explosives to ships' keels, were highly successful. One unit alone, the Tenth Light Flotilla, sank or damaged twenty-eight ships, including the battleships *Queen Elizabeth* and *Valiant,* the cruiser *York,* and over 110,000 tons of merchant shipping. The frogmen were used to great effect in the harbors of Alexandria and Gibraltar, where American merchantmen also encountered them.[2]

The SS *Esso Gettysburg* was the first American tanker to go into Gibraltar during the war, arriving on 29 August 1942, more than two months before the invasion of North Africa. Chief Mate Herman Kastber reported later, "At Gibraltar we were told to be very careful not to let bumboats come alongside, as in time of peace, to sell wine, etc. In several cases the enemy had used a bumboat to put a man overboard to attach a bomb to the bilge keel of a ship in the bay. We had orders to warn any bumboat away and then fire a shot across her bow. If this failed, we were to drop an anti-personnel depth charge—strong enough to blow a man out of the water within a radius of 50 feet, but not sufficiently powerful to harm the tanker."[5]

Merchant ships, loaded with war material and anchored at Gibraltar, were lucrative targets, and Italian frogmen made numerous daring raids against them. These units operated almost under the noses of the British defenders, one group operating from an innocent-appearing villa on the Spanish coast just two miles from the roadstead. All frogmen, of necessity, were superb swimmers, and they swam regularly across the bay to attach explosives to Allied ships. Another group operated from an old Italian merchant ship docked across the bay from Gibraltar. The ship had an underwater door so that frogmen and their torpedoes would be undetected, and it has been reported that the British never did learn where they had come from or where they had gone.

In November 1942 while waiting at Algiers for orders to move on, the AG crew aboard the SS *William Johnson* witnessed a daring attack by Italian frogmen. They broke the back of one ship, sank one, and damaged two others. Six frogmen were captured. Still more merchant ships were damaged by frogmen in Algiers in early December 1942.

Somewhat later, a Liberty ship, the SS *Harrison Gray Otis,* was moored in the harbor of Gibraltar. Around midnight the deck watch spotted a man floundering in the water nearby. When pulled out he was found to be an Italian frogman who had attached a mine to the hull of the ship. The

British, by then more experienced in such things, suggested that the engine should be turned over slowly, with the possibility that the propeller wash might dislodge it. The tactic did not work, as sometime later the mine exploded and damaged the *Otis* to such an extent that she was designated as a total constructive loss. Two other merchant ships were also mined that night. Later the SS *Patrick Harrison* was also mined and declared a total loss. Two British ships nearby in the harbor were also damaged by mines.

Only occasionally was there a lighter note in the war in the Med. HMS *Opportune,* which had performed nobly in seventeen North Russian convoys and had rescued survivors from the stricken SS *Henry Bacon* and towed the helpless SS *John Latrobe* from drifting into a minefield, also served in the Med. Able Seaman Len Phillips reports, "We were returning from the Mediterranean by way of the Bay of Biscay when a shadowing sub was caught by one of our aircraft, which had damaged the conning tower. We were dispatched to the scene to investigate. It was our intention to capture the sub intact, but this wasn't to be, as unknown to our boarding party, the sea cocks had been opened; fortunately the party had not yet gotten on board. All the German sailors were swimming about in the water or floating singing the German National Anthem. Our skipper said, "Let them finish," and then we picked them up and dispatched them as prisoners of war in the UK. The incident occurred 30 October 1942 and the submarine was U-517." Phillips has since exchanged correspondence with the U-boat commander, who became a high-ranking officer in the postwar Germany Navy.[4]

With the exception of the delivery of two deckloads of Spitfires by the USS *Wasp* to Malta, the Med had been almost exclusively a British show. In June 1942, however, two merchantmen with AG gun crews received a fiery initiation into the meat grinder that was Malta. The Dutch-flag *Tanimbar* and the American SS *Chant* were part of a five-ship convoy from Scotland carrying munitions, provisions, and medical supplies. The destination given the masters was said to be

Freetown, but the AG crews quickly got other ideas when they saw they were being escorted by ten destroyers and two cruisers, hardly a routine escort for five merchantmen. At Gibraltar a large tanker was added to the convoy, as was an additional escort of one battleship, two carriers, three more cruisers, eleven additional destroyers, four minesweepers and six motor launches. This awesome array of naval might must have raised unlimited speculation on the part of merchant crews and AGs as to what was ahead. It can be assumed they formed a firm conviction that they weren't going to enjoy it.

They didn't have long to wait for the action to begin; the convoy was spotted by aircraft within hours. Ammo was laid out, and the AGs remained at General Quarters the entire day and night of 13 June. Serious action began the next morning with an attack by fifty enemy aircraft—high- and medium-level bombers and torpedo planes. Both the *Chant* and *Tanimbar* fired at the aircraft and shot one down. A torpedo plane made a run on the *Tanimbar* and hit her amidships, but the plane was shot down. The ship was soon enveloped in flames and ordered abandoned; within five minutes she sank by the stern, but all the AGs were rescued. The *Chant* was strafed with no damage, and the gunners ate at their guns awaiting the next big attack, when forty-five dive-bombers and torpedo planes struck with no damage. The convoy proceeded slowly, coming under unsuccessful fire from shore batteries and from two Italian cruisers and three destroyers that remained at a discreet distance and caused no harm. However, the *Chant*'s luck was about to run out. In still another air attack she was hit amidships, and part of her hull plating blew off. When flames spread on the decks, the men were ordered to abandon ship. All the AGs made it, but several crewmen were lost. What was left of the battered convoy reached port, but a Polish destroyer was sunk entering the harbor.

Two AG officers and one gunner's mate were awarded the Silver Star, and the remaining members of the AG gun crews received commendations for their actions. This was the first of the many ordeals to be faced by AGs in the Med, and as they moved on to North Africa, Sicily, Salerno, Anzio, and southern France, they were to be hit with everything a determined enemy could throw at them.[5]

Operation Torch, the invasion of North Africa, was the launching of the first real American contribution to operations in the Med, a baptism of fire for American merchantmen and their AG crews. The invasion was three-pronged, with landings at Algiers, Oran-Arzeu, and Casablanca on the nights of 7 and 8 November 1942. The Moroccan phase was entrusted entirely to U.S. forces; the Algerian venture was a joint British-American operation. It was a tremendous undertaking. Over 700 ships were assembled for the invasion, to take place along 1,000 miles of coastline. The Western Task Force took off from the Norfolk, Virginia, area with one of the largest convoys ever assembled and traveled a devious course of some 3,100 miles to get to Casablanca. The Center Task Force, also composed of American troops, set sail from England, to land in the vicinity of Oran. The Eastern Task Force, of American and British troops, was to land near Algiers. Merchant ships of the Western Task Force alone carried twenty-two million pounds of food and ten million gallons of gasoline, and other major convoys were similar in nature. The logistics were staggering, but the biggest problem was getting the necessary material together. General Lyman Lemnitzer was then assistant chief of staff for Plans and Operations of Operation Torch and he reported his many frustrations, the most important being tied in with the Battle of the Atlantic: ". . . We finally picked the date for early September. Almost daily, however, our forecast got a torpedo in it somewhere because the Battle of the Atlantic was on. It was one of the most discouraging operations I think I have ever participated in. As a planner you counted on getting something, but it simply disappeared . . . for example, we had a ship sink in the Atlantic which lost all of the divisional artillery—I think it was the First Division."[6]

U.S. merchant ships, defended by armed guards, played an important role in the North African invasion. In the Oran area alone they defended some thirty ships that brought the munitions and supplies necessary to consolidate position and begin the push toward Tunis. They were the spearhead of what would become as many as 1,500 merchant ships in the Med at one time. Not a single merchant ship carrying AGs was lost in the invasion of Algiers, although a number got into action, firing on and shooting down enemy planes. The SS *Edward Rutledge* came under fire from shore batteries with no damage, and had no hesitation at shooting at planes (including one British aircraft that was dilatory in identifying itself). She was the only ship to effect landing of ammunition and gasoline under unfavorable sea conditions at Arzeu.[7]

George Prestmo of Mt. Vernon, Washington, was assigned to the *Rutledge,* a part of a large convoy, destination unknown. At Torpedo Alley a number of ships left the convoy, probably heading for Murmansk, while his ship continued to Ireland and into Liverpool. After unloading, carpenters came aboard and built a galley and latrine on the after deck and converted the after hold into sleeping quarters; landing craft were loaded on the forward deck.

When work was completed, American soldiers came aboard and moved into the hold; English sailors came aboard to operate the landing craft. Just before the ship sailed, word came that of the ships that had left the convoy at Torpedo Alley, fourteen had been sunk or were not accounted for. Prestmo continues with his story:

"We entered the Med in a convoy so big that ships were in sight in every direction. We stayed on our guns in the gun tubs all the time, sandwiches were brought to us. It was weird. We were all blacked out, sitting on our guns and on the Gibraltar side we could see lights on shore, and lights to our right which we were told was Tangiers.

"Early in the morning of 7 January, we stopped and landing craft were put over the side, with their English coxswains. The soldiers got into the landing craft and they took off in the dark. It was getting light, big guns were shelling off to our right, and huge flashes were seen on the horizon, a

British battleship shelling Oran. We and about twenty other ships pulled into a small harbor, Arzeu, French Algeria. We could see our soldiers on the shore. Suddenly a plane flew low over the beach and started strafing. We went all out on the guns, and shot it down, and I still have a piece of it that I got when we went ashore. It was a British Spitfire, piloted by a French collaborationist."

Life was not entirely grim in Operation Torch. "One day while on gangway watch, I saw one of our sailors and a Limey mess boy rolling a big keg of wine down the dock. I helped them get it aboard, and took it to the galley used by the soldiers and poured it into two big coffee makers. Officers on the ships wondered how we stayed so cheerful all the way back to Liverpool. As we were entering the Mersey River, some of the merchant seamen threw their Boatswain's Mate over the side; he was picked up by a dredge, but refused to come back.

"The *Rutledge* with another load of soldiers, left Loch Long, Scotland, on Christmas Day 1942. Our menu for Christmas was boiled cod fish, but as we went into the Irish Sea it was very rough, and the soldiers lined up on both sides of the deck throwing up over the rail. Their cooks had prepared turkey, dehydrated potatoes and gravy, but none of the soldiers could eat, so we were invited to eat their meal (much better than cod fish).

"As we proceeded into the ocean it was terribly cold, and the seas were so rough that we couldn't stand watch on the bow. We put on our life-saving rubber suits and gathered on the boat deck to stand watch. Ships around us began going up in big flames, a German wolfpack had gotten into the middle of our convoy and were picking off the tankers. I remember seeing three of them burning in the distance, and wondering which of my buddies were on them.

"In Oran we unloaded our troops, and one evening I heard a lot of depth charges and saw corvettes scooting around the harbor. Suddenly an Italian sub popped up and gave up. Later the harbor was bombed. I was a pointer on a 3-inch 50 and a piece of shrapnel passed by my head, between my hands, struck my right knee, tearing a big gash and buried itself in the trunnion of my gun. I got a Purple Heart, and the ship got a citation for our actions in French North Africa."[8]

Prestmo served in the armed guard from the beginning to the end (September 1941–45); he served on six ships and says he doesn't know anyone left who served any longer than he.

A mystery of sea warfare until quite recently was the disappearance of the SS *C.J. Barkdull,* a Panamanian-flag tanker carrying a crew of thirty-eight officers and men and an AG crew of twenty. She sailed from New York on 12 December 1942 in a convoy of forty-five ships, with strong naval escort, for a "secret destination," according to a report of the Standard Oil Co. of New Jersey. The vessel did not arrive at her destination, and on 30 January 1943 the War Shipping Administration reported her "long overdue and presumed lost." All that was known was that on 13 December she was seen to lose headway and drop out of the convoy. She was never heard from again, and her entire merchant crew and AG gun crew, under Ensign Meyer Stein, were lost. Years later it was determined that she had been sunk by the *U-632* on 10 January 1943, at an unknown point in the North Atlantic, and that her original destination had been Casablanca, French Morocco.[9] Today, even that is in doubt.

As one successful campaign in North Africa and the Med followed another, a flood of shipping carrying supplies, equipment, and manpower poured into the Med. If anyone expected easier going, they were quickly disillusioned, as the supply convoys faced hot opposition from determined *Luftwaffe* and U-boat opponents. The most costly attack on a convoy, in terms of lives lost on a single ship, was made against Convoy UGS-38, made up of eighty-six ships, off the Algerian coast en route to Bizerte on 20 April 1944. Striking at dusk, the most dangerous part of the day, German torpedo planes flashed in and launched their lethal cargo. The Liberty ship SS *Paul Hamilton,* carrying a cargo of high explosives and a large contingent of army air force personnel,

Survivors of a sunken ship await rescue. (National Archives)

was struck and blew to pieces in a violent explosion. The nearby SS *Fitzhugh Lee* had its deck covered with pieces of steel, debris, and oil and had all of its guns knocked out. When the huge cloud of smoke cleared, there was not a sign of the *Paul Hamilton,* passengers or crew. All had vanished in an instant. There were no survivors of the merchant crew of 47, the AG unit of 29, and the 504 army passengers. Several other ships were lost or damaged, but a number of enemy planes were destroyed or damaged, including the one that hit the *Paul Hamilton,* set afire by gunners on a ship it passed during its attack.

Some small degree of reprisal was achieved on 11 May 1944 when German planes attacked a fifty-six-ship convoy off Algiers. In a remarkable display of shooting, armed guard crews were credited with thirteen planes destroyed, five assists, and four probables. By this time many AG gunners were veterans of enemy attack. Ships involved in this action included the SS *Abraham Lincoln, Colin P. Kelly, Jr., Clement Clay, William Patterson, William Mulholland, Zachary Taylor, Thomas W. Bickett, Thomas L. Clingman, Stephen A. Douglas, Samuel Moody, Peger Zenger, John Stevens, James Whitcomb Riley, James W. Fannin, James W. Gillis, Grenville M. Dodge,* and *George Dern,* each of whom was credited with destroying or damaging the enemy attackers. The *James W. Fannin* had perhaps one of the most unusual experiences of the war. In addition to downing two planes, it caught a torpedo in its torpedo net, later removed at Malta.

The use of torpedo nets was largely restricted to areas around the British Isles and in the Mediterranean. Affixed to fore-and-aft booms, they protected the ship from #1 and #2 holds forward to #4 and #5 holds aft, leaving only a tip of the bow and stern unprotected. Swung outward by the booms on both sides of the ship, they were half-in and half-out of the water and protected the hull down to the keel; the basic purpose was to ensnare the screw of an incoming torpedo and prevent it from striking the ship, but there are few reports of the nets' effectiveness. The Liberty SS *Thomas Fitzsimmons* was outfitted with torpedo nets in Wales, at a time when she was calling at many ports in the British Isles; she also made use of them in the Mediterranean, but never had occasion to see how well they worked, although she participated in the invasions of Sicily, Salerno, Anzio, and South France.[11]

Indicative of the action in the Med is the U.S. Navy commendation given the armed guard unit aboard the SS *William T. Barry* for action against enemy aircraft while en route to Gibraltar on 13 August 1943: "A report of the experience reveals that the convoy of which your ship was a part was attacked by a large formation of German bombers which approached from dead ahead, coming out of the setting sun and flying very low over the water. As they flew down the columns of ships, launching their deadly missiles, the planes were met by an accurate and vicious barrage of shellfire which completely disrupted their plan of attack.

The navy gun crew of the *William Barry* performed brilliantly, shooting down three of the enemy and contributing to the destruction of three more, thereby insuring the safety of their ship and the successful completion of its mission. . . ."[12]

Creal "Irish" Gibson, of Jersey City, was a signalman 2/c, aboard the USAT *Santa Elena*. A former Grace Line liner operating in South American service, she was at that time carrying 1,965 Canadian troops and a contingent of nurses from England to Naples to participate in the Italian campaign. She was hit by a German torpedo plane and seriously damaged; she was then rammed by a fellow convoy member and subsequently sank. The experience was nothing new to Gibson. He had survived the sinking of the USS *Langley* in the Indian Ocean on 27 February 1942 and had been plucked out of the sea by the USS *Whipple* (DD 217) and transferred to the USS *Pecos*. The *Pecos* was sunk by enemy action on 1 March, and Gibson found himself once more in the water. Incredibly, he was not only pulled out again by the *Whipple*, but for the second time his savior was a close friend from the orphanage they had lived in before the war. In November 1942 Gibson was transferred to the Armed Guard Center, Brooklyn, and somewhat later reported aboard the *Santa Elena*.

Gibson was one of a forty-four-man AG crew; the *Santa Elena* was in a convoy of over twenty ships with destroyer escort, 27 miles west of Philippeville, Algeria, when enemy planes struck. The *Santa Elena* brought down one plane, but was hit by a torpedo that disabled her engines and steering gear and tore a hole about 20 feet in diameter in the port side. The ammunition magazine was pierced, but did not explode. About the same time a torpedo struck the Dutch-flag *Marnix Van Sint Algebonde*. Gibson reports, "I felt the whole ship shake from a direct hit. I was sitting on top the smoke-floats trying to launch them, to no avail. I remember the excitement and confusion of the soldiers bunched along the side rails and back on the fantail. I heard some sounds from the water just below me and heard that there were some men in the water. Without giving it any thought, I went off the fantail. I saw one man struggling and screaming for help and pulled him back to the side and had a rope thrown down and secured it to the soldier and they hauled him aboard. I was ready for the rope for me when I heard another call for help from not far distant. I left the line hanging and went to the other man, pulling him back by the collar of his life jacket, and got the line on him. When I got back on board I went to the signal bridge, and the Canadians were transferred to another ship without loss of a single man. After finishing my watch I heard a lot of screaming and saw a huge black object (the Dutch ship) bearing down on us from our starboard side. I grabbed an Aldis lamp and tried to signal them, but they rammed us just forward of the bridge. We were under tow at the time and all of a sudden the tow line parted and we rolled over to port, a number of us being thrown into the water. We were picked up by a destroyer escort within a half-hour and were put ashore." The *Santa Elena* had put up a good fight for survival, but the double blow was too much for her and she went down on 21 July 1944. Gibson received a citation from Secretary of the Navy James Forrestal for his rescue effort.[13]

Declassified Canadian government documents concerning the sinking of the *Santa Elena* corroborate Gibson's report and add some further details. One officer reports that "the work of the gun crew of the *Santa Elena* was excellent," but has some harsh comments on the ship's crew. Brigadier G. W. Hallenby confirms this, saying, "The loud speaker system was working and orders were given from the bridge to lower the lifeboats. These contained nurses and part of the crew. These crew members apparently had no idea of handling the boats. They were South American waiters and stewards, and in many cases the nurses had to take the oars. Orders were then given from the bridge to throw over the life rafts. This was very badly handled by the ship's crew. Rafts were thrown over indiscriminately and allowed to drift away before any of the troops could get aboard them . . . during the voyage there were many 'Fire Drills' and 'Abandon

Ship' drills, but apparently no proper practice of lowering lifeboats, scramble nets and rafts. It was apparent that the lifeboat crews were unfamiliar with the handling of boats." Still another officer reports, "There was general criticism of the behaviour of the crew of the *Santa Elena.* The moment they came alongside the *Monterey* they were the first up the ladders." In retrospect, it seems miraculous that not one person of the Canadian contingent was lost; however, there was one last plaintive comment, "The following afternoon the *Santa Elena* appeared in tow escorted by destroyers. At 1715 hours the tug seemed to slow up. Then the aft portion of the *Santa Elena* slowly sank by the stern, her bow rising from the water. She finally turned over on her starboard side and slowly settled and disappeared, a very depressing sight, with all our personal kit going down before our eyes." [14]

Battle action grew heavier as the merchant ships and their AG gun crews began to move eastward in support of the Allied movement on land. Enemy air attacks became heavier and more frequent, with increasing numbers of planes shot down by ship's gunners. The SS *William Wirt* compiled a spectacular record in a thirteen-ship convoy bound for Philippeville in January 1943. Carrying a heavy load of aviation gasoline, the *Wirt* was the first to fire on a group of attackers and sent four of them into the sea. One of the planes had put a bomb into #1 hold, which was filled with drums of gas, but providentially, it failed to explode. Another bomb hit and flooded #3 hold, but she stayed with the convoy. A day or so later the convoy was again attacked by waves of bombers and torpedo planes, but the *Wirt*'s luck still held. Next to come was a submarine, forced to the surface by depth charges. The *Wirt*'s gunners opened up on it along with an escorting destroyer, and the sub sank backward into the sea.

Through continuing waves of enemy attacks, the *Wirt* was undamaged, but finally one near-miss knocked the propeller shaft out of line and she had to return to England for repairs. [15]

The increasing effectiveness of the heavy defensive AG fire kept enemy planes from attaining advantageous positions to launch their bombs and torpedoes, and in this the *Wirt*'s sharpshooters were particularly outstanding.

On 16 March 1943 in Convoy UGS-6 bound for the Med, the SS *Benjamin Harrison*, which had miraculously survived the slaughter of Convoy PQ-17 to Murmansk in July 1942, was torpedoed off the Azores and eventually sunk by an escort. Incredibly, the escort was the USS *Rowan*, which had been one of the covering escorts of PQ-17 and had been forced to leave with the other escorts by order of the British Admiralty. The *Rowan* in turn was lost 9 September 1943 at Salerno. In the same convoy, the SS *Molly Pitcher* was torpedoed. Two AGs lost their lives, but the AG officer and other survivors stayed aboard with some of the ship's crew to try and save the vessel, to no avail.[16]

The war was far from being won, and there were many more ships to be lost or damaged, and lives to be lost. The Liberty SS *Nathaniel Greene*, battle-scarred survivor of PQ-18 to Murmansk and damaged by the explosion and annihilation of the nearby SS *Mary Luckenbach*, finally had her luck run out off Algeria while joining a passing convoy. German bombers attacked her with three torpedoes and in company with a U-boat, killing four crew members and wounding others. All seventeen AGs survived, but the ship was towed to port and declared a total loss. Another troop ship, the SS *William B. Woods*, carrying 400 troops and ammunition, was torpedoed, and exploded with the loss of over one hundred men.[17]

An unusual story of the war in the Med is told by "Pete" Burke, Philadelphia, who served on a number of ships as commodore's signalman. Assigned to the SS *John B. Hood*, they left New York for Norfolk, Virginia, to pick up fifty MPs, plus bombs for Sicily. The forward holds had been fitted out for Italian prisoners of war, hence the fifty MPs. "By the time we got into the Med, Italy had surrendered, so we unloaded our cargo, except for the MPs, and came back empty. For them overseas was just one big boat ride. After getting back to New York, 500 troops were put aboard, but the same night they were taken off, as we had received changed orders to pick up more cargo in Charleston, South Carolina. When we got back to Norfolk, there were the same 500 troops, shipped down by rail. We then sailed for Casablanca, 15 days, and that's when I was glad I was in the Navy, they were cooped up in the forward holds all that time. They would line up for chow, and by the time all got served, it was time to line up again. We arrived in Casablanca on 19 December 1943.

"Christmas Day some of us were drinking in a big bar in Casablanca. It was crowded with servicemen from half a dozen countries, the uniforms of Americans, English, Australian, French, Polish, Canadian . . . but one little guy at the end of the bar had a uniform that was different than anyone else. He was all by himself, so Mac and I thought we would buy him a drink to cheer him up. He turned out to be a German in the French Foreign Legion—with the magic of cognac we conversed with "Hans" in three languages, German, French and English, and began to sing, including some German drinking songs that I knew. Hans was reluctant to join in singing German drinking songs in a bar full of Allied servicemen, but booze has a habit of putting back-bone into the least of us, so he finally joined us, and we really turned up the volume with the Drinking Song from the *Student Prince* . . . even though there was a war going on with Germany, nobody in the bar seemed to give a damn. I guess we were all there for the same purpose, to drink and leave the war behind." [18]

Operation Torch had just been a prelude to what was to come, a step on the road to the invasion of Europe. To follow was a great military amphibious operation directed at the historic island of Sicily, a battleground of rival empires for centuries. Separated from the mainland of Italy only by the narrow Strait of Messina, capture of strategic Sicily was imperative to Allied plans. Operation Husky, under overall command of Lieutenant General Dwight Eisenhower, called for the landing of two major invasion forces on the island. The U.S. 7th Army was to move into the Gulf of Gela to the southwest, and the British 8th Army, battle-scarred veterans of the desert war, was to move in on the east coast. A vast armada of ships ferrying supplies for the operation from North Africa followed the invasion forces, which landed on 10–11 July 1943.[19]

Merchant ships supporting U.S. forces arriving at Gela were attacked almost immediately by shore batteries and planes. The SS *Robert Rowan* was straddled by the artillery fire, which caused no damage, but three bombs made direct hits and the ship began burning. The *Rowan* was carrying ammunition and a total of 421 merchant seamen, AGs, and army troops; passengers and crew were ordered to abandon ship, followed a few minutes later by the armed guards. Miraculously, all were clear of the ship when it was blown in half by a terrific explosion. The merchant crew and the armed guards were taken to Algiers and arrived just in time to witness the distintegration of a Norwegian freighter carrying munitions that caused much damage to the port and killed many. They were just two hundred yards from a Canadian ammunition ship that was set aflame and whose ammunition started to explode.

The SS *Nicholas Gilman* had a lot of action and some very close calls at Gela. She was first shelled from the beach by German tanks, causing some casualties, including an AG. In an early afternoon attack she experienced ten near-misses, followed in a second raid by five near-misses and a direct hit in her #1 hatch. Fire broke out but was brought under control. From 10–18 July the exhausted gun crew slept by their guns and were officially credited with two planes destroyed and one assist. She returned to Gibraltar where a number of ships nearby were damaged by explosives attached to the hulls by enemy frogmen.

Seven armed guards were wounded by shell fragments while serving the after 3″ gun on the SS *Joseph Pulitzer*. She escaped major damage and shot down two planes, and later carried supplies to Palermo. The SS *Lawton B. Evans* was slightly damaged by a number of near-misses, and returned to Bizerte where an unexploded shell made a hole in #1 hatch, wounding one AG, George J. Edel, seaman 1/c, who won the Silver Star for his action on this occasion. Wounded by a shell fragment, he returned to his gun station with a piece of steel still in his arm and helped bring down a German plane.

Enemy activity against the American forces eased off at Gela, but picked up sharply as more merchant ships arrived at Palermo. Two AGs on the SS *Samuel Huntington* and four on the SS *William Mulholland* were wounded by shell fragments. The SS *William W. Gelhard* was close to an ammunition ship that blew up at the dock; shells flew around the ship, and many fell on the decks. Three AGs were wounded, but many were saved when a quick-thinking AG officer threw a shell overboard just before it exploded. Bombs fell all around her, but did no damage. Members of the AG crew helped unload cargo to hasten the departure of the ship from Palermo; she made it, but had exhausted her luck and was sunk a short time later en route to Salerno.

The *William B. Travis* had survived a torpedo attack on the way to Palermo, in which two ships were hit. Returning to Bizerte she hit a mine that tore open the port side of #2 hold and caused casualties, including four AGs wounded. However, they concealed their injuries and returned to man their guns, and the *Travis* made Bizerte safely.

While the experience of the U.S. merchant ships on the west coast was not dull, the action involving ships supplying the east coast invasion forces at Avola was much more intense. From 10–14 July there were fifty air raids. The AG crew aboard the *Colin Kelly Jr.* ate and slept at their guns, and an AG officer never left the bridge for four days. The gun crew of "Coffin Corner Kelly" performed exceptionally; they shot down six enemy planes and scored contributory hits on four more, in spite of numerous shell fragments falling all around. The third mate was particularly praised for his performance, laughing, joking, and singing, inspiring the crew while hot shrapnel was bouncing all around them on the deck.

The most horrible experience of ships at Avola occurred when an enemy plane put two bombs into a hold full of ammunition on the SS *Timothy Pickering*, which had just arrived and still had troops aboard. The ship vanished in an awful explosion, only a towering smoke-filled cloud remaining. Of 192 men aboard the *Pickering* the only survivors were twenty-three men blown overboard in the initial explosion. The nearby SS *O. Henry* was hit by bits of the ship, and several men were killed—including one soldier, ironically hit by a flying truck wheel.[20]

Armed guard voyage reports give grim evidence of the severity of the battle for the eastern beachhead. Practically every merchant ship off the beaches had one or more close calls. Heavy and continuous fire from AG gun crews kept the bombing from being even more accurate and deadly. A postwar report written for the navy states that there was probably no action in the European theater in which merchant ships participated that was more dangerous or more bitterly fought than that at eastern Sicily.[21]

The thirty-four-man NAG crew aboard the SS *Esso Providence* under Ensign Sydney N. Wagner, must have thought that providence indeed was watching over their ship. After partially refueling three British naval vessels at Augusta, Sicily, on 24 August 1943, she was attacked by enemy aircraft, which scored a direct hit, but she was able to complete the discharge of her cargo of navy fuel oil. On 29 August she experienced four air attacks in two and a half hours. Badly damaged, emergency repairs were effected in Augusta. Wire cables were passed around the vessel to hold the extensive wreckage in place, and it was decided to try to proceed to Malta where more effective temporary repairs could be made. Rough seas and Force 5 winds combined to carry the emergency repairs away, and loose wreckage was pounding heavily. In order to steer the ship, the captain had to carry 15–21 degrees right rudder, and speed was reduced to 5 knots. After finally limping into Malta, on 19 October one of her ammunition lockers caught fire from undetermined cause. It could have been catastrophic, as the blaze threatened to explode fifty 5-inch shells, and 20-mm projectiles were flying all about. However, due to the heroism of Chief Mate Leslie H. Winder, who was severely burned, the fire was extinguished before it cost the lives of the crew and the ship. Winder was highly commended, but in his report he merely remarked, "Nothing interesting happened on this voyage. There was a fire and it was put out."[22]

After heavy fighting, the conquest of Sicily was completed on 8 August 1943, and in a reverse-Dunkirk, thousands of Axis defenders were successfully evacuated to the mainland. The ancient city of Salerno, on the gulf of the same name, was chosen as the next target of the Allied movement into Europe. The invasion of the Italian mainland was begun on 9 September 1943 under the code name Operation Avalanche. Soaring Churchillian rhetoric will ring and offer inspiration through the ages, but it unfortunately did not always conform to the actual state of affairs; certainly it did not to those who participated in the painful, slogging advance northward from the beaches of Salerno. There was nothing soft about his proclaimed "soft underbelly of Europe." Progress was slow, and a high price was paid for every mile; over 12,000 Allied troops were lost at Salerno alone, including some 5,000 Americans.[23]

As usual, the merchant ships followed the invasion barges and landing craft, carrying the vital, high-priority materiel without which no invasion force can survive in the face of a determined enemy. And determined it was, as Allied forces on land and sea soon found out. American merchant ships were faced with heavy and continuous air opposition from the moment they arrived. Although most had seen enemy action before, a report written for the navy says that AGs agreed that there had never been a worse experience than the "awful six and one-half days of death and destruction off Salerno." Armed guards remained at their battle stations the entire time, a grim struggle against both the enemy and complete physical exhaustion, while the fate of the beachhead hung in the balance. Ship after ship reported up to thirty or more air attacks, including the SS *George Matthews* (twenty-one), *Lewis Morris* (twenty-nine) *William Dean Howells* (thirty-eight), *Winfield Scott* (twenty-seven), and *James Woodrow* (over thirty) with near-misses too many to count. The *Hugh Williamson* appears to have been a favorite target for the enemy; her AG officer reported forty-eight bombing attacks, in which she destroyed nine planes. Her gunners shot the fin off a glider bomb that missed the ship by five feet, and then helped rescue men from other ships that were hit. In more "quiet" moments, they even helped unload cargo.[24]

The SS *Bushrod Washington,* loaded with army trucks, ammunition, and high-test aviation gasoline, was the first American merchant ship to be sunk, hit by a radio-guided aerial bomb on 14 September 1943 while anchored in the Gulf of Salerno about one mile from shore. Fire reached the ammunition hold and she exploded, destroying the forward part of the ship. Six crew members and one AG were killed and many others injured, but the casualties might have been much heavier if not for the heroism of Cadet/Midshipman John Herbert, who showed great resourcefulness in cutting loose a burning landing craft loaded with ammunition, after a bomb killed thirteen crewmen and other army stevedores. The ship was ordered abandoned and the AG gun crew trans-ferred to other vessels, including the SS *James W. Marshall,* to continue the fight. The *Marshall* also was badly damaged and later towed to Bizerte, still manned by most of the gun crew from the *Bushrod Washington.* Shortly after abandon-ing ship, the master of the *Washington,* the AG officer, and two members of the crew reboarded the vessel in an attempt to extinguish the fire and remove the dead and injured. How-ever, the fire was out of control and the vessel was ordered abandoned by a navy vessel, the USS *Hopi.*[25]

The next large group of merchant ships entering Salerno Bay received an equally warm welcome, some being at-tacked before they even dropped anchor. One of these was the SS *William G. Gerhard,* noted for its valiant action in Sicily. Carrying gasoline and field artillery, she was hit by a torpedo, and the crew was ordered to abandon ship. The AG officer learned that there were wounded AGs still aboard, and he returned to get them. Of the thirty-man detachment, two AGs were killed and six wounded. The ship sank a short time later.

Attacks on merchant ships at Salerno decreased as the

fighting moved north and the ships followed. The *Elihu Yale,* soon to be lost at Anzio, was in the first convoy to reach Naples. The SS *James Iredell* seemed to have a charmed life. She made it back after sustaining a torpedo attack, three direct bomb hits, concussion damage from an ammunition ship blown up just ahead of it, and after fighting a three-day fire in the hold. The battered, war-weary but valiant old ship finally met an ignoble end for a fighter of her caliber. She was deliberately sunk as part of the invasion breakwater of France on D-Day, but she served her country to the end.

German fighters and bombers were not the only hazard at Salerno. Al Hodge, who served in the AG crew on the SS *James Russell Lowell* stated that after dropping anchor at Salerno, the AG crew stood a modified General Quarters for seventeen days. One night while getting some sleep he was awakened by the severe vibration of the ship. Rushing on deck he observed that a terrible storm was in progress, the ship had both anchors down and the engines were running full speed ahead trying to keep from being blown onto the beach. When morning came, he saw ships scattered all over the anchorage, and several high and dry on the beach. On her return to Bizerte the *Lowell* was torpedoed, and the crew ordered to abandon ship. After pulling away, an injured man was noted on the forward 3″ 50-caliber gun, so the boat returned and Hodge and another AG went aboard to get the injured man. The *Lowell* was finally towed into port but was declared a total loss.[26]

Centuries ago the small fishing village of Anzio was a favorite resort for Roman gentry. Until World War II Anzio's chief claim to fame (or infamy) was that two of Rome's most unsavory emperors, Nero and Caligula, had been born there. However, there was nothing favorable about it to the Americans who suffered or died there, on land or aboard ship, in the dark days of a stalled Italian campaign in 1944. To those who survived, the mere mention of the name brings a strained expression and a frequent "What a nightmare!"

As originally planned the invasion was to be a brilliant, speedy, and successful end-run around the strongly German-held line, bringing an end to the months-long deadlock on that front by forcing the enemy to divert forces to the landings at Anzio-Nettuno. Instead it turned into a near-disaster. Although Italy had surrendered on 8 September 1943, the German Army fought a series of bloody rear-guard actions, the most effective at Monte Cassino, which blocked the Allied advance on Rome for five months at heavy cost in lives and ruined the timetable.

Anzio-Nettuno run together and are practically one city. The first surprise landings were quite successful against little opposition, but matters quickly got out of hand. The plan faltered when the Allies delayed pushing inland, allowing the Germans to consolidate their defenses. The result was a four-month horror story, with Allied forces pinned down on a small area of beaches, so flat that there were not even any rocks where Allied soldiers could find shelter, and with the enemy having the advantage of full observation from hills above. The tiny, shell-raked beaches offered no protection during the day, and the German raiders came overhead at night. Enemy flares and antiaircraft fire lighted the skies as bright as day. Sitting on a ship full of aviation gas or high explosives would not be conducive to calm nerves, but it did provide considerable incentive to work with vim while unloading.[27]

In addition to German 88s shelling the small beachhead and harbor, enemy bombers dropping a hail of explosives, and fast E-boats, the enemy brought in a new weapon, radio-guided glider-bombs, which possibly caused as much psychological as physical damage; U.S. Navy countermeasures succeeded in jamming and decoying many of the glider-bombs into the sea. However, there were many heart-stopping near-misses on the merchant vessels offshore, no doubt contributing to cases of "Anzio Anxiety" or "Nettuno Neurosis." Ashore, German propaganda leaflets were dropped that depicted a grinning skull covering Anzio harbor, titled "Beachhead—Death's Head!"[28]

While the situation was bad on the beach, it was little better on the ships delivering supplies and reinforcements.

To reduce the number of ships to be targets of enemy attacks, a regular shuttle service from Naples was inaugurated, but it was necessary to unload offshore, under regular attack. The Liberty SS *Elihu Yale* arrived off Anzio on 13 February amid air raids and shelling; she lay about one-half mile off the beach discharging shells into an LCT alongside when she was struck by a glider-bomb in the #4 hold. She exploded with a tremendous bang, followed by an enormous cloud of smoke rising high over the beachhead. Almost miraculously, only five men were killed, two AGs and three merchant crewmen, and four AGs were wounded.

Since an arriving large convoy offered too-attractive a target to the enemy, most ships arrived singly from Naples and left as quickly as they could be unloaded. Ships were kept moving around the roadstead when they were not being unloaded, and were moved into different positions overnight after the inevitable enemy reconnaissance planes departed, so as not to be in a known position, to preclude enemy gunners from finding the range. There was much shelling from German 88s; the SS *F. Marion Crawford* observed 200 near-misses in nine days as her captain shifted position regularly. The SS *John W. Brown* made several trips to Anzio and was regularly shelled from the hills. The *Brown* fought back with her 3″ guns, but the most effective deterrent was the appearance of American planes, at which time the German artillery ceased fire.

The SS *John Banvard* reported seventy-two alerts and twenty-five bombing attacks before two glider-bombs landed only ten yards from the ship, causing such heavy damage that the order was given to abandon ship. Lieutenant Lester Isenberg, USNR, Woodmont, Connecticut, was awarded the Navy and Marine Medal and Citation, and a commendation from Admiral Hewitt, CIC, U.S. Naval Forces, Northwest Africa waters for his action at the time.[29]

The extent of the ordeal of merchant ships at Anzio can be appreciated by their records. From 21–22 January, the SS *Hilary A. Herbert* reported seventy-five air raids and twenty-seven actual bombing attacks. She was so badly damaged by near-misses that she had to be beached, and then was hit by enemy artillery and missed by a glider-bomb by only 50 feet. Nevertheless, she eventually was towed to Naples for a full study of damage. Before she left she had shot down three planes, with two probably destroyed. The SS *Lawton B. Evans* was one of the first ships to arrive at Anzio. She had never seen action, and sixteen of the twenty-nine members of the AG gun crew had never been to sea before. When she left she had a veteran AG crew and five planes to her credit. Two ships that had seen a lot of action in the Mediterranean advance saw more at Anzio. The SS *Tabitha Brown* reported seventy-eight alerts from 31 January to 7 February, and the SS *William Mulholland* recorded sixty-two red alerts and was showered with shell fragments causing deck plates to crack. Both ships were credited with planes shot down or damaged as possibles. The SS *Edward Rutledge,* which had seen its share of action elsewhere, was the target of artillery, repeated air attacks, and a glider-bomb that landed 15 yards from the ship. The SS *James M. Wayne* visited Anzio four times and was the last ship to win the combat star for action at Anzio. In eleven days at Anzio the SS *Charles Goodyear* experienced every kind of attack the Germans could muster—bombing, submarine attack, aerial torpedoes, E-boats, mines, and shelling from shore. The AG was sent to General Quarters 106 times.[30]

While in the early stages of the action at Anzio, every ship had to defend herself, but eventually the Allies had so much antiaircraft weaponry on the beach that ships had orders not to fire at night unless they were attacked. With the brilliant German flares, and a sky filled with red tracers, plus 90-mm exploding overhead, one observer said that the harbor was "brighter than Yankee Stadium." It was dangerous for a ship to try to get away from the flares, because the phosphorescence of the water lighted up the wake of the ship and could attract a straddle pattern of bombs. Raid after raid came streaming over the harbor at night, because at dusk air cover had to be withdrawn.

Noted war correspondent Ernie Pyle reported that every

day and night a thin line of tiny boats ("Ducks") moved constantly back and forth between shore and ships at anchor a mile or so out in the harbor. "They reminded me of ants at work," he wrote.

The SS *Thomas Fitzsimmons* was in on the invasions of Sicily, Salerno, and Anzio. Herb Norch, who served as gunner in the AG crew, reports that the *Fitzsimmons* went in on the British side of the invasion of Sicily, but was held up because of the designation of its cargo and did not see action. It saw plenty of action on its next trip, carrying a load of ammunition and 500-pound bombs to Salerno, and making a number of trips to Anzio. Norch says that when Naples was opened, the *Fitzsimmons* unloaded its cargo directly onto trucks pulled alongside, which then headed directly to the front. The trucks would bring back wounded on their return trip, to be put aboard a hospital ship docked directly ahead of the *Fitzsimmons.* She later carried part of the 36th Division to Anzio. At Anzio the *Fitzsimmons* unloaded onto LCTs alongside while destroyers were running around laying a smoke screen. German 88s were very effective and came close, but the *Fitzsimmons* was not hit. Glider-bombs came frequently, but Norch says that frogmen were more of a problem. From Anzio the *Fitzsimmons* brought back refugees being evacuated to Naples, mostly women, children, and old men. One young woman gave birth aboard the ship, in blackout conditions. Delivery was accomplished in the officer's mess, with Norch and three others holding lights for the armed guard officer and the purser who performed the services of doctor; all went well except for Norch who sheepishly admits he passed out during the birth.[31]

Upon her first arrival at Naples with her vital cargo of ammunition and supplies, steam was required to operate the booms for unloading, but the utility engineer responsible for making steam refused to work as he had "other plans." Despite continued requests from ship's officers and port authorities, he remained adamant, although trucks were lined up awaiting loads. Finally the provost marshal and an army colonel came aboard, and when he still refused, the officer ordered him put in handcuffs; he was taken off the ship and never returned. Rumor had it that he was immediately drafted into the army.

In spite of the unceasing efforts of the enemy to drive the Allies into the sea to keep Hitler's promise, the beachhead steadily built up. The Liberty ships sailed on a well-established schedule, and an average of four Liberties was cleared every ten days. Over 500,000 tons of supplies were unloaded at Anzio, with a peak of 7,828 tons being unloaded on 29 March. The small fishing port had become one of the most important ports of the world. It will certainly never be forgotten by the men who served there.[32]

The little-known but disastrous enemy air attack on the relatively obscure Italian port of Bari on 2 December 1943 was an Allied merchantmen equivalent of Pearl Harbor from the standpoint of surprise to the defenders and the catastrophic loss of shipping. In a "battle" that lasted only twenty minutes, seventeen ships unloading supplies for the British 8th Army campaign up the Italian Peninsula were sunk or damaged beyond all repair. The loss of Allied lives, although heavy, was small by comparison with the casualties among the local population, many of which were the result of a strange cloud that spread over the area. It emanated from an American Liberty ship and was deadly World War I-type mustard gas. It was part of the cargo of the SS *John Harvey*, not known even to its officers, who died unaware. Bari also represented possibly the highest death rate of the U.S. Naval Armed Guard for any one action in both World War I and II.

Thirty Allied freighters and tankers were tied up at Bari, either unloading or waiting to discharge cargo, gasoline, explosives, and other supplies for the British drive north. Things had been going well, and the Bari area had become what was considered a quiet zone, but the cluster of ships discovered by German reconnaissance was too attractive a target to ignore. British Colonel Bradshaw arrived on the scene to brief AG officers on air defense and to ensure that no shots were fired at aircraft, unless positively identified as hostile "after" they dropped bombs. AG gun crews were ordered not to fire until given a signal to avoid shooting at friendly aircraft. When told that Captain A. B. Jenks of the Office of Harbor Defense did not feel so sanguine about the low possibility of air attack and actually expected one based on the recent appearance of a number of German reconnaissance planes, Colonel Bradshaw dismissed him as being "a nervous sort."

Captain Jenks was right in his premonition. The German air commander in the Balkans, Major General Peltz, advised of the arrival of the convoy, formulated a plan for a surprise attack on the harbor, utilizing a mass effort of bombers on one target. The result was all too easy. Defenses were inadequate at best, there was no radar warning and no indication of approaching planes until a few strips of radar-blocking tinfoil fell, some of them on Ensign Kay Vesole, AG officer on the SS *John Bascom*, who had already alerted his crew to be ready for anything. He reacted immediately, and the *Bascom*'s guns were the first to fire. (The story of Ensign Vesole's heroic action was covered in detail in chapter 6, "Gallant Ships, Gallant Men.")

The ships in the harbor were trapped; one by one they were hit and sunk or damaged. The American Liberty ship SS *Samuel Tilden*, last to arrive, was first to go under. She took a bomb hit in the engine room, and her cargo of gasoline and ammunition was quickly aflame. Thomas E. Harper, an AG from the SS *John L. Motley*, who had been ashore on liberty and was returning to his ship, reported that while he was running to the dock area an ammunition ship was hit and blew up, and he found himself "still running three feet in the air." Stopping at a British battery, he observed that the harbor was lighted up by a bright searchlight from ashore. He says the light was not directed toward planes in the sky but was focused right on the SS *Samuel J. Tilden*. Antiaircraft fire was also directed at the *Tilden*, reportedly killing and injuring some of the crew before the "enemy" finished it off.

Harper's ship, the SS *John L. Motley*, quickly became a raging inferno as did the SS *Joseph Wheeler*. The *John*

Bascom was hit in #3 and #5 holds and the boat deck by a stick of three bombs and was quickly sinking. Oil-covered water in the harbor was soon ablaze, and many men were burned as they tried to swim away from the flames. The *Motley* and the *John Harvey* exploded almost simultaneously with a terrific blast, followed quickly by a fatal explosion on the *Joseph Wheeler.* The SS *Lyman Abbott* was rolled over and her decks ripped open by the blast, but she survived. All around the harbor ships were exploding violently every few seconds; four British freighters, three Italian, and one Norwegian sank, and others were badly damaged.

It was the Liberty *John Harvey* that had cost the most lives in the disaster. Unknown to anyone except for a detachment of army chemical-warfare personnel aboard, she carried a load of 100 tons of mustard gas, authorized by President Roosevelt to be stockpiled at Bari for use in the event the Germans introduced poison gas. When the *Harvey* exploded, both the air and the water were contaminated. The chemical-warfare unit was all dead, and there was no one to warn of the hazard; it was not until 4 December that the presence of mustard gas in the water was proven and admitted, and by that time it was too late for many survivors on land or for those who had been exposed to it in the oily waters.

The cost of the Bari raid was colossal in terms of ships sunk or damaged, cargoes lost, the slowing of the British advance, plus hundreds of civilian and military casualties. A recap of casualties on the American ships alone shows an appalling picture:

SS *John Bascom*—four merchant crew, ten AGs lost, many injured.

SS *Joseph Wheeler*—twenty-eight merchant crew, fifteen NAG lost. The only survivors were one AG officer and twelve men ashore on liberty.

SS *John Harvey*—thirty-eight merchant crew, twenty-eight AG, and ten army personnel killed. The only two survivors were two men ashore at the time of attack.

SS *Samuel Tilden*—ten merchant crew, AG, and army
casualties, but all the AGs survived.

SS *Lyman Abbott*—two merchant crew, one AG, and one
army killed, almost all AGs wounded or suffered mustard gas burns.[33]

The Liberty SS *Louis Hennepin* was the only ship carrying AGs that escaped without material damage or casualties.
Searchers probing American ships after the attack found 38
bodies; 150 men from the ships were missing.[34]

Bad as it was, the Bari raid could have been worse. The
Lyman Abbott was also carrying a load of mustard gas, which
was not disturbed.

Jack Coleman, a signalman from Houston, Texas, served
on six Liberties and a Hog Islander. He made his second trip
to the steaming hot Persian Gulf in October–November
1944 on the SS *Daniel Carroll*. While in convoy approaching
the narrow Straits of Messina between Sicily and the toe
of the Italian "boot," the order was given to proceed through
the Straits in single line.

The *Daniel Carroll* was carrying 4,000 tons of TNT and
4,000 tons of foodstuffs, as was a sister Liberty about 1,000
yards ahead. Coleman does not recall her name, but he had
been "talking" to the signalman aboard it about Bombay as
they waited their turn to proceed. It was quiet and clear, a
"lazy day," according to Coleman. Suddenly, the ship ahead
exploded with a deafening roar. The concussion and shock
wave from the ill-fated ship was such that Coleman was
almost blown off the bridge and had to clutch the rail to
hold on.

Men on the *Daniel Carroll* rushed on deck shouting,
"What was that?" and looked anxiously over the sides. "Everyone was on lookout for a submarine," says Coleman, "but
there was no sign of such, and we decided that a stray floating mine had hit the ship. A column of dense black smoke
rose slowly to about 1,000 feet; there was no wind, so it was
very slow to disperse. When it did clear, we saw that there
was nothing left, and as we passed through the area where

the ship had been, there were only a few bits and pieces of flotsam. Destruction was total."[35]

Mines were an ever-present danger when encountered anywhere in the world. They could cause great structural damage even if the ship remained afloat. A vessel written off as a complete loss was labeled TCL (total constructive loss), but a ship able to return home for repair was a "state-side hit." There was no question as to the status of the Norwegian *Christian Michelsen;* she hit a mine off Bizerte on 26 September 1943, blew up and went down in less than a minute, with only three survivors.

The SS *Patrick Henry,* first of all the Liberties, was laid down on 30 April 1941 at the Fairfield Yard of Bethlehem Steel. Launched on 27 September, she was delivered on 30 December, a remarkable performance at that time. She went into service less than a month after Pearl Harbor. She was a rugged ship, and she had to be, for on her first voyage to the Middle East she steamed over 7,500 miles. That was the beginning of a twelve-voyage career that took her into some of the worst areas of the war, including the Murmansk run in the first convoy after disastrous PQ-17. Louis V. Ritter, Far Rockaway, New York, boarded her as a gunner in early 1944. Her destination was to be North Russia, but orders were changed and she headed south, traveling alone to Trinidad, Capetown, and Dakar, where the crew was restricted to the ship because of an outbreak of bubonic plague. They then went to Naples and to Leghorn. While Ritter was serving on 4-inch gun watch one night, the ship was rocked by a big explosion. He says, "I rang General Quarters, thinking the Germans were shelling the area. As it turned out, the British would throw dynamite in the water each night because of enemy frogmen. This time they hit some sort of an ammo barge and blew it up. The concussion shook the ship like a toy." Ritter feels badly that the *Patrick Henry* was not preserved, as she was not only historic but had a wonderful record, living through the entire war. He was very fond of the reliable old ship, and regrets that he had not been one of the original crew. The chief engineer stayed with her all through the war, and said that she ran like a charm and he hated to leave her. Rusty, tired, and worn out after seeing service in some of the worst action of the world, she was towed back to the place of her birth and ignominiously scrapped, a sad end for a gallant lady.[36]

An extraordinary incident at the end of the war in the Mediterranean has been described by Gunner's Mate 2/c DeWitt Welch; "We on the Liberty SS *Big Foot Wallace* were sailing to Brindisi. We received a radio message on 7 May that Germany had surrendered, and not to fire on any enemy ships. The next day we sighted some small craft going south. When we got close enough, we could see they were flying the flag of surrender. They finally passed us on our starboard side, five U-boats and eight E-boats (and we had been told the Adriatic was clean). As we passed the German flotilla we dipped our colors, and they did also," an exceptional exchange of courtesies at the end of the long and bloody Mediterranean conflict.[37]

During the war in the Mediterranean, a total of 413 merchant ships, of almost two million tons, were sunk by enemy action. The last U-boat success in the Mediterranean occurred on 18 May 1944; the *U-453* was herself sunk with all hands five days later. The Mediterranean, by any name, had exacted a terrible toll of lives, ships, and naval and air services of both Allies and Axis.[38]

CHAPTER SEVENTEEN
THE PACIFIC

The Atlantic isn't romantic,
and the Pacific isn't terrific.
—World War II Song

Although the Pacific was the largest battleground in World War II, stretching across nearly half of the globe, for the naval armed guard the Pacific theater of operations in the early stages could not begin to match the concentrated horror of the Murmansk run, with its combined attacks by the elements and the enemy, the violence and wolfpacks of the North Atlantic, or the incessant air and other attacks of the Mediterranean. By comparison, drawn by veterans of the North Atlantic, the Pacific was a veritable millpond as regards weather most of the time, and the Japanese never mounted the volume of attacks against merchant shipping as did the U-boats. However, the viciousness of their attacks and the treatment of survivors and prisoners was often barbarous.

Thomas Heggen caught the essence of much of the service in the obscure backwaters of the Pacific in his immensely popular post–World War II book, *Mr. Roberts,* later made into a play and then a movie starring Lieutenant Henry Fonda, USNR, playing a true-to-life Mr. Roberts. Heggen aptly described life aboard a decidedly unglamorous cargo ship, the famed "USS Reluctant": "For the most part it stayed in the regular run from "Tedium to Apathy and back, about five days each way. It made an occasional trip to Monotony . . ." However, just as the war, and death, caught up with Mr. Roberts at Okinawa, after he was finally relieved of duty on the "Reluctant," the full fury of Japanese suicidal attacks fell on the naval and merchant ships that were carrying troops and supplies to the Pacific campaigns. For most of the time, prior to the invasion of the Philippines and Okinawa, for the AG the Pacific was mainly an immense supply operation of cargo ships and tankers that brought supplies of war from the West Coast to Australia, New Zealand, and to such previously unknown ports as Noumea, Espiritu Santo, and the huge bases in the Eniwetok, Kwajalein, and Ulithi atolls. The voyages were usually long and often deadly boring. A few merchant ships were attacked by Japanese submarines off the West Coast shortly after Pearl Harbor, causing considerable panic in some areas, but they had no major successes. From 1942–43 Japanese submarines only managed to sink a little over 100,000 tons of merchant shipping in the entire Pacific. By comparison, American submarines in January 1944 alone sank 300,000 tons of Japanese shipping.[1]

One feature of the Pacific theater was that the NAG gun crews never knew their next destination; they could go around the world in one voyage, and often did, traveling alone most of the time.

One of the early assignments of many AGs in the Pacific was to the Aleutians, and anyone in that service would dispute the claim that the Pacific was a "millpond." Larry La Fontaine, Olympia, Washington, made three trips to the Aleutians and he recalls that the AG gun crew was always cold, with one to two inches of ice in their quarters. The guns would ice up and freeze immediately after being washed off, and it was necessary to chip off the ice. Winds of 100 mph were not uncommon, and a ship could roll 45 degrees. Of more immediate concern was their original foul-weather gear, which consisted of some clothes originally used in World War I. They bought parkas from the Eskimos to try and keep warm. While on the Aleutian run, La Fontaine served on the SS *Waipo* and the SS *R. J. Hanna,* a tanker; the "armament" on the *Waipo* consisted of seven Marlin World War I machine guns and an antique 4-inch gun on the stern, reportedly taken from a state park and refurbished. When he was transferred later to a new ship with a 5-inch/38, he says it was like going from a Model T to a Cadillac.[2] Howard Roberts, Tumwater, Washington, served on the SS *Yukon,* an ex-luxury liner that made two trips a month to Alaska; other AGs served on a number of old coal-burners on the run. All veterans of the Aleutians agree that if Balboa had discovered their area of operations, the "Pacific" would have had another name.[3]

The description of the Pacific as a millpond also would not have impressed navy recruit Carlin Montgomery, fresh from a solidly anchored farm in Texas. He began feeling queasy even when his new ship was tied to the dock in San Francisco, and he remained seasick during his entire seventeen-day voyage on the SS *Nampa Victory* to New Guinea. Carlin was assigned to an upper bunk, but a bunkmate in a lower position gladly traded places with him, tired of being the middleman between Carlin and his pail. The armed guard officer kept on Carlin continually with, "It's all in your head!", but Carlin got some degree of consolation when, during a ship-tossing typhoon, the lieutenant became equally ill. Painfully raising his head above the rail, Carlin inquired, "Is it in your head too, Lieutenant?" The question went unanswered, but Carlin noted that the lieutenant was notably cool to him for the rest of the voyage.[4]

Unlike some other unfortunates, Carlin eventually became adjusted to his seagoing home, and went "regular" navy after the war. However, he still blesses the name of the sympathetic messman who supplied him with stale bread and fruit, to which he attributes his early survival. Many other young recruits of the time also swear that stale bread, saltine crackers, and little pieces of fruit saved their lives in similar circumstances. Some forty years later, Carlin and his lieutenant had a pleasant reunion and laughed about the not-so-good old days.

Carlin was not alone in his problem; another AG gunner who does not wish attribution recalls, "At first I used to get terribly seasick, and frequently there was no place to go, so I would use rubber boots." He added quickly, "But I always made sure they weren't mine."

In the Pacific, the AGs found themselves on a wide variety of ships and transports. In the early stages of the Americans' return to the western Pacific, many found themselves on troop transports ferrying troops and supplies to Guadalcanal, unloading during the day and pulling away into Tulagi Bay at night to avoid attacks on Henderson Field by Japanese planes. "Washing Machine Charlie," a Japanese plane, was a regular visitor, not much feared although not entirely welcome. "Charlie's" pending arrival was easily identified by the uneven sound of his engine. He would come over every day at about the same time, drop a few bombs, and sputter slowly away.

An unpublished navy history of the NAG lists many merchant cargo ships with AG gun crews at Guadalcanal, but reports few and comparatively light air attacks and little damage; the Japanese were much more concerned with the intense struggle on shore.[5]

One of the more unusual stories of transporting troops to the Pacific involved the U.S. cavalry coming to the rescue, not of beleaguered settlers on the western plains, but of a confused, green NAG gun crew. The story is told by former Sergeant Bill McLaughlin of Mashpee, Massachusetts: "Our unit, the 110th (Horse) Cavalry of the Massachusetts National Guard, had been called into Federal service in January 1941, when it became obvious that war was imminent. As machine-gun sergeant I drilled my men intensively in the working of the .50-caliber machine gun. We boarded ship in Brooklyn with the rest of our group and Task Force 6814 sailed for Australia. By that time we were old hands with the new 50s. Once aboard the USAT *Argentina,* still being converted to carrying troops, and with a civilian crew aboard, we looked at the armament. A five-inch gun on the fantail was the heaviest weapon, with four three-inch fifties, two port and two starboard, with another facing forward on a raised gun platform over the bow. Along with these were six .50-caliber machine guns, water-cooled, spaced around the ship in gun tubs raised high above the deck. Climbing into the turret we checked to see the difference between the air-cooled models we had and the water-jacketed guns. What a surprise to find on the eve of our sailing that the guns were still packed in cosmoline; the heavy grease used for dead storage of weapons until use was never easily removed. To have sailed with them in this shape meant that they were useless for defense of any kind.

"We went to see the commander of the Armed Guard, composed of a dozen or so young sailors, mostly boots fresh out of Great Lakes, fine-looking bright lads of about eighteen. The Ensign quickly assured us that he had only recently come out of ROTC and knew nothing about machine guns. He referred us to the GM 1/c who was senior petty officer, an old China hand, but he finally admitted that while he knew 5″ and 3″ guns from stem to stern he knew nothing about machine guns. 'Would you like to volunteer for the Armed Guard?', he asked, and we jumped at the offer. After all, it meant no standing in line for chow, and as an added bonus we were quartered in the Children's Playroom on the boat deck directly over the swimming pool. And it kept away the boredom of a thirty-day cruise. We quickly became great friends with the Navy lads, and we drilled them in care and firing of the fifties.

"We thought we were heading for the Philippines, but Bataan fell before we were too far out, so we were saved from that fate . . . the Brits wanted us to go to Singapore, but someone succeeded in convincing FDR that the only convoy then afloat in the Pacific (ours) was more urgently required in New Caledonia to keep the Vichy French from siding with the Axis powers; a close call for all of us as Singapore also fell soon."[6]

It has been reported previously that there was a "mail buoy" at Ambrose Light off New York harbor; happily a similar service was also available in the Pacific. Herb Book, AG radioman aboard the SS *Frank B. Linderman* in 1943, reports: "While I had been through boot camp, Navy Radio School and Armed Guard Radio School, I was still green and innocent about ways of the sea. The trip was a long one to New Guinea. About three weeks out of port, the experienced sailors (AGs and merchant seamen alike) started the story that we would be passing a 'mail buoy' some time during the next day, and if we want to write letters home, they could be placed in the 'mail buoy,' and would be picked up by the next passing ship to the U.S. Of course we stayed up half the night feverishly writing letters. The next day, we were placed on watch, to be certain that we would not miss the 'mail buoy.' Then, it was mostly our fault when somehow we missed it! Another initiation into the ways of the sea."[7]

In the worldwide conflict featuring history's most sophisticated technology and ending with the detonation of the world's ultimate weapon, the SS *Virginian* was an anachronism. And so was her war cargo. The *Virginian* was built in happier days, in 1904, and originally was a coal-burner. She saw service in the Great War, and responded again to the call to the colors in World War II. She must have felt at least a bit mortified, however, by being assigned as a mule ship, a throwback to wars seemingly long past.

Gerald Sossamon, fresh off a farm in Mulberry, Arkansas, served as a gunner in the naval armed guard detachment on board the *Virginian*. To Gerald, mules were no problem; he had handled his father's beloved and highly efficient mule team for years while growing up. When off duty he would frequently go visit the mules, talk to them and scratch their noses, but he says the mules were a shock to the city boys on board, and they were scared to death of them.

The mules were being transported to New Guinea where the mountainous terrain and absence of roads made mechanized warfare impossible. The only way that the army field artillery could be moved into a position of strategic importance was by pack mule. So the old reliable SS *Virginian* was called upon to deliver the old reliable mule power.

Six hundred and one reluctant mules were loaded aboard the *Virginian,* above and below decks, and 599 mules were delivered where needed; two succumbed en route and presumably were buried honorably at sea. The trip was not all that easy, however. Because of the *Virginian*'s circuitous routing, the mules were at sea for almost three months, during which time their dispositions did not improve. Gerald Sossamon recalls the end of their odyssey with a smile, "When we finally reached Port Moresby, New Guinea, the mules virtually tippy-toed down the gangplank. But when their hooves touched solid ground they took off like rockets, kicking and running and dragging their helpless handlers all over the place. The handlers were taking sixteen-foot steps trying to hang on. It was quite a scene."[8]

Gerald sailed on many other ships during the war, including an ammunition carrier, a troop ship, and a tanker sailing alone, and he underwent kamikaze attacks, a collision at sea during a typhoon, and other action, but his favorite reminiscence is his voyage on the mule ship.

Things were not always so pleasant on the long hauls in the Pacific. Lieutenant Harold Bondhus, USNR, a NAG gunnery officer, recalls his first voyage: "Since I had spent part of three days at sea while at San Diego, I had the second-most sea duty of my seventeen-man gun crew. The gunner's mate had sailed through the canal and one day out of the canal they were sunk. So he was the 'saltiest' of the crew. With that inexperienced crew, and our terribly antique equipment, we had something new added to our experience. We were almost loaded when word went out that all were confined to the ship. I was told to prepare to have someone share my cabin and to find room for six more people with the crew. They then put a third of all the poison gas that the USA had on the foredeck. The added men were chemical warfare people from the Army. With great wisdom, they placed the Lewisite and mustard gas so that if there were a leak, the ship's motion would bring the gas into the living quarters, so, with the gas and ten million pounds of bombs, we were off towards Australia. However, they did detour us a bit. Since we had gas, they routed us way southeast of New Zealand. When we finally got to Brisbane, they unloaded the gas along with the rest of the cargo. The chemical warfare gang moved on. However, one of their people was actually a medical corpsman. The CW people did not know what to do with him so he stayed on the ship and went back and forth to New Guinea with us for about a year. Somehow, he could go someplace in Brisbane and get paid. Since we had no one who knew anything about medicine, I was glad to have him aboard. He never had a thing to do during that period and when we got back to Australia he was automatically on twenty-four-hour liberty. It could have been called the 'life of Reilly,' except his name was Cronin."[9]

Richard C. Hudnall, Agoura, California, spent all of his time in the Pacific as a striker and signalman 3rd class. His first ship in December 1943 was the transport SS *Meteor,* a C-2-type hull, which carried the 2nd and 4th marine divisions. The *Meteor* made all the Pacific islands, winding up at Tinian. It brought Jap prisoners back to Pearl Harbor and wounded marines to San Francisco. He was next assigned to a Norwegian tanker, MV *Ohio,* sailing under the Panamanian flag. The *Ohio* ran independently along the "roaring forties," extremely cold, windy, and stormy, carrying high-octane aviation fuel from South America to Australia and New Zealand. Due to the quick turn-around time, the Norwegian crew would take their leave aboard ship at sea. "They stood no watches, got up whenever they wanted to, had plenty of booze on board so they would stay drunk for two weeks. However, one officer, 4th Engineer, couldn't take it any more and committed suicide by jumping overboard while we were on the high seas. Contrary to orders, the ship did turn around to search for him, but not for long. The water was like ice, and he wouldn't have made it anyhow." Hudnall added that the ship had been built in Germany, and everything was in German or Norwegian including his signal book, International Code of Signals HO #1, and the navy radioman's typewriter had all kinds of strange characters on it.[10]

The *Ohio* had an interesting background; built for a Norwegian line, she ran out of Germany under fire when war broke out. Safely home, she again fled under fire when Germany invaded Norway. She then came under Panamanian registry, "but only the officers were Norwegian. Only the Second Officer could interpret the International Code Book for me if a message was not in Mersigs . . . what impressed me the most about the ship was that it was kept spotlessly clean, the officers demanded it of themselves and of the crew, and you could eat off the bilges in the engine room."

After one week of "gunnery training," mostly stripping

guns and seeing brief training movies, plus one day at sea watching gunnery practice, Al Gonzales, now of El Paso, Texas, was assigned to his first ship, the Dutch-flagged SS *Noordam,* and joined a forty-eight-man navy gun crew. The *Noordam* was a big ocean passenger liner that carried pilots, WACs, and nurses to New Guinea. She was protected by 5″ 38s bow and stern, two twenty-mm guns and one 50-caliber machine gun amidships. In comparison with later ships he served on, Gonzales says that it was "good duty," good food and comfortable quarters. "The officers were not too happy to have an Armed Guard gun crew aboard but the Indonesian crew was great," Gonzales says. At a later date, while in San Francisco picking up personnel heading westward, Lieutenant (j.g.) Henry Fonda, USNR, came aboard. He introduced himself to Gonzales and asked if he would show him the guns aboard ship. (Fonda had enlisted in the navy after Pearl Harbor and asked for gunnery training; although subsequently given a commission in air combat intelligence, he was still interested in gunnery.) Fonda inquired if Gonzales would give training in the maintenance procedure for .45-caliber revolvers for the newly graduated pilots aboard who had never had any experience with .45s, and he conducted classes for the pilots. Gonzales reports that Fonda, although even then a prominent Hollywood figure, was very quiet, pleasant, and efficient. He looked and acted just as he did in the highly successful film "Mr. Roberts." Another member of the navy gun crew confirms Fonda's pleasant attitude and adds that he took great interest in gunnery practice en route to his assignment in Hawaii.[11]

Manley Michler, Olympia, Washington, also served in Pacific transport duty. "After completing my training as a PhM I was assigned to the USS *Lurline,* a former luxury liner operated by the Matson Line between the west coast and the Hawaiian Islands. It had been converted into a transport, carrying 4,500 men to various theatres of action in the Pacific, and bringing wounded and other casualties back. Our staff consisted of thirty-eight enlisted men, and one Chief, and four doctors, three medical doctors and one dentist. We had a well-equipped sick bay and hospital for emergency operations, an X-ray room, and 135 beds. While we carried nurses to the war zones, there were no nurses on the *Lurline* staff.

"We traveled alone because of our speed, eighteen to twenty knots zigzagging and followed the invasions; we would invariably carry a full load of casualties back. These included a lot of mental cases which were hard to handle and required heavy watch. I made nineteen crossings of the Equator, San Francisco, Hawaiian Islands, Australia, New Zealand, and Bombay. On the return trips we traveled light and were about ninety-feet out of the water; the ship was top-heavy, and in storms we bounced up and down, pitching and tossing for days on end. The trip to Australia took seventeen to nineteen days and we made one trip a month on the average, down and back. It was good duty, the crew was the same as when it was in passenger liner service, accommodations were good, two to a room, and the food was excellent. My battle station was on the fantail with a 5″ gun, and because we were shorthanded, frequently Army gunners served in the gun crew.

"The only time we were accompanied was from Sydney and Bombay, carrying troops. We were assigned a fast Australian gun boat, as the Indian Ocean was a graveyard of ships. After VJ-Day, we picked up a lot of casualties from Burma, survivors of the 'Death Railroad' built by the Japanese and featured in 'The Bridge on the River Kwai.' They were in terrible shape, almost all litter cases. We also brought back a large number of Italian PWs to Sydney, but I never found out where they came from."[12]

The late Lee Rigg of Seattle, Washington, served as a gunner's mate on the SS *Phillip C. Shera* in the Pacific and recounted an amusing story of his greatest scare while in the AG. "We were sailing south of Australia and the ship was tossing and water was freezing on the bow, where I was sitting alone, all hunched down in my foul-weather gear, in the 20mm gun tub. All of a sudden there was this big noise alongside, and I was looking right in the eye of a whale! He was half out of the water, and he was blowing and good God, he scared me. I nearly fell overboard." On another voyage, loaded with gasoline and explosives, the ship stopped outside of Perth to pick up a harbor pilot. "When he came on board he asked matter-of-factly if we had our degaussers turned on. When someone said no, he said "My God, man, you're about to enter the biggest magnetic minefield in the Pacific!" He jumped right over the rail and the pilot boat picked him up. He came back later, in dry clothes, after we had turned on the degaussers." [15]

When gunnery officer George Miller and his NAG crew took over their duties in the Liberty SS *George Taylor*, they found that the last entry in the log made by the departing crew was, "There are five monkeys who remain with the Armed Guard crew." Puzzlement soon ended when the new crew found that there were indeed five monkeys who hung out in AG quarters, guntubs, or wherever they decided to be. They were the last of 800 monkeys carried for medical research at Johns Hopkins Medical School in a previous voyage. They had escaped from a broken cage and had remained aboard when their compatriots were unloaded in Brooklyn. "The monkeys stole food from the galley, and mess halls and from crew quarters," says George Miller, "but the Navy crew learned to live with them. However, one day in a scrap over a banana, one monkey grabbed the banana and jumped over the side with the others in hot pursuit. The first of the pursuers followed suit, but the other three hit the brakes and were saved. When the ship docked at Brisbane and the Health Authorities came aboard and saw one of the survivors, they quarantined the entire ship until some disposition could be made of the unwelcome guests. A team from Brisbane Zoo came aboard with dart guns allegedly loaded with tranquilizers and they finally caught up with the three. As they were carried ashore they looked more deceased than tranquilized, but we were assured that they would be on display in the Brisbane Zoo in a few days. However, when the Navy crew paid a visit to the zoo they were unable to find them, and there was considerable suspicion that their crewmates had been done in. We will never know, but living aboard ship for thirty-three days with five or three monkeys is some experience."[14]

One of the biggest drawbacks to AG service in areas such as the Pacific or Indian oceans was boredom. Weeks could go by without sight of land or another ship. The Esso tanker SS *John D. Archbold* spent months at sea, mostly in the Pacific, visiting many navy bases and making oiler rendezvous. Leaving New York on 4 November 1943, she did not return to a continental U.S. port for one year and twenty-six days, with little or no opportunity for shore leave. Occasionally when refueling oilers, the crew and AG were invited to see motion pictures shown nightly on such vessels, a "much needed diversion" according to the captain. From 15 September 1939 to 2 September 1945, she made seventy voyages and delivered 9,991,513 barrels of oil products.[15]

Other AG and merchant crews were more fortunate. On the SS *Capitol Reef,* Carlin Montgomery recalls that someone got the bright idea of building a swimming pool. With the approval of the ship's skipper, the pool was built on deck, just forward of the bridge, by both AGs and merchant crew. It was one-half saltwater and one-half freshwater and was enjoyed by all as the vessel shuttled from California to Guam, Saipan, Tinian, Kwajalein, Ulithi, and other bases in the Pacific.[16]

One of the dubious joys of service in the tropics is the never-ending supply of bugs of all types and sizes as well as flies. George Miller, now a newspaper columnist living in Tampa, Florida, was gunnery officer on the SS *George Taylor.* When in Milne Bay, New Guinea, a port officer came on board and had lunch with the captain and gunnery officer. George Miller picks up the story, "The flies just about carried the food off our plates. The port officer came back the next day with a one-pound can of aerosol fly spray. It worked. First time I had ever seen such an item . . . I put in a request for two cases, figuring there were twelve–twenty-four of those one-pound cans in a case. The next day Gunner's Mate Johnny Balchunas said there was a request for a boom to be put over the side to hoist aboard our supplies that had been ordered. On the dock there were two large wooden crates, and we soon learned that each crate had twenty-four ten-pound canisters of aerosol fly spray. We not only never had another fly on that ship, but we had trading rights to ice cream powder as well as ammunition as we moved through the Philippines. That fly spray was a great item for exchange for whatever was needed." [17]

Merchant vessels, ferrying men and supplies as American forces slowly and painfully slugged their way north toward Japan, were attacked on numerous occasions, including in Australia. Floyd Jones of Natural Bridge, Virginia, a gunner on the Liberty SS *Hall Young*, reports that while the *Young* was discharging high-octane gasoline, it fought forty-eight Japanese bombers attacking Darwin, destroying one. "We fired thirty rounds of 3" fifty at them rapid fire, and the last round I was so tired that I couldn't get my hand to the top of the shell, it went in the block and the rim almost cut my finger off. We didn't have any medics so the gun crew patched me up the best they could." [18] However, it was not until the landings at Leyte that the Pacific war became a nightmare of air attacks on merchant shipping. A navy report of the Leyte battle lists the names of over 120 merchant vessels that carried men and material to the landing area, of which five were lost, and lists others damaged in varying degrees. It was at Leyte that the enemy introduced large-scale attacks by kamikaze pilots. Armed guard gunners were credited officially with over one hundred planes destroyed, probably a conservative estimate, about twenty planes per each ship lost; 150 armed guards were casualties, and 14 were listed as killed or missing.

The nature of the campaign required that merchant vessels remain in Philippine waters for long periods of time before they could unload. There were many Japanese air bases nearby that could not easily be knocked out, and it was several days after an initial landing before shore-based AA defenses could be set up, so the ships had to fend largely for themselves. The navy report indicates that the battle of the

Philippines was the "most severe action in the Pacific for the Naval Armed Guard," and was comparable to some of the worst action in other theaters of operations, including Salerno, Anzio, and other parts of the Mediterranean. "While each ship has its own stories," the navy report adds, "perhaps no ship took more punishment than the Liberty SS *Benjamin Ide Wheeler,* which came under attack before even dropping anchor. She was defended for seventy-six days and her AGs went to General Quarters 353 times and underwent ninety-six bombing attacks, which included two hits by kamikazes." [19]

The voyage report of Lieutenant Earle Douglas Woodring, USNR, covering the period 29 August to 7 January 1945, when the ship had to be abandoned in Tacloban Harbor, is a model of clarity and detail. Unfortunately, it is not possible to reproduce the fifteen-page, single-spaced report verbatim, but it reports action so continuous and exhausting that it is a magnificent tribute to the courage and stamina of the AG crew, the merchant crew, especially Captain Dan J. Coughlin, and the army volunteers. Things started slowly. The *Wheeler* was laid over for fifty-three days in Hollandia, delayed because it was carrying low-priority navy cargo and had to shuttle to and from the (then) single dock to make way for higher-priority ships. The deadly boredom ended when the *Wheeler* finally discharged its cargo and loaded 267 officers and men of the army's 251st Engineer Construction Battalion and their equipment, supplies, and vehicles, and high-octane gasoline for Leyte Gulf. Young army PFC Russell Best wrote a long letter home in which he reported that he and others had volunteered to assist at the guns and had been thoroughly trained by the navy gun crew, with whom they became the greatest of friends and still visited at Leyte, again manning guns during enemy attack.

Traveling in a convoy of seventy ships, thirty-five merchant vessels plus escorts, the *Wheeler* arrived at the Philippines, to be greeted by enemy air attack before the ship was at anchor. There were 118 actual raids during the week 24–30 October. On 27 October the *Wheeler* was hit by a kamikaze for the first time and was so damaged that she lay in the harbor of San Pedro Bay for over two months. Signalman 3/c Bob Norling, now a retired editor of the *Boston Globe*, in a newspaper article later recalled the first kamikaze hit, ". . . twin-engine Betty bombers went after the airstrip near Tacloban and the ships anchored off Red Beach. A red glow appeared in a cloud ahead of us and in the next instant, out popped a bomber with one of its engines afire. It went into a dive straight at the *Wheeler*, we knocked off part of its left wing and set the second engine afire, but nothing was going to stop that pilot. He followed the tracer trails of our 20-mm fire right into the ship. There were two explosions, one bomb made a hole roughly eight feet square right at the waterline, a second blasted a gaping hole in the hull near the keel, and the ship sank slowly by the stern. The bottom of our anchorage wasn't that deep and although we were at an awkward up-angle, most of the ship was above water and it didn't hinder the gunner's ability to down enemy planes . . ." AG casualities were two dead and three wounded, "later we had three more dead in a fire and a severe case of combat fatigue."[20]

Efforts were made to repair the *Wheeler*, but were unavailing. Enemy attacks continued unabated, and on one occasion, the *Wheeler*'s gunners shot down two of four enemy planes, driving the other two off. Lieutenant Woodring wrote, "The four planes might have done considerable damage after the bad night if Corbin, GM 3/c, and his crew had not picked them up immediately and fired so effectively. . . . Unable to be repaired, the *Wheeler* was moved alongside the SS *Augustus Thomas* "fully loaded with ammunition and gasoline, to supply steam for unloading her. Her engine room was flooded by bombing, no merchant or gun crew aboard. Numerous anti-materiel bombs dropped near the two ships. No hits. The following day, 12 November, the crash-diving of eight ships in the harbor was observed. A number of anti-materiel bombs landed in the water off the starboard beam. A Jap winged toward us through heavy fire at 700 feet altitude, #9 and #10 guns fired six rounds, three close bursts. Plane crossed our stern trailing white smoke. The four port-side 20 mm fired, getting several hits. The plane pitched suddenly and crashed into the bay.

"On 18 November after several attacks, a Jap Betty made a long, fast glide over the center of the harbor and crashed the bridge and #4 hold of a Liberty, the SS *Gilbert Stuart,* anchored southeast of us, flaming gas streamed over the side of our ship. One bomb hit our ship on the starboard side passing within ten feet of #7 gun, one hit near the side of the boat deck of the SS *Thomas,* alongside. Three C-1s anchored next to us were crashed, including the SS *Alcoa Pioneer,* SS *General Fletcher,* and SS *Cape Romano,* fires soon put out . . . from 10 December–7 January 1945, when the Armed Guard unit was removed from the ship, enemy air attacks were less frequent, only 91 alerts . . ."

In his report Lieutenant Woodring gives highest praise to the master, Captain Coughlin, "who directed the efforts of the merchant crew after the Army soldiers were disembarked, kept all guns fully manned, and during the many alerts he helped keep binocular lookout on the bridge." He adds, "The Navy gun crew performance in action was of the highest quality including Signalman Norling for his skill in picking up, identifying and following reported planes in separate sectors and assisting as a junior gunnery officer."

It was decided on 22 December by WSA that the *Wheeler* was to be abandoned in Tacloban and used as a floating warehouse. The merchant crew was repatriated to the States and the navy crew taken to Hollandia and ordered into the AG pool for further assignment. The gallant crew was broken up, assigned to a number of ships that returned to Tacloban somewhat later.

The experience of the *Wheeler* is intended to serve as an example of the many merchant ships that saw heavy action in Leyte Gulf.

In his article in the *Boston Globe,* on the occasion of the fortieth anniversary of the kamikaze crash on the *Wheeler,* Bob Norling has the last word, "When we returned to Hollandia, many GIs in the area were saddened to learn of the

Wheeler's fate, not that they wept; they had fond memories of a vital war mission the *Wheeler* had performed five months earlier. That was in August 1944 when, after 54 days at sea from New York, we arrived at Hollandia with a most precious cargo—45,000 cases of beer for the GIs fighting in New Guinea's steaming jungles."[21]

One of the worst losses of life at Leyte Gulf was on the SS *Thomas Nelson,* hit by a bomb from a kamikaze that then crashed into the ship at the after end on 12 November. Explosion and fire took a terrible toll: over 240 army personnel were reported killed, wounded, or missing, and three AG killed, two missing, and two wounded, but the AG continued to fight and claimed destruction of one enemy plane after the crash.[22]

When the *Alcoa Pioneer* was hit by kamikaze, six AGs were killed, including the AG officer, and eight were wounded. Seaman 1/c Patrick Henry Stevens, badly burned, one arm almost severed, still manned his 20-mm gun from the burning gun tub. Stevens was awarded the Silver Star, and nine other AGs received the Bronze Star for heroism, still manning their guns when more than half the AG unit was killed or wounded.[23]

On the SS *Gus W. Darnell,* an AG gunner was blown overboard when the ship was torpedoed, but he climbed back up the anchor chain and through the hawsepipe to return to his gun station. On the SS *Jeremiah Daily* the AG officer gave his life when, severely burned, he returned to his gun station.

The Liberty ships SS *Adoniram Judson* and SS *Marcus Daly,* two of the earliest ships at Leyte, were awarded "Gallant Ship" citations. The *Judson*'s holds contained 3,000 barrels of high-octane gasoline, but she beat off Japanese attacks with 20-mm guns while her 3-inch kept high-level bombers at a safe distance. Heroism was the common denominator of the men of the merchant ships in the Battle of the Philippines.[24]

An interesting story is told by Captain Frank Pharr of the SS *Esso Rochester.* Carrying out a fueling mission in a convoy taking troops and supplies to General McArthur's forces locked in battle at Leyte, "We were met at Leyte by about forty or fifty Japanese planes which bombed and machine-gunned the landing soldiers and attacked vessels in the harbor. They set three Liberty ships afire. In practically all cases the attacking enemy aircraft were kamikaze squadrons. We heard a broadcast in English from a Japanese radio station. It was reporting a banquet given in honor of suicide fliers about to depart. They were told that it was their duty to land their planes on American ships. According to reports we heard from naval officers, inspection of Jap planes brought down ashore showed they did not have enough gasoline for a return trip." The *Rochester*'s navy gun crew received credit from the Navy Department for confirmation of destruction of a Japanese "Sally" medium bomber, which caused "the starboard engine to burst into flame. Seconds later the plane struck the water and sank almost instantaneously." According to Captain Pharr, the plane crashed about 100 feet off the port bow of the *Rochester.*[25]

Ivy R. Wells, Clinton, Arkansas, was an AG gunner on the SS *Sharon Victory,* a munitions ship that was part of General MacArthur's invasion force in his return to the Philippines. "We were docked at Tacloban, unloading when on 5 December 1944 the Japanese sent in paratroops to retake the airfields at Tacloban. We shot down a plane load of paratroops who were heading straight for MacArthur's headquarters and it crashed in flames. The *Sharon Victory* was the only merchant ship to down a plane load of paratroops."

Some of the bitterest action of the entire war in the Pacific as regards merchant shipping came at the invasion of Mindoro in late December 1944–early January 1945. More merchant seamen lost their lives in the Mindoro action than did army or navy men. The first of three merchant convoys arrived on 22 December, and attacks on them began immediately, including one by a surface force consisting of one battleship, six destroyers, and one cruiser. The attack was repelled by U.S. planes using recently unloaded bombs, with three destroyers sunk and another damaged, and the cruiser also damaged. Enemy air attack then increased in intensity, with disastrous results; on 28 December 1944 the SS *Lewis L. Dyche,* a munitions ship, was crashed by a kamikaze and exploded with the loss of all hands—forty merchant crewmen and twenty AGs. On 4 January 1945 the SS *John Burke,* also carrying munitions, was hit by a kamikaze and disintegrated with a blinding flash with loss of all on board, forty-one merchant seamen and thirty AGs. Four AGs were killed and seven wounded on the SS *John S. Clayton,* in addition to two merchant seamen killed and two wounded when the ship was hit by a skip bomb. The SS *William Sharon* was hit by a kamikaze, but was able to make it back to Leyte; however, four AGs, an army security officer and six merchant seamen were killed, and nine AGs and six merchant seamen wounded. The toll of men and ships was heavy, but when the SS *Henry M. Stephens* returned to Mindoro in March, she found the Japanese attacks had spent themselves.[26]

The SS *Francisco Morazan* also distinguished herself at Mindoro. Lieutenant John J. Hartley, AG commanding officer, reportedly fired ten tons of ammunition passed by the merchant crew, and claimed six planes shot down. Hartley received a commendation for "maintaining full efficiency and having a well-disciplined merchant crew as well as Navy gun crew."

With the bypassing of many Japanese bases in the South Pacific and the taking of the Philippines, U.S. forces continued to move inexorably toward the home islands of Japan, and Okinawa became a major strategic objective. The invasion of Okinawa was a long and costly operation. Hundreds of merchant ships moved northward in support of the invasion forces, including many of the new Victory ships, larger and faster than the faithful old workhorses of the seas, the Liberties, although they also were well represented. A new protective strategy for merchant shipping was employed, concealing them by smoke and ordering them not to fire at enemy planes unless directly attacked or inadequately protected by smoke. Particularly, they were ordered not to fire at night, as tracers on a dark night could easily spot them as targets, proven in the European theater at Anzio and other beachheads. A further reason was that American air coverage became so effective as time passed that there was a definite danger of shooting down our own planes. However, that did not prevent massive attacks by kamikaze pilots, which caused frightful damage, more to the navy than to merchant shipping, which was considered a lower priority. The "merchants" also came under attack from one- or two-man submarines (*kaitens*) as well as suicide boats, "skunk boats" to the Americans. Probably the happiest moment of the whole invasion was when the crew of the SS *William R. Davie* observed a kamikaze attack on some rocks jutting out of the sea nearby; the pilot apparently thought the rocks to be a large ship, and his last "Banzai" was wasted.[27]

The best shooting of any merchant ship was apparently done by the SS *Cornelius Vanderbilt,* which had four confirmed kills out of five attacking planes on 18 May, plus two more on 20 May. The American fighter screen became more and more effective until few penetrations were successful, although alerts were still common. However, in spite of the vast amount of air power directed against invasion ships, actual AG casualty losses of April–July 1945 were much less than in the Philippine campaign.

The SS *Uriah M. Rose* was anchored at Nagakasuka Wan from 14 May to 19 June. She carried a naval gun crew of only nine, plus two signalmen, "not sufficient to man the guns aboard ship," according to Lieutenant John M. Landis, USNR, in his voyage report. The merchant crew had to make up the vacancies, and were carefully trained as gunners, loaders and ammunition carriers. This combination outfit was at General Quarters eighty-one times, and had five actions against kamikaze attacks; one was downed only 50 feet from the *Rose,* blowing gasoline and parts over the ship from stem to stern. The gunners succeeded in blowing the wing off another attacker, which unfortunately was able to crash into another nearby ship, and drove off several others with intense fire. The *Rose* also was credited with several assists. To their dismay, however, on 28 May they observed a Japanese Betty sneak in out of range and crash itself into the SS *Mary Livermore,* killing the captain and four AGs, but the ship continued to fight even after the attack, although the gunnery officer was seriously wounded.[28]

When the gunnery officer was wounded, as ranking member of the armed guard crew of the SS *Mary A. Livermore,* GM1c Hilmer C. Schmidt took over as armed guard commander. His report to Commanding Officer, Armed Guard Center (Pacific) states that "At 1025 28 May 1945 at Okinawa, a Japanese suicide plane crashed into our ship on the starboard side of the bridge causing a terrific explosion and fire. No sooner had we placed the wounded [four dead, three wounded including the gunnery officer] aboard an LCI when general alarm was sounded again. The gun crew took stations, sending the four-inch [gun] crew to fill in the stations left by the casualties . . . another plane, presumed a Tony, made a direct attempt at our ship . . . the 3"50 sustained a direct hit, at range of 800 yards. He crashed into the bay about 400 yards off our port beam. Still another plane crossed from our port to starboard, numbers 3 and 9 20 mms opened fire, expending a drum each. He crashed into the water alongside two small Naval craft. The crew carried out their duties beyond the highest Naval tradition. Their courage cannot be emphasized too highly."

Sadly, in contrast, at Okinawa an AG officer report on one ship included the following, "The master became hysterical during fire and interfered with efficient work on the bridge, but this was soon overcome by simply ignoring his gunnery orders and concentrating on the enemy."

The *Uriah M. Rose*'s navy gun crew had previously received a high commendation by Kingdon S. Thomas, master, sent to the chief of naval operations, for the actions of then-AG commanding officer Lieutenant (j.g.) F. S. Szemela, for his complete cooperation during a one-year voyage, and particularly for the navy crew's aid in fighting a serious fire that could have had disastrous results from the explosion of 200 cases of land mines in the immediate vicinity of the fire. The navy crew fought the fire while the merchant crew was engaged in moving the *Rose* away from other nearby ships that could have been affected by an explosion. Captain Thomas ended with the remark, "This officer cannot be too highly recommended, and it has indeed been a pleasure to have had him with us."

Much time and study has been given the Japanese policy of using kamikazes in such numbers during the closing stages of the war. It stems from the centuries-old code of Bushido, a code of honor of the nobility dating to about 1785 that became the standard of conduct for the Samurai warrior class. Bushido led to "no surrender," and to the suicidal Banzai charges. The suicide policy became an instrument of policy, in the air and on the sea, with the use of kamikaze pilots and operators of human submarines, no more than human torpedoes. Kamikaze means the "Divine Wind," which blew away the invasion fleet of Kublai Khan in the fourteenth century. In World War II it was developed by Admiral Onishi in the summer of 1944, and was originally intended for suicide pilots to crash themselves into aircraft carriers; the Japanese Air Force followed suit by deliberately ramming into American B-29s. The program became particularly effective at Okinawa, where the Japanese (untruly) claimed 293 ships sunk, but did cause serious concern.[29] Japanese college students were called to the colors in 1943 and given glider training to learn the rudiments of flight; they were not expected to come back. The policy was first tried seriously in the Philippines, but then came Okinawa where it achieved its height. Some figures give a precise number of 4,615 kamikaze pilots who lost their lives, 2,409 from the Imperial Navy and 2,206 from the Imperial Army. With such philosophy, it can only be imagined what would have been the cost if the U.S. had proceeded with the actual invasion of Japan.[30]

A most interesting report is furnished by Donald P. Firer, Charlottesville, Virginia, a signalman on the SS *Pampero*. "I served on the SS *Pampero* from February to September 1945. She was a new C-2 freighter of 6,214 tons, under Captain D. H. Smith. Our runs were from the west coast to Saipan, Tinian and Guam. The trip to Tinian in July 1945 was a strange voyage. We loaded cargo under very stringent security control at Port Chicago, California. Personnel were closely checked when boarding or leaving. Army security officers were all over the *Pampero*. The scuttlebutt was that we were loading aerial mines. The cargo receiving all the security attention was loaded in the aft hold. The hold was sealed after loading by the security officers, one of whom remained on board.

"We sailed for Tinian, Mariana Islands, off all sea lanes, with our port and starboard lights on, all the way to Tinian. The security officer checked the sealed hold daily. Upon arrival at Tinian, although unloading docks were available, we unloaded the aft cargo onto LCIs quite a distance out in the harbor. Unloading was also accomplished under stringent security control. Afterward we docked to discharge our regular cargo. Crossing the Pacific, 100 miles off all sea lanes, with running lights on in wartime was indeed very strange. The Bomb was dropped in August, the Enola Gay departing from Tinian. Ironically, we returned to the States in late July 1945, hearing of VJ-Day while at sea. And we were blacked out on the return trip, no running lights on!

"Our gunnery officer, Lt. George S. Lawson, has written me that he has always had a hunch that we had some part of the atomic bomb aboard."[31]

Along with the joy that the ending of the war brought was a feeling almost of unreality, as described by Richard Hudnall. His last ship was the SS *Rice Victory*, on which he ended the war. He observes, "We had the weirdest feeling at night when they allowed lights to be on, after so many years of sailing under absolute darkness at night." However, victory in the Pacific was not the end of his career, he remained in the navy, retiring in June 1967.[32]

The relative ineffectiveness of the Japanese attack on merchant vessels is evidenced in the fact that only forty-eight American merchant ships are listed as sunk or damaged by Japanese submarines during the entire war. In contrast, American action, primarily by submarines, sank 2,346 Japanese merchant ships, totaling 8,618,109 tons, involving the death of some 30,000 Japanese merchant seamen.[33]

CHAPTER EIGHTEEN
THE WAR IN SOUTHERN WATERS

For a time there was quiet in Cape waters . . . only the regular hare-brained reports of U-boat sightings served as a reminder of war.
—L.C.F. Turner, Assistant Editor, Union War Histories[1]

While the North Atlantic, the Murmansk run, and the Mediterranean had the most concentrated and continuing heavy air and sea action in the war at sea, the South Atlantic, the Indian Ocean, and the Arabian Sea did not lack for Axis attention. The hundreds of black dots on war maps covering the area, each representing an Allied ship sunk, give graphic evidence of the presence and cost of war, even in some of the most remote regions of the globe. With the usual route to the south via the Suez Canal cut off by the violent struggle in the Mediterranean, much American merchant shipping bound for India and beyond was forced to take the long voyage around the Cape of Good Hope. Vessels sailing from the East Coast usually traveled one of three routes. Some sailed via South America, across the South Atlantic and around the Cape into the Indian Ocean, the Arabian Sea, and the Persian Gulf. Others transited the Panama Canal and went down the seemingly interminable bleak west coast of South America, around always-tempestuous Cape Horn, and into the South Atlantic. They would then hug the ice fields north of Antarctica to South Africa in hope of evading submarines and then proceed to the Persian Gulf, India, and Ceylon. A third route took some ships across the Pacific to Australia, and then on into the Indian Ocean. All voyages were long, the ships traveled alone and frequently went weeks or even months without seeing anything, land or another ship. With the presence of German surface raiders, the sighting of a ship on the horizon often meant a sudden change of course at maximum speed.

Those that went around the Horn were faced with other hazards, equally dangerous. The vicious combination of winds, storms, and unmarked rocks has long made Cape Horn noted as being a marine graveyard, littered with the bones of countless ships. Although famed Portuguese navigator Ferdinand Magellan discovered an inland passage in 1520 that provided some protection from the continuous storm of the outer route, during World War II this was cluttered with the wrecks of ships that had struck the rocks, and shipping was forced to go outside and confront some of nature's worst tantrums.

An armed guard officer who traveled around the Horn in an old Hog Islander wrote a graphic description of the experience: "Passageway, cabins, and mess rooms are generally flooded. The ship indulged in three movements, a roll, a pitch, and then a twist without a moment's let up. We were besieged by a terrific gale and for the greater part of the time the winds registered just one point below a hurricane. From the night of the 21st, beginning just east of Cape Horn, until the 25th when we finally got around the Cape my memories are just one big blur of pounding waves, howling wind, broken crockery, dancing tables, no sleep, cold, being constantly wet, wet food, wet beds, debris floating around on the ship, floating deck cargo and constant darkness. Fighting the waves consists of climbing to the very top of the first wave, hanging there precariously perched, then a sickening lurch as she falls over the crest and slides sideways down into the trough, rolling way over on her sides as she goes down. At the bottom she starts to right herself, gives a flip and starts climbing the next wave. This one is getting a little too much for her and she can't quite make the top, and tries to cut her way through the upper portion of the wave, takes on a big cargo of water, and as the crest of the wave goes tearing by,

A World War I Hog Islander rounding Cape Horn in 1943. (Courtesy of Q. M. Hunsaker)

slips and slides down into the trough again. The third wave is just too much for her, what with being tired from climbing the waves with a load of water on her decks, and this time she just gives up, lowers her head and blows straight into the wave. Hundreds of tons of water come pouring over her bow and smash the deck with a terrific thud, rattling the entire ship and shaking the ship like a dog shaking a rabbit. Then for three or four more waves she just wallows, almost drowned until a little breathing space between waves comes along and she has a chance to get her head out of the water, roll on her side to pour the water off, and get her feet under her again, ready to take on the next bunch of waves. She was a brave old girl and after knowing all the things that have happened in moderate storms to some of the new Liberty ships, I am thankful that this ship is not one of them."[2]

Rounding the Horn west to east was just as traumatic. Walter Peters of Brownwood, Texas, signalman 3/c, was aboard the new Liberty, SS *Jeremiah H. Wadsworth*. In the rough seas the *Wadsworth* suffered seven cracks in her hull, fortunately all above the waterline. Peters adds, "After making it around the Horn, insult was added to injury— we were torpedoed and sunk en route to Capetown."[5] The *Wadsworth* was not an exceptional case. Enemy action picked up dramatically in the South Atlantic when Dönitz's U-boats, which had enjoyed such success on the United States's east and Gulf coasts and the Caribbean, were driven southward by the late introduction of an effective convoy system and air cover. The U-boats then shifted their attention to waters off South America where the many ships traveling alone made attractive and still vulnerable targets. Although a master chess player in the "game" of war, Dönitz outsmarted himself; he infuriated Brazil by sinking a number of Brazilian ships, and Brazil joined the war, providing the United States with bases for American surface units, naval aircraft, and even the slow-moving, ungainly appearing blimps that proved superb in protecting convoys. The United States presence was in the form of the Fourth Fleet, under Vice Admiral Ingram, headquartered at Recife. It covered a vast theater of operations, and before defenses reached maximum effectiveness, ship losses were heavy.

The story of the SS *Jeremiah H. Wadsworth* is an interesting one. She was carrying 6,000 tons of cargo and a deck load of trucks and had got almost into the Indian Ocean when on 27 November 1942, she ran out of luck. Walter Peters picks up the story: "Suddenly there were two violent explosions, two torpedoes had hit the ship. The order was shouted 'commence firing!', but the initial response at the bow gun was 'at what?', we couldn't see anything as the attack had come from the stern. The ship began going down by the bow, and the captain ordered to abandon, but we finally saw a periscope and kept firing until we had to jump for it. I had set up my life jacket for just such an emergency, papers, cigarettes and other personal effects, but it was in my quarters, and I had to dive into the water without it. . . . We swam about for what seemed a long time before we were picked up by the captain's boat. There were three lifeboats and we set out to find the Bos'n who had been blown off the bridge by the explosion. After four hours we found him, still blowing his whistle. Shortly thereafter the U-boat surfaced alongside the boats and an officer inquired if anyone was hurt, fortunately not the case. The three boats were separated by three violent storms in a row, and we found ourselves alone in the middle of a blank expanse of ocean; our lifeboat capsized twice, but we were able to right it each time . . . after six cold days, with the winds coming off the ice fields to the south, we were spotted by the SS *John Lykes*. It came close to being a miracle as the *Lykes* was running far behind schedule. She had previously picked up so many survivors of sunken ships that she had to divert course and land them at Port Elizabeth.

"The *Lykes* had to maintain radio silence and could not communicate that she had picked up survivors, so that by the time we reached land the Navy had already sent telegrams to our next of kin reporting we were missing in action. They were never notified that we had survived; although we sent cables, mine never arrived. When I arrived home on leave my uncle answered the doorbell, took one look at me, and promptly fainted. While we had been incredibly lucky, on return to duty I heard some bad news. One of the Navy crew had been sunk three times before and was "torpedo happy" even on board. This time had pushed him over the edge and he had to be taken out of the service and hospitalized. I never heard how he made out."[4]

While serving in the SS *Fitz John Porter*, about 500 miles off the coast of Brazil, Larry LaFontaine of Olympia, Washington, was on the bow watch. The sea was light by a full moon and LaFontaine saw a torpedo miss the bow. He informed the captain, who said it was "just porpoises." LaFontaine then informed the gunnery officer, who ordered him to return to his 20-mm gun on the bow. He says, "I did, but the next 'porpoise' got us, knocked the 4″ gun off its mounts and put a big hole in #5 hold. The ship started to go down, one of our gunners had been hit, we tried to find him but couldn't, and the captain ordered abandon ship." The convoy had lost thirteen ships, but the *Porter* crew was comparatively lucky; survivors were picked up by a Brazilian ship and taken to Recife. "We were the first survivor crew the authorities had seen and they didn't know what to do with us, so they put us in jail until matters could be straightened out, which took a couple of days." LaFontaine had previously had a close call aboard the SS *William H. Seward* in the Indian Ocean, when they were trailed by a large ship that did not acknowledge signals, but followed every change of course of the *Seward*. They lost it at night, and upon arrival at Aden they heard from an air force report that the stranger was a German raider.[5]

Coxswain 3/c Warren Chapman sailed on a tanker that became one of the early casualties in the southern waters. It was his first voyage, and nearly his last. He was in charge of the ship's small AG gun crew, and they fired at a submarine cruising slowly on the surface; the sub submerged to cheers and shouts of victory, but Chapman figured it would be back at night when it would have all the advantage. He was right. "Suddenly there was a terrific roar, and the whole ship shook as if it were about to fall apart. I got to the aft gun and found it was a wreck, the whole deck was twisted out of shape. The ship was listing badly and the crew began lowering boats. But our orders from the Navy were not to quit the ship until it was certain that there was no possibility of putting up a fight. I was checking the gun to see if anything could be done with it when the second torpedo hit, and that was it . . . we were in lifeboats about thirty-six hours before being picked up . . . my 'initiation' was over." However, his troubles weren't, for he was next assigned to the Murmansk run on another tanker. On the fourteenth day out his ship caught a torpedo and broke in half. It is not known if he survived the war.

What is reported to be one of the longest open-boat trips in World War II is the saga of the officers and men and the armed guard crew aboard the SS *Roger B. Taney,* en route from southwestern Africa to Bahia, Brazil. She was hit by three torpedoes, and a Navy Department report of survivors says she was believed to have been sunk at night, as she was not in sight at daybreak. Donald Zubrod, purser, has reported that the *Taney*'s merchant crew and AG wound up in two lifeboats, twenty-six in one and twenty-eight in the other. One boat, under command of the first mate, was picked up after twenty-one days, but the second, under Captain Tom Potter, went through an ordeal ranging from dead calm to raging storms for forty-two days, during which they sailed 2,600 miles before being picked up. Zubrod, who was aboard Captain Potter's boat, reports, "Our boat contained thirteen AGs, one of whom was Sam Lo Presti, goal-tender of the Chicago Blackhawks hockey team in 1940–41. He was Gunner's Mate, and was a very strong individual, mentally and physically. I have vivid recollections of him spearing a thirty-five-pound fish around the thirty-sixth day, the first real food we had had up to then and the last until we were picked up." Captain Potter kept a log of the ordeal, and in it is reference to Lo Presti's dolphin, boiled and cooked over an oil fire in a bucket by Tex Miller, the ship's baker, and rationed, "with thanks to God for good fortune."[6]

While not as long, one of the most harrowing ordeals at sea involving women and children was the experience of those aboard the SS *West Lashaway,* bound for Fall River, Massachusetts, from West Africa. Carrying a cargo of tin, copper, and a secret cache of gold, with a merchant crew of thirty-seven, an AG gun crew of nine and nine passengers, she was torpedoed on 30 August 1942 about 350 miles east of Trinidad. Among the passengers was Mrs. Ethel Bell, a missionary in West Africa. There had been no time to send an "under attack" distress call, as the vessel sank in two minutes, with heavy loss of life. Mrs. Bell, her own two children and two others, plus fourteen men drifted on an 8 × 10-foot raft for nineteen days. Her son Robert later wrote a gripping account of the ordeal; swollen feet, immersed in seawater constantly, led to festering sores that grew into ulcers. Scabs could not form because of constant soaking and the pain never let up. A navy signalman, the only AG survi-

vor of the sinking, died on the raft. The captain became de-
ranged and also died; both were put overboard. Through it
all Mrs. Bell never lost faith in God and of rescue, and on
18 September they were found by HMS *Vimy*, but they had
one more shattering experience. The raft was shelled by mistake, in belief that it was a submarine, but fortunately the
aim of the gunners was off, the mistake discovered in time,
and the seventeen survivors rescued.[7]

While southern waters offered a greater chance of survival than the frigid waters of the Arctic, they also led to
more suffering from being adrift in an empty sea for extended periods. None could match the ordeal of Seaman 2/c
Basil Dominic Izzi, South Barre, Massachusetts, and two
merchant seamen of the Dutch liner *Zaandam*, an epic
of endurance and triumph of the human spirit. Their incredible story had been lost with the passage of years until
discovered by Bob Norling, former AG signalman, a retired
editor of the *Boston Globe*. The *Zaandam*, a 10,909-ton passenger liner, formerly engaged in the Rotterdam-New York
service, had been fitted out as a troop transport in early
1942 and was assigned a naval armed guard gun crew of
unknown size. On 2 November 1942, traveling about 300
miles off the Brazilian coast, she was struck by two torpedoes and sank within minutes; only 168 of 299 aboard were
saved. Originally, five survivors were aboard a life raft, but
AG officer Lieutenant (j.g.) James Maddox, USNR, and gunner Franklin Beazely died before rescue; Izzi and the two
Dutch seamen survived for eighty-three days on the raft
before they were found. A detailed account of their experience was written in 1943 and later published in an anthol-
ogy of war accounts, *The New Yorker Book of War Pieces*. The
piece did not list the ship involved, as was customary during
wartime, and the ship's name was but recently located by
Norling and verified in a terse navy report, excerpts of which
follow:

"Three ships passed them by without noticing the raft
and its five occupants. Their food lasted sixteen days, and
water for less than a week longer. They caught a shark by

using their toes for bait, and bringing the shark into a noose which they had formed from a line from the life raft. They ate fifteen birds which they caught and used the entrails to catch fish. They ate sea snails and chewed seaweed. They caught rain in a piece of canvas. They even made a checkerboard of sorts . . . When picked up by PC-576 on their eighty-third day, about seventy miles off the coast of Brazil, the three survivors were 'skeletons with bronze skin wrapped around them.' They gained thirteen pounds in thirteen hours after rescue . . ."

Gunner Beazely died first. Lieutenant Maddox almost lived to see his wife and home in Indiana, where he had been a college instructor, and of which he had talked often as they whiled away the hours and days. Maddox died on the seventy-sixth day. Their ordeal on the open sea has been described as the longest on record.[8]

The effectiveness of the German intelligence network in Argentina was evidenced by the sinking of two ships, the Liberty SS *William Gaston* and the *John Carter Rose*. Lieutenant Commander Harold J. McCormick, USNR, now of Stamford, Connecticut, was gunnery officer of the *Gaston*, and he has reported how the *Gaston* was trailed from Buenos Aires by an Argentine-flag freighter, an old coal-burner, which took position on the same course, about a mile off the starboard quarter of the *Gaston*. The small freighter doggedly followed the *Gaston*, running as a neutral, turning on her running lights at dark. That the stranger followed all course changes of the *Gaston* led her master, Captain Harry W. Chase, to observe, "The damn fools are following us to Africa!" But suddenly on Sunday 23 July, the Argentine changed course and disappeared. At sunset, with the navy crew standing its usual General Quarters watch, the *Gaston* was hit by a torpedo on the starboard quarter and quickly began to settle by the stern. Seas were too rough to abandon ship immediately, but at dawn the *Gaston* was struck by a second torpedo and began going down fast. Lifeboats were floated by the rising seas, and the crew took to them. The AG crew was still on deck but took to a raft in time. Survivors were spotted by a navy Mariner-class plane and were soon picked up by the USS *Matagorda,* a seaplane tender. All aboard the *Gaston* survived.[9]

On 8 October 1942, the *John Carter Rose* was torpedoed 850 miles east of Trinidad, while traveling alone. A survivor in the water was picked up by a U-boat and transferred to a lifeboat. However, he first was reportedly shown a piece of paper with the names of both the *Rose* and the *Gaston,* and was asked which ship was his. The lifeboats were then furnished first-aid supplies, cigarettes, and brown bread and given the course to Venezuela.

Since Argentina was technically "neutral," Axis vessels had the legal right to enter Argentine harbors. John Dunkerly, AG coxswain aboard the SS *John C. Spencer,* reports that they were traveling alone to Capetown, via Cape Horn. "We pulled into Buenos Aires on Easter Sunday—and a U-boat followed us in. It must have been a shock to the captain, who was reported to have lost several ships on the Murmansk run."[10]

One of the slowest voyages across the Atlantic since the days of sail must have been the SS *Cape Neddick*'s return to the United States from Capetown, South Africa. Gunnery officer Lieutenant Michael Gurda, USNR, now an attorney in Middletown, New York, reports that the *Neddick,* carrying troops and material for Egypt, had to take the long way, via the Panama Canal, South Atlantic, around the Cape to Egypt and back via the South Atlantic. Approximately 500 miles south of Capetown the ship was attacked by a German submarine. "We spotted the submarine and fired the 5″ 38 and the machine guns. A torpedo struck the starboard side of our ship just under the bridge; the ship listed very badly, since the hole in the side was approximately 40 feet by 60 feet. A second torpedo missed the ship by about 30 feet. The captain gave the order to abandon ship, and about sixty men went into the lifeboats. As senior Naval representative, we took command of the ship and kept firing the guns until the sub disappeared. The next morning we picked up the lifeboat and limped to German East Africa to a town named

Torpedo damage to the SS *Cape Neddick*. With temporary repairs she crossed the South Atlantic to the United States at 3 knots. (Courtesy Lt. Michael Gurda, USNR)

Swakopmund. We subsequently moved the ship to Capetown where it could not be repaired, but was reinforced so that we could cross the Atlantic. It took three months, traveling at three knots per hour, to Hampton Roads. The cargo of ammunition, jeeps, tanks and aircraft parts had been saved!" Several men were wounded but none killed in the attack. The *Cape Neddick* was subsequently repaired and put back into service. She had previously carried General Patton's officers and tanks to Casablanca and had made six North Atlantic crossings before she was hit. Lieutenant Gurda was cited and received the Purple Heart for his action during the attack.[11]

The sinking of the SS *Dona Aurora* was unique in many respects. She had a Filipino master and merchant crew, and a twelve-man navy AG crew. She was one of the very few AG-manned ships sunk by an Italian submarine, the *Enrique Tazzoli*, while en route Capetown to Baltimore on Christmas Day 1943. Three AG survivors made it to the coast of Brazil after thirty-one days on a raft. Sadly, one of the three, S 2/c Earl Ward was lost only a short distance from shore. The story was told later by S 2/c Dodrill, Ridgley, West Virginia, to Ward's fiancée. The AG gun crew boarded the *Dona Aurora* in Brooklyn, and they proceeded in convoy to Scotland. However, the captain was very unhappy about plugging along at eight knots, as his ship was capable of making eighteen. He received permission to leave the convoy in Scotland and go on by himself, and he reached Bombay. On return they loaded bauxite in Mombasa, East Africa, and at Durban they picked up twelve survivors from another ship that had been sunk. Just before leaving Capetown, Ward checked the two lifeboats and life rafts for water, survival equipment, and food and found that they needed replenishing, of crucial importance as they soon learned. On Christmas morning Dodrill gave the alarm of an approaching torpedo, but it was too late, and the ship went down in seven minutes. The Italian captain of the submarine surfaced and after an exchange with survivors, took a civilian, John Oliver, nationality and address unknown, aboard the submarine.

Cow hides in the cargo began drifting to the surface and immediately attracted sharks, which tore the hides apart and ate them and then tried for two days to overturn the raft, but were beaten off. Each man received one rye-crisp cracker soaked in saltwater and washed down with freshwater three times a day. At night the ocean spray kept them wet and cold; during the day they suffered from the heat of the sun. They drifted 700 miles and found themselves stranded on a sandbar. For six hours they tried to work the raft loose, to no avail. In the morning they noticed land not far off. The water appeared to be only about waist deep and Dodrill and Ward decided to wade ashore to find help; the third AG, Joe Schopmeyer, had been injured so badly that his foot was twisted backward, and he could not make the attempt. Moving in toward shore they fell into deep water just as the tide was going out. Ward could not swim well and was carried out by the tide. Dodrill watched him disappear, an emotional shock after feeling that they were so close to safety after their long ordeal. Dodrill washed ashore where he was found by a native. Later on, Schopmeyer somehow worked the raft loose and he floated in. They were on an island at the mouth of the Amazon, and they stayed with the natives for about two weeks to regain strength. Then the natives took them to Belém, where they contacted the navy and were brought home.

While on the raft they saw twenty-two airplanes and seven ships, but apparently they were never seen. The two survivors found that they had been listed as missing, as were seven other members of the navy gun crew. Nothing further was heard of the civilian survivor of two sinkings who was taken aboard the submarine.[12]

Fortunately, merchant ships and their AG gun crews were not always victims. Two that were not were the Liberty SS *Charles Willson Peale* and the SS *Columbian.* Lieutenant (j.g.) Roscoe E. Johnson, USNR, and his gun crew, in the *Peale* with merchant volunteers, put up such a good fight, and the master maneuvered the ship so skillfully that they drove off a submarine and made port safely. The *Columbian* encountered a submarine on the surface off the coast of Brazil at midnight; both vessels fired, and a shot from the *Columbian*'s 4″ stern gun scored a direct hit, followed by another hit, and the submarine ceased fire. Ensign Merrill R. Stone, Jr., commander of the AG gun crew, credited the master for the fine maneuvering of the ship, which enabled the gunners to get good position and range.[13]

The situation in the Indian Ocean and Arabian Sea, however remote, could not be conducive to the peace of mind of the men aboard merchant ships plying the area. Most ships traveled alone, and what convoys were available were poorly escorted. Japanese submarines were active in the Indian Ocean and Arabian Sea in 1942; they made seventy attacks on merchant shipping and sank twenty ships; thirty-one of the attacks were made in the first three months of the year, and took a toll of a possible fifteen ships. In June, Japanese subs made sixteen attacks, but they dwindled off rapidly, and by December they were made only occasionally.[14] However, what they lacked in number they more than made up for in viciousness and in the sadistic treatment of survivors; details are furnished elsewhere. Nevertheless, the Japanese submarine force proved surprisingly inept and of minor significance. Not so Dönitz' U-boats, which were highly successful in operating in the area. Until late in the war they were routed from submarine bases in France down the west coast of Africa, around the Cape of Good Hope and into the Indian Ocean. The Mozambique Channel proved to be a happy hunting ground. Between September 1942 and the summer of 1943, twenty-eight U-boats, operating on a rotation basis, sank 117 Allied ships with a loss of only 3 subs. When they became available, Dönitz sent the new Type-IX U-boats into the Indian Ocean, two groups of which were later dispatched to give the Japanese help in Eastern waters. The key to the early success of the U-boats was refueling at sea and replenishing supplies by use of supply ships such as the *Charlotte Schliemann* and large "milch-cow" submarines. Their success went downhill following the destruction of the supply vessels and the loss of German submarine bases in France, but before that there was more than enough hazard for the lone travelers, as well as some extraordinary experiences for the men of the merchant vessels.[15]

The *U-181*, under command of Lieutenant Commander Wolfgang Luth, was highly successful in both the Indian Ocean and the Far East before his strange death on shore late in the war.

The SS *Alice F. Palmer*, a Kaiser-built Liberty, was launched in 1943, and Arno L. Grasty of Houston, Texas, was a member of the AG gun crew. He recalls, "They were loading her while they were still painting her." Her first voyage took her to Australia, India, and Ceylon, and she was heading for Durban, South Africa, in ballast, about 130 miles southeast of Madagascar when the torpedo hit. Grasty ran to his assigned gun, but realized quickly that there was no need to be there; there was no electricity and the shaft on the ship had been broken and was making a terrible roar. The captain ordered abandon ship, and Grasty found himself with twenty-one others in a standard-size 23-foot lifeboat, built to hold sixteen men. There were eleven AG men and eleven merchant seaman aboard the boat. "The German U-boat surfaced and asked if there were any injured and if we had provisions. When asked the name of the ship, someone answered '*H. M. Storey*,' a ship I had been on for nine months and which had been sunk several months before. They told us we were only ninety miles off the coast, but they might as well have said 9,000 as none of us figured we'd make it because of storms." While available food was strictly rationed, a flying fish landed in Grasty's lap and, cut into bait, enabled them to catch a big dolphin, which they ate raw but it tasted good. Sixteen days later they drifted in sight of land, having been blown back and forth for days by shifting winds. They landed in Bazaruto Island on 26 July, and found that it was a Portuguese penal colony, including murderers, but the survivors found them very friendly and helpful. "They brought us water and stuff to cook and built a fire and put a big pot over it and made mush from cornmeal; when it was about ready, one reached down and grabbed a handful of sand and put it into the pot. Someone asked why he did this, and he replied, 'Chickens eat sand; good for people too.' The only inhabitant who wasn't there for crime was a lighthouse keeper, who got in touch with the mainland, and we were picked up the next day." [16]

Just before they made shore the men in the lifeboat saw a number of whales lying off the beach; they got so close that the men could smell their breaths, and there was unanimous agreement that "whales have halitosis!" The whales were enormous, and Grasty said, "They went down just before we got to them. What we didn't realize, although the whales were trying to let us know, was that we were still in mighty deep water." Grasty credits a fellow AG, Bos'n E. M. (Mac) Dale, for their survival, as he allowed for a number of contingencies before leaving the ship and handled the lifeboat surely in the turbulent seas. Dale's back hurt him, but it was not until he was brought back to the United States that it was found that he had a fracture of the spine that required several months hospitalization.

One of the other lifeboats was spotted by a PBY Catalina after three days, and the twenty survivors were taken aboard the plane. However, the hull of the plane was damaged in attempting to take off with the heavy overload, which included two depth charges; the plane had to taxi on the water for eighteen hours until they reached the coast of Madagascar, and then it was demolished in the surf. The gallant British pilot was threatened with court-martial for disobeying orders and landing at sea in such fashion, but Dale heard that he had been cleared, only to be killed shortly thereafter.

The U-boat that had sunk the *Palmer* was the *U-177*, commanded by Lieutenant Robert Gysae, later to become a flotilla admiral in the postwar German Navy. A member of the merchant crew tracked him down after the war, and they exchanged pleasant correspondence, in which Gysae commented whimsically that he was surprised to find the ship was the *Alice F. Palmer,* as he had reported the name of the ship, "as the crew told us!"

Lieutenant Commander Harold McCormick, USNR, reports on an unusual experience: "On one of our passages from the Persian Gulf to Australia, we ran into heavy weather, and one of my navy seamen was thrown against a steel stanchion and broke his collarbone. As we had no doctor or medical corpsman on board, the boy faced several weeks of pain and the likelihood of improper bone-mending. We were not authorized to break radio silence except every third night to give our position and a local weather report, but I persuaded the captain to let me append a report of an injured seaman. Within a few hours, our tanker received a message from a British station in India, ordering us to change course and head for a point in the Equator in the middle of the Indian Ocean. No land was indicated on navigational charts and we assumed we were going to rendezvous with a naval vessel. The following morning, a low, thin line of palm trees appeared directly ahead of us. Within an hour or so, a blinker light mounted in the trees signalled us to proceed on a precise course, which led us through a narrow channel between two islands and into a broad deep-water lagoon. Later we learned that it was Addu Atoll, and that the British Navy was holding it as an emergency fleet anchorage. One island was a leper colony, another had a small medical clinic with its own generator for X-ray equipment, plus a modern weather station staffed by a small crew of British and American technicians. A doctor set the seaman's shoulder, we took a swim in the surf, had British tea (and brandy) and then resumed our voyage to Australia."[17]

Everyone who has seen "South Pacific" on stage or screen has fallen in love with Bali Hai, but "Lieutenant Cable" of Philadelphia really won the prize. In real life, however, Lieutenant Gordon Morton of Detroit, Michigan, came close, according to Robert Ruark. Sunk somewhere in the Indian Ocean, survivors made land in seventeen days. "Sure enough," says Ruark, "out came the natives in outriggers and the lifeboat was towed through a break in the coral reef." The island was Kavaratti, in the Laccadive group, and the king of the island undertook to entertain the survivors, stuffing them with food; there was the expected tropical moon, soft breezes sighing through the palms, the throb of native drums and native chants. Finally the Americans were taken to a coastal village from where they were sent to Ceylon and a rest camp. Ruark reports that as Morton left, he felt vaguely uneasy, conscious of something missing. "I kept expecting Dorothy Lamour in her sarong to turn up," he said.[18]

Certainly one of the most unusual examples of eliminating boredom on a merchant ship on a long voyage was the building of sailboats by the AGs and merchant crew aboard the SS *James H. Johnson* en route from Calcutta to Lourenço Marques in East Africa. AG gunner DeWitt Welch of Georgia and George Kauffman, bos'n mate 1/c of Alpena, Michigan, bunked together and found they had a lot in common.

DeWitt was from a long line of carpenters, and George was from a family with generations of experience building boats on the Great Lakes. Seeing fine wood, including Douglas fir, being discarded in Calcutta, "Yankee" and "Georgia Boy" conceived the idea of building a sailboat. Obtaining the Danish captain's permission, they scrounged lumber from the docks, tarpaulins from the army to make sails, and nails from the ship's locker. Seeing what they were doing, the ship's bos'n got permission from the captain, and the crew also began work. By the time they got to Mozambique, both boats were ready except for masts, so George and DeWitt scouted up a lumber dealer and found just the right size piece and kind of wood for a mast. They and ship's crewmen walked through the center of town carrying long pieces of wood on their shoulders, to the gapes of onlookers. Being a master woodworker, George turned out masts that looked "like they had been turned out on a lathe." With the captain's permission the boats were lowered over the side by ship's boom, masts and sails installed, and both boats worked perfectly. Even the captain joined the crew in sailing about in various ports where they had long waits to be loaded or unloaded, to the envy of crew from other waiting ships and even land detachments. When the *Johnson* was about to sail for home, George and DeWitt were approached by a United States Army contingent who asked them to sell their boat and offered a handsome price, but they decided to give the boat to the army group, on the basis that ordinary nails had been used in construction and in time would rust out and the boat would fall apart.[19]

Late in 1942, after the destruction of Convoy PQ-17 and the delay until the darkness of fall of the hard-hit and costly PQ-18, the Allied Powers were faced with a critical logistical problem—how to deliver enough war material and supplies to the U.S.S.R. to keep it in the war. Things were going badly for the beleaguered Soviet forces, and there was a growing danger of a Russian collapse. To escape the combined plagues of vicious weather and incessant enemy attacks from above and below the sea against convoys to Murmansk and Archangel an alternative or supplemental route had to be developed. The only feasible alternative available was to the south, via the Indian Ocean, Arabian Sea, and Persian Gulf, and through the "back door" of Russia via Iran and Iraq.

While merchant shipping did not have to run the gauntlet of enemy harassment encountered steadily on the North Russian run, it was quickly found that there were also formidable problems to the south. The greatest of these was the unloading, storing, and transporting of supplies arriving on a steadily increasing number of Allied ships to the primitive ports along the Gulf. These ancient installations had to be modernized, and docks, terminals, and transport facilities developed from scratch. Getting the goods from port to the Russian border was another nightmare. The Shah of Iran, distrusting his neighbors, had built a railroad, but of a different gauge from connecting lines in Iraq and Russia. Both roadbed and rolling stock were so archaic that the capability of the railroad was only about 200 tons per day, if all went well. The road system was equally bad; brand new tires on convoy trucks being delivered to the U.S.S.R., loaded with cargo, blew out in as little as 10 miles from port. The combination of rocks, holes, incredible heat, and heavy overload proved deadly to the transportation services. Tempers (and temperatures) of American transport personnel were not cooled when Russian "allies" refused to permit them to cross the Russian border, at which point trucks and cargoes were turned over to the Russian crews.

The flood of materiel arriving by sea overwhelmed even improved new port facilities, where found, and port delays of weeks or even months to unload were standard. The average turn-around time for a ship was fifty-five days at one time, but some unfortunate crews were stranded for up to three months or more. One AG crew must have thought they were part of the "Forgotten Convoy" in Murmansk, except for the difference in climate, having to wait an unnerving 124 days to unload and head out of the hellish Gulf. Lucky ships with priority cargo, such as aviation supplies and ammunition, were unloaded sometimes within a few days, a mixed blessing to long-delayed crews who weren't always overjoyed to have them in the immediate neighborhood. The heat was so intense that it was necessary for AG crews to put wet blankets over ammunition as protection from the blazing sun.

The personal-discomfort quotient, if such were ever considered, must have registered at the top of the scale. In addition to 125-degree-and-above heat, plus humidity, the ubiquitous yellowish-brown dust sifted into everything. It irritated eyes, nose, and mouth; it intruded into food, machinery, and instruments. Although seafaring men have never been noted for welcoming hurricanes, many a man in the Persian Gulf would have positively enjoyed a hurricane and its heavy rains to wash down both selves and ships.

At time of writing, millions of American television viewers have become familiar with the haze-obscured pictures of tankers being convoyed by United States naval units in the Persian Gulf. Although living conditions aboard ship have been greatly improved since World War II, even now it is difficult. During the war, life was unbearable below deck and almost as bad on a ship's upper deck. The heat is so enervating that heat stress is a major problem even today.

Bob Williams, The Dalles, Oregon, was a Murmansk veteran who later found himself in the Persian Gulf. Signalman 3/c on the SS *William L. Marcy,* he had experienced thirty-seven days of darkness and wild weather in which his ship rolled thirty-seven degrees and the hull cracked. The break ran across the main deck, and down 8 feet on the starboard side and 16 feet on the port side. The crew used a winch to pull the pieces together as far as possible, and the *Marcy* limped along at two knots for four days, traveling alone, before they made port in Belfast. He wasn't too enthusiastic about going back to Murmansk, but his luck didn't improve a lot, for his next ship, the SS *Eli Whitney,* carrying food and clothing to the Russians, headed for the Persian Gulf. His introduction to the Gulf was not heartening. The *Whitney* ran into a dust storm that lasted almost a week. Visibility was zero, and the blowing sand burned faces because it hit with such force. It was so hard on eyes and nose that it was impossible to stand watch for four hours. "Two of us switched watch after one hour as we needed water so badly. Coming into port at Bandär Shapur we were really lost, we couldn't see lights, and buoys looked like native fishing craft. The heat was so intense that unloading would start at dawn and stop at 1:00 P.M. as we couldn't stand the heat. A number of us got heat stroke but stayed on the boat as there was no place else to go." [20]

When the SS *Thomas J. Rusk* reached the Persian Gulf, she waited six weeks before unloading began. Gunnery officer Lieutenant Commander Norman Alston reports, "The temperature would get to ninety degrees before the sun rose, and official temperature reading by the U.S. Army contingent ashore would reach 140 degrees during the day." As a veteran of many a Texas sandstorm, Alston says that the Abadan variety makes a West Texas sandstorm look feeble by comparison, and what's more, Persian Gulf sand is coarse, rather than the fine dust of the Chihuahua Desert. The heat was so intense that when the *Rusk* reached the Indian Ocean, and temperatures plunged to 70 degrees, the crew began breaking out the foul-weather gear originally issued for harsher climates. The *Rusk*'s voyage was a real time-consumer, forty-six days from Panama to Perth, six weeks in Abadan, and forty-six more days from Abadan to Bahia, Brazil, the first stop en route back, with no liberty stops in between. [21]

Such was the destination of hundreds of ships and their AG crews, after a long and hazardous journey. A total of 385 ships were lost on the Persian Gulf run; in 1941 only twenty ships were lost to the Axis powers, but as the volume of shipping increased, Dönitz countered by sending more U-boats into the area, and in 1942, 205 ships were lost, the high-water mark of submarine activity in the Indian Ocean and Arabian Sea. With improved defensive measures, losses fell to eighty-two in 1943, fifty the following year, and only three in 1945. [22]

A forerunner of current convoy operations in the Persian Gulf, the Esso Tanker SS *E. G. Seubert* was torpedoed on a dark night in 1944, while proceeding from Abadan and Hormuz in convoy. Two other tankers in the convoy were also torpedoed and destroyed. The *Seubert* sank in about twelve minutes with the navy gun crew still aboard the burning ship. She sank suddenly and all hands still on deck were washed overboard; three members of the AG gun crew were lost and others injured.[23]

What story of war, since the days of the Spanish Main, would be complete without a mystery "treasure ship," lost with its cargo of riches intact, just waiting to be discovered, à la Spanish galleons of old in the Caribbean Sea. World War II is no exception; the Liberty ship SS *John Barry,* traveling alone, was en route from Aden to Ras at-Tannurah in the Persian Gulf when she was torpedoed by the *U-859* on 28 August 1944, about 125 miles off the coast of Saudi Arabia in the Arabian Sea. The *Barry* was carrying a full load of general cargo and could not be distinguished from any other hundreds of Liberties plying the ancient trade routes of the Middle East. However she was not just the ordinary weather-beaten cargo carrier; she had a special extra load—$26 million in silver bullion, confirmed by a navy report.[24]

The *Barry* was struck about 1800 hours between the #2 and #4 holds, on the starboard side. A second torpedo hit moments later, and the *Barry* sank quickly. The merchant crew of forty-one officers, men, and the navy gun crew of twenty-seven abandoned ship, with the exception of two crewmen who were lost. All survivors were rescued quickly.

The *Barry* was owned by WSA and operated by Lykes Brothers Steamship of New Orleans, but Lykes now has no records pertaining to the ship. A former member of the merchant crew, interviewed in the NMU *Pilot,* reported that when he boarded the ship no one would tell the destination, leading to protests, but rumors really started flying when "about 28 million dollars" in bullion was brought aboard. The *Barry* joined a Med convoy, went through the Suez Canal and stopped at Aden. The crewman remembered the *Barry* as a "good ship," but too heavily loaded at the bow, and hard to steer. He was at the wheel one night, in bright moonlight, the ship making a zigzag course when he saw a torpedo coming in amidships. Then there was a ball of fire, and when he came to, the ship was dark, except for the light of the moon. Only one lifeboat was left, and he recalled the AG officer losing two fingers trying to release a boat full of water. Then a second torpedo hit and the *Barry* broke apart. The radio operator threw his emergency kit into the water, fished it out, and was able to get off an SOS. Survivors were picked up by two nearby ships and landed at Khorramshahr, Iran, on 6 September, whence they were repatriated.[25]

The extreme length of the run to the Persian Gulf when the Suez was closed brought about some unexpected complications. Frank Davis, a veteran merchant mariner, says, "I was on the Liberty, SS *Philip Livingston,* and we returned from Iran in October 1943. Ship and crew had been out for eleven months. On arrival in New York, our AG crew had to be bused to the Navy Yard and fitted with new uniforms. Their average age was nineteen, and during the time they had all gained twenty to thirty pounds. They gave the chow, which was good and plentiful, just plain hell, especially the ten pound cans of Spam and six-pound buckets of peanut butter, along with fresh baked bread. We did run out of food on the way back, and it must have been a nightmare for them as we had no peanut butter. I admired those kids (and they were kids), they strained their eyes out, day and night, looking for the devil and prayed for action."[26]

India was a major destination for merchant ships with AG crews, and is the location of some unique experiences. One of the important details of war is to maintain friendly relations with Allies, and so the opportunity to demonstrate good will and build rapport was welcomed by the gun crew of the SS *Big Foot Wallace* while in Calcutta. Once again we turn to the words of DeWitt Welch, gunner's mate: "The stevedores had just about finished unloading us except for the sulphur in #5 hold. It was powdered and in 50-pound bags. We had been informed that a party of British officers had heard about our new 5″ 38-caliber gun and were interested in learning more about it. The British officers came aboard about 10 A.M. The Lieutenant met them at the gangway and showed them back to the stern where the gun was located. My crew was already on the gun deck. The British came up the ladder and spread out around the gun, about ten of them, all in tropical whites.

"I made my speech about the gun, but they acted like they didn't believe me when I told them how fast it operated. I told them I would call the engine room and have the power turned on and they would see how fast it was. I had all my crew at battle stations. I had to go behind the ready boxes to the telephone to call the engine room. When I got to the phone, I could see down in #5 hold and smoke was beginning to pour out of the hold. The stevedores were yelling and reaching up the ladder out of the hold, so instead of telling the engine room to put power on the gun, I told them to put pressure on the fire mains. There was a fire hydrant on the port and starboard corners of our gun crew quarters, just a few feet from #5 hold. I told my crew to go down and break out the fire hoses. They all got down the ladder and turned on the fire hydrant after they got the hose stretched out. Water began pouring into #5, but they were all on the same hose; under 200 pounds pressure the hose was difficult to control.

"I yelled and told some of them to get the hose on the other side working. All the officers had lined on the other side trying to see what was going on, but we still hadn't seen anything but a lot of smoke. All of my crew except one man let go of the first hose at the same time. He held on but the nozzle pointed straight up and away from the hold. A couple of my men returned to help him and finally got it pulled down and swung it around. However, before they got it under control it hit the British officers. They just about drowned those officers with that stinking, muddy river water. By that time, my other boys had the other hose going and the smoke began to clear up. The merchant crew deck hands and a couple of Mates showed up and took over, but the British decided they had seen all they wanted to see, and left the ship, looking considerably the worse for wear. That afternoon the captain and our Lieutenant came back to the stern and told us how much they appreciated what we did and the way we handled it."[27]

DeWitt did not indicate why he thought it took the captain so long; perhaps the captain had a hard time stopping laughing. Whatever, at the end of the voyage, DeWitt's last before discharge, he received a note from Captain John Hansen, master of the SS *Big Foot Wallace*. It said, "For cheerfully rendered service. Thank you and the best of luck." Enclosed was a twenty-dollar bill.

The United States Naval Armed Guard has never been rated with West Point or Annapolis as regards turning out a top-flight marching unit. However, the AG gun crew in the SS *William H. Moody* had a most unique honor. They were invited to participate in the great "Victory Parade" held by the Royal Navy in Bombay 14 May 1945. Rick Whalen, Hyattsville, Maryland, reports that in their unaccustomed whites, led by lieutenant (j.g.) George T. Bayley, USNR, they passed in review before a host of dignitaries including the governor of Bombay, Sir Henry Knight, who took the salute. A photograph of the occasion shows the smart unit "Eyes Right" while passing the reviewing stand. The AG unit received commendations and congratulations from Rear Admiral Oliver Bevir, RN, senior officer of the Royal Navy establishment.[28]

One of the most heart-warming stories out of India involved AG Joe Morgan of Kansas. After having survived twenty Atlantic crossings, he made a voyage to India. One evening in Calcutta, across a table, he saw a familiar face— his brother, who was in India with the 90th Army Division.

CHAPTER NINETEEN
JAPANESE SUBMARINE
WARFARE/ATROCITIES

As a result of orders from Commander
SW Area Fleet, Vice Admiral Yakasu,
survivors were murdered when the
Richard Hovey, Bevar and Jean Nicolet
were sunk . . .
—Dr. Jürgen Rohwer
  German Naval Historian[1]

No account of the war in the Pacific, Indian Ocean, and Arabian Sea could fail to take note of the often-barbaric actions of the submarine force of the Imperial Japanese Navy, as a result of which a number of top-ranking naval officers were charged after the war as war criminals and either were executed or committed hara-kiri.

At the start of the war Japan had the finest fleet of long-range submarines in the Pacific, and the largest in the world in its I-400 series. The I-class was of 3,300 tons or more, capable of carrying two or more seaplanes and of cruising to California and back without refueling. Until the advent of the nuclear submarine, they were the largest ever built.[2] They were originally intended to attack the Panama Canal and destroy Gatun Lock, but the mission was never carried out for a number of reasons, including an increasing shortage of fuel. In 1944, because of the heavy losses of submarines, they were converted to *kaiten* carriers (human torpedoes), their aircraft deck hangars and catapults removed, and fitted out to carry four or more *kaiten*s. The Japanese not only had the largest submarines, their torpedoes were far superior to both American and German torpedoes in the early stages of the war, as were their night binoculars, until American radar changed the odds.[3]

By the time of Pearl Harbor, the Japanese had 64 submarines ready for action and subsequently built 126 new boats, but they were surprisingly ineffective and contributed little of significance to the Japanese war effort. Many were ultimately converted from offensive to defense assignments and merely became supply ships for bypassed garrisons, stripped of torpedoes, shells, and guns to make room for supplies. After Guadalcanal, thirty-eight were so employed, of which twenty were sunk.[4]

Japanese submarine warfare policy was almost entirely different from the German strategy of sinking as many cargo carriers and tankers as possible, to deny supplies to the hard-pressed Allies. Although they had some early successes, their efforts were relatively unimpressive, and comparatively few merchantmen were sunk. However, in contrast to German submarine commanders, who frequently were reported to have offered medical aid, provisions, cigarettes, and direction to nearest land, Japanese treatment of survivors, both military and civilian, was often sadistic. One of the ghastliest Japanese atrocities occurred on land; after the capture of Wake Island, the master and mate of the MS *Justine Foss* were among ninety-eight American civilians, mostly construction workers, captured and brutally executed by order of Rear Admiral Shigematsu Saikabara. The prisoners were blindfolded, seated with their hands tied behind their backs in a single line facing seaward. Japanese guards opened fire with rifles and machine guns until all were dead. The bodies were dumped into a tank trap. The admiral was subsequently tried, convicted, and hanged as a war criminal on 10 June 1947.[5]

The nature of Japanese warfare on survivors of sunken ships became evident as early as 8 December 1941 when the SS *Capillo* was attacked by Japanese planes off Corregidor. Three lifeboats were destroyed by strafing. On 23 December 1941, the SS *Montebello* was torpedoed and shelled off the coast of California; the lifeboats were machine-gunned, but no one was hit. Then came the unlucky Panamanian-flag SS *Donerail,* torpedoed en route from Fiji to Vancouver by the *I-10* (*Kayahara*). The sub surfaced and used its deck gun;

twenty shells were poured into the sinking ship while passengers and crew were endeavoring to escape. Sixteen were killed and many wounded; survivors set out in a riddled lifeboat, and sixteen died in a thirty-eight-day voyage. Tragically, the survivors made it to Tarawa, then under Japanese control, and were taken prisoner.[6] On 14 March 1943 the British hospital ship *Centaur* was torpedoed and sunk by the *I-37*, under command of Lieutenant Commander H. Nakagawa, although the ship was clearly marked and lighted. Loss of life amounted to 268. This was followed by the British *Daisy Moeller*, torpedoed by *RO-110*, Lieutenant Kasuro Ebato, on 14 December 1943. Of 127 on board, 55 were killed by the ramming and strafing of lifeboats and rafts.[7]

The Dutch-flag *Tjisalak* was torpedoed by the *I-8*, under Commander Tatsunosuke Ariizumi, who ordered the execution of ninety-eight survivors. This was just the beginning for Ariizumi. Later promoted to captain, he achieved further infamy in his treatment of survivors of the ill-fated American Liberty ship SS *Jean Nicolet* on 2 July 1944.

The *Jean Nicolet*, carrying army general cargo from San Pedro–Colombo, Ceylon, and Calcutta, was traveling alone in the Indian Ocean when she was hit by two torpedoes on the starboard side and developed a severe list. On order of Captain David M. Nillson, the ship was abandoned by its merchant crew of forty-one, twenty-eight NAGs, thirty passengers, and one army medic. The sub surfaced, and the commander ordered all boats and rafts alongside; almost all the survivors were taken aboard the large deck—except a few on a small raft who were able to get away in the darkness. What transpired next is a true horror story, fully documented by accounts of the few survivors. In an affidavit dated 25 October 1944, Charles E. Pyle, first engineer swore, "First, the Japs shot the youngest member of the crew, a boy of seventeen as a warning, then for four hours they subjected us to beatings. They bound the hands of those who showed signs of life and left unbound only twenty-three of us whom they had beaten so badly they had to give us up for dead. . ."[8]

A United States Navy report stated that they forced the

captives to run a gauntlet of pieces of pipe, pistols, and knives and bayoneting; some were taken to the after section, bayoneted and shoved overboard, after the taking of all of their possessions. Those left alive, hands bound behind them with lines, were left to die when the sub suddenly submerged after hearing an approaching aircraft. During the horror Captain Ariizumi was reported in the conning tower cheering his men on. A number of lives were saved because of a navy gunner who had secreted a knife in his trousers, cut himself loose, and then freed others still alive in the water. The navy AG officer and five of his gunners had not responded to the order to come alongside the *I-8* and tried to pull away in the tiny raft, but the Japanese turned a searchlight on them and opened fire; one man was lost, but the others flattened themselves on the raft and the Japanese assumed they had been killed and cut off the light. They could clearly hear the cries of their shipmates aboard the submarine. They were spotted by a patrol plane and some hours later were picked up by an Indian frigate. Of the one hundred men aboard the *Jean Nicolet,* only twenty-three survived. Nineteen members of the naval armed guard crew were among those brutally slain.[9]

One of the armed guard survivors was Radioman 3c Cullie Stone, Tulsa, Oklahoma. He had enlisted as soon as he was eighteen, and his first ship was the SS *Jean Nicolet.* He reports, "We had made several trips to the war zone before having any trouble. On 2 July 1944, when we were about ten days from Calcutta, we spotted smoke on the horizon off the starboard beam four times during the day. The captain thought it might be an enemy submarine, waiting for sundown before attacking us and he was correct. Five minutes after general quarters we were hit with two torpedoes. I went to my battle station on the bridge and no one was there, to my surprise. I then climbed down to my assigned lifeboat and no one could confirm abandon ship for the navy crew. I went back on ship and found the captain in his quarters. I asked if the navy was to abandon ship and his answer was, "For God's sake, yes." My responsibility was to take the portable

transmitter to the lifeboat, which I did. It seemed that everything was going to be all right; four lifeboats and two rafts
had been lowered safely. All of the men had left the ship and
we had only minor injuries. Our distress call and position
had been received in Bombay, as I learned later.

"Suddenly we heard machine gun fire, and someone
said, 'I see a submarine bearing on us.' The sub had shelled
our ship and she was burning. The sub then turned toward
the boats and rammed our lifeboat. The Japanese captain
said in English, 'Come aboard one at a time. Hurry up or you
will get shot,' and he repeated the threat. A seventeen-year-
old crewman screamed and was immediately shot. A Lithua-
nian crew member, whose name I do not recall, demanded
to be taken to the captain, and he too was shot. The Japanese
picked up 96 men, all from the *Jean Nicolet*, except for a
few others who were on a small rubber raft and were able
to hide in the darkness. When the 96 were taken aboard,
the Japanese machine-gunned the life boats. Two Japanese
grabbed me by each arm and another searched me, taking
my shoes, watch, dog tag and belt. We were tied up four
abreast, hands tied behind our backs, seated forward of the
conning tower.

"The submarine set a course and the Japs formed a gauntlet, aft of the conning tower, where the victims had to run
between two lines of men with clubs and other weapons.
The men were beaten until believed dead and then thrown
into the ocean one at a time. I was in the middle of the men
on the forward deck. They had beaten all the men behind
me and the two men on my left. I was the next to run the
gauntlet. To my right was the ship's carpenter, 'Chips.' He
had gotten loose in about 15 minutes after being tied. He
asked me if I had been praying, and I said that I didn't know
how, but he told me to pray to God that we would not die.
The sub apparently picked up something on her radar and
sounded the alarm for a crash dive. Chips tried to untie me
but he couldn't get my hands loose and he was swept away
by a wave. I bounced along the superstructure and suddenly
thought about the huge propellor at the stern of the sub.

I kicked my feet trying to get away from the prop. I called out for someone to come and untie my hands and a man came to help me but he could not untie me. He said he would get a knife and come back; one of the armed guard crew had been able to secrete his knife and after cutting himself loose was able to cut the bonds of a number of men in the water.

"I would struggle to get free, give up, tell my parents and sister goodbye, let my body sink into the ocean and kick my feet to come up for air. I remembered my friend telling me to pray and I told my God that if He would let me go home I would go to Sunday School. As I continued to strain at the ropes they fell from my wrists and my hands became free. (Three months later I still had a ring of scabs around each wrist.)

"I guessed that I had been in the water for about one hour. My ship was eight or ten miles away and burning brightly. I had no doubt that I could swim to the ship. I swam for what might have been fifteen hours and was about 100 yards from the ship when it sank. During my swim I experienced nausea and vomiting, muscle cramps and the sting of a Portuguese man-of-war. I was the fourth person to make it back to a raft from the ship. We were on the raft for two days, during which time I saw many huge sharks. In the survival gear we had two five gallon cans of water and two wool blankets, rubberized on one side. During the day we stayed under the blankets to protect ourselves from the sun. We were completely naked, having removed our clothes to make the big swim. We were picked up by a Ceylonese patrol boat. Of the hundred men on the *Jean Nicolet,* only twenty-three or four survived; some of the survivors were men believed to have been beaten to death and thrown overboard.

"The experience changed my life. I learned a good lesson—*Trust in God and Never Give Up.*"

The Liberty SS *Henry Knox* was also sunk in the Indian Ocean on 19 June 1943 by the *I-37* (Kamimoto) en route to the Persian Gulf with a load of fighter planes, gunpowder, and other war materiel. The gunpowder exploded, and several men were killed or wounded trying to release the boats.

Three boats and some rafts drifted free. The Japanese submarine surfaced and questioned the survivors. The Japanese then checked the boats, took the charts, mast, sail, and emergency bundles and left. In this case no men were hurt and the forty-one survivors from the explosion eventually rowed their boats to the Maldives.[10] The SS *William K. Vanderbilt* was torpedoed off Fiji on 16 May 1943 by the *I-19* (Kinashi). The AG gun crew stayed aboard, hoping to get a shot at the submarine, but they were forced to leave when a second torpedo hit, taking to the rafts or walking off the stern and being picked up by lifeboats. The submarine surfaced and cruised among the survivors, machine-gunning one lifeboat and two rafts; the men aboard hid under the rafts and were saved. Although the submarine passed within twenty feet, it was dark and the men were not observed. The *I-29* (*Izu*) had sunk the SS *Paul Luckenbach* several months earlier, but all survived; the submarine was itself sunk on 26 July 1944 by the USS *Sawfish.*[11]

Two days out of Bombay, homeward-bound, the SS *Richard Hovey* was struck by a torpedo fired by the *I-27*, under command of Lieutenant Commander T. Kusaka. The navy gun crew under Lieutenant Harry Chester Goudy, USNR, manned their guns immediately and remained at their stations until the vessel was in such imminent danger of sinking that they were forced to abandon ship. A navy report dated 20 July 1944 reports, "Surfacing close at hand, the Jap submarine shelled first the ship and then the survivors. Four members of the crew including the Master were taken prisoners aboard the submarine after it had rammed and overturned one lifeboat and taken another in tow. Many of the Navy gunners were in the shark-infested waters from two to four hours, concealing themselves behind and under rafts and lifeboats while the submarine's guns were shelling them and later struggling to keep afloat until rescued by shipmates. Lieutenant Goudy gathered seventeen members of the gun crew and twenty-one members of the ship's crew, including several officers and immediately assumed command of the group . . ."

Unknown to Lieutenant Goudy, another lifeboat, under command of Chief Mate Richard Evans, badly shot up and carrying fifteen men, had also escaped destruction. They were found and picked up by the SS *Samcalia,* a British ship, on 1 April and taken to Karachi. They were luckier than the men in Lieutenant Goudy's boat, who spent sixteen days under a blazing sun before being picked up by a British ship, the SS *Samuta.* Seaman 1/c Philip Fittipaldi, a member of the gun crew did not survive the ordeal. Seriously burned, his condition got progressively worse, and he died on the morning of 10 April and was buried at sea.

A navy report submitted to the secretary of the navy (Board of Decorations and Awards) highly praised Lieutenant Goudy and the men under his command. An extraordinary feature of the ordeal was that, at Lieutenant Goudy's suggestion, Arthur Drechsler, junior assistant engineer, constructed an ingenious still, and making use of one of the ship's rafts as fuel was able to distill fifty to sixty gallons of potable water. This greatly alleviated suffering from thirst, heat, and crowded quarters during the sixteen days in which they were adrift.[12]

On 30 October 1944, the last civilian Liberty ship, carrying food, explosives, and a deckload of trucks, was sunk by a Japanese submarine in the Pacific. The SS *John A. Johnson* was torpedoed by the *I-12* (Captain Kaneo Kudo). The submarine surfaced and repeatedly rammed and strafed the *Johnson*'s lifeboats and tried to catch survivors in the water in the vessel's screws; ten of the forty-one men in the *Johnson,* including five naval guards, were lost in the inhuman incident. The sinking of the *Johnson* between California and Hawaii came as a shock to naval authorities, as there had been no such problems for a long while.[13]

Treatment given survivors of merchant ships who were taken prisoner or turned over to the Japanese military by German raiders was equally barbarous; many were worked to death or died in unmarked prisoner ships being taken to Japan. An army report on Americans who escaped from a torpedoed Japanese transport 23 October 1944 relates that

Japanese guards deliberately fired on the Americans trapped in the holds, seeking to escape; others were hunted down and killed in the water as they sought to swim to nearby shore. A survivor of another unmarked Japanese ship torpedoed on 7 September 1943 reports that there were 750 American prisoners aboard, held in the hold. The Japanese turned machine guns on those who got into the water. Thirty prisoners were caught, taken to another prison ship and systematically shot; however, before they got to him, he slipped his bonds and was able to escape.[14]

If there were a Hall of Infamy for sadistic behavior of Japanese submarine commanders, certainly a high place would have to go to Tatsunosuke Ariizumi, commander of the *I-8,* who ordered the murder of survivors of the *Jean Nicolet* and the Dutch ship *Tjisalek.* However, possibly because of his "gallantry" in action, he was promoted and made commander of the 1st SM Division, based at Truk. Close to the end of the war, he put to sea with the *I-400, I-401, L-13,* and *L-14,* with eight aircraft on board, to make a kamikaze attack on the big American base at Ulithi, but the mission was called off because of the cease-fire. Ariizumi was sought as a war criminal, but evaded prosecution by committing hara-kiri before the *I-401* was turned over to the United States authorities on 27 August 1945.[15]

Between 1945 and 1951 Allied military commissions condemned 920 Japanese to death and sentenced some 3,000 others to prison for various terms for being guilty of war crimes, but many sentences were subsequently reduced. One of the most heinous was Captain Hiroshi Iwanami, commanding officer of a naval hospital on Truk Atoll, whose actions in performing medical experiments on American POWs were termed diabolical sadism. The testimony at his, and other, trials was nauseating; he was convicted and sentenced to be shot, and it was carried out, an easy death for a man convicted of inhuman torture. Postwar records show that 27 percent of the prisoners of the Japanese died in captivity.[16]

Other infamous Japanese submarine commanders who deserved "war criminal" status for their treatment and murder of survivors of sunken ships were lost during the course of the war along with their vessels. Included are Lieutenant Commander H. Nakagawa (*I-37*), Lieutenant Kasuro Ebato (*RO-110*), Lieutenant Commander T. Kusaka (*I-27*), Lieutenant Kaneo Kudo (*I-12*) and Lieutenant Commander Nishiuchi (*I-26*).[17]

CHAPTER TWENTY
TOWARD VICTORY
IN EUROPE

I have nothing to offer you but blood,
toil, sweat and tears . . .
—Winston S. Churchill, 13 May 1940

The hundreds of thousands of men, trucks, jeeps, guns, and the mountains of food, munitions, and supplies of war all had to be brought to England by ship preparatory to staging the world's greatest invasion. As has been related, many did not make it, but those aboard the ships that did soon learned what the people of England had suffered through during the long years of the Battle of Britain. While many fine books have been written on the subject, perhaps the observations of one armed guard officer might provide a more personal insight into what the English bore with such fortitude. London was a particularly dangerous port for merchant ships carrying supplies. The general orders governing their action during air attacks were for them to remain dark and silent rather than fire guns and attract attention, a difficult order to obey. The London Blitz was bad enough, but then came the second Blitz, with rockets; the nights were full of rockets, flares, searchlights, flaming planes, shell bursts, huge fires in the city, and the crash of explosives, leveling everything near where they landed. Gilbert Robinson, a lieutenant, USNR, at the time, vividly recalls such action: "During July of 1944 (I will never forget that date) we pulled into the West India Dock area in London. We were not there long before we were initiated into the German buzz bombs. There were acres of warehouses when we arrived, and our cargo was unloaded into the warehouses, but by the time we left to come back to the States, the warehouses were completely gone, wiped out, blown out and burned out. All that was left were the upright steel beams that had supported the structures. While officially made light of, buzz bombs were wreaking havoc on London and the southern coastal area. They hit ships, docks, hotels, taverns, churches, and the 2,000-pound burst of liquid air was a terrible explosion.

"The concussion of a nearby hit split the seams of a Liberty ship setting just ahead of us. It is still horrifying to describe the scene after a U.S. LST took a direct hit. They had just finished loading and had pulled up the ramp to head for France with some 200 Canadian soldiers; 37 United States officers and enlisted men, and all aboard met instant death. The LST faintly resembled a tin can after exploding a giant firecracker inside it.

"We assisted in rescue work in many areas, and one of the worst hits was a fire station at the end of our slip. Everyone in the building was killed, and pieces of bodies were everywhere. We never did find the head of one unfortunate victim. We picked up several large containers (the size of 50-gallon oil drums) of metal shrapnel from the deck of our ship as a result of one 48-hour blitz the West India Dock received while we were there, but fortunately had only two men wounded. The buzz bomb blast was horizontal, and when it hit it exploded. It did not penetrate to any depth, but the concussion in a horizontal direction (all directions) was ghastly. Everything in the proximity was leveled. At night, it was a spectacular sight to see the high-power searchlights spotting and chasing the buzz bombs. Our crew did a lot of rescue work when we could leave the ship on liberty, much of it outside London, to the south, which also took a fearful pounding. The worst aspect of the whole nightmare was seeing the children who were victims. . . .

"Buzz bombs were easy to hit, but not to destroy. At first you waited to see where it was going to land and then dove for cover. The later V-2 rockets were much worse, they hit before the sound reached you."[1]

The long-awaited invasion of Western Europe began on 6 June 1944, to be forever known as "D-Day." The invasion fleet consisted of thousands of naval vessels, merchant ships, and landing craft. Supply ships needed harbors, then held in German hands, so the solution was to build artificial ones, protected by artificial breakwaters called "Gooseberries," which consisted of specially placed sunken ships. Seventy-six ships were selected, including twenty-seven merchant ships, many battle-scarred survivors of previous hard campaigns. Perhaps the best known was the Liberty SS *James Iredell,* which had compiled an astonishing record for endurance and damage under continuing attack in the Mediterranean.

Manned by volunteers, it was expected that the Gooseberry ships would be subject to furious enemy attack while being placed, and that subsequent supply ships would also be violently attacked. According to an unpublished navy account, however, losses to merchant ships in the invasion and later were less than anticipated, although they were attacked by E-boats, planes, and shore batteries. Mines were a constant and major danger.[2] The *Luftwaffe* had lost much of its punch, so devastingly effective in the Mediterranean and the Murmansk runs earlier. The loss of aircraft and experienced pilots through attrition, along with the shortage of fuel, reduced its effectiveness to a major degree. Captain Otto Werner, commander of the *U-953,* has reported that most of the few U-boats available were wiped out before they could attack the invasion fleet. Many had been deployed elsewhere, including twenty-two in Norwegian fjords. Others operating from French bases had been sunk in the month preceding the invasion. The revolutionary new Walter boats, which carried six torpedo tubes instead of four, plus fourteen spare torpedoes, were fast underwater and had new, improved schnorkels, never became operational, although it was a near thing. If they had been available, they might easily have prolonged the war, with the Allies once again playing "catch-up."[3]

The naval AG gun crews who were on the ships that formed the breakwater did not just go in and out. They stayed aboard the scuttled ships and manned their guns for up to several weeks before being relieved by army personnel. They were targets for anything thrown their way, especially shelling by shore-based 88-mm guns. Many AGs were wounded, but none were killed according to navy records, and they shot down a number of enemy planes attacking the beachhead. AG gun crews involved in this operation were later returned to the United States. The commander of the United States Naval Forces in Europe highly commended the armed guard personnel for their participation in placing the breakwater ships and then defending them until relieved.[4]

In connection with D-Day, C. A. "Pete" Burke, veteran signalman of many ships, tells of the AG commanding officer on the SS *William Tyler Page,* Lieutenant R. Gordon Webber, USNR. "We arrived in Liverpool on 4 May 1944. Lt. Webber was reassigned. When he came aboard to get his gear, he invited three gunner's mates, the other signalman and myself into his quarters where he produced a bottle of Scotch. I asked him if he needed a good signalman, but he replied, 'I wouldn't wish this assignment on my worst enemy.' He then left without saying what the assignment was, but later I heard that he had been put in charge of a skeleton AG crew that sailed with a small merchant crew on an old rustbucket tanker that they scuttled at the Normandy beachhead. The merchant crew was immediately taken off, but the AGs were stranded on the scuttled ship all through the invasion and weren't relieved until days later."[5] Burke's ship also had some problems; there were no lighters and no stevedores in Normandy to unload the cargo, and the AGs volunteered to help the unloading onto Higgins boats and Army DUKs. "Being inexperienced, and trying to load a small craft that was bobbing up and down was like being on a pogo stick. We got sprayed with chloride of lime when the lid of a drum popped off, but none of us got it in our eyes and we doused off with water with little ill-effect. We returned from Normandy on 5 July. While entering Falmouth harbor, the current swept us into a British freighter and its anchor flipped up on our deck. No one was injured but the skipper of the Limey ship and our ship got into a big argument, just like two motorists who had bumped fenders; but the two ships were locked together because the anchor was really jammed into us and couldn't be freed."

The SS *Eleazar Wheelock* became the best-known vessel off Omaha Beach. One of hundreds of Liberties riding at anchor, she was "honored" by being designated NOIC (Naval Officer in Charge). She didn't go anywhere, and didn't do much of anything, but she lay there in the same spot for weeks on end, described by Lieutenant Commander Max Miller, USNR, as being "like a relative who is never invited to a dance, but always to a house cleaning." Then came The Storm, about two weeks after D-Day, which created absolute havoc along the beachfront at Utah Beach. So many vessels and parts of vessels were tossed up on the beach that it took weeks to clean up the debris so that supplies could be brought in. Needless to say, the navy crew aboard the *Wheelock* was cordially invited to that "house cleaning." [6]

Supply ships had many close calls, and a number were hit and damaged, but mines were the principal danger to the incoming vessels and took a heavy toll. On 29 June alone, four ships struck mines, and army casualties occurred on the SS *H. G. Blasdell* and others aboard the SS *James N. Farrell.* Men on the incoming ships also had a fine view of German buzz bombs heading for England where they caused terrible damage and many casualties.

N. Paul Cronin, now an attorney in Aberdeen, Maryland, was AG commanding officer on the SS *Charles Morgan* and describes his experience shortly after D-Day: "On 6 June 1944, our ship, loaded with men and equipment, sailed from Barry, Wales, and arrived off Utah Beach in the early morning 8 June. We were under attack during the evening of 7 June and later from shore batteries after we anchored. Unloading of the ship commenced 8 June and was completed on 9 June. We were prepared to sail back to England the next morning. At 0410 on 10 June, a bomb dropped by an unidentified plane fell into #5 hatch. The ship went down by the stern, but stayed otherwise afloat. At 1100 hours, when the ship was in danger of sinking, my crew transferred to a Higgins boat. We estimated that seven or more soldiers of the Port Squad which unloaded our ship were killed and a similar number wounded. Luckily, none of my Navy crew were either killed or wounded. An LST took us to Portland, England, on 11 June, and we were returned to New York."[7]

Mike Molinari of Brooklyn, New York, was a gunner on the Liberty ship SS *Andrew Carnegie,* being loaded with supplies for the European invasion—K-rations, uniforms, shoes, airfield landing-strip mats, jeeps, trucks and parts, and ammunition. After loading they anchored in the Hudson River for two weeks, along with four other Liberties. Life aboard was so boring that Mike and some shipmates decided to go for a swim. They almost made it to Europe ahead of their ship because the strong current was sweeping them out to sea. Rescued before they passed the submarine nets, they were given "Hell" by their AG lieutenant for their foolhardiness. The lieutenant himself, however, became part of another escapade after reaching Europe. The invasion was slowly pushing inland while they were being unloaded by army DUKs, and since there wasn't much action offshore, the lieutenant suggested that those who were not on watch hitch a ride on a DUK and go ashore. So, ten men and the gunnery officer went ashore, and Molinari reports: "We were walking on the beach and passed bombed-out tanks, wrecked LCIs, and dead men lying all over the beach. We then walked inland a bit and crossed some fields to a wrecked farmhouse. We noticed that some farm animals were all bunched up around a big tree back of the house. There were a number of signs in German which we could not understand, and didn't learn until later that they were warnings that the fields were mined. Suddenly, two Army privates jumped out of a foxhole and ordered us to halt. They then took us to a command post, and the CO yelled, 'What the Hell do you think you're doing here?' Our lieutenant said that we were just sight-seeing as it was awfully boring on ship. The CO then said, 'Look around the tent and see all the dead soldiers piled up like cordwood. We trained three years to get here today, and I wish I was home, and you are out to see the sights!' Then he told the sergeant, 'Feed 'em and get them back to their ship.' After several days, they were still eating K-rations and it wasn't like the good food we got on ship. They put us on a truck and took us back to the beach, but German snipers were shooting at us all the way. After we got back aboard we said that at least we had set foot on the European mainland, something we could tell our grandchildren." Molinari, although still a kid in years, was by then a seasoned veteran of the Murmansk run, a Caribbean hurricane that had so damaged his tanker that it barely made it to port, and other hazards of the AG. However, he never has forgotten his "stroll" on Utah Beach.[8]

Jim Bennett, signalman CPO (Ret.) had been aboard the SS *Charles W. Elliott,* but had moved on by the time the *Elliott* struck two mines on 28 June 1944 off Juno Beach, Normandy. She was towed to deeper waters by a salvage tug and was last seen by survivors at 1500 hours entirely submerged except for the bow. Later that day she was finished off by German aircraft. Bennett had previously served on ten round-trip convoys crossing the Atlantic, on shuttle duty between Casablanca and Bizerte during the North African campaign, and finally wound up trapped in Antwerp on Christmas Day 1944 dodging V-bombs during the Battle of the Bulge—and he never lost a ship or got a scratch. He considers himself one of the luckiest men in the naval armed guard.[9]

Carrying C-rations, trucks, jeeps, and airfield landing mats, the SS *Thomas Fitzsimmons* arrived at Omaha Beach on 13 June, after having been held back from the invasion on D-Day by the low priority of its cargo. During that period she moved almost entirely around the British Isles as there was no space available in any harbors en route. Upon arrival at Normandy, Herb Norch, AG gunner, reported that the beach looked like a junk yard, and many bodies were still floating in the water in full gear. While there for a period of twelve days unloading, a tremendous storm hit the area, and it was littered with additional debris and beached ships that took several weeks to clear up. However, Norch expressed great admiration for the efficiency of the unloading opera-

An artist's rendering of the sinking of the Liberty ship SS *William Gaston*, torpedoed 24 July 1944 by the *U-861* off the coast of Brazil. This painting was commissioned by LCDR Harold J. McCormick, USNR, who was the gunnery officer aboard the *Gaston*. (Courtesy Herbert Hewitt)

tion, "The Coast Guard knew the cargo of each ship and ordered it to a precise position." [10]

During the first month after D-Day, more than one million men were landed, along with some 183,000 vehicles and 650,000 tons of supplies. Not all was carried by the merchant ships; a high percentage was brought ashore by the squat LSTs, also known as "Large, Slow Targets." A Mr. John Niedermair was reported to have worked out the concept for the LST in about a half-hour. A former LST commander was quoted as saying that, based on his experience, he wished that Niedermair had spent "at least another half-hour on his design." [11]

With victory in Europe and the ending of convoys in the

The Naval Armed Guard gun crew from the SS *William H. Moody*
march in a victory parade in Bombay, India, on 14 May 1945. (Courtesy Rick Whalen)

Atlantic and elsewhere, 86,198 armed guards were transferred to fleet duty, to serve in LSTs, LCIs, PT boats, destroyer
escorts, and larger ships in preparation for the anticipated invasion of Japan, which was fortunately not required, saving
a potentially horrendous number of casualties.

During the war, most armed guards went from ship to
ship, but incredibly, the entire AG crew aboard the SS
Thomas Fitzsimmons—signalman, coxswain, and gunnery
officer—stayed together during their whole period of service beginning in 1942, not being broken up until November 1944 when they were transferred to fleet duty and were
dispersed.

CHAPTER
TWENTY-ONE
"THE NAVY
REGRETS . . ."

No roses bloom on a sailor's grave . . .
—Anon.

In the preceding pages the story of the United States Naval Armed Guard has been told, in part. Much of the story is from official records, but a large portion has been taken from oral or written accounts of those who made it safely home. By necessity, only a few of the 1,810 young men who gave their lives for their country have been mentioned, but all deserve equal honor. Therefore, the writer has selected two to represent the gallantry and sacrifice of all. One is an enlisted man, the other an officer, both volunteers. They came from widely divergent backgrounds and from different areas of the country, but they exemplify the many who did not return. One died with all his shipmates, armed guard and merchant seamen, when their ship sailed into oblivion, never to be heard from again. The other lost his life after almost four years at sea, in sight of the coast of the United States, the last armed guard to die in the last American ship to be sunk by a German submarine in the Atlantic—just three days before victory in Europe. These two honored armed guards were Lieutenant (j.g.) Carl Zeidler, USNR, Milwaukee, Wisconsin, descendant of German immigrants, who gave up his post as mayor of Milwaukee to enter the service of his country, and Lonnie Whitson Lloyd, of rural Franklin County, North Carolina, one of five brothers who, one by one, went to war in defense of their once-separated nation.

LONNIE WHITSON LLOYD, BM 2c, USNR

Whitson, as he is still best known, born on 26 November 1918, was the eldest of five brothers who worked and played together on the family farm in North Carolina. Life was hard there, as it was everywhere else in the days of the Great Depression, still known locally as "Hoover Times." Cotton was selling at near five cents a pound, and even high-grade tobacco brought only fifteen cents per pound. But with the exuberance of youth, in what spare time they had they played baseball, their passion. Within ten days of Pearl Harbor, Whitson volunteered for the navy and was sworn in 30 December 1941. He was sent to the Naval Training Center, Norfolk, and after recruit training was sent on to the Armed Guard School, Little Creek, Virginia. After three weeks of additional training he was assigned to gun crew #131E aboard the SS *Mormacdale* and shipped out of Beaumont, Texas. The country boy from the farm where he and his brothers had "raised tobacco and a little hell" quickly saw a lot of the world. His very first voyage took him to Capetown, South Africa, the blazing Persian Gulf, and Mozambique, where his ship ran into a typhoon that lasted six days.

When he returned to Baltimore, he was assigned to the SS *Expositor,* aboard which he made coxswain on 1 October 1942, en route to Murmansk in the first convoy to North Russia. The *Expositor* was an old Hog Islander, built in 1919, and she carried a complement of thirty-eight merchant crew and eleven armed guards. The Murmansk run quickly became known as the equivalent of a suicide run, and the crew of the *Expositor* soon found out why: only six ships in the convoy made it home safely, over twenty being lost. The *Expositor*'s luck ran out on the return voyage when she was torpedoed in the North Atlantic on 22 February 1943, causing the boilers to explode. Six merchant seamen and three armed guards were killed, but the survivors could have been considered doubly lucky, as on the outbound voyage the *Expositor* had carried a cargo consisting of 10,000 rounds of 75-mm and 37-mm shells and 5,000 cases of TNT.[1] On an earlier voyage, near Iceland on 5 July 1942, German U-boats sank seven ships in a convoy and damaged another. A lookout on the *Expositor* saw a sub conning tower in the center of the convoy, just a few yards off the ship's starboard quarter. When the submarine changed course, the 4-inch gun on the *Expositor* was brought to bear, and the top of the conning tower was blown off; a torpedo was avoided by backing the ship at full speed, according to a navy report. At that time, the report states, the AG crew on the *Expositor* consisted only of four gunners, a signalman striker, and one officer.[2]

When the *Expositor* was later torpedoed, Whitson Lloyd was knocked unconscious and was pulled from the sea into a lifeboat by some of the crew, forty-eight of whom were rescued by HMCS *Trillium* and put ashore at St. John's, Newfoundland. After returning from a rest camp, Whitson was assigned to the SS *Joseph P. Bradley,* on which he voyaged to the South Pacific. The diary he had kept on the *Expositor* had been lost, but he resumed his recording of events: "Japs sank a few ships ahead of us last night . . . having my bathing suit ready for a swim." It was then off again to the Persian Gulf where "men were falling out every day, temperature 172 degrees, awful sandstorm last night." Then a notation, "Italy surrendered today. We are going alone to South America," followed by, "Food nearly out, eggs rotten, salt water showers, raider reported ahead." The trip on the *Bradley* turned into a trip around the world, "Five months and three days at sea out of seven and one-half months, 33,000 miles."

Assigned upon return to the SS *Eugene Hale,* he continued the diary, and on 22 February he noted, "It was one year ago today that I was torpedoed." In the Mediterranean he wrote, "Tank got loose in the hold, AGs volunteered to go down and help lash it down, about to break through." Then followed waves of submarine and air attacks, "Another sub attack, we spend most of our time at our gun, three attacks last night . . . haven't had any sleep for two nights, four attacks today and they will be back . . . Some boys going to sleep eating at their guns, thirty-six hours at battle station, but storm may give us a break. Only lost eight ships so far."

Later . . . "Arrive Sicily tomorrow, don't know if we will live ten minutes from now, been under attack for a week." When the *Hale* later arrived at Bari, Whitson reported, "Thirty-six ships sunk in the harbor."

Somewhat earlier he had written, "We are expecting another air raid any minute, well, that's been my life for over two years. I've never told everything or about all the action I have seen, and never will, but some day somebody will tell about the war—if America could only see what's going on they would appreciate what we are doing, ships sunk everywhere, planes shot down lying on the beach, parts of them sticking out of the water."

The boy had become a man; he was fiercely proud of his ship, and he wrote a very good poem about her, an excerpt of which is:

"Her Master's hand is steady,
And her course is straight and true,
And her destination Victory,
As she proudly sails for you . . ."[3]

Whitson Lloyd served aboard the *Hale* until 9 November 1944 when, after home leave, he was assigned to the SS *Black Point*, a 5,300-ton collier on a coastwise run from Boston to Galveston. He was in charge of a five-man AG crew. In the meantime, his two younger brothers, Charles and L. D., had also enlisted in the navy and volunteered for the armed guard. With memories of the five Sullivan brothers still fresh, one can only wonder at the fortitude of Maggie Pearce Lloyd as she watched all of her sons go off to war. Previously, Willis had enlisted in the marine corps, and Jack had gone into the merchant marine.

It must have seemed a relief to Whitson Lloyd to have gotten away from incessant sea and air attack, in what was thought to be a quiet area, but his extraordinary luck was about to end. On 5 May 1945 off Point Judith, Rhode Island, the *Black Point* was hit by a torpedo and went down quickly. Whitson was blown overboard, and his body was never re-

The Wall of the Missing at the Cambridge American Cemetery and Memorial at Cambridge, England. (Courtesy William Stilinovich, whose brother Joseph's name is inscribed here)

covered. The *Black Point* was sunk by the *U-853,* under command of Oberleutnant Helmut Frömsdorf. It will never be known why the *U-853* attacked the *Black Point.* On 4 May Grosadmiral Karl Dönitz had sent a radio message to all U-boats, "As from 5 May, 0800 hours cease fire x for U-boats at sea attacks forbidden x break off immediately pursuit of enemy." Perhaps Frömsdorf never received the message, perhaps he was a fanatic who wanted just one more kill. Regardless, his attack on the *Black Point* cost him his own life, along with fifty-four of his men, the same day that Whitson Lloyd and eleven of his shipmates perished. The sinking of the *Black Point* so close to shore attracted the immediate attention of a number of U.S. Navy vessels, including the USS *Atherton* (DE 169) and USS *Moberly* (PF 63), and the pursuit was on. Sonar picked up the submarine on the bottom and depth charges were dropped incessantly. Their attack was relentless and at last the *U-853* met its end. To this day it still sits upright on a mud and sand bottom, bow pointed to the sea. The top of the conning tower lies ninety feet from the surface, some torpedoes still in the tubes. The U-boat was located and explored by divers in 1953, only seven miles from Block Island. It has become a center of some controversy because various individuals wish to salvage the U-boat and put it on exhibit; the German government prefers to leave it where it is, with the remains of the crew left undisturbed in their "iron coffin"; this view is also shared by many in the United States.[4]

Although Whitson Lloyd's body was never recovered, in the little Lloyd family graveyard in North Carolina, a simple stone monument commemorates him, erected by his brothers.

LT. (JG) CARL ZEIDLER, USNR

In the early 1940s, if anyone appeared to be on a clear track to national political recognition and influence, it would seem to be Carl Zeidler, of Milwaukee, Wisconsin. Tall, handsome, an excellent orator, with a singing voice of professional quality, he became the highly popular mayor of Milwaukee at the age of thirty-two and seemed to have an unbounded future. However, as for so many other bright and talented young men of the time, Fate had other plans.

Zeidler was a descendant of one of the many German and Austrian families who emigrated to the United States in the 1870s to build a new life in a free world. His family settled in Wisconsin, on a point south of the Fox River, broke ground, built a new home, and raised a number of strong, healthy children. Carl's father was Mike Zeidler, who became known as the "smiling barber" in Milwaukee's old West Side. Carl was born on 4 January 1908 and had a normal childhood, marked by a love of stories of faraway places told by seafaring men who frequented his father's shop. Those stories held him spellbound.

He was thrilled when at age twelve he was able to get a *Milwaukee Journal* paper route, and a once-shy boy became gregarious in nature. He loved meeting people, and in turn was liked by all. During his period in West Division High

School, he was an outstanding athlete in football and track, and because of his strong, clear voice, became a featured member of the Glee Club; he also played piano and violin and became active in dramatics and won his first election as senior class treasurer. Since his family was of moderate circumstances, he worked his way through school as a gas station attendant and "baggage smasher" for Northwestern Railroad, and did well enough scholastically to win a scholarship at Marquette University. He also became an insurance adjuster, continued his activity in athletics, and somehow found time to become an outstanding member of the debating team. And, once again, his voice proved a valuable asset. He picked up extra money by singing at weddings, funerals, or at any church that would call him.

Voted "One of the Most Likely to Succeed," by his college classmates, he went to Marquette Law School, where he obtained his degree in 1931, the bottom of the Great Depression. Active in civic affairs and with a broad base of contacts, he obtained an appointment as sixth-assistant district attorney at twenty-eight and shortly thereafter was admitted to practice before the State Supreme Court.

In 1940, the young politically inexperienced Zeidler was talked by friends into running for mayor against an incumbent who had held the post for twenty-four years, and had a well-oiled political machine. With a campaign chest of only $150.00, he entered the campaign, speaking anywhere people would listen. His eloquence and charm were such that in the primary, and as a complete political neophyte, he received 50,000 votes and went on to challenge Mayor Dan Hoan. The mayor didn't take the challenge seriously, and laughed off the "Boy Scout," but in the general election Zeidler received 112,000 votes to his opponent's 100,000. Zeidler was inaugurated on 16 April 1940, at age thirty-two, and rapidly became a very active and popular leader. After Pearl Harbor, although he could easily have obtained an exemption from military service because of his position, he applied for a commission in the navy and was sworn in as a lieutenant (j.g.) USNR on 7 April 1942, two years to the day of his inauguration as mayor.

He was ordered to the South Boston Navy Yard for training and assignment to the naval armed guard; he refused the thought of any relatively safe duty.

Zeidler's departure for military service was unplanned as a civic event, but some 20,000 people lined the street as he led a group of forty-eight army air cadets to the train, accompanied by the Police Department Band and a color guard of the American Legion.[5]

A fellow classmate in the first AG class in Boston was Lieutenant (j.g.) Charles Odegaard, later to become president of the University of Washington. Dr. Odegaard recalls having dinner in New York the night before they were to go to sea. Zeidler had received some ribbing about having been the guest of Mayor Fiorello LaGuardia at dinner the night before. Odegaard recalls his wife, Betty, asking a general question, "What are you doing?" She was startled to hear him respond, "I'm starting the last chapter in the life of Zeidler." She tried to put a good face on it, but felt that it was a strange premonition. Carl sailed the next day on the SS *La Salle*, to his death. By a strange coincidence, a third classmate, Lieutenant (j.g.) Joseph Rohr, who also attended the dinner, was also to be lost soon on the SS *Mallory*.[6]

The *La Salle* was never heard from again, beyond a point in the Canal Zone. It was one of the mysteries of the war, a voyage into oblivion. It was not until years later that the story of the death of the *La Salle* and all her crew began to be pieced together. After a long search, Carl's brother Frank, also to become mayor of Milwaukee, obtained some details.

The *La Salle*, loaded with ammunition and aircraft parts, was routed from Balboa, Canal Zone, down the western part of South America, and around the continent's southern tip and into the Atlantic to avoid submarines, and simply disappeared. No radio distress signal was ever received. A Coast Guard report indicated that the *La Salle* probably was lost about 400 miles southeast of Capetown, South Africa. German records studied after the war indicated that a munitions ship was torpedoed at about that position on 7 November 1942 by the *U-159*, commanded by Captain Helmut Witte. The ship was misidentified at the time as the SS *Umtali*, but eventually it became evident that it was actually the *La Salle,* which was bound for Capetown and was estimated to have been at that identical position.[7] The National Archives supplied Frank Zeidler with translated information from a German publication that confirmed the supposition.

The submarine's log gives a clear picture of the sighting and tracking of the *La Salle,* then unidentified. The first torpedo missed, believed to be because of torpedo failure, but the second scored a direct hit, and the log states, "Munitions steamer when hit was atomized . . . a burning column rose hundreds of meters high. Minutes long, it hailed broken pieces on the submarine through which three men on the bridge were lightly injured . . . on the whole much luck. Signed—Witte." Lost with the ship were Captain Willam A. Sillars, thirty-eight other crew members, and thirteen armed guards including lieutenant Zeidler. There were no survivors.[8]

A portrait, almost life-size, of Lieutenant (j.g.) Zeidler was presented to the City of Milwaukee to hang in the Milwaukee Memorial Center. It has been called a fine likeness of Zeidler ". . . in the joyousness of young manhood, his rebellious hair slightly rumpled . . ."

Lieutenant (j.g.) Carl Zeidler, BM 2/c Whitson Lloyd, and the more than 1,800 other young members of the naval armed guard lost at sea are in good company—adventurers, explorers, warriors, and other brave men who have dared the elements or the enemy . . . and lost.

EPILOGUE

World War I was to be "The war to end all wars"; World War II was to guarantee a war-weary world the "Four Freedoms" and a bright post-war future. But the lofty aims of the Atlantic Charter and the 1942 United Nations agreements were soon to evaporate in the reality of the postwar world.

A seemingly ironic development was the reaction of leaders of the U.S. Navy and others to the trial and conviction as a war criminal of their most dedicated and dangerous foe in the war at sea. Grand Admiral Karl Dönitz was arrested by the Allied Control Commission on 23 May 1945, and found himself, along with his former chief, Grand Admiral Erich Raeder, among other high Nazi officials in the dock at Nuremberg, to be tried as war criminals by the victorious Allies. Dönitz was charged on three counts: conspiring to wage aggressive war, waging aggressive war, and "violation of the laws of war at sea." Famed Rear Admiral Daniel V. Gallery, USN, took vociferous objection to the trial, calling the court "loaded" and the trial a travesty of justice. He pointedly asked how any military commander could wage war without being aggressive, unless he were a traitor to his country.[1] Admiral of the Fleet Chester W. Nimitz submitted a sworn statement to the Tribunal, in answer to questions put to him by Dönitz's counsel; he stated that American submarines had waged unrestricted warfare in the Pacific from the first day of the U.S. entry into the war. To the embarrassment of Great Britain, an order of the Admiralty dated 8 May 1940 stating that all vessels in the Skagerrak should be sunk on sight, without warning, was also brought into the evidence.

Both German admirals were convicted, Raeder to life imprisonment and Dönitz to ten years in Spandau Prison. Dönitz served his full term, 1946–56, during which he wrote his *Memoirs*. He died in 1958. Raeder was freed in 1955.

What sort of man was Dönitz? British author Peter Padfield in *Dönitz: The Last Fuehrer* apparently felt that he could be termed "The Devil's Admiral," responsible for the staggering toll of young men he sent to their deaths, including members of his own family.[2] Rear Admiral Samuel E. Morison, USN, regarded him as a "capable tactician who fought fair."[3] As a military professional, "lean in appearance, brief in speech, stern in demands," he was able to inspire the loyalty of his submarine force until the very end, even though they faced the fact that one boat in three sent out on patrol would not return.[4]

In 1976, H. K. Thompson, Jr., and Henry Strutz gathered and recorded the views of some 400 American and foreign military leaders, diplomats, and historians on Dönitz's trial and conviction. Included were statements by many flag-rank officers of the U.S. Navy and U.S. Naval Reserve; they registered strong objection to the trial and verdict on grounds that, as a professional military officer, Dönitz performed his duties as should be expected, and that the verdict set a dangerous precedent.[5] Admiral Gallery, in his book *Twenty Million Tons Under the Sea,* stated bluntly that a code of war had been established for war at sea that might embarrass us in the future.[6]

At question in a future conflict would be the need of a reactivated U.S. Naval Armed Guard service. From a war's-end position of having the greatest strength in its history, the

U.S. Merchant Marine has again fallen on parlous times. By VJ-Day, it had 4,421 vessels with a carrying capacity of more than 45 million tons; the May 1986 issue of *Proceedings*, published by the U.S. Naval Institute, reported a total of 390 American-flagged vessels, carrying less than 6 percent of American exports and imports, and down from a total of 441 vessels in 1984.

In view of the circumstances it would appear that re-activation of the naval armed guard service for a third time would not be required. Lending support to this possibility, a number of prominent American naval scholars are reported convinced that in spite of its formidable submarine fleet, the Soviet Union would not set attack on merchant shipping in the North Atlantic as a major objective in event of a U.S.-Soviet conflict.

NOTES

Chapter 1. The Great War 1914–1918

1. Josephus Daniels, *Our Navy at War*, 174–86.

2. Robert H. Ferrell, *Woodrow Wilson and World War I*, 35.

3. James Connally, *The U-boat Hunters*, foreword, vi.

4. Richard Hough, *The Great War at Sea 1914–1918*, 171–74; Robert H. Ferrell, *Woodrow Wilson and World War I*, 36; Sir John Jellicoe, *The Submarine Peril*, page not available.

5. Captain B. H. Liddell Hart, *The Real War 1914–18*, 12. Hart prophetically stated in the early (1930) edition of his book, "Removal of the submarine menace should not lead to an underestimate of its powers in the future," 31. However, Captain Donald MacIntyre, RN, in his book *The Naval War Against Hitler* reports that as late as 1937 the naval staff reported, "The submarine will never again present us with the problem we were faced with in 1917," 57.

6. Elting E. Morison, *Admiral Sims and the Modern U.S. Navy*, 342–43.

7. E. B. Potter, *Illustrated History of the U.S. Navy*, 137.

8. Clark G. Reynolds, *Command of the Sea*, 466.

9. Elting E. Morison, *Admiral Sims & the Modern U.S. Navy*, 338.

10. Frank Simonds, *History of the World War*, page not available.

11. Robert L. Lansing, *War Memoirs of Robert L. Lansing,* 99–100, 222–25.

12. Captain Scott W. Pitt, USN, "Estimate of the Situation Arming Merchant Vessels With Naval Guns for Defense," 1 March 1917, Naval Records Collection of the Office Of Naval Records & Library, National Archives (RG 45) Box 523/525.

13. Ensign Ralph Hornblower, USNRF, "The Armed Guard Section," 25 October 1918, National Archives (RG 45) Box 520.

14. "Arming of Merchant Vessels for Armed Guard Service," 11 August 1919, Naval Records Collection (1911–1927), National Archives (RG 45); Report of James Delaney, CGM USN, to CNO, 11 January 1919, Box 520.

15. Robert H. Ferrell, *Woodrow Wilson & WWI,* 39–41.

16. John M. Brinin, *The Sway of the Grand Saloon,* 104, 121, 380, 393, 431; William H. Callahan, telephone interviews 8 February and 25 April 1987.

17. Josephus Daniels, *Our Navy at War,* 175–86; Ensign Ralph Hornblower, USNRF, in "The Armed Guard Section" added, "No accurate figures of the effectiveness of the policy of furnishing AGs can be compiled because of the nature of submarine warfare . . . enough, however, is definitely known to prove beyond doubt that AGs have saved many ships which would otherwise have been lost."

18. "Ships, Having Armed Guards, Captured and Sunk by Gunfire/Bombs Placed on Board/Other Causes," dated 5 March 1920 (no attribution), National Archives (RG 45) Box 520.

Chapter 2. The Road to War (1939–1941)

1. E. B. Potter, *Illustrated History of the U.S. Navy,* 162.

2. Louis L. Snyder, *The War 1939–45,* 125; Robert T. Elson, *Prelude to War,* 185.

3. Joseph F. Lash, *Roosevelt and Churchill (1939–41),* 243.

4. Potter, *Illustrated History,* 161–63.

5. Ted Morgan, *FDR,* 526.

6. Haynes Johnson, "FDR, Reagan and Risks," *Washington Post,* 3 June 1987, 23; Clare Booth Luce, *Time,* 19 October 1987, 23.

7. Terry Hughes and John Costello, *The Battle of the Atlantic,* 186.

8. Robert Carse, *Cold Corner of Hell,* 2–3.

9. Admiral Ernest J. King, USN, and Commander Walter Whitehall, USNR, *Fleet Admiral King,* 445.

10. Edward R. Stettinius, *Lend-Lease,* 5.

11. Herbert Willet, Director Research & Reports, Foreign Economic Administration "Lend-Lease," *Americana Encyclopedia*, 428–29.

12. History of the Naval Armed Guard Afloat—WW II (OP 414), Director of Naval History, Fleet Maintenance Division (undated, unpublished).

13. *Great Soviet Encyclopedia*, vol. 14, translation of third edition, 369–70.

14. Ibid., "Roosevelt, Franklin D.," 271.

Chapter 3. Naval Armed Guard Organization and Training

1. Leonard Layton, correspondence, 29 April 1987.

2. Edward Quin, interview, 10 April 1987.

3. George Prestmo, interview, 17 October 1987, and correspondence.

4. Floyd James, correspondence, 9 May 1987.

5. History of Naval Armed Guard Afloat—WW II (OP 414), Director of Naval History, Fleet Maintenance Division (undated), chap. I, 1–7.

6. Michael Molinari, voluminous correspondence, 1987.

7. Albert Gonzales, interview, 15 March 1987.

8. Irving Brownell, correspondence, 6 May 1987.

9. Herbert Norch, numerous interviews, 1987.

10. Firal Millhoupt, "Armed Guard Pointer" (Newsletter), April 1987.

11. History of NAG Afloat, 48.

12. Dr. Walter Havighurst, *The Miami Years*, 212–22.

13. History of NAG Afloat, 53.

14. James Bennett, correspondence, 31 August 1987.

15. Eugene Book, correspondence, 17 December 1987.

16. Armed Guard Officer Voyage Report, SS *Dunboyne*, National Archives (RG 38).

17. Captain Arthur Moore, *A Careless Word . . . A Needless Sinking*, 98.

18. C. A. "Pete" Burke, correspondence, 1 September 1987.

19. Lieutenant Commander Paul Kincade, USN, interview, 12 April 1987 and correspondence.

20. Manley Michler, interview, 11 October 1987.

21. James Handy, correspondence, 25 August 1987.

22. Captain Stansel DeFoe, USN (Ret.), correspondence, 9 September 1987.

23. Lieutenant Commander Norman Alston, USNR, interview, 15 September 1987 and correspondence.

24. Lieutenant Commander Harold J. McCormick, USNR, correspondence, 20 June 1987.

25. Carl G. Ossman, correspondence, 21 August 1987.

26. Lieutenant Commander Gilbert Robinson, USNR, voluminous correspondence, 1987.

27. N. Paul Cronin, correspondence, 21 August 1987.

28. Irving Kaplan, correspondence, 22 May 1987.

29. Harold Bondhus, correspondence, 25 October 1987.

30. William C. Schofield, *Eastward the Convoys,* 13–14.

31. Dr. Charles E. Odegaard, unpublished memoirs dated 6 May 1962, copy furnished by author, 28 October 1987.

32. Lieutenant Robert Ruark, USNR, "They Called 'Em Fish Food," *Saturday Evening Post,* 6 May 1944, 39–45.

33. History of the AG Center (Pacific), Appendix H. 12th ND Administrative History (13 November 1945), 128.

34. U.S. Naval Training School, AG Center, NOLA, "Training Review," October 1945.

35. Richard E. Williams, correspondence, 15 December 1987.

36. William P. Watson, correspondence, 17 January 1988.

37. History of NAG Afloat in WW II (OP 414), 86–88.

38. Robert Ruark, 45.

39. Warren Chapman, "Floating Firecrackers," *Mechanix Illustrated,* September 1945. (Page illegible.)

40. C. A. Burke, correspondence, 12 June 1987.

41. "Arming of Merchant Ships and Armed Guard Service," Appendix I and III, U.S. Naval Administration in World War II, Office of the CNO, covering period 7 December 1941–30 September 1945.

The elimination of gunnery training at Great Lakes Training Center (see note 37) because winter conditions on the Great Lakes were not suitable for gunnery practice would have proved ironic to veterans who served in the North Atlantic during winter, or on the Murmansk run at almost any time. To them service in the Great Lakes would have compared favorably with duty in the Caribbean.

The strange bit of advice offered Lieutenant Odegaard, note 31 ("Shoot the Bastards"), perhaps has been traced belatedly. John Cusick of Sun City, Arizona, wrote that he was formerly a deck officer in the merchant marine. A classmate was first mate on a ship that arrived in Montevideo, Uruguay, to be greeted by a longshoremen's strike. The NMU crew aboard cooperated by withholding power from the winches. The master and first mate supported charges against the crew upon return to the United States. The men were tried and convicted in the U.S. District Court of Maryland, and the conviction was upheld by the Circuit Court of Appeals. As a result, the two officers were blacklisted. The master wound up as a lecturer at the Boston AG Officer's School. Cusick adds, "I was told that he constantly denigrated merchant marines and scared the wits out of the officer/students."

Chapter 4. The "Other Navy" at Sea

1. Robert Ruark, "They Called 'Em Fish Food," *Saturday Evening Post,* 6 May 1944, 39.

2. Dr. Charles E. Odegaard, "Memoirs of My Service in the U.S. Navy 1942–46," dated 6 May 1962, copy furnished by author.

3. Harold Bondhus, correspondence, 25 October 1987. In reporting on his problems with a 1907 5″ 50-caliber gun, he also wrote that a friend of his had the mate to his gun. At his first stop in the Fijis, he got a direct order from the Port Director that "Under no circumstances should your gun be fired. It is of much greater danger to the crew than it would possibly be to the Japanese."

4. Lieutenant Commander Beverley Britton, USNR, "The Navy's Stepchildren," *Proceedings,* December 1947.

5. Lieutenant Commander Gilbert Robinson, correspondence, 20 July 1987.

6. Robert Ruark, 45.

7. Lieutenant Commander Leo Blackburn, USNR, correspondence, 22 June 1987.

8. Lieutenant Commander Gilbert Robinson, correspondence, 20 July 1987.

9. Lieutenant Commander Norman Alston, USNR, interview, 5 March 1987, correspondence, 12 August 1987.

10. Dr. Charles E. Odegaard, unpublished memoir.

11. Captain Henning Lind, SS *Woodbridge N. Ferris* to Captain William Coakley, U.S. Naval Armed Guard Center, Brooklyn, N.Y.

12. DeWitt Welch, correspondence, 20 June 1987.

13. Herbert Norch, interview, 15 September 1987.

14. James Bennett, correspondence, 14 October 1987, with permission to quote from his article, "Forgotten Heroes," *Sea Classics,* August 1987.

15. Raymond Roy, correspondence, 15 October 1987.

16. Letter of PFC Russell Best, made available by former S 3/c Robert Norling.

17. DeWitt Welch, correspondence, 2 September 1987.

18. DeWitt Welch, correspondence, 12 July 1987.

19. Lieutenant Commander Norman Alston, USNR, correspondence, 12 August 1987.

20. Thomas Hedge, correspondence, 15 May 1987.

Chapter 5. The Ships They Sailed

1. *History of the Armed Guard Center (Pacific)*, 12th ND Administrative History, 13. Naval Armed Guards were furnished 5,114 U.S. flag and U.S.-owned foreign flag vessels, plus 1,122 foreign-owned merchant ships, including Panamanian, British, French, Norwegian, Danish, Dutch, Greek, and even one Chinese-flag vessel.

2. Robert H. Ferrell, *Woodrow Wilson and World War I*, 100. Hog Islanders were built at a new yard in a former swamp on the Delaware River, near Philadelphia. The first Hog Islander was launched 5 August 1918, but not delivered until after the Armistice.

3. Walter Peters, interview, 6 March 1987.

4. Gerald Sossaman, interview, 11 March 1987; correspondence, 5 September 1987.

5. Joseph Kushner, interview, 11 April 1987.

6. Edward Krupski, correspondence, 15 August 1987.

7. Lieutenant Commander Leo Blackburn, USNR, correspondence, 22 June 1987.

8. Dr. Charles E. Odegaard, correspondence, 12 April 1987.

9. James Handy, correspondence, 25 August 1987.

10. Walter Peters, interview, 6 March 1987.

11. *Ships of the Esso Fleet in WW II*, Standard Oil Company of New Jersey (New York, 1946), foreword.

12. Rosalio Martinez, interview, 6 March 1987.

13. Frank Belsito, correspondence, 25 July 1987.

14. Captain Arthur Moore, *A Careless Word . . . A Needless Sinking*, 217.

15. "Liberty Ship," American Society of Mechanical Engineers, 18 September 1944.

16. David E. Dorn, "Ships for Victory," *Proceedings*, February 1985, 69–75.

17. David G. Sudhalter, "How 'Hurry-up Henry' Helped Win the War," *The Retired Officer*, August 1986, 35–37.

18. "Background Material on Bethlehem Steel Corporation's Fairfield Yard," Public Affairs Department, Bethlehem Steel Corporation, Baltimore, Maryland.

19. "The U.S. Merchant Marine at War," final report to the President by the Administrator, U.S. Maritime Commission, 15 January 1946. Also listed were Victory ships (571), tankers (673), "reefers," standard cargo and passenger ships (548), 242–45.

20. Dewitt Welch, correspondence, 21 August 1987.

The U.S. Maritime Commission Report referred to in note 19 gave dramatic evidence of the miracle of production in American shipyards, from twenty-eight ships built in 1939 to a total of 5,558 by 1 September 1945. They were delivered from eighty yards. In 1944 the WSA reported that an average of one ship left U.S. ports every thirty minutes, and some 5,000,000 tons of merchant shipping were in shuttle service in various war theaters. In 1943 alone there were 2,976 Lend-Lease sailings, of which 328 were to Russia.

Two excellent books on Liberty ships are: *Liberty Ships* by John Gorley Bunker, and *The Liberty Ships* by L. A. Sawyer and W. H. Mitchell. A fascinating account of tanker operations, featuring individual ships, is *Ships of the Esso Fleet in World War II*, published by Standard Oil Company of New Jersey, which has been used extensively in this account. The monumental history of the tremendous losses of the U.S. Merchant Marine in World War II, *A Careless Word . . . A Needless Sinking*, by Captain Arthur R. Moore, has been essential to the writer in providing authentic detail and verifying information provided after a lapse of over forty years by individual members of the Naval Armed Guard, Merchant Marine, and others. Captain Moore's book reports particulars on the loss of over 750 ships and thousands of merchant seamen and Navy Armed Guards. Published by the American Merchant Marine Museum at the U.S. Merchant Marine Academy, Kings Point, New York, in 1983, with revisions in 1984 and 1985, it has been out of print, but happily was revised and reprinted in 1988, with additional detail recently discovered.

The last Liberty ship of original configuration in operating condition is the SS *Jeremiah O'Brien*, open to the public at her home berth, Pier Three East, Fort Mason, Golden Gate National Recreational Area, San Francisco, California. She was brought out of mothballs and completely restored to her original configuration, including guns, eight 20-mm and a 5″/38 caliber mounted on her stern. She has been designated a National Monument and placed on the National Register. Several times a year special sailings are arranged, one recently by the U.S. Navy Armed Guard Veterans of World War II.

Efforts are under way at the time of writing to restore another Liberty, the SS *John W. Brown*, last surviving East Coast Liberty; it will serve as an operational Merchant Marine memorial, berthed in Baltimore.

Chapter 6. Gallant Ships, Gallant Men

1. History of the Naval Armed Guard Afloat in World War II (OP 414), Director of Naval History, Fleet Maintenance Division (undated), 14, 69.

2. U.S. Merchant Marine Academy Catalog, 10. By the end of the war the academy had graduated 6,634 officers of the U.S. Merchant Marine, who also held commissions in the U.S. Naval Reserve.

3. Captain Arthur R. Moore, *A Careless Word*, rev. ed. 1985, Merchant Marine Museum, Kings Point, N.Y., 551–53. The proper spelling of SS *Nathaniel Greene* is *Nathanael*. However, several sources, including her official "Gallant Ship" citation, used *Nathaniel*; thus, that spelling is used here to avoid confusion.

4. Ibid.

5. Ibid.

6. History of the Naval Armed Guard Afloat in WW II, 14–15; *Dictionary of American Naval Fighting Ships*, (hereafter cited as DANFS), Naval Historical Center, Washington, 1981, 492.

7. *DANFS*, vol. 7, 142; Davenport (Iowa) *Daily Times*, 13 March 1944, 1.

8. Copy of posthumous citation and award of Navy Cross; copy of navy announcement renaming destroyer DD 878 in honor of Ensign Kay K. Vesole, USNR, dated 11 November 1944.

9. Navy Department press release "Heroism of Armed Guardsmen Told in Citations," dated 10 August 1944.

10. Davenport (Iowa) *Daily Times*, 13 March 1944, "Crew Members Tell How Ensign Vesole Died Heroically," 1.

11. *DANFS*, vol. 1, 142; Letter of Commendation, Chief of Naval Personnel, Board of Awards, dated 25 February 1943.

12. *DANFS*, vol. 8, 324; Navy press release, 12 March 1943, Citation Navy Cross; summary of statements of survivors of SS *Stephen Hopkins*, (date illegible), signed by Lieutenant H. V. Stebbins, USNR.

13. *DANFS*, vol. 7, (1968) reprint 1977, 320; citation Navy and Marine Corps Medals.

14. *DANFS*, vol. 8, (1981), 73–74.

15. Statement of Naval Service, Navy Dept., Bureau of Navigation (NAV-3654VP-95325), 4 May 1942, citation Silver Star posthumously.

16. *DANFS*, vol. 4, (1969), Statement of Naval Service, 26 July 1943; (Code 103623; Pers-22246-CJB 22 March 1944). Quote, Letter of Commendation signed by Secretary of the Navy Frank Knox dated 21 August 1942, later replaced by Silver Star. The official Navy citation was in error. Ensign Marshall was serving aboard the SS *Merrimack*, not "a U.S. Naval vessel."

17. William Schofield, *Eastward the Convoys*, 22–24; Captain Arthur R. Moore, *A Careless Word*, 191.

18. *Our Navy*, December 1942 (no page number available), Silver Star awards and Letters of Commendation to named 20-man NAG gun crew.

19. *Ships of the Esso Fleet in WW II*, 454–60.

20. Letter of Commendation from CNO, dated 17 April 1944.

21. Letter of Commendation from CNO, dated 17 April 1944.

22. *The Bulletin Board* (unspecified date), "Battle Stars for Armed Guard Crews," listing several hundred ships carrying NAGs "which have taken part in engagements up to 25 September 1944 warranting the award of battle stars to their naval personnel was announced recently in three letters from BuPer's to the COs of Armed Guard Centers." The list did not include the SS *Stanvac Calcutta*, which had received a citation as a "Gallant Ship" for its gallant fight against the German raider *Stier*.

23. Letter from an official of the Awards and Special Projects Branch to family member of a C/M killed in action, "The Navy's policy in such cases is to authorize Navy medals only to those Merchant Marine personnel who attended the Merchant Marine Academy, graduated, and accepted a commision as Ensign, USNR, without a break, in service. Since your brother's service does not meet this criteria, Navy medals may not be authorized. This fact in no way detracts from the value of your brother's service to our country." The identity of the writer has purposely been withheld; the request had been for a Purple Heart, appropriate campaign medals and a Victory Medal, to be presented to the U.S. Merchant Marine Academy in the name of the cadet/midshipman.

Chapter 7. The Convoys

1. Martin Middlebrook, *Convoy,* 16–17; Terry Hughes and John Costello, *The Battle of the Atlantic,* 204–7; Barrie Pitt, *Battle of the Atlantic,* 156.

2. Admiral Ernest J. King, USN, and Commander Walter Whitehall, USNR, *Fleet Admiral King,* 457. King's reported opposition to convoys has been stated to be erroneous in implication; as CINCLANTFLT before December 1941, he was responsible for inaugurating USN convoy operations in the North Atlantic, and the reason for the delay in establishing coastal convoys was that available resources were more needed to protect oceanic convoys, in effect since the summer of 1941. Even so, British reproach of the U.S. for not accurately measuring the extent of submarine danger along the U.S. East Coast or taking adequate measures to ensure protection of shipping was made repeatedly, including by Winston S. Churchill in his book *The World Wars,* vol. 1, 416, and in Captain Donald MacIntyre's book *The Naval War Against Hitler,* 326–27.

3. Captain Stephen Roskill, RN, later official Royal Navy historian, *Churchill and the Admirals,* 190–97, 217, 233–34, 270.

4. Admiral Ernest J. King, USN, and Commander Walter Whitehall, USNR, *Fleet Admiral King,* 454–55.

5. Dr. Jürgen Rohwer, *Critical Convoy Battles of March 1943,* 9–30.

6. Cornelius A. Burke, correspondence, 29 April 1987.

7. James Bennett, correspondence, 15 July 1987.

8. Walter Peters, interview, 6 March 1987.

9. Kenneth Cauble, interview, 12 October; correspondence, 1 November 1987.

10. Louis Ritter, correspondence, 1 August 1987.

11. Captain Arthur R. Moore, *A Careless Word,* 187.

12. Grady Railback, correspondence, 10 May 1987; interview, 10 April 1987.

Convoy tactics are well covered in *The Battle of the Atlantic,* Hughes and Costello, and detailed coverage of the battle for convoys SC 122 and HX 229 is provided in *Convoy* by Martin Middlebrook.

Chapter 8 The Sea Raiders

1. *History of Naval Armed Guard Afloat in World War II* (OP 414) (undated), 92.

2. Lowell Thomas, *Raiders of the Deep* (page number not available).

3. *Harper's Pictorial Library of the World War,* 187–89. A new book on the exploits of the *Emden* was published by the Naval Institute Press, Annapolis, in 1988, *The Last Gentleman of War* by R. K. Lockner (translation by Thea and Harry Lindauer).

4. Edwin P. Hoyt, *The Raider Wolf,* 143–50.

5. L. C. F. Turner, H. R. Gordon-Cummings, and J. E. Betzler, *The War in Southern Waters,* 20–23, 260–61.

6. *History of the NAG Afloat,* 85.

7. Ibid., 86–92.

8. Ibid.; Captain Arthur R. Moore, *A Careless Word,* 322–23.

9. George W. Duffy, correspondence, 20 July 1987.

10. Lieutenant Commander Edward Anderson, USNR, correspondence, 17 August 1987; *History of NAG Afloat,* 87–88.

11. *History of NAG Afloat,* 90–92; Captain Stephen Roskill, RN, *The War at Sea,* 109. Also see the chapter "Gallant Ships, Gallant Men."

12. Navy Department, Division of Naval Intelligence, CI Branch, "Log of #1 Life Boat of SS *Stephen Hopkins,* dated 12 January 1942, signed by Lieutenant H. S. Burch, USNR.

In researching an account such as this, one comes across many poignant stories. One such was a letter written in 1945 by the young bride of a navy gunner aboard the SS *American Leader.* They had been married for only two months before he enlisted in the navy, to be reported "Missing in Action" shortly, and finally reported "Killed" by the Navy Department. After the war she received a letter from one of his shipmates saying that her husband had been a POW in a Japanese work camp in Java. While being transported in an unmarked prison ship to Japan, the ship was sunk by an American submarine, unaware that it was carrying prisoners, and her husband was lost. The young woman was writing a shipmate to request any possible details of her husband's experience in the camp or of his death. She wondered wistfully if he had received any of her mail or packages. Her letter, in clear and beautiful handwriting, was particularly moving when she wrote, "It seems so wonderful to walk down the streets and see all the boys home again . . . but I know that I can be ever so proud of him and that he gave his life for us at home."

Chapter 9. Other Hazards

1. *Ships of the Esso Fleet in World War II*, 478–82.

2. Captain Arthur R. Moore, *A Careless Word . . . A Needless Sinking*, 409–10.

3. Ibid., 410.

4. Ibid., 417.

5. DeWitt Welch, correspondence, 25 April 1987.

6. Edward Quin, interview, 6 March 1987.

7. Raymond Roy, correspondence, 1 December 1987.

8. "Typhoon," DESA (Destroyer Escort Sailors Association) News, January/February 1983, 10.

9. Robert Heitzinger, interview, 12 October 1987; correspondence, 5 December 1987.

10. Irving Brownell, correspondence, 20 June 1987.

11. Captain Arthur R. Moore, *A Careless Word . . . A Needless Sinking*, 421.

12. Raymond Roy, correspondence, December 1987; Peter Britton, "Nightmare Waves Are All Too Real," *Smithsonian*, February 1978, 60–63.

13. Michael Molinari, correspondence, 12 August 1987.

14. Glen Kittleman, correspondence, 12 November 1987.

15. Albert Gonzales, interview, 20 March 1987.

16. John Gorley Bunker, *Liberty Ships*, 144; Captain Arthur R. Moore, *A Careless Word*, 397.

17. John J. Pohl, correspondence, 25 October 1987.

18. Riccard Whelan, correspondence, 19 August 1987.

19. Eugene Meadows, correspondence, 20 September 1987.

20. Captain Arthur R. Moore, *A Careless Word*, 319.

21. Ibid., "Additions and corrections," updated insert, September 1985.

22. Lieutenant Commander Harold J. McCormick, USNR, correspondence and FBI monograph, "German Espionage World War II—Latin American," Chapter 6 Argentina (undated) obtained by McCormick under Freedom of Information Act, 1988.

23. "Oregon Victory Ship Attacked in 'Mistaken Identity' Case," *Oregon Journal*, 8 November 1944.

Chapter 10. Relations with the Merchant Marine

1. Norman J. Adams, "Why the U.S. Requires a Merchant Marine," *Marine Progress*, July 1935; reprinted in *Naval Engineers Journal*, March 1986.
2. "Caught Short with Too Few Ships," NMU *Pilot*, May 1987, 6.
3. *Todd Shipyards in Peace and War*, Todd Shipyards Corporation, 11.
4. C. B. Mitchell, *Every Kind of Shipwork*, 45.
5. *History of the Naval Armed Guard Afloat in WW II*, (OP 414), undated, preface, 2.
6. Rear Admiral Samuel E. Morison, USN, *The Battle of the Atlantic*, vol. 1, 300.
7. John Gorley Bunker, *Liberty Ships*, 34–35.
8. Charles Dana Gibson, *Merchantman? Or Ships of War*, 131; Samuel E. Morison, *Battle of the Atlantic*, 299.
9. The source of this old personal account did not wish to be identified.
10. George W. Duffy, correspondence, 21 July 1987.
11. Robert Ruark, "They Call 'Em Fish Food," *Saturday Evening Post*, 6 May 1944, 37–39.
12. Lieutenant Commander Beverley Britton, USNR, "Navy's Stepchildren," *Proceedings*, December 1947.
13. Edward Anderson, correspondence, 5 July 1987.
14. Wells Bain, correspondence, 12 November 1987.
15. Commander E. Ellsburg, USN, *Under the Red Sea Sun*, 31–32.
16. James Hoffman, correspondence, 5 August 1987; Captain Arthur R. Moore, *A Careless Word . . . A Needless Sinking*, 518.
17. *Ships of the Esso Fleet in World War II*, 202.
18. Harry Koch, correspondence, 18 April 1987.
19. Frank E. Davis, correspondence, 12 September 1987.
20. Walter Peters, interview, 6 March 1987.
21. Robert Chamberlin, correspondence, 21 June 1987.
22. *Ships of the Esso Fleet*, 126.
23. Ibid., 177.
24. Lieutenant Commander Robinson, correspondence, 12 September 1987.

Chapter 11. Hell Below Zero: The Murmansk Run

1. R. H. Dawson, *Decision to Aid Russia—1941,* 284.

2. *History of Naval Armed Guard Afloat in World War II* (undated) (OP 414).

3. John Sheridan, *Linda and the Gunner's Mate,* based on his personal experience/correspondence; *History of NAG Afloat,* 21.

4. NAG Officer's Voyage Report SS *Dunboyne* to CNO (date illegible) signed by Ensign Rufus T. Brinn, USNR. National Archives, Code MR CRR, Box 175.

5. George T. Smith, letter to C. A. Lloyd, dated 3 April 1986; Captain Arthur R. Moore, *A Careless Word . . . A Needless Sinking,* 315.

6. Warren Chapman, "Floating Firecrackers," *Mechanix Illustrated,* September 1943, 53, 155–56.

7. Irving Kaplan, correspondence, 29 April 1987, and copy of his voyage report to CNO, dated 30 January 1944.

8. Joseph E. Hecht, correspondence, 28 March 1988.

9. Louis Vigh, correspondence, 12 May 1987.

10. *History of Naval Armed Guard Afloat,* 39–41. The SS *Nathaniel Greene, Virginia Dare* and *William Moultrie* were designated "Gallant Ships."

11. *Ships of the Esso Fleet in World War II,* 326.

12. William Leonard Phillips, RN, voluminous correspondence with author 1987–88; John Gorley Bunker, *Liberty Ships,* 67–69. Able Seaman Phillips tried for years to discover the fate of the baby he had rescued from the lifeboat. Through the assistance of the British Broadcasting Company (BBC) and the Norwegian government, in 1988 he was put in touch with the now-grown lady. She is the last of the refugee survivors of the lifeboat and is still living on the remote Isle of Soraya; naturally she remembers nothing of the ordeal, except what she had been told as a child. The reunion was widely featured by British and Norwegian news media and TV.

13. Captain Arthur R. Moore, *A Careless Word,* 186, 323–35.

14. William L. Phillips, RN, correspondence, 6 November 1987.

15. *History of NAG Afloat,* 16–18; NAG Officer's Voyage Report to CNO dated 17 March 1943, signed by Lieutenant (jg) William A. Carter, USNR, National Archives, Code MR CRR (RG 38), Box 547.

16. Ernest Sanders, correspondence, December 1987; "Convoy to the Top of the World," *Stars and Stripes,* 15 February 1943.

17. James Blalock, interview, 3 April 1987.

18. Winston S. Churchill, *The Hinge of Fate,* 750; Records of

Arming Merchant Ships Section, Fleet Maintenance Division, Office of the CNO.

Chapter 12 The PQ-17 Disaster

1. Captain Stephen Roskill, RN, *Churchill and the Admirals*, 52.
2. Ibid., 130. Roskill reports that Admiral Tovey registered "vigorous protests" over summer convoys, and warned that disaster would take place if instituted, but constant pressure from Stalin led Churchill to overrule Tovey's valid objections. Captain Donald MacIntyre, RN, in *The Naval War Against Hitler* devotes chapter 9, "Disaster in the Barents Sea," to the Arctic convoys. He reported that the First Sea Lord, Admiral Sir Dudley Pound, wrote Admiral Ernest King, "The whole thing is a most unsound operation with the dice loaded against us in every direction." But the desire of Churchill and Roosevelt to meet the demands of Stalin was the deciding factor, and in June 1942, Convoy PQ-17 was assembled in Iceland, one of the most calamitous episodes of the naval war, 271.
3. Rear Admiral Samuel E. Morison, USN, *The Battle of the Atlantic*, 179–80.
4. Dr. Jürgen Rohwer, *Chronology of the War at Sea 1939–1945*, 229–32.
5. Ibid., 231.
6. Winston S. Churchill, *The Second World War*, vol. 4, "The Hinge of Fate," 262–66.
7. Robert Carse, *Cold Corner of Hell*, 144–45. S 1/c Wright was awarded the Silver Star for gallantry in this action.
8. Captain Arthur R. Moore, *A Careless Word . . . A Needless Sinking*, 308.
9. Kenneth Clasen, correspondence, May 1987; "Wartime Survivors Remember Convoy Fate," Marilyn J. Shaw, Goldsboro (NC) *News-Argus*, 30 June 1985, Section C, 1.
10. NAG Officer Voyage Report to CNO (dated 15 August 1942) signed by Lieutenant (j.g.) Morton E. Wolfson, USNR, National Archives, filed under ship (RG 38).
11. Captain Arthur R. Moore, *A Careless Word*, 554.
12. David Irving, *The Destruction of PQ-17*. Report of difficulties with crew confirmed by NAG Officer Voyage Reports of 3 November 1942, covering both outbound and inbound voyages, signed by Ensign Howard E. Carraway, USNR. National Archives, filed under SS *Troubadour* (RG 38).
13. Captain Arthur R. Moore, *A Careless Word*, 43.

14. John E. Sexton, correspondence, 6 October 1987, and his NAG Officer Voyage Report to CNO dated 14 July 1942, furnished by him.

15. Robert H. Wolff, interview, 12 December 1987, correspondence, 5 January 1988.

16. Dr. Jürgen Rohwer, *Chronology of the War at Sea 1939– 1945*, 232.

17. Captain Arthur R. Moore, *A Careless Word*, 544–45.

18. Jacques Mordal, *25 Centuries of Sea Warfare*, 360–69; General S. M. Shtemenko, *The Last Six Months*, 20–23. Shtemenko writes that the loss of PQ-17 was due to "politics and hostility of Britain toward the USSR." Such attitude was part of the "cataract of abuse and fault from the Soviet Government" reported by Churchill in *The Hinge of Fate*, 263.

19. Winston S. Churchill, *The Hinge of Fate*, 575.

20. Ibid., 264–65.

21. Robert Carse, *Cold Corner of Hell*, 262.

22. Winston S. Churchill, *The Hinge of Fate*, 266. Rear Admiral Hamilton, RN, was excoriated for his withdrawal, but he did so under the direct order of Admiral Sir Dudley Pound, First Sea Lord. Roskill reports that by 1943 Pound was a very sick man, unfit to carry out his heavy responsibilities; he suffered a stroke that led to his resignation, and he died on 21 October 1943.

23. Captain Reinhart Reche, FGN (Ret.), correspondence dated 26 August 1987. He reports that his boat, the *U-255* ("Fox Boat"), was on her first patrol and "scored four ships of PQ-17, with a total of 25,544 GRT. With her skilled crew she fought under three COs in the Arctic, later in the Atlantic, and finally was the last U-boat in the Bay of Biscay until the end of World War II." Captain Reche, who was noted for his assistance of survivors in lifeboats, ended the war at Narvik, control point for Arctic U-boats, until at the end the six remaining U-boats on patrol went to England under escort. After the war Captain Reche became a high-ranking NATO naval officer.

Chapter 13 Stranded in Russia: The Forgotten Convoy

1. John Sheridan, correspondence, 3 August 1987.

2. Edward Quin, interview 15 April 1987.

3. Eugene Meadows, correspondence, 8 December 1987.

4. Arthur MacLaren, correspondence, 25 October 1987.

5. Hilary Makowski, correspondence, 11 September 1987.

6. *Ships of the Esso Fleet in World War II,* 151–54; confirms name as *Beaconhill* (not *Beacon Hill*).

7. John Mitchell (deceased). His diary was given by his mother to his friend and shipmate Hilary Makowski; she had refused previous offers to buy it for commercial use. The diary was made available for use in this account by Hilary Makowski.

8. Hilary Makowski, correspondence, 11 September 1987.

9. Max Jones (deceased). The information provided was in an interview on 9 May 1987, and permission to include it was graciously given by his daughter Mrs. Brenda J. Farrell.

10. AG Veterans of WW II, "Pointer," Spring 1987.

11. C. A. Burke, "Yuletide in Murmansk," *Philadelphia Bulletin,* 24 December 1978. Permission to quote furnished during the course of voluminous correspondence with writer in 1987.

The stirring WW II movie *Action in the North Atlantic,* to which MacLaren refers in reference 4 concerned the ordeal of a Liberty ship en route to Murmansk. It depicted the arrival of the battle-scarred merchant ship in Murmansk, greeted by enthusiastic cheers of well-dressed, arm-waving crowds lining the waterfront, hardly in accord with the reality reported by veterans of the Murmansk run. However, MacLaren and several other merchant seamen who served on the run visited Murmansk again in 1987 and received a much different reception from the unfavorable accounts reported in this volume.

Chapter 14. – The Battle of the Atlantic

1. Winston S. Churchill, *Memoirs of the Second World War,* 410.

2. Barrie Pitt, *The Battle of the Atlantic,* 22.

3. *History of NAG Afloat in WW II* (OP 414), 80.

4. Grossadmiral Karl Dönitz, *Memoirs,* 133.

5. Winston S. Churchill, *The Hinge of Fate,* 125.

6. Barrie Pitt, *The Battle of the Atlantic,* 22.

7. Winston S. Churchill, *The Hinge of Fate,* 125.

8. General Lyman Lemnitzer, USA, interview in *Military History* (October 1986), 45.

9. Dr. Jürgen Rohwer, *Critical Convoy Battles of March 1943,* 16–33; Grossadmiral Karl Dönitz, *Memoirs,* 146.

10. Terry Hughes and John Costello, *The Battle of the Atlantic,* 140–54.

11. NAG Officer Voyage Report to CNO, dated 31 January 1943, signed by Ensign G. B. Watkins, USNR; Summary of Statements of Survivors, dated 2 April 1943, signed by Lieutenant (j.g.) Robert B. Fulton, USNR, National Archives, Record Group 38, Box 382.

12. John Mitchell (deceased). Diary given by his mother to his close friend and shipmate, Hilary Makowski.

13. *Ships of the Esso Fleet in WW II*, 177–86.

14. Ibid., 406–8.

15. George Prestmo, interview, 12 October 1987; correspondence, 2 November 1987.

16. Summary of Statements of Survivors, dated 30 April 1943; survivor Edward P. Rego, correspondence of 1 July 1987; Terry Hughes and John Costello, *The Battle of the Atlantic*, 264–72.

17. Captain Arthur R. Moore, *A Careless Word . . . A Needless Sinking*, 305.

18. Edward Rego, correspondence, 1 July 1987.

19. Dr. Jürgen Rohwer, *Axis Submarine Successes 1939–1945*, 156.

20. David Kahn, *The Code Breakers*, 465–68.

21. Press release, Public Information Office, 5th ND, 16 September 1945, 10.

22. Dr. Jürgen Rohwer, *Axis Submarine Successes*, 153–60.

23. John Gorley Bunker, *Liberty Ships*, 86–109; Grossadmiral Karl Dönitz, *Memoirs*, 327–30. Dönitz quotes Captain Stephen Roskill (RN) as saying, "The Germans never came so near to disrupting communications between the New World and the Old as in the first twenty days of March 1943." Possibly the two best books on the subject are Martin Middlebrook's *Convoy*, and Dr. Jürgen Rohwer's *Crucial Convoy Battles of March 1943*. In the preface to the English edition of his book, Dr. Rohwer states that the two books complement each other very well—Middlebrook's emphasis being on the fate of the participants of the battle on both sides, and Rohwer's book dealing with more strategic and leadership problems. Captain Arthur R. Moore's outstanding reference book, *A Careless Word . . . A Needless Sinking*, furnishes details on each of the American merchant ships sunk in the battle.

23. William Stilinovich, correspondence, 2 June 1987, and a number of telephone interviews.

24. Captain Arthur R. Moore, *A Careless Word*, 187.

25. Herbert Werner, *Iron Coffins*, 327.

26. Grossadmiral Karl Dönitz, *Memoirs*, 329; Martin Middlebrook, *Convoy*, 101.

27. Grossadmiral Karl Dönitz, *Memoirs,* 341.
28. Captain Stephen Roskill, RN, *War at Sea,* vols. 1–3 (London: HM Stationery Office).
29. Grossadmiral Karl Dönitz, *Memoirs,* appendix.

Chapter 15. The Yankee Turkey Shoot

1. Terry Hughes and John Costello, *The Battle of the Atlantic,* 100.
2. U.S. Navy press release, Public Information Office, 5th ND, 16 September 1945.
3. Ibid.
4. Herbert Werner, *Iron Coffins,* 75.
5. *Ships of the Esso Fleet in World War II,* 177–86.
6. Winston S. Churchill, *The Hinge of Fate,* 108–19.
7. M. Schuyler Jr., "How We Closed the Port of New York," *Sea History,* summer 1987, 50–51.
8. *Atlanta Journal,* 2 February 1987; reprint of piece by Daniel Christensen, *Miami News,* date and page unspecified.
9. *Ships of the Esso Fleet,* 106–10.
10. Ibid., 295–99.
11. Ibid., 335–40.
12. Ibid., 433–40.
13. Ibid., 423–25.
14. Associated Press (delayed) 19 September 1943.
15. Theodore Taylor, *Fire on the Beaches,* 194–99.
16. Francis E. Davis, correspondence, 10 October 1987.
17. Theodore Taylor, *Fire on the Beaches,* 194–99.
18. *Ships of the Esso Fleet,* 343–44.
19. Edward Hogan, correspondence, 22 June 1987.
20. Nathan Miller, *The U.S. Navy: An Illustrated History,* 337–38.
21. James D. Handy, correspondence, 5 August 1987.
22. *Ships of the Esso Fleet,* 310–16. Scholars dispute Dönitz's "tonnage warfare" concept, that it makes no difference where the tonnage was sunk, just so long as it went to the bottom. In a frontispiece to volume 10 of his monumental *History of U.S. Naval Operation in World War II,* Samuel E. Morison quotes Dönitz's war diary of 31 December 1942: "The tonnage war is the main task for submariners, probably the most decisive contribution of submarines to winning the war. This war on merchant shipping must be carried out where the greatest success can be achieved with

the smallest losses." Morison felt that the "integral tonnage" strategy was a failure, but added, "Let us never forget that the initial successes and surprises by the U-boats fell not far short of rendering Germany invincible on the seas, while her arms were carrying everything before them on the continent of Europe." (*The Two Ocean War,* 564.)

23. Theodore Taylor, *Fire on the Beaches,* 84.

24. Winston S. Churchill, *The Hinge of Fate,* 84.

25. *Ships of the Esso Fleet,* 207–8.

26. Ibid., 212–18.

27. Ibid., 310–18.

28. Ibid., 252, 261, 274, 393, 413.

29. Ibid., 241–43.

30. Ernest Sanders, correspondence, 31 December 1987.

31. Lieutenant Commander Paul Kincade, USN (Ret.), interview, 9 April 1987, and correspondence 15 December 1987.

32. Edward Knopf, interview, 10 October 1987; correspondence 12 December 1987.

33. Captain Reinhard Hardegen, KTB *Newsletter,* February/ March 1987, 11.

Chapter 16. The Mediterranean

1. Ernle Bradford, *Siege: Malta,* 193–97, 288. Bradford reports that for the period August 1940 through August 1942, twenty-two of fifty-five ships sailing in convoy were sunk, eleven turned back vs. only one sunk and one turned back out of thirty-one ships traveling alone; he attributes this to the use of old and small ships that hugged the coast until they made their final dash to Malta, a striking illustration of Axis control of the air in the early days of the war.

2. John Gorley Bunker, *Liberty Ships,* 120; *The Mediterranean* (New York: Time-Life Books), 120–45. High praise for the valor and skill of the 10th Light Flotilla is found in Captain Donald MacIntyre's book *The Naval War Against Hitler,* 199.

3. *Ships of the Esso Fleet in World War II,* 454–60.

4. William Leonard Phillips, RN, correspondence, 10 May 1987.

5. Samuel E. Morison, *History of U.S. Naval Operations in World War II,* vol. 1, *Battle of the Atlantic,* 193–97, 301–3; *History of the NAG Afloat in World War II,* (OP 414), 93–101.

6. General Lyman Lemnitzer, USA, interview, "Pressed for Any Victory," *Military History,* 6 October 1986, 45.

7. *History of NAG Afloat,* 104–6.

8. George Prestmo, interview, 10 October 1987; correspondence, 12 December 1987.

9. *Ships of the Esso Fleet,* 421–23.

10. John Gorley Bunker, *Liberty Ships,* 111–23; Captain Arthur R. Moore, *A Careless Word . . . A Needless Sinking,* 217.

11. Herbert Norch, interview, 1 December 1987.

12. Letter of Commendation to Feral Carney, S 1/c, USNR, from CNO, dated 8 September 1944.

13. Creal Gibson, interview, 23 August 1987; *The Little Creek Pointer,* 2 July 1944, 3, presentation of Commendation Ribbon to S 2/c Gibson.

14. Directorate of History, National Defense Headquarters, Ottawa, File 1325-500G "Report on Air Attack on Allied Convoy in Mediterranean Sea 6 November 1943, E. W. Haldenby, Brig.: supplemental statements by Captain E. B. Cobby (COMD HQ CDN BASE RFT GROUP, CMF) and Captain E. G. Radley.

15. *History of NAG Afloat,* 115.

16. Ibid., 118–19.

17. Captain Arthur R. Moore, *A Careless Word . . . A Needless Sinking,* 200.

18. Cornelius Burke, correspondence, 15 September 1987.

19. *History of NAG Afloat,* 122–29.

20. Ibid., 134–35.

21. Ibid., 135.

22. *Ships of the Esso Fleet,* 486–91.

23. *History of the NAG Afloat,* 158–65.

24. Ibid., 158.

25. Ibid., 161.

26. Albert Hedge, correspondence, 12 December 1987.

27. *History of NAG Afloat,* 170–75.

28. *DESA NEWS,* November/December 1982, "Top Secret Operation," 11–14; Winford Vaughn-Thomas, *Anzio,* 132–49.

29. *Armed Guard Pointer* (Brooklyn Armed Guard Center Bulletin) 11 May 1945, 10, presentation of award to Lieutenant (j.g.) L. Isenberg, USNR, by Admiral Hewitt.

30. *History of NAG Afloat,* 170–75.

31. Herbert Norch, interview, 1 March 1988.

32. William L. Allen, *Anzio: Edge of Disaster,* 124–25.

33. *History of NAG Afloat,* 166–69; John Gorley Bunker, *Liberty Ships,* 121–23; Glen Infield, "Night We Poisoned Our Own Troops," *Saga,* October 1964, 22–23, 82–83, and "America's Secret Poison

Gas Tragedy," *True* magazine, July 1961, 98–100. (Also see chapter 6, *Gallant Ships, Gallant Men.*)

34. Captain Arthur R. Moore, *A Careless Word,* 151, 155, 161, 251.

35. J. Coleman, interview, 12 April 1987.

36. Louis V. Ritter, correspondence, 14 October 1987.

37. DeWitt Welch, correspondence, 16 September 1987.

38. Dr. Jürgen Rohwer, *Chronology of the War at Sea 1939–1945,* 515.

Chapter 17. The Pacific.

1. John Costello, *The Pacific War (1941–45),* 562.

2. Larry La Fontaine, interview, 15 October 1987.

3. Howard Roberts, interview, 15 October 1987.

4. Carlin Montgomery, interview, 12 March 1987; correspondence, 15 July 1987.

5. *History of the NAG Afloat in WW II* (OP 414), 186–89.

6. William McLaughlin, correspondence, 18 June 1987.

7. Eugene Book, correspondence, 12 August 1987.

8. Gerald Sossaman, correspondence, 9 February 1987; interview 15 March 1987.

9. Lieutenant Commander Harold Bondhus, USNR, correspondence, 15 October 1987.

10. Richard Hudnall, correspondence, 25 October 1987.

11. Albert Gonzales, interview, 13 March 1987.

12. Manley Michler, interview, 10 October 1987.

13. Lee Rigg, (deceased), the *Armed Guard Pointer,* October 1987, release authorized by Mrs. Lee Rigg.

14. George Miller, interview, 9 December 1987; correspondence, 2 March 1987.

15. *Ships of the Esso Fleet,* 409–12.

16. Carlin Montgomery, correspondence, 8 March 1988.

17. George Miller, correspondence, 10 February 1988.

18. Floyd Jones, correspondence, 9 May 1987.

19. *History of NAG Afloat,* 255.

20. NAG Officer Voyage Report to CNO of 24 March 1945, signed by Lieutenant Earle Douglas Woodring, USNR.

21. Robert Norling, "A Kamikaze Scored on My Liberty Ship," *Boston Globe,* 11 May 1985, 11.

22. *History of the NAG Afloat,* 214.

23. Ibid., 213.

24. Ibid., 196.

25. *Ships of the Esso Fleet,* 383–92.

26. *History of NAG Afloat,* 228.

27. Ibid., 242.

28. NAG Officer Voyage Report to CNO of 20 July 1944, signed by Lieutenant John M. Landis, USNR. National Archives, RG 38, Box 665.

29. Edwin Hoyt, *Japan's War,* 173, 249, 309, 344, 356, 389.

30. Denis Warner, *The Sacred Warriors,* New York, 339.

31. Donald P. Firer, correspondence, 25 September 1987.

32. Richard C. Hudnall, correspondence, 25 October 1987.

33. Captain Arthur R. Moore, *A Careless Word . . . A Needless Sinking,* 549; John Costello, *The Pacific War,* Appendix B, quoting U.S. official figures.

Chapter 18. The War in Southern Waters

1. L. C. F. Turner, H. R. Cummings-Gordon (RN Ret.) and J. E. Betzler, *War in the Southern Oceans, 1939–45,* 20.

2. The officer from whose journal the description of rounding the Horn was taken did not wish to be identified. However, he gave the writer permission to use it.

3. Walter Peters, interview, 15 March 1987.

4. Ibid.

5. Larry La Fontaine, interview, 14 October 1987.

6. Donald Zubrod, correspondence, 7 September 1987; Statement of Survivors, dated 31 March 1943, signed by Ensign John C. N. Guibert, USNR, National Archives, RG 38, Box 563; John Gorley Bunker, *Liberty Ships,* 103–5.

7. Robert W. Bell, *In Peril on the Sea* (no page number available); Captain Arthur R. Moore, *A Careless Word . . . A Needless Sinking,* 298.

8. Mark Murphy, "Eighty-Three Days," *The New Yorker Book of War Pieces,* New York (1947), 202–30; *History of the NAG Afloat in WW II,* (OP 414), 76–77.

9. Lieutenant Commander Harold J. McCormick, USNR, correspondence, 9 December 1987; FBI monograph, German Espionage Monograph, Latin America (1946), chapter 6, "German Espionage in Argentina," 137–77, Modern Military Field Branch, National Records Center, Suitland, Md. The FBI monograph reports many

high-ranking Argentine government officials, diplomatic and military, collaborated actively with German agents in Argentina. Prominently included was then-Colonel Juan Domingo Peron, later to become president of Argentina and husband of the glorified Evita. In a chart, "German-Argentine Collaboration in Bolivian Revolt of December 20, 1943," 177, Colonel Peron is listed as an active participant in the conspiracy to install a pro-German regime in Bolivia.

10. John Dunkerley, interview, 9 December 1987.

11. Michael Gurda, correspondence, 9 March 1988.

12. E. Ross, correspondence, 12 June 1987, based on interview with Arthur Dodrill, July 1984; Captain Arthur Moore, *A Careless Word*, 549.

13. Samuel E. Morison, *History of U.S. Naval Operation in WW II*, vol. 10, 224.

14. Dr. Jürgen Rohwer, *Axis Submarine Successes 1939–1945*, 258–77.

15. Edward Schnepf, "Die Erste Monsoons," *Sea Classics* (date not shown), 34.

16. Arno Grasty, unpublished memoir of the sinking of the SS *Alice F. Palmer;* Summary of Statements by Survivors, date illegible; letter of Captain George Pedersen to E. M. Dale of 13 September 1943; letter of Flotillenadmiral Robert Gysae of 23 October 1974 to Allen S. Hedrin.

17. Lieutenant Commander Harold J. McCormick, correspondence, 15 April 1988.

18. Robert Ruark, "They Called 'Em Fish Food," *Saturday Evening Post*, 6 May 1944, 39.

19. DeWitt Welch, correspondence, 12 November 1987.

20. Robert Williams, interview, 13 October 1987.

21. Lieutenant Commander Norman Alston, interview, 9 March 1987.

22. John Gorley Bunker, *Liberty Ships*, 137.

23. *Ships of the Esso Fleet*, 496–501.

24. John Gorley Bunker, *Liberty Ships*, 137; NAG Officer Voyage Report to CNO, dated 16 October 1944, signed by Lieutenant (j.g.) John C. Kelley, USNR; Summary of Statements of Survivors, dated 5 October 1944, signed by Lieutenant (j.g.) Barbara Conrad, USNR. The navy reports were obtained from the National Archives by E. Bates McKee, formerly on the staff of the New York Port Director. He also furnished the writer with Report of the Special Com-

in the gun tubs and wait for the sub to surface and then open fire—our only chance." The SS *Benjamin D. Wilson* observed two submarines identified as Italian, which submerged, but did not attack, and reported a scout plane, possibly from a submarine, but the trip to Madras was uneventful.

Reference: Correspondence dated 1 July 1989 and copy of the Armed Guard officer's log (declassified) received from former Radioman 3/c Robert J. Villares.

Chapter 20. Toward Victory in Europe

1. Lieutenant Commander Gilbert Robinson, correspondence, 20 July 1987.
2. *History of NAG Afloat in WW II* (OP 414), 176–85.
3. Herbert Werner, *Iron Coffins,* 227.
4. *History of the NAG Afloat,* 180.
5. Cornelius Burke, correspondence, 9 October 1987.
6. Lieutenant Commander Max Miller, USNR, *The Far Shore,* 46–55.
7. N. Paul Cronin, correspondence, 29 June 1987.
8. Michael Molinari, correspondence, 1 June 1986.
9. James Bennett, correspondence, 21 August 1987.
10. Herbert Norch, interview, 15 March 1988.
11. Melvin Barger, "Getting the Goods to the Beach," *Surface Warfare,* January/February 1988, 11.

Chapter 21. "The Navy Regrets . . ."

1. Captain Arthur R. Moore, *A Careless Word . . . A Needless Sinking,* 98; Felix Reisenberg, *Sea War,* 169.
2. *History of the NAG Afloat in WW II* (OP 414), 27.
3. Lonnie Whitson Lloyd, unpublished diary, made available for this account only by his brother Charles A. Lloyd, one of the three Lloyd brothers who served in the NAG. In relation to the controversy over raising the *U-853,* he added that the family shared the belief that the remains of the crew of *U-853* should remain undisturbed.
4. Bill Reynolds, "U-boat Still Attracting Attention," DESA *News,* January/February 1983, 11–12.
5. Frank Zeidler, a voluminous package of newspaper clip-

pings from Milwaukee papers concerning the life, political career, and death of his brother, Lieutenant (j.g.) Carl Zeidler, USNR.

6. Dr. Charles E. Odegaard, unpublished memoir of his service in the NAG in WW II.

7. Frank Zeidler, correspondence, 3 November 1987, concerning his postwar efforts to learn more of his brother's death; clipping from the *Milwaukee Journal,* 2 July 1985, "Sub's Log Details Loss of Carl Zeidler's Ship," no page indicated.

8. Dr. Jürgen Rohwer, *Axis Submarine Successes 1939–1945,* concerning misidentification of SS *La Salle* by commander of *U-159,* 265; Captain Arthur R. Moore, *A Careless Word,* 169.

Epilogue

1. Rear Admiral Daniel V. Gallery, USN, *Twenty Million Tons Under the Sea,* epilogue, 22.

2. Peter Padfield, *Dönitz: The Last Fuehrer,* foreword.

3. Rear Admiral Samuel E. Morison, USN, *The Two-Ocean War,* 563.

4. Captain John M. Waters, Jr., USCG, "What Manner of Men Were They?", *Sea History,* spring 1985, 24.

5. H. K. Thompson, Jr., and Henry Strutz, ed., *Dönitz at Nuremberg: A Reappraisal;* Rear Admiral D. V. Gallery, *Twenty Million Tons,* epilogue, 23.

BIBLIOGRAPHY

Primary Sources

Interviews and Correspondence

Alline, John (C)
Ashworth, Vice Admiral Frederick, USN (Ret.) (C)
Anderson, Lieutenant Commander Edwin L., USNR, (I & C)
Alston, Lieutenant Commander Norman, USNR, (I & C)
Bain, Wells, (C)
Belsito, Frank (I & C)
Bennett, James J. (C)
Blackburn, Lieutenant Commander Leo, USNR, (C)
Blalock, James (I & C)
Bondhus, Harold M., Lieutenant Commander, USNR (C)
Book, H. E. (C)
Brownell, Irving (C)
Braynard, Frank O. (C)
Burke, Cornelius A. (C)
Callahan, William J. (telephone interviews)
Carleton, James (I & C)
Cauble, Kenneth (I & C)
Chamberlin, Robert (C)
Clasen, Kenneth S. (C)
Coleman, "Jack" (I & C)

Cronin, N. Paul (C)
Cusick, John (C)
Dale, C. K. (C)
Dale, E. M. (deceased—family supplied tape & correspondence)
Davies, James, (I)
Davis, Francis E. (C)
DeFoe, Captain Stansel, USN (Ret) (C)
Driscoll, John A. (C)
Duffy, George W. (C)
Dunkerley, John (I & C)
Firer, Donald P. (C)
Fox, Rev. Ruston (telephone)
Gibson, Creal (telephone & correspondence)
Golos, Henry J. (C)
Gonzales, Alfred R. (I & C)
Grasty, Arno L. (I & C)
Gullage, Leo J. (I & C)
Gurda, Michael, Lieutenant Commander, USNR (C)
Handy, James D. (C)
Harrison, E. G. (C)
Hecht, Joseph E. (C)
Hedge, Thomas J. (C)
Heitzinger, Robert (I & C)
Hoffman, James D. (C)
Hogan, Edward (I & C)
Hogan, Robert R. (C)
Hudgins, George V. (C)
Hudnall, Richard C. (C)
Hunsaker, Q. M. (I & C)
Jones, Clifton E. (C)
Jones, Floyd (C)
Jones, Max (I)
Kaplan, Irving, Lieutenant Commander, USNR (C)
Kincade, Lieutenant Commander Paul B., USN (Ret.) (I & C)
Kittleman, Glen B. (I & C)
Knopf, Edward K. (I & C)
Koch, Harry A. (C)
Krupski, Edward J. (C)
Kushner, Joseph (I & C)
La Fontaine, Larry (I & C)
Layton, Leonard (C)

Leoni, Nicholas (C)
Lloyd, Charles A. (I & C)
Makowski, Hilary (C)
Martinez, Rosalio T. (I & C)
McCormick, Lieutenant Commander Harold J., USNR (C)
McKee, Bates E. (telephone & correspondence)
MacLaren, Arthur (I & C)
McLaughlin, William J. (C)
Meadows, Eugene D. (C)
Michler, Manley (I & C)
Millhoupt, Firel W. (C)
Miller, George H. (I & C)
Molinari, Michael (C)
Montgomery, Carlin (I & C)
Norch, Herbert (I)
Norling, Robert (telephone & correspondence)
Odegaard, Dr. Charles E. (C)
Ossman, Carl G. (C)
Peters, Walter (I & C)
Phillips, William L., RN (C)
Pohl, John J. (C)
Prestmo, George (I & C)
Quin, Edward E. (I & C)
Railsback, Grady (I & C)
Reche, Captain Reinhart, FGN (Ret.) (C)
Rego, Edward (C)
Rice, Chester W. (C)
Rigg, Lee (deceased—material authorized by wife) (C)
Ritter, Louis V. (C)
Roberts, Howard (I & C)
Robinson, Gilbert, Lieutenant Commander, USNR (I & C)
Ross, E. (C)
Roy, Raymond J. (C)
Sanders, Ernest M. (C)
Sexton, Lieutenant Commander John E. (telephone & correspondence)
Sheridan, John E. (C)
Sossaman, Gerald D. (I & C)
Stilinovich, William (telephone & correspondence)
Stone, Cullie (telephone & correspondence)
Suggett, Robert (I)

Trowbridge, Lieutenant Commander Le Roy, USNR (C)
Vigh, Louis (C)
Villares, Robert J. (C)
Watson, William P. (C)
Wells, Ivy R. (C)
Welsh, DeWitt (C)
Whalen, Riccard (C)
Williams, Richard E. (C)
Williams, Robert E. (I & C)
Wilmot, Lieutenant Commander King A., USNR (C)
Wolff, Robert H. (I & C)
Zeidler, Frank A. (C)
Zubrod, Donald E. (C)

U.S. Government

History of Naval Armed Guard Afloat in World War II (OP 414), Director of Naval History, Fleet Maintenance Division (undated, unpublished). Operational Archives Branch, Naval Historical Center.

History of the AG Center (Pacific), Treasure Island, San Francisco. Appendix H (12th Naval District, 13 November 1945), unbound. Office of Naval History.

Dictionary of American Naval Fighting Ships. Vols. 1, 4, 7, 8. Naval Historical Center, Washington, D.C.

"Estimate of the Situation Arming Merchant Vessels with Naval Guns for Defense." 1 March 1917, Captain W. Pitt Scott, USN. Naval Records Collection of the Office of Naval Records and Library, National Archives (RG 45) Box 523/525.

"The Armed Guard Section," 25 October 1918, Ensign Ralph Hornblower, USNR. National Archives (RG 45) Box 520.

"Ships having Armed Guards, Captured and Sunk by Gunfire/Bombs Placed on Board/Other Causes," 5 March 1920. National Archives (RG 45) Box 520.

"Arming of Merchant Vessels for Armed Guard Service," (1919) Office of Naval Records and Library. National Archives (RG 45).

"Exchange of Destroyers for Air and Naval Bases." U.S. Department of State Bulletin, 7 September 1940. El Paso Public Library, Government Records.

"The U.S. Merchant Marine at War," final report of the Administrator, WSA, 15 January 1946, El Paso Public Library, Government Records.

"Navy Purchases of Middle East Oil" Senate Report, Part V, 22 April 1943 and 28 April 1948. National Archives, serial unknown, copy furnished by source.

"German Espionage Latin America" (Chapter 6—"Argentina") FBI Monograph (1946), Modern Military Field Branch, National Records Center, Suitland, Md.

"Sinkings in 5th Naval District" Office of CNO, press release 16 September 1945. Location unknown, copy furnished by source.

Numerous Armed Guard Officer Voyage Reports to CNO, National Archives, Filed by ship (RG 38).

"Summaries of Statements of Survivors," National Archives, filed by ship. (RG 38).

Secondary Sources

Books—WWI

Blair, Clay. *Silent Victory.* Philadelphia/New York: Lippincott Co., 1975.

Brinin, John M. *The Sway of the Grand Saloon.* New York: Delacorte Press, 1971.

Commager, Henry Steele. *Documents of American History, 9th Edition.* Englewood Cliffs, New Jersey: Prentice Hall, 1973.

Connally, James B. *The U-Boat Hunters.* New York: Charles Scribner Sons, 1918.

Daniels, Josephus. *Our Navy at War.* U.S. Navy: Pictorial Bureau, 1922.

Emmon, Frederick. *The Atlantic Liners.* New York: Bonanza Books, 1977.

Ferrell, Robert H. *Woodrow Wilson and World War I.* New York: Harper and Row, 1985.

Hart, Captain B. Liddell *The Real War 1914–1918.* Boston: Little, Brown & Co., 1930 and 1964.

Hoehling, A. H. *Lost at Sea.* Harrisburg: Stackpole Books, 1984.

Hough, Richard. *The Great War at Sea 1914–18.* London: Oxford University Press, 1983.

Hoyt, Edwin. *Raider Wolf.* New York: Paul S. Eriksson Pub., 1974.

Jellicoe, J. R. *The Submarine Peril.* London: Her Majesty's Stationery Office, 1924.

Lansing, Robert. *War Memoirs of Robert Lansing.* New York: Bobbs-Merrill Co., 1935.

McMaster, John B. *The U.S. in World War (1918–20).* New York: D. Appleton, Co., 1920.

Miller, William H. *The Great Luxury Liners.* New York: Dover Publications, 1981 reprint.

Morison, Elting E. *Admiral Sims and the Modern U.S. Navy.* Boston: Houghton Mifflin Co., 1942.

Potter, E. B. *Illustrated History of the U.S. Navy.* New York: Crowell, 1971.

Reynolds, Clark W. *Command of the Sea.* New York: William Morrow & Co., 1974.

Simonds, Frank H. *History of the World War.* New York: Doubleday Page & Co., 1919.

Thomas, Lowell. *Raiders of the Deep.* New York: Garden City Publications, 1928.

Winston, John. *Convoy.* London: Michael Joseph, Publications, 1920.

Books—World War II

Ships of the Esso Fleet in World War II. New York: Standard Oil Co. of New Jersey, 1946.

Allen, William L. *Anzio: Edge of Disaster.* New York: Elsevier-Dutton, 1978.

Beach, Captain Edward L., USN., *The U.S. Navy.* New York: H. Holt & Co., 1986.

Bell, Robert W. *In Peril on the Sea.* Garden City: Doubleday & Co., 1984.

Berry, Lieutenant Robert B., USNR. *Gunners Get Glory.* New York: Bobbs-Merrill Co., 1943.

Bradford, Ernle. *Siege Malta.* New York: William Morrow & Co., 1986.

Breuer, William C. *Operation Torch.* New York: St. Martins Press, 1985.

Buchanan, Russell A. *The U.S. and World War II, vol. 2.* New York: Harper and Row, 1964.

Buell, Thomas. *Master of Sea Power.* Boston: Little, Brown & Co., 1980.

Bunker, John G. *Liberty Ships.* New York: Arno Press, 1980.

Carpenter, D., and N. Polmar. *Submarines of the Imperial Japanese Navy.* Annapolis: Naval Institute Press, 1986.

Carse, Robert. *Cold Corner of Hell.* New York: Doubleday-Garden City, 1969.

Churchill, Winston S. *The Hinge of Fate.* Boston: Houghton Mifflin Co., 1950.

———. *Memoirs of the Second World War.* Boston: Houghton Mifflin, 1959.

Costello, John. *The Pacific War (1941–44).* New York: Rawson Wade, 1971.

Dawson, R. H. *The Decision to Aid Russia—1941.* Durham, North Carolina: University of NC Press, 1959.

Dönitz, Grossadmiral Karl. *Memoirs.* Cleveland: World Publishing, 1958.

Dower, John W. *War Without Mercy.* New York: Pantheon Books, 1986.

Ellsberg, Commander E., USN. *Under the Red Sea Sun.* New York: Dodd, Mead & Co., 1946.

Elson, Robert T. *Prelude to War.* New York: Time-Life Books, 1977.

Gallery, Rear Admiral Daniel V., USN. *Twenty Million Tons Under the Sea.* Chicago: Henry Regnery Company, 1957.

Gibson, Charles D. *Merchantman? Or Ship of War.* Camden: Ensign Press, 1986.

Havighurst, Walter. *The Miami Years.* New York: G. P. Putnam Sons, 1958.

Hoehling, A. *The Great War at Sea.* New York: Thomas Crowell Co., 1965.

Holmes, Captain W. J., USN. *Undersea Victory.* New York: Doubleday, 1966.

Hoyt, Edwin P. *Japan's War.* New York: McGraw-Hill Book Co., 1986.

Hoyt, Edwin P. *U-Boats Offshore.* New York: Stein & Day, 1978.

Hughes, T. & J. Costello. *Battle of the Atlantic.* New York: Dial Press, 1977.

Irving, David. *Destruction of PQ-17.* New York: Simon & Schuster, 1968.

Ito, Masanori. *The End of the Imperial Japanese Navy.* New York: Berkley Press, 1984.

Kahn, David. *The Code Breakers.* New York: Macmillan, 1967.

King, Admiral Ernest J., USN, & Commander Walter Whitehill, USNR. *Fleet Admiral King.* New York: W. W. Norton, 1952.

Lash, Joseph P. *Roosevelt & Churchill (1939–41).* New York: W. W. Norton, 1976.

Maclean, Allistair. *HMS Ulysses.* New York: Doubleday & Co., 1956.

Middlebrook, Martin. *Convoy.* London: Penguin Books, 1976.

Miller, Lieutenant Commander Max, USNR. *The Far Shore.* New York: McGraw-Hill, 1945.

Miller, Nathan. *US Navy: An Illustrated History.* New York: American Heritage Publishing, 1977.

Mitchell, C. B. *Every Kind of Shipwork.* New York: Todd Shipyards Corp., 1981.

Montserrat, Nicholas. *The Cruel Sea.* New York: Alfred A. Knopf, 1966. Reprint, Annapolis: Naval Institute Press, 1988.

Moore, Captain Arthur R. *A Careless Word . . . A Needless Sinking.* Kings Point, New York: American Merchant Marine Museum, 1983/1985.

Mordal, Jacques. *25 Centuries of Sea Warfare.* New York: Charles N. Potter, 1965.

Morgan, Ted. *FDR.* New York: Simon & Schuster, 1985.

Morison, Samuel E. *History of U.S. Naval Operations in World War II.* Boston: Little, Brown & Co., 1947 and 1975.

———. *The Two Ocean War: A Short History of the U.S. Navy.* New York: Ballantine Books, 1972.

Morris, Eric. *Salerno.* New York: Stein & Day, 1983.

Noli, Jean. *The Admiral's Wolfpack.* Garden City: Doubleday, 1974.

Padfield, Peter. *Dönitz: The Last Fuehrer.* New York: Harper & Row, 1986.

Piccigallo, Philip. *The Japanese on Trial (1945–1951).* Austin: University of Texas Press, 1979.

Pitt, Barrie. *Battle of the Atlantic.* New York: Time-Life Books, 1980.

Reisenberg, Felix. *Sea War.* New York: Rinehart, 1956.

Rohwer, Jürgen. *The U-Boat Wars—1939–45.* Annapolis: Naval Institute Press, 1983.

———. *Critical Convoy Battles of March '43.* Annapolis: Naval Institute Press, 1973.

———. *Axis Submarine Successes—1939–45.* Annapolis: Naval Institute Press, 1983.

———. *Chronology of the War at Sea (1939–45), vol. 1 & 2.* New York: Arco Publishing, 1972.

Roskill, Captain Stephen, RN. *Churchill and the Admirals.* New York: William Morrow Co., 1978.

Sawyer, L. A., & E. Mitchell. *Liberty Ships.* Cambridge, Maryland: Cornell Maritime Press, 1970.

Schofield, William G. *Eastward the Convoys.* Chicago: Rand McNally, 1965.

Shtemenko, General S. M. *The Last Six Months.* New York: Double-day & Co., 1977.

Sheridan, John M. *Linda and the Gunner's Mate.* New York: Carlton Press, 1985.

Sill, V. R. *American Miracle.* New York: Odyssey Press, 1947.

Snyder, Louis L. *The War 1939–1945.* New York: Simon & Schuster, 1960.

Stettinius, Edward R. *Lend-Lease.* New York: Macmillan Co., 1944.

Sulzberger, C. L. *Picture History of World War II.* New York: Time-Life Books, Inc., 1950.

Taylor, Theodore. *Fire on the Beaches.* New York: W. W. Norton, Inc., 1958.

Thompson, H. K. and H. Strutz. *Dönitz at Nuremberg: A Reappraisal.* New York: Amber Publishing Co., 1976.

Tolischus, Otto D. *Through Japanese Eyes.* New York: Cornwall Press, 1945.

Turner, L. G. F., H. R. Gordon-Cummings, and J. E. Betzler. *War in the Southern Oceans.* London: Oxford University Press, 1961.

Vaughn-Thomas, W. *Anzio.* New York: Rinehart & Winston, 1961.

Warner, Denis. *The Sacred Warriors.* New York: Van Nostrand Reinhold, 1982.

Waters, Captain John M., USCG. *Bloody Winter.* Princeton: Van Nostrand, 1967.

Werner, Herbert A. *Iron Coffins.* New York: Holt, Rinehart & Winston, 1969.

Whipple, A. B. *The Mediterranean.* New York: Time-Life Books, 1981.

Periodicals

"Liberty Ship." *American Society of Mechanical Engineers,* 18 September 1984.

Anderson, N. O. "Why the U.S. Requires a Merchant Marine." *Naval Engineers Journal.* March 1986, reprint of July 1935.

Barger, Mervin D. "Getting the Goods to the Beach." *Surface Warfare,* January/February 1980.

Bennett, James. "Forgotten Heroes." *Sea Classics,* August 1987.

Bennett, Ralph K. "The Toshiba Scandal." *Reader's Digest,* December 1987.

Britton, Lieutenant Commander Beverley, USNR. "Stepchildren of the Navy." *Proceedings,* December 1947.

Burke, C. A. "Yuletide in Murmansk." *Philadelphia Bulletin,* 24 December 1978.

Chapman, Warren. "Floating Firecrackers." *Mechanix Illustrated,* September 1943.

Demars, Vice Admiral Bruce, USN. "Supersub of the 1990's." *Sea Power,* 9 August 1987.

Dorn, David R. "Ships for Victory." *Proceedings,* February 1985.

Giaccone, Joseph. "Oral History of the S.S. *John Barry."* NMU *Pilot,* May 1987.

Guillen, Michael. "The S.S. John Brown." *Sea History,* Autumn 1986.

Hoyt, Edwin P. "Predator Beyond All Rules." *Military History,* February 1985.

Johnson, Haynes. "FDR, Reagan and Risks." *Washington Post,* 3 June 1987.

Kimmelman, Donald. "Wintry Murmansk." *Philadelphia Inquirer,* 5 February 1984.

Meyer, S. M., Jr. "How We Closed the Port of New York." *Sea History,* summer 1987.

Millar, Ian. "The Sea Raider Michel." *Sea Classics,* June 1985.

Norling, Bob L. "Kamikazes Scored On My Liberty Ship." *Boston Globe,* March 1985.

Ruark, Lieutenant Robert, USNR. "They Called 'Em Fish Food." *Saturday Evening Post,* 6 May 1944.

Sudhalter, D. L. "How Hurry-Up Henry Helped to Win the War." *The Retired Officer,* August 1986.

Memoirs

Odegaard, Dr. Charles E. "Memo of My Service in the USN 1942–46." Unpublished memoirs 6 May 1982.

Grasty, Arno L. "Sixteen Days in a Lifeboat." Unpublished memoir.

Miscellaneous

Great Soviet Encyclopedia (vol. 14). Translation of third edition, El Paso Public Library: Collier McMillan, London.

INDEX

Abadan, 344–45
Achee, Willie, 150
Aconit, 230
Addu Atoll, 340
Aden, 92, 329, 345
Africander, 182
Aldersdale, 196
Aleutians, 302–3
Alexandria, 260, 270
Algiers, 275
Alston, Lieutenant Commander Norman, USNR, 36, 58, 68, 344
Alther, 2/M George, 166
American Merchant Marine Museum, 125, 387
Ames, Ensign M. K., USNR, 253
Anderson, Lieutenant Commander Edward, USNR, 110, 130–34, 163
Anzio-Nettuno, 279, 290–95, 314, 319
Archangel, 171, 188, 192, 197–99, 202, 210–15, 341
Ariizumi, Commander Tatsunosuke, 351–52, 357
Armed Ship Bill, 5
Arnold, Lieutenant John S., II, USNR, 108–9
Aruba, 232, 262

Arzeu, 276
Asdic, 14, 224
Atlantis (Ship No. 16), 124–26
Avola, 286
Azerbaijan, 195, 205

B-Dienst, 227, 234, 237, 244
Bahia, 344
Bain, Wells, 163
Baker, BM 2/C Wayne, USN, 186
Balchunas, G/M Johnny, 312
Bandär Shapur, 344
Barber, Commander J. Lee, 185
Bari, 295–98, 371
Barker, Moses, 137
Barnes, S 2/C Ted, 137
Bass, Coxswain Charles J., 262
Bauer, Commodore Herman, 3
Bayley, Lieutenant George T., USNR, 348
Bazaruto Island, 338
Bear Island, 173, 191, 193, 211
Beazely, Franklin, 331–32
Behrendt, Yeoman 3/C D., 129
Belém, 336
Bell, Mrs. Ethel, 330
Belsito, Lieutenant Frank, USNR, 83
Bennett, Jennings J., 127

Bennett, Jim, 30, 64–65, 116, 365
Benson, Rear Admiral William S.,
    USN, 4
Besse, Captain W. F., 166
Best, PFC Russell, 65, 314
Bethlehem Steel, Fairfield Yards,
    86–89, 387
Bevir, Rear Admiral Oliver, RN, 348
Bizerte, 285–86, 289–90, 299, 365
Blackburn, Lieutenant Com-
    mander Harold, USNR, 56, 73
Blalock, Jim, 188
Bletchley Park, 227–28
Bogart, Humphrey, 8, 213
Bombay, 310, 348, 352, 355
Bondhus, Lieutenant Harold, USNR,
    39, 51, 307
Book, Herb, 305
Borum, Lieutenant John R., USNR,
    102
Bourg, S., 198
Boyce, Bob, 102
Boyer, Paul, 137
Bradford, Ernle, 269
Bradshaw, Colonel, 295
Breck, Wallace, 136–37, 168
Brennan, Ensign John J., USNR, 106
Brewton, Ensign Elmer C., USNR,
    263
Brindisi, 300
Brinn, Ensign Rufus T., 32, 174–75
Brisbane, 301, 311
Britton, Lieutenant Commander
    Beverley, USNR, 51, 162
Bronstein, S1/C Harry, 263
Brooklyn AG Center, 24, 38, 66, 171,
    231
Brownell, Irving, 28, 145
Buck, Captain Paul, 136–37
Buenos Aires, 332
Bullock, S 2/C Virgil, 137
Burke, C. A. "Pete", 33–34, 48, 115,
    221, 283, 362

Calcutta, 340, 346–47, 351–52
Callahan, BM William C., 8
Cameron, James C., 103
Camp Shelton, VA. *See* Little Creek
Cape Horn, 325–27, 333

Cape of Good Hope, 270, 337
Capetown, 333, 369, 375–76
Carraway, Ensign Howard E.,
    USNR, 201–3
Carroll, Ensign Charles, USNR, 199
Carter, Lieutenant William A., 186
Casablanca, 217, 284, 365
"Cash & Carry Act," 13
Cauble, Kenneth, 117, 122
Centaur, 351
Chamberlin, C/M Arthur, Jr., 136,
    165, 168
Chapman, BM 1/C Warren, NAG,
    47, 175–76, 329
Charlotte Schliemann, 133, 337
Chase, Captain Harry W., 332
Cheyne, Stout R., 261
Christian Michelsen, 299
Churchill, Winston S., 3, 16–18, 111,
    189, 206, 208, 250, 261, 399; Ad-
    miralty protests over Arctic con-
    voys, 395; Battle of the Atlantic,
    224–25, 231; comments on PQ-17
    disaster, 206–8; complaints re
    lack of U.S. convoy escorts, U.S.
    East Coast, 261; requests for U.S.
    aid, 16
Clasen, Kenneth E., 196–97
Clee, Ensign Gilbert, USNR, 45
Cleveland, Captain Edward,
    USNR, 27
Coakley, Captain William J., 61, 174
Coastal Command (Caribbean),
    260–61
Code Breaking, 227–28, 234, 237,
    244
Coleman, Jack, 298
Colombo, 351
Convoys: experimental, 3, 112; ob-
    jections to, 2, 3, 381, 385; organi-
    zation of, 113–15, 390, 398; U.S.
    reluctance to adopt, 111–12, 114;
    use of blimps, 256–58; CU-15,
    140–41; HX-21, 105; HX-228, 234;
    HX-229, 119–20, 237–39, 244;
    KS-520, 120, 153; MSK-9, 154;
    ONS-144, 175; PQ-8, 170; PQ-13,
    120, 170, 175; PQ-14, 175; PQ-17,
    119, 173, 178–79, 185–86, 190–

209, 283, 395–96; PQ-18, 180, 187, 341; QP-13, 185, 192–93; QP-14, 208; RA-53, 186; RA-64, 184–85; SC-122, 119, 237, 239; UGS-38, 83

Copassaki, Chief Boatswain's Mate Andrew, 7

Coughlin, Captain Dan J., 314, 316

Cox, Seaman 2/C T.P., 134

Cramm, Ensign Kendall, USNR, 165

Cronin, Lieutenant N. Paul, USNR, 38, 363

Cronk, S/Eng. George, 137

Croteau, Norman, 184–85

Cunningham, Sir Andrew, RN, 112

Curaçao, 232, 252

Curran, Joseph, 159

Dale, Boatswain's Mate E. M. "Mac," 338

Daniels, Secretary of the Navy Josephus, 1, 10, 382

Davis, Frank E., 167, 254, 346

Death Railroad, 310

Deazmond, Velton L., 262

DeFoe, Captain Stansel E., USN, 36

Delaney, Chief Boatswain's Mate James, 8, 382

Delaney, Coxswain Leonard D., 263

DEMS, 158

Destroyers for Bases, 16

Diller, George, Sr., 150

Dodd, Commander, RN, 235

Dodrill, S 2/C Arthur, 335

Domonkos, Michael, 256

Dönitz, Gross Admiral Karl: admitted loss of Battle of Atlantic, 245, 398–99; breaking of U-boat communications, 245; convoy battle with SC-122/HX-229, 244; differences with Hitler, 223–24; named successor to Hitler, 246; Nuremberg Trials, 377–78; operations in southern waters, 337, 344; order to U-boats to cease fire, 372; replacement of Grand Admiral Raeder, 246; report of Allied merchant vessels sunk by U-boats, 247; report of U-boats lost, 247; use of *B-Dienst*, 227,

234, 244; use of Italian submarines, 227–28; World War I service, 223; mentioned, 3, 119, 222–26, 228–29, 253–55, 260, 327, 372

Dowding, Commodore J. C. K., RNR, 190, 196, 205

Drechsler, Arthur, 356

Dryer, Ensign W., USNR, 130

Duffy, George W., 128–30

Dunkerly, Coxswain John, 333

Ebato, Lt. Kasuro, 351, 358

Edel, S 1/C George J., 285

Eisenhower, Lieutenant General Dwight D., USA, 284

Ellis, Captain T. C., 234

Ellsberg, Commander Edward, USN, 164

Enigma, 227–28

Eopolucci, John J., 7

Evans, Chief Mate Richard, 356

Firer, Donald P., 322

Fittipaldi, S 1/C Phillip, 356

Fonda, Henry, 301, 309

Forrestal, Secretary of the Navy James, 99, 281

Forsdal, John J., 251

Frankel, Captain S. B., USN, 206, 220

French Fleet, 270

Freundlick, Junior Engineer Frank, 139

Frömsdorf, Oberleutnant Helmut, 372

Gallery, Rear Admiral Daniel V., USN, 377–78

Garner, Bob, 150

Gawlik, S 1/C Walter A., 139

Gerlach, Captain Horst, 135

German Surface Fleet: *Admiral Hipper*, 193; *Admiral Scheer*, 193; *Bismarck*, 193; *Emden*, 123, 391; *Lutzow*, 193; 1939 status, 13–14; *Scharnhorst*, 211, 213; Sea Raiders, 123–37, 391; *Tirpitz*, 191, 193–94, 207; Versailles Treaty Limitations, 12

Gibson, Signalman 2/C Creal "Irish," 280
Gilbride, John T., 157
Gilman, Ensign H. P., 108
Goldstein, Coxswain David, 101
Gonzales, Al, 28, 149, 309
Goudy, Lieutenant Harry Chester, USNR, 355–56
Grasty, Arno L., 337
Graves, Captain Edward L., 195
Grayson, Rear Admiral Cary, USN, 4
Great Lakes Naval Station, 29, 46, 384
Great Soviet Encylopedia, 19–20
Grills, Lieutenant N. G., 257
Gulfport Training Station, 98. See NOLA
Gurda, Lieutenant Michael, USNR, 333–34
Gysae, Lieutenant Robert, 339

Hallenby, Brigadier General G. W., 281
Hamilton, Rear Admiral L. H. K., RN, 190–91, 194
Handy, James D., 35, 80, 109, 258
Hansen, Captain John, 348
Harper, Thomas E., 296
Hart, Captain B. H. Liddell, 2, 381
Hartley, Lieutenant John J., 319
Hecht, SMC Joseph E., 178
Hedge, Thomas, 68
Heggen, Thomas, 301
Heitzinger, Radioman 3/C Bob, 143–44
Herbert, Cadet/Midshipman John, 289
Herzog, Lieutenant William Randolph, USNR, 104–5
Hewitt, Admiral C. I. C., USN, 292
Hey, Daniel, USN, 251
Hicks, Lieutenant Robert B., USNR, 32
Hill, Lieutenant Commander, 241
Hitler, Adolf, 13, 73, 75, 124, 190–91, 193, 222–24, 245–46, 269, 295
Hoan, Dan, 374
Hodge, Al, 290

Hoffman, C/M Jim, 165
Hoge, Vice Admiral Friedrich, 134
Hog Island, 69–70, 156–58, 387
Hopkins, Harry, 261
Houghton, Lieutenant Edward W., 232
Howard, B. B., 166
Hudnall, Richard C., 308, 323
"Huff-Duff" (High Frequency Direction Finding), 225, 229, 245

Ingram, Vice Admiral Jonas, USN, 327
Irving, David, 201
Isenberg, Lieutenant Lester, USNR, 292
Italian Navy: submarines, 226, 276, 335–36; Surface Force, 269; 10th Light Flotilla, 270–72, 400
Iwanami, Captain Hiroshi, 357
Izzi, S 2/C Basil Dominic, 331

Jackson, A. C., 242
Jan Mayen Island, 180, 191, 193
Japan: atrocities, 349–57, 406–7; kamikazes, 313, 322; merchant marine losses, 323; submarines, 302, 323, 349–57
Jellicoe, 1st Sea Lord Sir John, RN, 3
Jenks, Captain A.B., 296
Johnson, Lieutenant Roscoe E., USNR, 336
Johnson Debt-Default Act, 18
Jones, Floyd, 23–24, 313
Jones, Max, 220

Kaiser, Henry J., 36, 86–88
Kaplan, Lieutenant Irving, USNR, 38, 176–78
Karlsson, Captain Gustav O., 130–32, 163
Kastber, Chief Mate Herman, 271
Kauffman, George, 340
Kincade, Lieutenant Commander Paul, USN, 33–34, 264–65
Kindl, Coxswain Fred J., 233
King, Fleet Admiral Ernest J., USN, 111–13

Kittleman, Glen, 147
Knight, Sir Henry, 348
Knopf, Ed, 266–67
Koch, Harry, 166
Kreimar, William A., 101
Kretschmer, Kapitan Otto, 119, 228
Krupski, Ed, 72
Kudo, Captain Kaneo, 356, 358
Kusaka, Lieutenant Commander T., 355, 358
Kushner, Joseph, 71–72

LaBounty, Captain, 34
Lafferty, Joseph, 8–10
LaFontaine, Larry, 302, 328–29
LaGuardia, Mayor Fiorello, 375
Land, Admiral Emory S., USN, 85, 157
Landis, Lieutenant John M., USNR, 320
Laney, Jimmy, 266–67
Lansing, Secretary of State Robert, 5
Lawson, Lieutenant George S., USNR, 323
Layman, Bob, 220
Layton, Leonard, 22
Lemnitzer, General Lyman, 274
Lend-Lease: Lend-Lease Act, 18; sailings, 387; Soviet lack of appreciation, 19–21; volume of aid, 383
Liberty ships, 69, 387; background, 84–86; design, 84–88; problems, 85–88; production technique/volume, 86–89
Lind, Captain Henning, 61
Little Creek, VA, 23, 24, 38, 40, 42, 46
Lloyd, C. A., 61, 407
Lloyd, Lonnie Whitson, 368–76
LoPresti, Sam, 330
Luce, Clare Booth, 16
Luth, Lieutenant Commander Wolfgang, 267, 337
Lyman, 2/M Joseph, 136

MacArthur, General Douglas, 317
McCormick, Lieutenant Commander Harold J., 37, 153, 332, 339
McIllwane, Lieutenant Robert, USNR, 108
MacIntyre, Captain Donald, RN, 244, 381
MacLaren, Art, 213
McLaughlin, Sergeant Bill, 304
Maddox, Lieutenant James, USNR, 41, 331–32
Makowski, Hilary, 214, 218–19
Marshall, Ensign Hunter, USNR, 107
Martinez, Rosalio, 81–82
Meadows, Eugene, 151, 212
Merchant shipping losses: Battle of the Atlantic, 247; British, 247; Japanese, 323; Liberty ships, 81; *Luftwaffe*, 222–24, 246, 277–83, 360–61; Murmansk run, 189, 205, 206; Mediterranean, 300; sunk by U-Boats, 247; tankers, 81; U.S., 387; U.S. 5th Naval District, 267; U.S., WW I, 10
Miami University, 29–30
Michler, Manley, 34, 309
Miller, C/M George, 165
Miller, Lieutenant Commander Max, USNR, 363
Miller Lieutenant George, USNR, 311–12
Miller, Tex, 330
Millhoupt, Firal W., 29
Mitchell, John, 215, 231
Mlodzik, A., 130
Mogenson, Seaman 2/C C., 130
Molinari, Mike, 27, 146–47, 364–65
Molotov, V. M., 207
Montgomery, Carlin, 303, 312
Moore, Captain Arthur R., 387
Morgan, Joe, 348
Morison, Rear Admiral Samuel E., USN, 159, 161, 378
Morton, Lieutenant Gordon, 340
MS *Justine Foss*, 350
MS *Sawokla*, 126–27
MS *Spidolene*, 117
Muldrow, J. C., 134

MV *American Leader*, 126–29, 391
MV *Blenheim*, 73, 74, 75

Nakagawa, Lieutenant Com-
    mander H., 351, 358
National Maritime Union, 159;
    NMU pilot, 345, 405
Neely, Ensign E. S., USNR, 186
Nerger, Captain Karl, 123–24
Neutrality Act, 14; changes, 19; eva-
    sion of, 14–17, 19, 384
New Yorker Book of War Pieces, 331
Nibouar, GM E/C John, 260
Niedermair, John, 366
Nillson, Captain David M., 351
Nimitz, Admiral Chester W., 378
Nishiuchi, Lieutenant Com-
    mander, 358
NOLA, 27, 44, 46, 62, 101
Norch, Herb, 28, 63, 294, 365
Norling, Signalman 3/C Bob, 315–
    16, 331
North Carolina Shipbuilding
    Corp., 96
Novaya Zemlya, 196, 197, 199, 200,
    205

Odegaard, Lieutenant Commander
    Charles E., USNR, 40, 42, 49–50,
    53, 59, 75, 375
O'Hara, Cadet/Midshipman Ed-
    win, 110, 125, 136–37, 165
Oliver, John, 335
Operation Avalanche, 288
Operation Husky, 285
Operation *Paukenschlag*, 248–49,
    267
Operation *Rösselsprung*, 191
Operation Torch, 226, 274, 276, 281,
    284
Oppacich, Peter, 252
Ossman, Lieutenant Carl G.,
    USNR, 37

Padfield, Peter, 378
Panama Transport Co., 261
Patton, General, 334
Peck, Chief Eng., 183
Peltz, Major General, 296

Peron, Colonel Juan, 404
Perrierre, Commander Lothar Jon
    Arnauld de la, 2
Person, John O., 261
Peters, Walter, 80, 117, 167, 327
Petersen, SM 2/C Herbert A., 187
Pharr, Captain Frank, 317–18
Phillips, Able Seaman William L.,
    RN, 184–85, 272, 395
Pilling, Ensign Frank, USNR, 240
Poche, Captain James, 250
Pohl, John J., 151
Port Chicago explosion, 150
Ports of call: Darwin, 322; Durban,
    335, 337; Eniwetok, 302; Espiritu
    Santo, 302; Fiji, 350; Gela, 284,
    285, 286; Gibraltar, 270, 271, 272,
    273, 275, 285; Gooseberry Break-
    water, 361; Guadalcanal, 35, 303,
    304; Guam, 312, 322; Halifax,
    N. S., 103, 114, 174, 175; Hol-
    landia, 314, 317; Hormoz, 345;
    Hvalfjord, 190; Karachi, 356;
    Kwajalein, 302, 312; Khorram-
    shahr, 346; Leyte, 301, 312, 317–
    19; Loche Ewe, 145, 171, 177, 179,
    180; Liverpool, 163, 276, 362;
    London, 359–60; Lourenço Mar-
    ques, 340; Malta, 171, 268, 269,
    272, 287, 400; Madagascar, 339;
    Mindoro, 318–19; Mombasa, 335;
    Murmansk, 170–89, 190–209,
    283, 299, 301, 329, 341–43, 369;
    Molotovsk, 171, 177, 179, 202, 210,
    215–18; Naples, 280, 290, 292–
    94, 299; New Guinea, 303, 306,
    307, 308, 309, 312; New Cale-
    donia, 305; Noumea, 302; Oki-
    nawa, 301, 319–22; Omaha Beach,
    363–65; Oran, 93, 274, 276; Pa-
    lermo, 285–86; Panama Canal,
    349; Perth, 311, 344; Phillippe-
    ville, 280–82; Port Elizabeth,
    328; Ras Al-Tannurah, 345; Reyk-
    javik, 171, 178, 201, 203; Rio de
    Janeiro, 257; Saipan, 312, 322;
    Salerno, 279, 288–90, 294, 314;
    San Pedro Bay, 315; Sicily, 258,
    279, 284, 287, 288, 294, 371; Singa-
    pore, 305; St. John's, Newfound-

land, 74, 103, 370; Suez Canal, 268, 270, 324, 345; Sydney, 310; Tacloban, 314, 315, 316, 318; Tinian, 308, 312, 322, 323; Trinidad, 257, 261, 262, 330, 333; Tunis, 275; Truk, 357; Ulithi, 302, 312, 357; Utah Beach, 363–65; Wake Island, 350; Windward Passage, 260, 264, 265

Potter, Captain Tom, 330
Potter, E. B., 3, 13, 15
Pound, Admiral Sir Dudley, RN, 195, 207
Prestmo, George, 23, 233, 275, 277
Pyle, Charles E., 351
Pyle, Ernie, 293

Q ships, 4
Quin, Ed, 22–23, 141–42, 211

Raeder, Grand Admiral Erich, 191, 246, 377
Railsback, Grady, 121
Ramsey, Admiral Lord, RN, 16
Reche, Captain Reinhart, 208, 396
Rego, Seaman 1/C Edmund P., 109, 235
Rehse, Henry, 251
Richardson, Charles, 168–69
Rigg, Lee, 310
Ritter, Louis V., 120, 299
Roberts, Howard, 302
Robinson, Lieutenant Commander Gilbert, USNR, 38, 54, 57, 169, 359
Rohr, Lieutenant Joseph, 375
Rohwer, Dr. Jürgen, 350
Roosevelt, President Franklin D., 171, 261, 297; declaration of neutrality, 14; destroyers for bases, 15; evasion of Neutrality Act, 14–17, 19, 384; "fireside chats," 18, 37; line of demarcation, U.S. Navy and air patrols, 20; support of Arctic convoys, 271, 395; "ugly ducklings," 85
Roskill, Captain Stephan R., RN, 112, 134
Roy, PFC Ray, 65, 142, 145–46, 392
Royal Navy: HMT *Ayrshire*, 202;

HMS *Bluebell*, 183; HMS *Curacoa*, 142; HMS *Devonshire*, 126; HMS *Duke of York*, 191; HMS *Eskimo*, 181; HMS *Harvester*, 234, 235; HMS *Impulsive*, 187; HMS *Lotus*, 196; HMS *Mansfield*, 241; HMS *Onslaught*, 182; HMS *Opportune*, 184, 185, 272; HMS *Queen Elizabeth*, 270; HMRS *Rathlin*, 195; HMS *St. Elston*, 90; HMS *Sydney*, 123; HMS *Valiant*, 270; HMS *Verain*, 175; HMS *Victorious*, 191; HMS *Vimy*, 331; HMS *Volunteer*, 237; HMS *York*, 270

Ruark, Lieutenant Robert, USNR, 42–43, 46, 49, 55–56, 162, 340
Ruud, Karl O., 139

Saikabara, Rear Admiral Shigematsu, 350
Sanders, Ernie, 188, 263–64
Sarrazin, Hartswohl E., 130, 132
Schmidt, GM 1/C Hilmer C., 321
Schniewind, Admiral, 193
Schofield, Lieutenant William C., USNR, 40
Schopmeyer, Joe, 335
Schwinn, H. H., 242
Scott, Captain W. Pitt, USN, 5–6
Selness, Captain T. C., 253
Sexton, Lieutenant John E., USNR, 204, 208
Shayer, Radioman 3/C William H., 199
Sheridan, G/M 2/C John, 171–72, 174, 210
Ships, merchant (SS):
  Abraham Lincoln, 279
  Adoniram Judson, 95–96
  Alamar, 185
  Albert Watts, 7
  Alcoa Pathfinder, 153
  Alcoa Pioneer, 316–17
  Alcoa Puritan, 143
  Alcoa Ranger, 121, 199–200, 206
  Alexander H. Stephens, 149
  Alexander White, 68
  Alice F. Palmer, 337
  Aramis, 133

Ships, merchant (SS) (*continued*)
Ariaga, 261
Artigas, 214, 217
Augustus Thomas, 315–16
Aztec, 7
Beacon Hill, 214–15
Benjamin Brewster, 256
Benjamin Harrison, 204–5, 209, 283
Benjamin Ide Wheeler, 65, 314–17
Benjamin Wilson, 405–7
Bering, 214
Big Foot Wallace, 92, 346–48
Black Point, 371–72
Bluefields, 253
Brant County, 235
Brilliant. See destroyer escort
John R. Borum, 96, 103
Brookfield, 147
Brunswick, 263–64
Bullfinch, 61
Bushrod Washington, 289
Byron D. Benson, 143
C. J. Barkdull, 277
C. O. Stillman, 262
Caloria, 72
Camp Fire, 179
Cape Neddick, 333–34
Cape Romano, 316
Capillo, 350
Capital Reef, 312
Carleton, 196, 203
Cedar Mills, 95
Chant, 272–73
Charles Goodyear, 293
Charles McAllister, 187
Charles Willson Peale, 336
Chilore, 253
Chr. J. Kampmann, 263
Christopher Newport, 194, 203
Cities Service Toledo, 35, 258–59
City of Omaha, 214, 220
Clement Clay, 279
Colin P. Kelly, Jr., 279
Columbian, 336
Compana, 7
Connecticut, 126
Cornelius Vanderbilt, 326
Courageous, 34

Daisy Moeller, 351
Dalhousie, 133
Daniel Carroll, 298
Daniel Morgan, 196, 197, 198, 199
Daniel Webster, 237
David Bushnell, 51
Dominican Victory, 154
Dona Aurora, 334
Donbass, 198, 199
Donerail, 350
Dunboyne, 32, 172, 174, 175
E. A. Bryan, 150
E. G. Seubert, 344–45
Earleston, 196
Edward Chambers, 71
Edward Rutledge, 275, 276, 293
Ehrenfels, 153
El Capitan, 203
El Coston, 76, 77, 78, 79, 80
Eli Whitney, 343
Elihu Yale, 292
Empire Byron, 196
Empire Dawn, 129
Empire Tide, 199, 200, 201
Esso Aruba, 262
Esso Augusta, 249–51
Esso Baltimore, 253
Esso Baton Rouge, 250
Esso Bolivar, 168, 232
Esso Boston, 254
Esso Concord, 116
Esso Gettysburg, 163, 270
Esso Houston, 261
Esso Manhattan, 252
Esso Philadelphia, 146
Esso Providence, 287
Esso Richmond, 148, 165, 166
Esso Rochester, 317–18
Esso Williamsburg, 232
Eugene Hale
Excello, 153
Executive, 186
Expositor, 32, 369, 370
F. Marion Crawford, 292
Fairfield City, 196–97
Fitzhugh Lee, 278
Fitz John Porter, 328–29
Francis Scott Key, 214, 219
Francisco Morazan, 319

Frank B. Lindermann, 305
Franklin L. Lane, 262
Frederick L. Dau, 23, 141
Frederick R. Kellogg, 263
Gemstone, 133
George Ade, 253
George Dern, 279
George Leonard, 242
George Matthews, 288
George Taylor, 311–12
George W. Clymer, 126
Gilbert Stuart, 316
Gloucester Castle, 133
Granville, 242
Grenville M. Dodge, 279
Gulf Disc, 237
Gulf King, 259
Gulfoil, 256
Gus W. Darnell, 317
H. H. Rogers, 232
H. M. Storey, 338
Hall Young, 313
Harrison Gray Otis, 271
Harry G. Seidel, 261
Harry Luckenbach, 165, 239, 241, 247
Heffron, 185
Heinrich V. Riedemann, 261
Henry Bacon, 183
Henry George, 121
Henry Knox, 354
Henry M. Stephens, 319
Henry Villard, 142, 211
Henry Wynkoop, 151, 212
Hilary A. Herbert, 292
Honomu, 196, 209
Hoosier, 203
Horace Gray, 182
Hugh Williamson, 178, 179, 243, 288, 289
Ile de France, 65
Irenee DuPont, 239, 241, 242
Ironclad, 202, 205
Irving McDowell, 151
Israel Putnam, 214
J. Pinckney Henderson, 139, 163
J. A. Mowinkel, 253
J. H. Latrobe, 185
J. H. Senior, 139

J. L. M. Curry, 90, 186
Jacksonville, 152
James Bowie, 89
James C. Oglethorpe, 238
James C. Cameron, 83
James Carter Rose, 332–33
James H. Johnson, 340–41
James Iredell, 290
James M. Wayne, 293
James Russell Lowell, 290
James W. Denver, 236
James W. Fannin, 279
James W. Gillis, 279
James W. Marshall, 289
James Whitcomb Riley, 279
James Woodrow, 109, 235, 288
Jean, 237
Jean Nicolet, 351–54, 357
Jeremiah Daily, 317
Jeremiah H. Wadsworth, 327
Jeremiah O'Brien, 387
John A. Johnson, 356
John B. Hood, 283
John Banvard, 292
John Barry, 345, 346, 401, 405–6
John Bascom, 97–102, 296, 297
John Burke, 319
John C. Spencer, 333
John Clayton, 319
John D. Archbold, 34, 48, 312
John Harvey, 295, 297
John L. Motley, 296
John L. Luckenbach, 7
John Lykes, 328
John Morgan, 140
John Penn, 181–82
John Randolph, 185
John Stevens, 279
John W. Brown, 292, 388
John Witherspoon, 199, 203
Johnny Walker, 179
Jon Sedgewick, 68
Jonathan Sturges, 165, 230
Joseph P. Bradley, 370
Joseph Pulitzer, 285
Joseph Wheeler, 296–97
Joshua L. Chamberlain, 149
Junyo Maru, 130
Kaganovich, 124

Ships, merchant (SS) (*continued*)
    Kentucky, 182
    Kim, 124
    Kofresi, 237
    Komet (Ship No. 45), 124
    Komoran (Ship No. 41), 126
    Kungsholin, 65
    L. B. Drake, 262
    La Salle, 155, 163, 375, 376, 408
    Larranga, 170
    Lawton B. Evans, 285, 293
    Leda, 263
    Lenin, 124
    Lewis L. Dyche, 319
    Lewis Morris, 288
    Liberator, 253
    Louis Hennepin, 298
    Lurline, 309–10
    Lusitania, 4
    Lyle Park, 8
    Lyman Abbott, 297–98
    M. F. Elliott, 262
    MacBeth, 182
    Madoera, 230
    Mallory, 375
    Manchuria, 8
    Marcus Daly, 95, 317
    Margaret Lykes, 75, 149, 237
    Marnix Van Sint Algebonde, 280, 281
    Mary Livermore, 320–21
    Mary Luckenbach, 149, 180, 182
    Massmar, 185
    Matthew Luckenbach, 120, 242
    Meanticutt, 179
    Merrimack. See DE *Hunter Marshall,* 97, 106
    Meteor, 308
    Michel (Ship No. 28), 125, 126, 127, 128, 129, 130, 131
    Mihiel, 141
    Mobile City, 214
    Molly Pitcher, 283
    Mongolia, 7
    Montana, 140
    Montebello, 350
    Monterey, 282
    Moreni, 7
    Mormacdale, 369

    Mormactern, 150
    Mount Vernon (former *Kronprinzessin Cecile*), 8
    Murfreesboro, 140
    Nampa Victory, 303
    Nashbulk, 141
    Nathaniel Greene, 95, 96, 283
    Nathaniel Hawthorne, 107
    Navarino, 195
    Nicholas Gilman, 285
    Noordam, 309
    Norlina, 7
    Norvess, 248
    O. Henry, 287
    Ohio, 308
    Olambala, 265
    Olapana, 121, 200
    Oregonian, 182
    Otho. See DE *John J. Brennan,* 97–106
    Owen Wister, 171–72, 210
    Pampero, 322–23
    Pan Atlantic, 199
    Pan Kraft, 196
    Pan New York. See DE *William R. Herzog,* 97–104
    Pan Rhode Island, 237
    Patella, 133
    Patrick Harrison, 272
    Patrick Henry, 87–89, 179–80, 299, 300
    Patrick J. Hurley, 97, 105, 106
    Patrick Walsh, 97, 98, 99, 105
    Paul H. Harwood, 182–83
    Paul Hamilton, 83–84, 277–78
    Paul Luckenbach, 355
    Paulsboro, 8
    Paulus Potter, 196, 200
    Penelope, 261
    Peter Kerr, 196, 204, 209
    Peter Zenger, 279
    Phillip C. Shera, 310
    Philip Livingston, 346
    Pinguin (Ship No. 33), 126
    Portero del Llano, 255
    President Grant, 81–82
    President Monroe, 24
    Queen Elizabeth, 65
    Queen Mary, 65, 142, 145, 146

Quinault Victory, 150
R. J. Hanna, 302
R. P. Resor, 251
R. W. Gallagher, 259
Raymond Clapper, 117
Rice Victory, 323
Richard Alvay, 179
Richard Bland, 185, 186, 192
Richard Hovey, 355, 356, 406
River Afton, 17, 190, 196
Robert E. Peary, 89
Robert H. Harrison, 122
Robert P. Harper, 135
Robert Rowan, 285
Robert Tuttle, 249
Robin Tuxford, 36
Roger B. Taney, 329
Salinas Victory, 82
Samcalia, 356
Samuel Chase, 203, 204, 205, 208
Samuel Huntington, 286
Samuel Moody, 279
Samuel Parker, 38, 95
Samuel Tilden, 296, 297, 298
Samuta, 356
San Demetrio, 248
San Fabian, 263
Santa Elena, 280, 281, 282
Santa Maria, 169
Sea Train Texas, 45
Sharon Victory, 318
Silver Sword, 202, 205, 208, 209
Sinclair Opaline, 254
Southern Prince, 240
Stalin, 124
Stanvac Calcutta, 125–26, 130–
   35, 163
Stephen A. Douglas, 279
Stephen C. Foster, 237
Stephen Hopkins, 95, 96, 97, 103,
   104, 110, 125, 126, 134, 135, 136,
   137, 138, 165, 166, 167, 168, 391
Stier, 125, 126, 132, 133, 134, 135,
   137, 138, 165
Suriname, 265
T. A. Moffett, Jr., 252
Tabitha Brown, 293
Tachira, 266
Tanimbar, 272, 273

Tannenfels, 134, 135
Tekoa, 240
Thomas A. Barry, 65
Thomas Fitzsimmons, 279, 294
Thomas Hartley, 213, 214, 215,
   218, 231
Thomas J. Rusk, 37, 58, 344
Thomas L. Clingman, 279
Thomas Nelson, 317
Thomas Scott, 182
Thomas Sumter, 264
Thomas W. Bickett, 279
Thorshavet, 263
Timothy Pickering, 165, 166,
   286–87
Tjisalak, 351, 357
Tomohaku Maru, 129
Trondanger, 264
Troubadour, 201, 202, 205
Uckermark, 128, 129
Unicoi, 253
Uriah M. Rose, 320–21
Uruguay, 141
Vacuum, 7
Vaterland (later SS *Leviathan*), 8
Virginia Dare, 68, 95, 181
Virginian, 71, 306
Waipo, 302
Walter Q. Gresham, 238, 243
Washington, 195, 196, 200
Wade Hampton, 163, 175
West Lashaway, 330
Willard Hall, 188
William B. Travis, 286
William B. Woods, 283
William C. Gorgas, 165, 233, 234,
   235
William C. Humphrey, 126, 127
William Clark, 179
William Dean Howells, 288
William Eustis, 237
William Gaston, 37, 153, 332
William H. Seward, 239
William H. Moody, 151, 348
William H. Welch, 145
William Hooper, 195
William J. Worth, 66, 131
William Johnson, 271
William K. Vanderbilt, 355

Ships, merchant (SS) (*continued*)
William L. Marcy, 343
William Moultrie, 95, 96
William Mulholland, 279, 293
William Patterson, 279
William R. Davie, 320
William Sharon, 319
William T. Barry, 279
William W. Gerhard, 289
William Wirt, 282–83
Winfield Scott, 288
Winston-Salem, 121, 200, 205
Wolf, 123, 124
Woodbridge N. Ferris, 39, 61, 176, 177, 178
Yaka, 175
Yukon, 302
Zaafaram, 121, 196
Zaandam, 331
Zachary Taylor, 279
Sillars, Captain William A., 376
Sims, Rear Admiral William S., USN, 3, 4
Sisson, Lieutenant Fred U., USNR, 166
Smith, Captain D.H., 322
Smith, George T., 175
Smith, William L., 199
Solsbury, Durard, 150
Sondergaard, 2/Eng. Harry, 139
Sossaman, Gerald, 70, 306–7
Stalin, Josef, 206
Stark, Admiral Harold R., CNO, USN, 17
Stein, Ensign Meyer, USNR, 277
Steinbeck, John, 142
Stettinius, Edward R., 170
Stevens, S 1/C Patrick Henry, 317
Stilinovich, Bill, 239–40
Stilinovich, Joe, 239, 241
Stone, Ensign Merrill R., Jr., USNR, 336
Stone, Radioman 3/C Cullie, 352
Stringer, M.E., 242
Strutz, Henry, 378
Stull, Captain Elmer J., 96
Sullivan, Captain George T., 198–99
Szemela, Lieutenant F.S., USNR, 321

Tait, Captain A.A., RN, 235
Taylor, Ray Don E., 242
Thomas, Kingdon S., 321
Thomas, Lieutenant Charles C., USN, 7
Thompson, H.K., Jr., 378
Todd Shipyards Corp., 88, 156–57
Topel, R.A., 242
Torpedo Alley, 231, 275
Torpedo Junction, 249
Tovey, Admiral Sir John, RN, 191–92, 207
Trahan, S., 198
Treasure Island, 24, 27, 39, 43
Treaty of Versailles, 12, 13, 223
Tresek, R.J., 240, 242
Trojer, Korvetten Kapitän, 235
Turner, L.C.F., 324

U.S. Army: Armed Guard, 65, 142, 145, 146; chemical warfare units, 149, 297, 298, 307; Engineer Construction, 251st Bn, 314; Horse Cavalry, 110th (Mass. National Guard), 304; Transport Service, 1034th, 142, 145, 146; volunteer gunners, 310
U.S. Maritime Commission (War Shipping Administration), 26, 29, 95, 157, 159, 277, 387
U.S. Merchant Marine: Academy (Kings Point), 95, 125, 165, 168, 287, 359; casualties, 95; between WW I–WW II, 159; citations, 95, 168; distinguished service medal, 168; "Gallant Ships," 95; history, 156, 393; manpower, 157,169; present status, 379; sailings, 387; ships, 387; veterans' benefits, 167, 168
U.S. Naval Academy, 36
U.S. Naval Armed Guard: Arming Merchant Ships Section, 26, 27; Bureau of Naval Personnel, 26; Bureau of Ordnance, 26; Bureau of Ships, 26; Naval Training School (Local Defense), 41, 98; Naval Training Schools (Radio),

29, 30, 31; organization and training, WW II, 22, 48; reactivation, 18, 19; service on American-flag ships, 386; service on foreign-flag ships, 386; total strength, 48; training centers, 23, 24, 27, 29, 30, 31, 36, 38, 39, 40, 41, 42, 43, 46, 62, 101, 401; WW I, 5, 11, 384
U.S. Navy Ships: USS *Atherton* (DE 169), 372; USS *Belknap*, 230; USS *Block Island*, 116; USS *Charger*, 39; USS *Dover*, 42; USS *Dubuque*, 25; USS *Eagle*, 25; USS *Greer*, 16; USS *Hunter Marshall*, 97; USS *John J. Brennan*, 97; USS *John R. Borum*, 96; USS *Kay K. Vesole*, 97–98; USS *Kearny*, 17; USS *Kenneth Willett*, 97; USS *Matagorda*, 333; USS *Moberly* (PF63), 372; USS *Paducah*, 25; USAT *Patrick Walsh*, 97; USS *Pennsylvania*, 8; USS *Philadelphia*, 197; USS *Quincy*, 106; USS *Reuben James*, 17; USS *Rowan*, 191, 209, 283; USS *Sawfish*, 355; USS *Tang*, 129; USS *Tuscaloosa*, 191, 200, 206; USS *Wainwright*, 191; USS *Washington*, 191; USS *Wasp*, 272; USS *Wichita*, 191, 207; USS *William R. Herzog*, 97; YMS 20, 250
U-Boats: Enigma, 227–28; "Happy Time," 228; losses, 247; production, 223–24; schnorkels, 229; status WW I, 2, 11; tactics, 119, 223–25, 228–29, 249, 255, 260, 399–401; Walter boats, 245–46; 361; *U-39*, 223; *U-68*, 223; *U-110*, 227–28; *U-123*, 267; *U-144*, 234; *U-159*, 375, 408; *U-161*, 260; *U-162*, 260; *U-177*, 339; *U-181*, 337; *U-230*, 249; *U-255*, 86, 192, 199–200, 203, 396; *U-376*, 205; *U-408*, 192; *U-511*, 251; *U-652*, 17; *U-757*, 235; *U-853*, 372, 407; *U-859*, 345; *U-953*, 361
USAT *Argentina*, 304
USAT *General Fletcher*, 316

USAT *Uruguay*, 141
Vesole, Ensign Kay K., USNR, 97–98, 100–102, 296
Vigh, Louis, 181
Von Bernstorff, Ambassador Johann, 5
Von Luckner, Count Felix, 123, 128
Von Ruckteschell, Captain Helmut, 126, 128
Von Zwatowski (*sic*), Captain, 128

Wagner, Ensign Sydney N., USNR, 287
Walker, Lewis, 184
Wall, Captain, 39
Walsh, Lieutenant Patrick J., USNR, 105–6
War Shipping Administration. *See* U.S. Maritime Commission
Ward, S 2/C Earl, 335
Watkins, Ensign G.B., USNR, 230
Watson, Lieutenant William P., USNR, 45
Webber, Lieutenant R. Gordon, USNR, 362
Weiss, S 1/C Otto H., Jr., 287
Welch, DeWitt, 66–68, 91, 141, 300, 340, 348
Welch, Lieutenant Brian, USNR, 196
Wells, Ivy R., 318
Werner, Lieutenant Herbert, 243, 249, 361
Whalen, Rick, 151, 348
Willett, Lieutenant (j.g.) Kenneth M., USNR, 103–4, 136
Williams, Richard E., 44
Williams, S 3/C Bob, 343
Willkie, Wendell, 16
Wilson, President Woodrow, 4–6, 12, 14, 16; policy of U.S. neutrality, 4; request to arm merchant ships, 5; request for declaration of war, 6; "Fourteen Points", 13
Winder, C/M Leslie H., 287
Witte, Captain Helmut, 375
Wolff, G/M 3/C Robert H., 204

Wolfson, Lieutenant Morton E.,
     USNR, 197–98
Woodring, Lieutenant Earle Doug-
     las, USNR, 314–16
Woods, G.E., 242
Wright, Hugh, 194

Wright, Rear Admiral W.D., USN,
     207
Zeidler, Frank A., 376, 407–8
Zeidler, Lieutenant Carl, USNR,
     155, 368, 373–76
Zubrod, Donald, 330

The Naval Institute Press is the book-publishing arm of the U.S. Naval Institute, a private, nonprofit professional society for members of the sea services and civilians who share an interest in naval and maritime affairs. Established in 1873 at the U.S. Naval Academy in Annapolis, Maryland, where its offices remain today, the Naval Institute has more than 100,000 members worldwide.

Members of the Naval Institute receive the influential monthly naval magazine *Proceedings* and substantial discounts on fine nautical prints, ship and aircraft photos, and subscriptions to the Institute's recently inaugurated quarterly, *Naval History.* They also have access to the transcripts of the Institute's Oral History Program and may attend any of the Institute-sponsored seminars regularly offered around the country.

The book-publishing program, begun in 1898 with basic guides to naval practices, has broadened its scope in recent years to include books of more general interest. Now the Naval Institute Press publishes more than forty new titles each year, ranging from how-to books on boating and navigation to battle histories, biographies, ship guides, and novels. Institute members receive discounts on the Press's more than 300 books.

For a free catalog describing books currently available and for further information about U.S. Naval Institute membership, please write to:

Membership Department
U.S. Naval Institute
Annapolis, Maryland 21402

or call, toll-free, 800-233-USNI.